MORE
LETTERS
OF NOTE

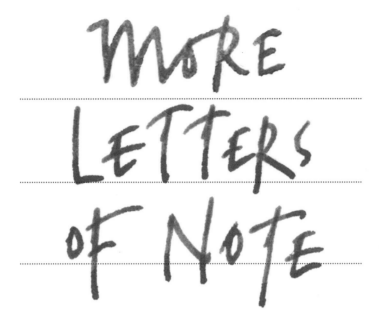

MORE LETTERS OF NOTE

COMPILED BY **SHAUN USHER**

CANONGATE

unbound

This paperback edition published in 2017 by Canongate Books

First published in Great Britain in 2015 by Canongate Books Ltd in conjunction with Unbound

Canongate Books Ltd., 14 High Street, Edinburgh EH1 1TE
www.canongate.co.uk

Unbound, Unit 18, Waterside, 44–48 Wharf Road, London N1 7UX
www.unbound.com

1

Cover design and typesetting by Here Design

British Library Cataloguing-in-Publication Data
A catalogue record for this book is available on request from the British Library

ISBN 978 1 78689 169 3

Repro: syntax21.co.uk

Printed in China by imago.

For Karina

CONTENTS

INTRODUCTION   xv

001 TORTURING THE SAXOPHONE   2
ROBERT CRUMB TO MATS GUSTAFSSON

002 FOR LOVE AND HONOR   4
HOLLIS FRAMPTON TO MOMA

003 DEAR ONE   10
RACHEL CARSON TO DOROTHY FREEMAN

004 I'LL RAP YOUR HEAD WITH A RATCHET   12
STEVE ALBINI TO NIRVANA

005 SORROW COMES TO ALL   16
ABRAHAM LINCOLN TO FANNY MCCULLOUGH

006 I SEE NO BEAUTY IN LOPSIDED TRUE LOVE   18
ELIZABETH SMART TO GEORGE BARKER

007 MY EARTHLY MISSION IS ALREADY FULFILLED   20
VIVIAN ROSEWARNE TO HIS MOTHER

008 KING SEQUOIA   23
JOHN MUIR TO JEANNE CARR

009 HUSBAND UNTIL DEATH   29
ABREAM SCRIVEN TO HIS WIFE

010 BREAK BREAK BREAK   30
SYLVIA PLATH TO HER FAMILY

011 1984 VS. A BRAVE NEW WORLD   32
ALDOUS HUXLEY TO GEORGE ORWELL

012 MY HEART ALMOST STOOD STILL   36
HELEN KELLER TO THE NEW YORK SYMPHONY ORCHESTRA

013 GO TO HELL WITH YOUR MONEY BASTARD   39
ASGER JORN TO THE GUGGENHEIM

014 THE PARAKEET HAS A GOITER   40
BRIAN DOYLE TO VARIOUS

015 ALONG WITH THIS LETTER COMES A PLAY   42
SHELAGH DELANEY TO JOAN LITTLEWOOD

016 EVERYONE IS EXPECTING ME TO DO BIG THINGS   44
JACK TRICE TO WHOM IT MAY CONCERN

017 WITH GREAT RESPECT, MARGE SIMPSON   46
MARGE SIMPSON TO BARBARA BUSH

018 SLOWLY, QUIETLY, NEVER GIVING UP   48
CARL SANDBURG TO MARGARET SANDBURG

019 SHE WAS THE MUSIC HEARD FAINTLY AT THE EDGE OF SOUND   49
RAYMOND CHANDLER TO LEONARD RUSSELL

020 I EMBRACE YOU WITH ALL MY HEART   50
ALBERT CAMUS TO LOUIS GERMAIN

021 I HAVE RESOLVED TO ESCAPE   52
WINSTON CHURCHILL TO LOUIS DE SOUZA

022 WITH MANY GOOD WISHES FOR OUR HOUSE   54
LION FEUCHTWANGER TO THE OCCUPANT OF HIS HOUSE

023 LETTER TO THE DEAD   58
SHEPSI TO INKHENMET

024 YOU'RE OFF, BY GOD!   60
RICHARD BURTON TO ELIZABETH TAYLOR

025 THE TALE OF PETER RABBIT   62
BEATRIX POTTER TO NOEL MOORE

026 YOUR EAGER MOTHER   69
JESSIE BERNARD TO HER UNBORN CHILD

027 THE MATCHBOX   70
SYLVIA TOWNSEND WARNER TO ALYSE GREGORY

028 ALL THIS I DID WITHOUT YOU   72
GERALD DURRELL TO LEE MCGEORGE

029 NOTHING TO EAT BUT THE DEAD   76
VIRGINIA REED TO MARY KEYES

030 TIGER OIL MEMOS   80
EDWARD "TIGER MIKE" DAVIS TO HIS STAFF

031 I LONG FOR FREEDOM   92
HANNAH GROVER TO CATO

032 JANIS JOPLIN LIVES!   93
JANIS JOPLIN TO HER PARENTS

033 BECOMING TOM CLANCY   96
TOM CLANCY TO HIS FRIENDS

034 THE JL123 ISHO   111
FLIGHT 123 PASSENGERS TO VARIOUS

035 DARE TO STAND ALONE   114
BUD WILKINSON TO JAY WILKINSON

036 ARKELL v. PRESSDRAM   116
PRIVATE EYE TO GOODMAN DERRICK & CO.

037 THE OUTSIDERS   118
JO ELLEN MISAKIAN TO FRANCIS FORD COPPOLA

038 I CAN'T LOOK YOU IN THE VOICE   123
DOROTHY PARKER TO PASCAL COVICI

039 DO NOT BE SO BLOODY VULNERABLE   124
NOËL COWARD TO MARLENE DIETRICH

040 FROM HEAVEN   126
PAUL REVERE OSLER TO GRACE OSLER

041 CAT FANCY   135
AYN RAND TO CAT FANCY MAGAZINE

042 NEW FANGLED WRITING MACHINE   136
SAMUEL CLEMENS TO ORION CLEMENS

043 AMERICA'S YOUNGEST AMBASSADOR   137
SAMANTHA SMITH TO YURI ANDROPOV

044 SLEEP WELL MY LOVE   140
BRIAN KEITH TO DAVE

045 THIS IS MY LAST VISIT   142
WILLIAM BURROUGHS TO TRUMAN CAPOTE

046 BROWN IS AS PRETTY AS WHITE   144
W. E. B. DU BOIS TO YOLANDE DU BOIS

047 EVERY OUNCE OF MY ENERGY   146
BERTRAND RUSSELL TO SIR OSWALD MOSLEY

048 THIS WRETCHED COMEDY AS A MAN!   147
LILI ELVENES TO "CHRISTIAN"

049 THERE ARE TWO WAYS IN WHICH THIS CAN BE DONE   150
BERTHA BREWSTER TO DAILY TELEGRAPH

050 YOURS SINCERELY, ALBUS DUMBLEDORE   152
J. K. ROWLING TO STEVEN ARMES

051 I'VE GOT A HUNCH   155
THOMAS WOLFE TO MAXWELL PERKINS

052 WE ARE UNINTELLIGIBLE   156
JACK LONDON TO ANNA STRUNSKY

053 GENTLEMEN, I JUST DON'T BELONG HERE   158
URSULA LE GUIN TO JOHN RADZIEWICZ

054 I MISS LORINA BULWER   159
LORINA BULWER

055 MY REAL NAME IS DAVID JONES   163
DAVID BOWIE TO SANDRA DODD

056 A NEW PAGE IN MOTION PICTURE HISTORY   164
SAMUEL GOLDWYN TO WALT DISNEY

057 I LOVED THE BOY   166
WILLIAM WORDSWORTH TO ROBERT SOUTHEY

058 A PILE OF 5000 CATS AND KITTENS   168
FREDERICK LAW OLMSTED TO HIS SON

059 IT MUST BE NICE TO BE A BABY   170
DAISY WHITE TO JOEL WHITE

060 I HAVE LOST A TREASURE   176
CASSANDRA AUSTEN TO FANNY KNIGHT

061 A RIPPLE OF FLAME   184
EDITH WHARTON TO W. M. FULLERTON

062 FINAL, COMPLETE AND IRREMEDIABLE DEFEAT   186
HUGH DOWDING TO WINSTON CHURCHILL

063 A FORCE FOR EVIL   189
RICHARD HELMS TO DENNIS HELMS

064 YOU ARE A BEAST   190
MICHELANGELO DI LODOVICO BUONARROTI SIMONI
TO GIOVAN SIMONE BUONARROTI SIMONI

065 IT'S BURNING HELL WITHOUT YOU   192
DYLAN THOMAS TO CAITLIN THOMAS

066 I DRANK TOO MUCH WINE LAST NIGHT   194
JANE AUSTEN TO CASSANDRA AUSTEN

067 LET US BLAZE NEW TRAILS   196
BILL BERNBACH TO HIS COLLEAGUES

068 YOUR TYPE IS A DIME A DOZEN   198
HUNTER S. THOMPSON TO ANTHONY BURGESS

069 WE CAN CHANGE THE WORLD   200
JOHN LENNON TO ERIC CLAPTON

070 YOU ARE A TRUE MAN   210
BRAM STOKER TO WALT WHITMAN

071 WHAT DO YOU TAKE ME FOR?   214
NANNI TO EA-NASIR

072 REMEMBER?   216
BREECE D'J PANCAKE TO JOHN CASEY

073 I HOPE YOU DON'T FEEL TOO DISAPPOINTED   218
ERIC IDLE TO JOHN MAJOR

074 AN INSTRUMENT OF JOY   220
MARGARET MEAD TO ELIZABETH MEAD

075 WE PRESS YOU CLOSE AND KISS YOU WITH ALL OUR STRENGTH   222
ETHEL AND JULIUS ROSENBERG TO THEIR SONS

076 HOW DID YOU GET INVENTED?   224
ARCHBISHOP OF CANTERBURY TO LULU

077 WHY I AM AN ATHEIST   226
MINNIE PARRISH TO BLUE-GRASS BLADE

078 YOURS IN DISTRESS   228
ALAN TURING TO NORMAN ROUTLEDGE

079 OH MY ASS BURNS LIKE FIRE!   231
MOZART TO MARIANNE

080 TERRY TOMA   237
DAWN POWELL TO MABEL POWELL POCOCK AND PHYLLIS POWELL COOK

081 DO NOT REMAIN NAMELESS TO YOURSELF   240
RICHARD FEYNMAN TO KOICHI MANO

082 I SEE HIM IN THE STAR   242
EMILY DICKINSON TO SUSAN DICKINSON

083 I AM DESPERATE TO HAVE SOME REAL FUN   247
PETER SELLERS TO SPIKE MILLIGAN

084 THE WHITE HOUSE   248
ABIGAIL ADAMS TO HER DAUGHTER

085 YOUR ORGANIZATION HAS FAILED   250
ELEANOR ROOSEVELT TO DAR

086 ON BUREAUCRATESE AND GOBBLEDYGOOK   252
ALFRED KAHN TO HIS COLLEAGUES

087 I THINK I NO HOW TO MAKE PEOPLE OR ANIMALS ALIVE   255
ANTHONY HOLLANDER TO BLUE PETER

088 YOU RANG MY MOTHER   259
MICHAEL J. MOLLOY TO JEFFREY BERNARD

089 PEOPLE SIMPLY EMPTY OUT   260
CHARLES BUKOWSKI TO JOHN MARTIN

090 A STRING OF VERITABLE PSYCHOLOGICAL PEACHES   262
CARL JUNG TO JAMES JOYCE

091 THE APPALLING HORROR   264
FLORENCE NIGHTINGALE TO WILLIAM BOWMAN

092 YOU ARE A HOMOSEXUAL AND MAY NEVER CHANGE   268
FELICIA BERNSTEIN TO LEONARD BERNSTEIN

093 I NEVER STUDIED GRACE   270
CHARLES LAMB TO JACOB VALE ASBURY

094 I DO NOT LIKE SCOLDING PEOPLE   272
KATHERINE MANSFIELD TO ELIZABETH BIBESCO

095 MAKE YOUR SOUL GROW   274
KURT VONNEGUT TO XAVIER HIGH SCHOOL

096 THERE ARE NO REAL REWARDS FOR TIME PASSING   275
MARTHA GELLHORN TO ERNEST HEMINGWAY

097 I AM THE DEAD ONE   278
SPIKE MILLIGAN TO GEORGE HARRISON

098 LIKE A TREE IN FULL BEARING   280
CHARLOTTE BRONTË TO W. S. WILLIAMS

099 YOU GAVE ME A VALUABLE GIFT: YOU TOOK ME SERIOUSLY   282
HOWARD CRUSE TO DR. SEUSS (AND VICE VERSA)

100 THE MISERABLE'S NAME IS MAN   286
VICTOR HUGO TO M. DAELLI

101 WE WERE NOT FOUND WANTING   290
CHARLES JACK PRICE TO HIS STAFF

102 SHEER ENCHANTMENT   291
SOPHIE SCHOLL TO LISA REMPPIS

103 I HAVE NEVER SEEN ANYTHING LIKE IT   292
BARNUM BROWN TO PROFESSOR OSBORN

104 ENERGY EQUALS MASS TIMES THE SPEED OF LIGHT SQUARED STOP   299
BUCKMINSTER FULLER TO ISAMU NOGUCHI

105 I THINK YOU'RE A DAMN FOOL   300
NORMAN MAILER TO HIS FATHER

106 THE GREATEST MUSICAL PLEASURE I HAVE EVER EXPERIENCED   303
CHARLES BAUDELAIRE TO RICHARD WAGNER

107 I KNOW WHAT TASTE IS AND WHAT VULGARITY IS   309
TENNESSEE WILLIAMS TO JOSEPH BREEN

108 I WOULD LIKE TO GIVE YOU YOUR OWN HISTORY   311
JUAN GELMAN TO HIS GRANDCHILD

109 THIS IS QUITE TRUE   314
EVELYN WAUGH TO LAURA WAUGH

110 I SHALL EXPECT YOU, SISTER   316
CLAUDIA SEVERA TO SULPICIA LEPIDINA

111 LET ME ALONE   318
KATHERINE ANNE PORTER TO HART CRANE

112 F**K THA POLICE   320
THE FBI TO PRIORITY RECORDS

113 I HAVE ALWAYS BEEN TALKED ABOUT   321
ANSEL ADAMS TO NANCY NEWHALL

114 GROW UP AS GOOD REVOLUTIONARIES   326
CHE GUEVARA TO HIS CHILDREN

115 WE HOPE YOU SHALL TRY...   328
JESSICA MITFORD TO HERSELF

116 I DON'T ENJOY THIS WAR ONE BIT   330
DAVID FOSTER WALLACE TO DON DELILLO

117 I SHALL ALWAYS BE WITH YOU   332
MILADA HORÁKOVÁ TO HER DAUGHTER

118 P.S. THIS IS MY FAVORITE MEMO EVER   337
MATT STONE TO THE MPAA

119 DEAR FRIENDS ALL   338
HENRY JAMES TO 270 FRIENDS

120 MY MOTHER DECLARED MY BEDROOM A DISASTER AREA   340
ANDY SMITH TO RONALD REAGAN

121 THANKS, MR. EDISON   342
W. C. LATHROP TO THOMAS EDISON

122 THE MOST EXTRAORDINARY SCENE   343
CAPTAIN REGINALD JOHN ARMES TO HIS WIFE

INDEX   353

ACKNOWLEDGEMENTS   355

SUBSCRIBERS   357

PERMISSION CREDITS   364

Dear Reader,

It's two years since my last letter to you; two long years since
I was introducing the first volume of Letters of Note to the world,
unbearably excited and overwhelmingly proud to finally be waving off
the physical incarnation of a mammoth four year project that began as
a website. More than anything, though, I was nervous, for here was I,
in the fast-moving digital age of ebook readers and emails, trying
to captivate the plugged-in population with a hardcover book on the
subject of old-fashioned correspondence. Letters of Note already had
a dedicated following from its early days online, but what of the
wider public--surely that was a reach too far? As delighted as I was
to be holding such a beautiful book, I feared I was about to swim
against a pixelated tide.

Thankfully, I could not have been more wrong, and to say the past
two years have been a whirlwind would be a huge understatement. Indeed,
it is a testament to the enduring, universal appeal of letters and the
stories they tell that the first book is now being enjoyed in all
corners of the world, in many different languages, by people of all ages
and backgrounds and persuasions. As someone who spends most of his wakin
-g hours championing, researching, and thinking about the power of
letters, to see such a positive reaction has been indescribably gratifyi
-ng, and to imagine that even a small fraction of you may have been
inspired to write your own letters makes every single second of those
years of research worthwhile. And this is all without mentioning Letters
Live, a series of events inspired by the book in which a diverse cast of
talented performers read these letters of note on stage and breathe
life into them in a way I had barely even considered.

Thanks to its many moving parts, producing a book like this is a
logistical nightmare that nearly breaks me and my editor into tiny
pieces, but one of the most enjoyable tasks is deciding on the letters
to be featured. I'm clearly biased, but I can safely say that this
second volume of letters, telegrams and memos is every bit as impressive
as the first, if not more so, We have an enthusiastic letter written by
a young David Bowie in response to his first piece of fan mail; J.K.
Rowling's reply, in character as Albus Dumbledore, to a Professor of

Colloid and Polymer Science who applied to become Defence Against the
Dark Arts Professor at Hogwarts; from 1930, a missive from Lili Elvenes
in which she describes her relief at finally being able to undergo
surgery in what was one of the first cases of gender reassignment; a
long letter sent by Tom Clancy to his friends just as fame approached,
in which he speaks of his rapidly changing life; an embroidered letter
of such incredible dimensions that it spans several fold-out pages; the
charming illustrated letter that introduced Peter Rabbit to the world,
written by Beatrix Potter to a five-year-old boy; a letter from legendar
-y "dinosaur hunter" Barnum Brown, in which he describes having just
discovered the Tyrannosaurus rex; Florence Nightingale's harrowing
account of the "appalling horror" of the Crimean War, written in 1854,
and many, many more. As with the first book, you are soon to embark
upon a rollercoaster ride that soars as high as it does low, travelling
back in time as far as 2000BC to read an ancient Egyptian letter to
the dead and coming as close as 2014 to enjoy a wonderfully entertaining
letter by Robert Crumb.

There really is no correct way to consume this book. Read it from
front to back, from back to front, or simply pick letters at random;
whichever one you land on will offer you a snapshot of history in a
format that we cannot afford to let die. When you're finished, pass the
book on, pick up a pen, and write some letters of your own.

Yours in letters,

Shaun

SHAUN USHER
Letters of Note

TORTURING THE SAXOPHONE

ROBERT CRUMB to MATS
GUSTAFSSON
2014

In 2014, celebrated Swedish
free jazz saxophonist
Mats Gustafsson sent a
copy of his forthcoming
album to one of his idols,
the legendary comic book
artist, record collector and
musician Robert Crumb.
Gustafsson's upcoming
record was a compilation
of his experimental
interpretations of some jazz
classics by people such as
Duke Ellington, Lars Gullin,
and the Ayler brothers, and
he sought Crumb's opinion.
Crumb, baffled, pulled no
punches and responded
with this brutally honest
letter. In honour of the
critique, Gustafsson named
his next album *Torturing
the Saxophone*, and proudly
reprinted the letter amongst
the liner notes.

Gustafsson:

I finally gave a listen to those LPs and the CD you sent me, of your own saxophone playing and some Swedish modern jazz. I gotta tell you, on the cover of the CD of your sax playing, which is black and has no text on it, I wrote in large block letters, in silver ink, "Torturing the Saxophone—Mats Gustafsson." I just totally fail to find anything enjoyable about this, or to see what this has to do with music as I understand it, or what in God's name is going on in your head that you want to make such noises on a musical instrument. Quite frankly, I was kind of shocked at what a negative, unpleasant experience it was, listening to it. I had to take it off long before it reached the end. I just don't get it. I don't understand what it is about.

You actually go on TOUR with that stuff. WOW. People actually... sit... and... LISTEN... to that. I mean, they voluntarily go to the place, maybe even PAY... PAY to hear that stuff. And then they sit there, quietly, politely... and LISTEN. Unbelievable. I should go myself sometime and see this. Witness it with my own eyes.

I don't say these things with the intention to insult you. You seem to be a perfectly nice, civilized guy with a good sense of humor. I am speaking the plain truth of my reaction to the records and CD you sent. That this noise could give anyone any aesthetic pleasure is beyond my comprehension, truly. Is this the logical end of improvisational music? Is this where it ends up? Where does it go from this point? Is there any audience for this "free jazz" besides other guys who play it and maybe their wives who must patiently endure it?

I just don't get it. Am I too un-hip? Am I a square from Delaware? A hick from Battle Crick? A shmuck from Keokuck?

—R. Crumb

*Facing page: Cartoonist
Robert Crumb, 1985*

FOR LOVE AND HONOR

HOLLIS FRAMPTON to
MoMA
January 7th, 1973

In December of 1972, Donald
Richie, then film curator
at the Museum of Modern
Art in New York, wrote to
artist Hollis Frampton and
suggested that they organise
a retrospective of his work
at this most prestigious of
museums. To an artist of any
standing, this would be
a tempting offer; however,
Frampton took issue with
one particular line in the
proposal, a single detail of
Richie's which rendered
the suggestion entirely
unattractive: "It is all for
love and honor and no
money is included at all…"
Unwilling to work without
financial reward, Frampton
responded at length with a
rousing letter that has since
become legendary in the art
world for reasons which are
plain to see.

It's fair to assume that
a fee was later agreed:
MoMA's Hollis Frampton
retrospective ran from
March 8–12, 1973.

Box 99
Eaton, New York 13334

January 7, 1973

Mr Donald Richie
Curator of Film
The Museum of Modern Art
11 West 53 Street
New York, New York 10019

Dear Donald:

I have your letter of December 13, 1972, in which you
offer me the honor of a complete retrospective during
this coming March. Let me stipulate at the outset that
I am agreed "in principle", and more: that I appreciate
very deeply being included in the company you mention.
I am touched to notice that the dates you propose fall
squarely across my thirty-seventh birthday. And I am
flattered by your proposal to write notes.

But, having said this much, I must go on to point out some
difficulties to you.

To begin with, let me put it to you squarely that anyone,
institution or individual, is free at any time to arrange
a complete retrospective of my work; and that is not something that requires my consent, or even my prior knowledge.
You must know, as well as I do, that all my work is distributed through the Film-Makers' Cooperative, and that it is
available for rental by any party willing to assume, in
good faith, ordinary responsibility for the prints, together with the price of hiring them.

So that something other than a wish to show my work must
be at issue in your writing to me. And you open your
second paragraph with a concise guide to what that 'something' is, when you say: "It is all for love and honor and
no money is included at all...".

All right. Let's start with love, where we all started.
I have devoted, at the nominal least, a decade of the
only life I may reasonably expect to have, to making films.
I have given to this work the best energy of my conscious-
ness. In order to continue in it, I have accepted...as
most artists accept (and with the same gladness)...a standard of living that most other American working people hold
in automatic contempt: that is, I have committed my entire
worldly resources, whatever they may amount to, to my art.

Of course, those resources are not unlimited. But
the irreducible point is that I have made the work,
have commissioned it of myself, under no obligation
of any sort to please anyone, adhering to my own best
understanding of the classic canons of my art. Does
that not demonstrate love? And if it does not, then
how much more am I obliged to do? And who (among the
living) is to exact that of me?

Now, about honor: I have said that I am mindful, and
appreciative, of the honor to myself. But what about
the honor of my art? I venture to suggest that a time
may come when the whole history of art will become no
more than a footnote to the history of film...or of
whatever evolves from film. Already, in less than a
century, film has produced great monuments of passionate
intelligence. If we say that we honor such a nascent
tradition, then we affirm our wish that it continue.

But it cannot continue on love and honor alone. And
this brings me to your: "...no money is included at all...".

I'll put it to you as a problem in fairness. I have made,
let us say, so and so many films. That means that so and
so many thousands of feet of rawstock have been expended,
for which I paid the manufacturer. The processing lab
was paid, by me, to develop the stuff, after it was
exposed in a camera for which I paid. The lens grinders
got paid. Then I edited the footage, on rewinds and a
splicer for which I paid, incorporating leader and glue
for which I also paid. The printing lab and the track
lab were paid for their materials and services. You
yourself, however meagerly, are being paid for trying
to persuade me to show my work, to a paying public, for
"love and honor". If it comes off, the projectionist
will get paid. The guard at the door will be paid.
Somebody or other paid for the paper on which your letter
to me was written, and for the postage to forward it.

That means that I, in my singular person, by making this
work, have already generated wealth for scores of people.
Multiply that by as many other working artists as you
can think of. Ask yourself whether my lab, for instance,
would print my work for "love and honor": if I asked them,
and they took my question seriously, I should expect to
have it explained to me, ever so gently, that human beings
expect compensation for their work. The reason is simply
that it enables them to continue doing what they do.

But it seems that, while all these others are to be paid
for their part in a show that could not have taken place
without me, nonetheless, I, the artist, am not to be paid.

And in fact it seems that there is no way to pay an
artist for his work <u>as an artist</u>. I have taught, lectured,
written, worked as a technician...and for all those collat-
eral activities, I have been <u>paid</u>, have been compensated
for my work. But <u>as an artist</u> I have been paid only on the
rarest of occasions.

I will offer you further information in the matter:

Item: that we filmmakers are a little in touch with one
another, or that there is a "grapevine", at least, such
as did not obtain two and three decades ago, when The
Museum of Modern Art (a different crew then, of course)
divided filmmakers against themselves, and got not only
screenings, but "rights" of one kind and another, for
<u>nothing</u>, from the generation of Maya Deren.

Well, Maya Deren, for one, <u>died young</u>, in circumstances
of genuine need. I leave it to your surmise whether her
life might have been prolonged by a few bucks. A little
money certainly would have helped her work: I still recall
with sadness the little posters, begging for money to help
her finish THE VERY EYE OF NIGHT, that were stuck around
when I was first in New York. If I can help it, that won't
happen to me, nor to any other artist I know.

And I <u>know</u> that Stan Brakhage (his correspondence with
Willard Van Dyke is public record) and Shirley Clark
did not go uncompensated for the use of their work by
the Museum. I don't know about Bruce Bailey, but I doubt,
at the mildest, that he is wealthy enough to have travelled
from the West Coast under his own steam, for any amount of
love and honor (and nothing else). And, of course, if any
of these three received <u>any</u> money at all (it is money
that enables us to go on working, I repeat) then they
received an <u>infinite</u> amount more than you are offering
me. That puts us beyond the pale, even, of qualitative
argument. It is simply an unimaginable cut in pay.

Item: that I do not live in New York City. Nor is it,
strictly speaking, "convenient" for me to be there during
the period you name. I'll be teaching in Buffalo every
Thursday and Friday this coming Spring semester, so that
I could hope to be at the Museum for a Saturday program.
Are you suggesting that I drive down? The distance is
well over four hundred miles, and March weather upstate
is uncertain. Shall I fly, at my own expense, to face an
audience that I know, from personal experience, to be,
at best, largely unengaging, and at worst grossly provincial
and rude?

Item: it is my understanding that filmmakers invited to
appear on your "Cineprobe" programs currently receive
an honorarium. How is it, then, that I am not accorded
the same courtesy?

Very well. Having been prolix, I will now attempt
succinctness. I offer you the following points for
discussion:

1] It is my understanding, of old, that the Museum of
Modern Art does not, as a matter of policy, pay rentals
for films. I am richly aware that, if the museum paid
us independent film artists, then it would be obliged
also to pay rentals to the Hollywood studios. Since we
all live in a free-enterprise system, the Museum thus
saves artists from the ethical error of engaging in un-
fair economic competition with the likes of Metro-Goldwyn-
Mayer. (I invite anyone to examine, humanely, the logic
of such a notion.) Nevertheless, I offer you the opportunity to pay me, at the rate of one-half my listed catalog
rentals, for the several screenings you will probably
subject my prints to. You can call the money anything
you like: a grant, a charitable gift, a bribe, or divid-
ends on my common stock in Western Civilization...and I
will humbly accept it. The precise amount in question is
$266.88, plus $54.-- in cleaning charges, which I will
owe the Film-Makers' Cooperative for their services when
my prints are returned.

2] If I am to appear during the period you propose, then
I must have roundtrip air fare, and ground transportation
expenses, between Buffalo and Manhattan. I will undertake
to cover whatever other expenses there may be. I think
that amounts to about $90.--, subject to verification.

3] If I appear to discuss my work, I must have the same
honorarium you would offer anyone doing a "Cineprobe.
Correct me if I'm wrong, but I think that comes to $150.--.

4] Finally, I must request your earliest possible reply.
I have only a limited number of prints available, some
of which may already be committed for rentals screenings
during the period you specify. Since I am committed in
principle to this retrospective, delay might mean my
having to purchase new prints specifically for the
occasion; and I am determined to minimize, if possible,
drains on funds that I need for making new work.

Please note carefully, Donald, that what I have written
above is a list of requests. I do not speak of demands,
which may only be made of those who are forced to negotiate.

But you must understand also that these requests are
not open to bargaining: to bargain is to be humiliated.
To bargain in this, of all matters, is to accept humiliation on behalf of others whose needs and uncertainties
are greater even than mine.

You, of course, are not forced to negotiate. You are free.
And since I am too, this question of payment is open to
discussion in matters of procedure, if not of substance.

I hope we can come to some agreement, and soon. I hope
so out of love for my embattled art, and because I honor
all those who pursue it. But if we cannot, then I must
say, regretfully, however much I want it to take place,
that there can be no retrospective showing of my work at
The Museum of Modern Art.

Benedictions,

Hollis Frampton

DEAR ONE

RACHEL CARSON to
DOROTHY FREEMAN
September 10th, 1963

Published in 1962, *Silent Spring* was a pioneering book that alerted the public to the devastating harm being caused by fertilisers and pesticides – a hugely important exposé which, in the eyes of many, triggered the modern environmental movement. In 1960, as she worked on the book, its author marine biologist Rachel Carson was diagnosed with the cancer that would eventually, in 1964, take her life. Seven months before she died, with her health failing, Carson spent a morning at the coast with her dear friend Dorothy Freeman, watching the migration of monarch butterflies; that afternoon, she wrote her friend a letter.

September 10, 1963

Dear One,

This is a postscript to our morning at Newagen, something I think I can write better than say. For me it was one of the loveliest of the summer's hours, and all the details will remain in my memory: that blue September sky, the sounds of the wind in the spruces and surf on the rocks, the gulls busy with their foraging, alighting with deliberate grace, the distant views of Griffiths Head and Todd Point, today so clearly etched, though once half seen in swirling fog. But most of all I shall remember the monarchs, that unhurried westward drift of one small winged form after another, each drawn by some invisible force. We talked a little about their migration, their life history. Did they return? We thought not; for most, at least, this was the closing journey of their lives.

But it occurred to me this afternoon, remembering, that it had been a happy spectacle, that we had felt no sadness when we spoke of the fact that there would be no return. And rightly—for when any living thing has come to the end of its life cycle we accept that end as natural.

For the Monarch, that cycle is measured in a known span of months. For ourselves, the measure is something else, the span of which we cannot know. But the thought is the same: when that intangible cycle has run its course it is a natural and not unhappy thing that a life comes to an end.

That is what those brightly fluttering bits of life taught me this morning. I found a deep happiness in it—so I hope, may you. Thank you for this morning.

Rachel

I'LL RAP YOUR HEAD WITH A RATCHET

STEVE ALBINI to NIRVANA
1992

Although they only existed for a mere seven years and released just three albums, Nirvana were a band of immeasurable influence in the music world thanks in no small part to "Smells Like Teen Spirit", a single track on *Nevermind*, their second album. It was this song that brought them out into the open, going on to sell millions of copies and win countless awards, its iconic video seemingly broadcast on MTV every 20 minutes for the next six months.

A year after *Nevermind*'s release, the band got to work on what would be their final album, *In Utero*, produced by Steve Albini, outspoken engineer extraordinaire. Shortly before they formally agreed on his involvement, Albini wrote to Nirvana and laid bare his philosophy in a pitch letter that is fascinating from start to end.

Kurt, Dave and Chris:

First let me apologize for taking a couple of days to put this outline together. When I spoke to Kurt I was in the middle of making a Fugazi album, but I thought I would have a day or so between records to sort everything out. My schedule changed unexpectedly, and this is the first moment I've had to go through it all. Apology Apology.

I think the very best thing you could do at this point is exactly what you are talking about doing : bang a record out in a couple of days, with high quality but minimal "production" and no interference from the front office bulletheads. If that is indeed what you want to do, I would love to be involved.

If, instead, you might find yourselves in the position of being temporarily indulged by the record company, only to have them yank the chain at some point (hassling you to rework songs/sequences/production, calling-in hired guns to "sweeten" your record, turning the whole thing over to some remix jockey, whatever...) then you're in for a bummer and I want no part of it.

I'm only interested in working on records that legitimately reflect the band's own perception of their music and existance. If you will commit yourselves to that as a tenet of the recording methodology, then I will bust my ass for you. I'll work circles around you. I'll rap your head in with a ratchet...

I have worked on hundreds of records (some great, some good, some horrible, a lot in the courtyard), and I have seen a direct correlation between the quality of the end result and the mood of the band throughout the process. If the record takes a long time, and everyone gets bummed and scrutinizes every step, then the recordings bear little resemblance to the live band, and the end result is seldom flattering. Making punk rock records is definitely a case where more "work" does <u>not</u> imply a better end result. Clearly you have learned this yourselves and appreciate the logic.

About my recording methodology and philosophy:

#1: Most contemporary engineers and producers see a record as a "project," and the band as only one element of the project. Further, they consider the recordings to be a controlled layering of specific sounds, each of which is under complete control from the moment the note is conceived through the final mix. If the band gets pushed around in the process of making a record, so be it; as long as the "project" meets with the approval of the fellow in control.

My approch is exactly the opposite.

I consider the band the most important thing, as the creative entity that spawned both the band's personality and style and as the social entity that exists 24 hours out of each day. I do not consider it my place to tell you what to do or how to play. I'm quite willing to let my opinions be heard (if I think the band is making beautiful progress or a heaving mistake, I consider it part of my job to tell them) but if the band decides to pursue something, I'll see that it gets done.

I like to leave room for accidents and chaos. Making a seamless record, where every note and syllable is in place and every bass drum beat is identical, is no trick. Any idiot with the patience and the budget to allow such foolishness can do it. I prefer to work on records that aspire to greater things, like originality, personality and enthusiasm. If every element of the music and dynamics of a band is controlled by click tracks, computers, automated mixes, gates, samplers and sequencers, then the record may not be incompetent, but it certainly won't be exceptional. It will also bear very little relationship to the live band, which is what all this hooey is supposed to be about.

#2: I do not consider recording and mixing to be unrelated tasks which can be performed by specialists with no continuous involvement. 99 percent of the sound of a record should be established while the basic take is recorded. Your experiences are specific to your records; but in my experience, remixing has never solved any problems that actually existed, only imaginary ones. I do not like remixing other engineer's recordings, and I do not like recording things for somebody else to remix. I have never been satisfied with either version of that methodology. Remixing is for talentless pussies who don't know how to tune a drum or point a microphone.

#3: I do not have a fixed gospel of stock sounds and recording techniques that I apply blindly to every band in every situation. You are a different band from any other band and deserve at least the respect of having your own tastes and concerns addressed. For example, I love the sound of a boomy drum kit (say a Gretsch or Camco) wide open in a big room, especially with a Bonhammy double-headed bass drum and a really painful snare drum. I also love the puke-inducing low end that comes off an old Fender Bassman or Ampeg guitar amp and the totally blown sound of an SVT with broken-in tubes. I also know that those sounds are inappropriate for some songs, and trying to force them is a waste of time. Predicating the recordings on my tastes is as stupid as designing a car around the upholstery. You guys need to decide and then articulate to me what you want to sound like so we don't come at the record from different directions.

#4: where we record the record is not as important as how it is recorded. If you have a studio you'd like to use, no hag. Otherwise, I can make suggestions. I have a nice 24-track studio in my house (Fugazi were just there, you can ask them how they rate it), and I'm familiar with most of the studios in the Midwest, the East coast and a dozen or so in the UK.

13

I would be a little concerned about having you at my house for the duration of
the whole recording and mixing process (if only because you're celebrities, and
I wouldn't want word getting out in the neighborhood and you guys having to put
up with a lot of fan-style bullshit); it would be a fine place to mix the
record though, and you can't beat the vittles.

If you want to leave the details of studio selection, lodgings, etc. up to me,
I'm quite happy to sort all that stuff out. If you guys want to sort it out,
just lay down the law.

My first choice for an outside recording studio would be a place called
Pachyderm in Cannon Falls, Minnesota. It's a great facility with outstanding
acoustics and a totally comfy architect's wet-dream mansion where the band
lives during the recordings. This makes everything more efficient. Since
everybody is there, things get done and decisions get made a lot faster than if
people are out and about in a city someplace. There's also all the posh shit
like a sauna and swimming pool and fireplaces and trout stream and 50 acres and
like that. I've made a bunch of records there and I've always enjoyed the
place. It's also quite inexpensive, considering how great a facility it is.

The only bummer about Pachyderm is that the owners and manager are not
technicians, and they don't have a tech on call. I've worked there enough that
I can fix just about anything that can go wrong, short of a serious electronic
collapse, but I've got a guy that I work with a lot (Bob Weston) who's real
good with electronics (circuit design, trouble shooting and building shit on
the spot), so if we choose to do it there, he'll probably come along in my
payroll, since he'd be cheap insurance if a power supply blows up or a serious
failure occurs in the dead of winter 50 miles from the closest tech. He's a
recording engineer also, so he can be doing some of the more mundane stuff
(cataloging tapes, packing stuff up, fetching supplies) while we're chopping
away at the record proper.

Some day I'm going to talk the Jesus Lizard into going up there and we'll have
us a real time. Oh yeah, and it's the same Neve console the AC/DC album Back in
Black was recorded and mixed on, so you know its just got to have the rock.

#5: Dough. I explained this to Kurt but I thought I'd better reiterate it here.
I do not want and will not take a royalty on any record I record. No points.
Period. I think paying a royalty to a producer or engineer is ethically
indefensible. The band write the songs. The band play the music. It's the
band's fans who buy the records. The band is responsible for whether it's a
great record or a horrible record. Royalties belong to the band.

I would like to be paid like a plumber: I do the job and you pay me what it's
worth. The record company will expect me to ask for a point or a point and a
half. If we assume three million sales, that works out to 400,000 dollars or
so. There's no fucking way I would ever take that much money. I wouldn't be
able to sleep.

14

I have to be comfortable with the amount of money you pay me, but it's your
money, and I insist that you be comfortable with it as well. Kurt suggested
paying me a chunk which I would consider full payment, and then if you really
thought I deserved more, paying me another chunk after you'd had a chance to
live with the album for a while. That would be fine, but probably more
organizational trouble than it's worth.

Whatever. I trust you guys to be fair to me and I know you must be familiar
with what a regular industry goon would want. I will let you make the final
decision about what I'm going to be paid. How much you choose to pay me will
not affect my enthusiasm for the record.

Some people in my position would expect an increase in business after being
associated with your band. I, however, already have more work than I can
handle, and frankly, the kind of people such superficialities will attract are
not people I want to work with. Please don't consider that an issue.

That's it.

Please call me to go over any of this if it's unclear.

-Steve

If a record takes more than a week to make,
somebody's fucking up.
Oi!

15

SORROW COMES TO ALL

ABRAHAM LINCOLN to
FANNY McCULLOUGH
December 23rd, 1862

As the American Civil War
raged in December of 1862,
US President Abraham
Lincoln received word
that Lieutenant Colonel
William McCullough, whom
he had befriended many
years ago whilst working
as a lawyer in Illinois, had
recently been killed in battle,
leaving behind a distraught
22-year-old daughter so
suffocated by grief that she
was barely able to function.
Her worrying refusal to
eat and inability to sleep
prompted a mutual friend,
David Davis of the Supreme
Court, to make Lincoln, who
long ago had played with her
as a child, aware of Fanny's
deep depression. This
compassionate letter was
Lincoln's response.

Executive Mansion,
Washington, December 23, 1862.

Dear Fanny

It is with deep grief that I learn of the death of your kind and brave Father;
and, especially, that it is affecting your young heart beyond what is common in
such cases. In this sad world of ours, sorrow comes to all; and, to the young, it
comes with bitterest agony, because it takes them unawares. The older have learned
to ever expect it. I am anxious to afford some alleviation of your present distress.
Perfect relief is not possible, except with time. You can not now realize that you
will ever feel better. Is not this so? And yet it is a mistake. You are sure to be happy
again. To know this, which is certainly true, will make you some less miserable now.
I have had experience enough to know what I say; and you need only to believe it,
to feel better at once. The memory of your dear Father, instead of an agony, will yet
be a sad sweet feeling in your heart, of a purer and holier sort than you have
known before.

Please present my kind regards to your afflicted mother.

Your sincere friend
A. Lincoln

Facing page:
Abraham Lincoln in 1865

I SEE NO BEAUTY IN LOPSIDED TRUE LOVE

ELIZABETH SMART to
GEORGE BARKER
September 27th, 1946

Elizabeth Smart was in her 20s when she first met and fell for fellow poet George Barker; despite his already being married, by 1941 she was pregnant with the first of their four children. Smart and Barker's unorthodox relationship was a famously rocky affair due in no small part to their excessive drinking and Barker's repeated empty promises to leave his wife, Jessica. In September of 1946, Smart left him once again, and not for the last time. This was her parting letter. Their relationship eventually waned and Smart brought up the children on her own. George Barker remarried and went on to have fifteen children by four different women.

27th September 1946

I do not think that I want to lie down in your crowded bed for bouts of therapeutic lovemaking. Loving you, I see no beauty in lopsided true love. It really is in sorrow & not anger that I say: I do not want you any more because I simply cannot bear it. It isn't only the unfaithfulness. It's the loneliness, the weeks and months of being alone, really cut off from you, receiving perhaps a postcard saying I fuck you as you pause for breath in fucking somebody else. It would have been better if I had married before I met you, because then you could have given me a few months of fulfilling attentions which is all, apparently, that women need, & then I could have returned to the someone who, possibly, would have cared for me. For you do not want the responsibility even of love & by this I do not mean either money or guilt.

I realize that if you had cared about me the small necessary amount you would not have left me alone with so much pain, but would have contrived to find some other way of doing what you had to. This is the depths & the final & the end of my misery & degradation & if I say goodbye to you now I will be able to keep from being bitter because I am so grateful to you for your last few moments of frankness.

Dearest George, I will NOT give up the belief in true love or if you will romantic love—IT IS possible I KNOW. I never *wanted* anyone since you. IT IS possible to cometh to rest in someone—but you have not evidently had enough pleasure and power. Maybe I want the middle-aged things now. I've had my fuck, but I've lost my love. My womb won't tear me to pieces now, maybe, but my heart certainly will. Goodbye. Elizabeth.

Facing page: Canadian poet and novelist Elizabeth Smart, 1952

MY EARTHLY MISSION IS ALREADY FULFILLED

VIVIAN ROSEWARNE to HIS MOTHER
1940

In May of 1940, a 23-year-old RAF Flying Officer named Vivian Rosewarne was killed during the Battle of Dunkirk when the Wellington bomber that he was co-piloting was shot down above Belgium. Shortly after Rosewarne's death, his commander, Group Captain Claude Hilton Keith, discovered an unsealed letter amongst his belongings, to be forwarded to his mother in the event of his death. Such was its impact in private circles that the next month Vivian Rosewarne's mother gave permission for it to be published anonymously in *The Times* (pictured here) to wide acclaim. In fact, the letter was so popular that it was soon published in book form; 500,000 copies were sold that year alone.

Dearest Mother:

Though I feel no premonition at all, events are moving rapidly and I have instructed that this letter be forwarded to you should I fail to return from one of the raids that we shall shortly be called upon to undertake. You must hope on for a month, but at the end of that time you must accept the fact that I have handed my task over to the extremely capable hands of my comrades of the Royal Air Force, as so many splendid fellows have already done.

First, it will comfort you to know that my role in this war has been of the greatest importance. Our patrols far out over the North Sea have helped to keep the trade routes clear for our convoys and supply ships, and on one occasion our information was instrumental in saving the lives of the men in a crippled lighthouse relief ship. Though it will be difficult for you, you will disappoint me if you do not at least try to accept the facts dispassionately, for I shall have done my duty to the utmost of my ability. No man can do more, and no one calling himself a man could do less.

I have always admired your amazing courage in the face of continual setbacks; in the way you have given me as good an education and background as anyone in the country: and always kept up appearances without ever losing faith in the future. My death would not mean that your struggle has been in vain. Far from it. It means that your sacrifice is as great as mine. Those who serve England must expect nothing from her; we debase ourselves if we regard our country as merely a place in which to eat and sleep.

History resounds with illustrious names who have given all; yet their sacrifice has resulted in the British Empire where there is a measure of peace, justice and freedom for all, and where a higher standard of civilization has evolved, and is still evolving, than anywhere else. But this is not only concerning our own land. Today we are faced with the greatest organized challenge to Christianity and civilization that the world has ever seen, and I count myself lucky and honoured to be the right age and fully trained to throw my full weight into the scale. For this I have to thank you. Yet there is more work for you to do. The home front will still have to stand united for years after the war is won. For all that can be said against it, I still maintain that this war is a very good thing: every individual is having the chance to give and dare all for his principle like the martyrs of old. However long the time may be, one thing can never be altered – I shall have lived and died an Englishman. Nothing else matters one jot nor can anything ever change it.

TUESDAY JUNE 18 1940

Special Articles: PAGE
The Collapse In France   9
Bridge   9
"Old and True."—CXXXVI   9
Obituary: Sir Arthur Harden, F.R.S.,
  Mr. E. S. Holl, Mr. J. A. Pearson, and
  Fallen Officers   9

Illustrations:
The New French Government   8

Correspondence:
An Airman to his Mother   7
A Wordsworth Sonnet (Mr. D. A. G.
  Wilson)   7
Canning on Perseverance (Mr. A. Behr)   7
Nazi Strength and Weakness (Mr. G.
  Young)   7
Farm Work and Defence (Lord Lyming-
  ton)   7
Mobilizing the Unfit (Dame O. Buller)..   8
Saving Gift Stamps (Mrs. M. Lowry)   ..   8
Excess Profits Tax (Mr. C. Andrews, Sir
  W. Trinton, and Mr. C. M. Hall)   8
Returned Employees (Mr. F. R. Greo()..   8
Fracture Clinics (Sir G. Harris)   ..   8
Offers of Service (Mr. A. L. Goodday)..   8
Wedding Rings (Mrs. E. M. Parr)   ..   8
Week-end Munition Work (Mr. J. F.
  Diamond)   8
Points from Letters:—A Prayer for
  Courage; Letters from Evacuees; In-
  cendiary Bombs; Cyclists and Civil
  Defence; Whit-Monday; National
  Prayer; Poultry Stocks; Fenly Hay;
  Irish Children; Savings Certificates;
  Lawn Mowings

Index to News Pages:
BROADCASTING: PAGE 8

Art Exhibitions   ..   4   Imperial & Foreign   ..   11
Auctions To-day   ..   5   Law Report   ..   11
Court Circular   ..   9   News in Brief   ..   4
Crossword Puzzle   ..   5   Parliament   ..
Ecclesiastical News   ..   9   Notices   ..   2
Entertainments   ..   6   Sporting   ..   2
Estate Market   ..   5   The Times of 1840   ..   4
Finance   ..   10 & 11   University News..   11
Home News   ..   3   Wills & Bequests..

TO-DAY'S ARRANGEMENTS

TO-DAY'S NEWS

THE WAR

FINANCE AND COMMERCE

WE FIGHT ON

"If necessary for years, if necessary alone."

AN AIRMAN TO HIS MOTHER

THE FIGHT WITH EVIL

"MY EARTHLY MISSION IS FULFILLED"

Per Ardua ad Astra

TEXT OF THE LETTER

Dearest Mother,—

THE COLLAPSE IN FRANCE

WORN-OUT TROOPS

CRIPPLING EFFECT OF REFUGEES

From Our Military Correspondent

MARSHAL PÉTAIN'S ACTION

THE FRENCH FLEET

CONTROL OF PORTS

From Our Naval Correspondent

NAZI STRENGTH AND WEAKNESS

TO THE EDITOR OF THE TIMES

GORDON YOUNG, Reuter's Special
Correspondent in France.
By telegraph from Ankara, June 17.

A WORDSWORTH SONNET

TO THE EDITOR OF THE TIMES

DENIS A. G. WILSON.

CANNING ON PERSEVERANCE

TO THE EDITOR OF THE TIMES

ALEXANDER BEHR.

You must not grieve for me, for if you really believe in religion and all that it entails that would be hypocrisy. I have no fear of death; only a queer elation ... I would have it no other way. The universe is so vast and so ageless that the life of one man can only be justified by the measure of his sacrifice. We are sent to this world to acquire a personality and a character to take with us that can never be taken from us. Those who just eat and sleep, prosper and procreate, are no better than animals if all their lives they are at peace.

I firmly believe that evil things are sent into the world to try us; they are sent deliberately by our Creator to test our mettle because He knows what is good for us. The Bible is full of cases where the easy way out has been discarded for moral principles.

I count myself fortunate in that I have seen the whole country and known men of every calling. But with the final test of war I consider my character fully developed. Thus at my early age my earthly mission is already fulfilled and I am prepared to die with just one regret: that I could not devote myself to making your declining years more happy by being with you; but you will live in peace and freedom and I shall have directly contributed to that, so here again my life will not have been in vain.

Your loving son,

———————————

KING SEQUOIA

JOHN MUIR to JEANNE
CARR
Circa 1870

Born in 1838 in Scotland,
John Muir was 11 years
old when his large family
uprooted and moved to
Fountain Lake Farm in
Wisconsin, USA. It was
whilst growing up on that
farm, now recognised as a
National Historic Landmark
thanks to his work, that
Muir fell in love with the
wilderness and decided
to dedicate his life to its
preservation and promotion,
later becoming the country's
most famous conservationist
and "The Father of Our
National Park System".
Muir held a particular
affection for Yosemite
National Park and spent
months of his life wandering
amongst its giant sequoias,
a majestic species of tree,
larger than any other, to
which Muir felt a spiritual
connection; this incredible
letter, written to a friend
as he took such a trip, was
penned by Muir with ink
made from the sap of those
same, beloved sequoias.

Squirrelville,
Sequoia Co.
Nut Time

Dear Mrs. Carr

Do behold the King in his glory, King Sequoia! Behold! Behold! seems all I can say.
Some time ago I left all for Sequoia and have been and am at his feet; fasting and
praying for light, for is he not the greatest light in the woods, in the world? Where
are such columns of sunshine, tangible, accessible, terrestrialised? Well may I fast,
not from bread, but from business, book-making, duty-going, and other trifles, and
great is my reward already for the manly, treely sacrifice. What giant truths since
coming to Gigantea, what magnificent clusters of Sequoiac becauses. From here
I cannot recite you one, for you are down a thousand fathoms deep in dark political
quagg, not a burr-length less. But I'm in the woods, woods, woods, and they are in
me-ee-ee. The King tree and I have sworn eternal love – sworn it without swearing,
and I've taken the sacrament with Douglas squirrel, drunk Sequoia wine, Sequoia
blood, and with its rosy purple drops I am writing this woody gospel letter.

I never before knew the virtue of Sequoia juice. Seen with sunbeams in it,
its colour is the most royal of all royal purples. No wonder the Indians
instinctively drink it for they know not what. I wish I were so drunk and Sequoical
that I could preach the green brown woods to all the juiceless world, descending
from this divine wilderness like a John the Baptist, eating Douglas squirrels and
wild honey or wild anything, crying, Repent, for the Kingdom of Sequoia is
at hand!

There is balm in these leafy Gileads – pungent burrs and living King-juice for
all defrauded civilization; for sick grangers and politicians; no need of Salt rivers.
Sick or successful, come suck Sequoia and be saved.

Douglas squirrel is so pervaded with rosin and burr juice his flesh can scarce
be eaten even by mountaineers. No wonder he is so charged with magnetism! One
of the little lions ran across my feet the other day as I lay resting under a fir, and
the effect was a thrill like a battery shock. I would eat him no matter how rosiny for
the lightning he holds. I wish I could eat wilder things. Think of the grouse with
balsam-scented crop stored with spruce buds, the wild sheep full of glacier meadow
grass and daisies azure, and the bear burly and brown as Sequoia, eating pine-burrs
and wasps' stings and all; then think of the soft lightningless poultice-like pap
reeking upon town tables. No wonder cheeks and legs become flabby and fungoid!
I wish I were wilder, and so, bless Sequoia, I will be. There is at least a punky spark
in my heart and it may blaze in this autumn gold, fanned by the King. Some of my
grandfathers must have been born on a muirland for there is heather in me, and
tinctures of bog juices, that send me to Cassiope, and oozing through all my veins
impel me unhaltingly through endless glacier meadows, seemingly the deeper and
danker the better.

See Sequoia aspiring in the upper skies, every summit modelled in fine
cycloidal curves as if pressed into unseen moulds, every bole warm in the mellow

amber sun. How truly godful in mien! I was talking the other day with a duchess and was struck with the grand bow with which she bade me goodbye and thanked me for the glaciers I gave her, but this forenoon King Sequoia bowed to me down in the grove as I stood gazing, and the high bred gestures of the lady seemed rude by contrast.

There goes Squirrel Douglas, the master spirit of the tree-top. It has just occurred to me how his belly is buffy brown and his back silver grey. Ever since the first Adam of his race saw trees and burrs, his belly has been rubbing upon buff bark, and his back has been combed with silver needles. Would that some of you, wise – terribly wise – social scientists, might discover some method of living as true to nature as the buff people of the woods, running as free as the winds and waters among the burrs and filbert thickets of these leafy, mothery woods.

The sun is set and the star candles are being lighted to show me and Douglas squirrel to bed. Therefore, my Carr, goodnight. You say, "When are you coming down?" Ask the Lord – Lord Sequoia.

Squirrelville
Sequoia Co
Nut time

Dear Mrs Carr   Do behold the King
in his glory, King Sequoia. Behold!
Behold! seems all I can say
Some time ago I left all for Sequoia. I have
been & am at his feet fasting & praying
for light, for is he not the greatest light
in the woods—in the world. Where is such
columns of sunshine, tangible, accessible,
terrestrialized. Well may I fast, not
from bread but from business, from
bookmaking, duty doing & other trifles.
& great is my reward already for the manly treely
sacrifice. What giant truths since coming to gigantea,
What magnificent clusters of Sequoic becauses
From here I cannot recite you one, for you
are down a thousand fathoms deep in dark
political gnaze, not a burr length less—
But I'm in the woods woods woods, & they
are in me-ee-ee. The King tree & me have
sworn eternal love—sworn it without semaria
& I've taken the sacrament with Douglas squirrel
drank Sequoia wine, Sequoia blood, & with

its rosy purple dress I am writing this woody gospel letter,. I never before knew the virtues of Sequoia juice, seen with sun=beams in it, its color is the most royal of all royal purples No wonder the Indians instinctively drink it for they know not what — I wish I was so drunk & Sequoical that I could preach the green brown woods to all the juiceless world, descending from this divine wilderness like a John Baptist eating Douglass squirrels & wild honey or wild anything, crying, Repent for the Kingdom of Sequoia is at hand — There is balm in these leafy Gileads,— pungent burrs & living King-juice for all degraded civilization, for sick Grangers & politicians, no need of Salt Rivers, sick or successful — Come suck Sequoia & be saved. Douglass Squirrel is so pervaded with rosin & burr juice his flesh can scarce be eaten even by mountaineers no wonder he is so charged with magnetism. one of the little lions ran across my feet the other day as I lay resting under a fir, & the effect

was a thrill like a battery shock, I would
eat him no matter how rosiny for the
lightening he holds. I wish I could eat
wilder things. Think of the grouse with
balsam scented crop stored with spruce
buds, the wild sheep full of glacier
meadow grass, & daisies azure. & the
bear burly & brown as Sequoia, eating
pine burs & wasps stings & all — then
think of the soft lightningless poultice-like
pap reeking upon town tables. No wonder
cheeks & legs become flabby & fungoid —
I wish I were wilder & so bless Sequoia
I will be — There is at least a punky
spark in my heart & it may blaze in
this autumn gold, fanned by the King —
Some of my grandfathers must have
been born on a muirland for there
is heather in me, & tinctures of bog juices,
that send me to Cassiope, & oozy through
all my veins — impelling me unhaltingly
through endless glacier meadows, seeming
the deeper & danker the better —

4

See Sequoia aspiring in the upper skies
every summit modelled in fine cycloidal
curves as if pressed into unseen moulds —
Every bole warm in the mellow amber sun,
how truly godful in mien. I was talking
the other day with a dutchess & was struck with
the grand bow with wh she bade me goodbye
& thanked me for the Glaciers I gave her,
but this forenoon King Sequoia bowed
to me down in the grove as I stood gazing
& the highbred gestures of the lady seemed
rude by contrast.

There goes Squirrel Douglass the master ~~spirit~~
of the treetop. It has just occurred to me how
his belly is buffy brown, & his back silver-
gray. Ever since the first Adam of his race
saw trees & burrs, his belly has been rubbing
upon buff bark, & his back has been combed
with silvery needles. Would that some of you
wise, terribly wise social scientists might dis =
= cover some method of living as true to nature as
the ~~buff people of the~~ woods running as free
as the winds & waters among the burs
& filbert thickets of these leafy mothery woods.

The sun is set & the star candles are being
lighted to show me & Douglass Squirrel to bed
therefore my Carr goodnight. You say, When are you
coming <u>down</u>? Ask the Lord — Lord Sequoia —

HUSBAND UNTIL DEATH

ABREAM SCRIVEN to HIS
WIFE
September 19th, 1858

In 1858, an educated Georgia
slave named Abream Scriven
was abruptly parted from his
wife Dinah and their children
when his master, Reverend
Charles Colcock Jones, sold
him to a trader based many
miles away in New Orleans.
As he waited for his departure,
heartbroken, Scriven
handwrote a farewell letter to
Dinah. A reply arrived but its
contents are unknown. Her
subsequent attempts to have
her husband brought back
failed; it's believed that they
never saw each other again.

Savannah Sept the 19. 1858

Dinah Jones
    My Dear Wife
    I take the pleasure of writing you these few lines with much regret to
inform you that I am Sold to a man by the name of Peterson a treader and Stays in
new orleans. I am here yet But I expect to go before long but when I get there
I will write and let you know where I am. My Dear I want to Send you Some things
but I donot know who to Send them By but I will try to get them to you and my
children. Give my love to my father & mother and tell them good Bye for me. and if
we Shall not meet in this world I hope to meet in heaven. My Dear wif for you and
my Children my pen cannot Express the griffe I feel to be parted from you all.
I remain your truly
    husband until death
    Abream Scriven

*Below: A slave trade
business in Whitehall Street,
Atlanta, Georgia, 1864*

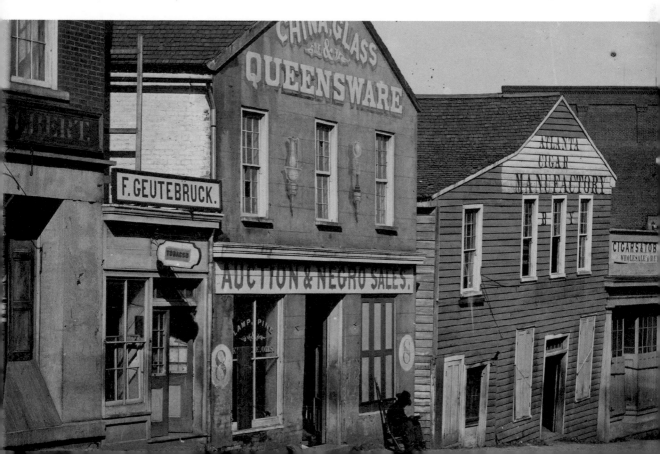

BREAK BREAK BREAK

SYLVIA PLATH to HER
FAMILY
January 5th, 1953

While in Ray Brook, New
York in January of 1953,
aged 20 and without any
previous skiing experience
to speak of, future Pulitzer
Prize-winning poet and
author Sylvia Plath took
leave of her senses and
decided to plummet down a
slope recommended only for
advanced skiers, let alone
those who could barely
stand in the snow. She later,
in a letter, described the
moment at which all control
was lost as "a sudden brief
eternity of actually leaving
the ground, cartwheeling [...]
and plowing face first into a
drift". The result was a badly
broken leg on which a heavy
cast would sit for the next
two months. Sylvia's family
were soon alerted by
telegram.

January 5, 1953

BREAK BREAK BREAK ON THE COLD WHITE SLOPES OH KNEE
ARRIVING FRAMINGHAM TUESDAY NIGHT 7:41. BRINGING
FABULOUS FRACTURED FIBULA NO PAIN JUST TRICKY TO
MANIPULATE WHILE CHARLESTONING. ANYTHING TO PROLONG
VACATION. NORTONS WERE PLANNING TO MEET ME SO WHY NOT
CALL TO CHECK. MUCH LOVE. YOUR FRACTIOUS FUGACIOUS
FRANGIBLE SIVVY.

1984 vs. A BRAVE NEW WORLD

ALDOUS HUXLEY to
GEORGE ORWELL
October 21st, 1949

In October of 1949, a few
months after the publication
of George Orwell's dystopian
masterpiece, Nineteen
Eighty-Four, he received
a letter from fellow author
Aldous Huxley,
a man who, 17 years
previous, had seen his
own nightmarish vision of
society published,
in the form of *Brave New
World,* a book also now
considered a classic. Having
recently finished reading
Orwell's novel, Huxley had
a few words to say. What
begins as a letter of praise
soon becomes a brief
comparison of the two
novels, and an explanation
as to why Huxley believes
his own, earlier work to be a
more realistic prediction.

Wrightwood
Cal.

October 21st 1949

Dear Mr Orwell,

It was very kind of you to tell your publishers to send me a copy of your book.
It arrived as I was in the midst of of a piece of work that required much reading and
consulting of references; and since poor sight makes it necessary for me to ration
my reading, I had to wait a long time before being able to embark on Nineteen
Eighty-Four. Agreeing with all that the critics have written of it, I need not tell
you, yet once more, how fine and how profoundly important the book is. May I
speak instead of the thing with which the book deals — the ultimate revolution?
The first hints of a philosophy of the ultimate revolution — the revolution
which lies beyond politics an economics, and which aims at total subversion of
the individual's psychology and physiology — are to be found in the Marquis de
Sade, who regarded himself as the continuator, the consummator, of Robespierre
and Babeuf.. The philosophy of the ruling monority in Nineteen Eighty-Four is
a sadism which has been carried to its logical conclusion by going beyond sex and
denying it. Whether in actual fact the policy of the boot-on-the-face can go on
indefinitely seems doubtful. My own belief is that the ruling oligarchy will find less
arduous and wasteful ways of governing and of satisfying its lust for power, and that
these ways will resemble those which I described in Brave New World. I have had
occasion recently to look into the history of animal magnetism and hypnotism, and
have been greatly struck by the way in which, for a hundred an fifty years, the world
has refused to take serious cognizance of the discoveries of Mesmer, Braid, Esdaile,
and the rest. Partly because of the prevailing materialism and partly because of
prevailing respectability, nineteenth-century philosophers and men of science were
not willing to investigate the odder facts of psychology. Consequently there was
no pure science of psychology for practical men, such as politicians, soldiers an
policemen, to apply in the field of government. Thanks to the voluntary ignorance
of our fathers, the advent of the ultimate revolution was delayed for five or six
generations. Another lucky accident was Freud's inability to hypnotize successfully
and his consequent disparagement of hypnotism. This delayed the general
application of hypnotism to psychiatry for at least forty years. But now psycho-
analysis is being combined with hypnosis; and hypnosis has been made easy and
indefinitely extensible through the use of barbiturates, which induce a hypnoid and
suggdestible state in even the most recalcitrant subjects. Within the next generation
I believe that the world's rulers will discover that infant conditioning and narco-
hypnosis are more efficient, as instruments of government, than clubs and prisons,
and that the lust for power can be just as completely satisfied by suggesting people

Wrighówood
Cal.

October 21st 1949

Dear Mr Orwell,

It was very kind of you to tell your publishers to send me a
copy of your book. It arrived as I was in the midst of
of a piece of work that required much reading and consulting of xxfxxxxxx
references; and since poor sight makes it necessary for me to ration my
reading, I had to wait a long time before being able to embark on Nineteen Eighty-Four. Agreeing with all that the critics have
written of it, I need not tell you **how** , yet once more, how fine and how
profoundly important the book is. May I speak instead of the x thing
with which the book deals --- the ultimate revolution? The first hints
of a philosophy of the ultimate revolution --- the reveolution which
lies beyond politics an economics, and which aims at the total
subversion of the indiväual's psychology and physiology --- are to be
found in the Marquis de Sade, who regarded himself as the continuator,
the consummator, of Robespierre and Bxbxfxxxxxxxx Babeuf..
The philosophy of the ruling monority in N,neteen Eighty-Four is
a sadism which has txxxxxxxxxxxxxxxxxx been carried to its logical
conclusion by going beyond sex and denying it. Whether in
actual fact the policy of the boot-on-the-face can go on indefinitely
seems dloubtful. My own belief is that the ruling oligarchy will find
less arduous and wasteful ways of xx governing and of
satisfying its lust for power, and that these ways will be--- xfixthxxhindxxm
resemble those which I described in Brave New World. I have had
occasion recently to look into the history of animal magnetism and
hypnotism, and have, been greatly struck by the fxxtxxhxxxxxxxxxxx
way in which, for ahundred an fifty years, the world has refused to
take serious cognizance of the dicooverieq of Mesmer, Braid,
Esdaile and the rest. Partly because of tprevailing
materialism and partly because of prevailing respectability,
nineteenth-century philosophers and men of science waxxkxxxxxxxxxxxxx
were not willing to investigate the odder facts of psychology.
Consequently there was no pure science of psychology for practical
men, such as politicians, soldiers an policemen, to apply in the
field of government. Thanks to the voluntary ignorance of our
fathers, the wxxkxxxxxxxxxxxxxxxxxx fxxxxxxxxxxxxx   advent of the
ultimate revolution was delayed for five or six generations.
Another lucky accident was Freud's kxxxxfixxxxxxx inability to
hypnotize successfully and his consequent disparagement of hypnotism.
This delayed the general application of hypnotism to psychiatry for at
least forty years. But now (xxxtxxxthxxxxtxxkxxxfxxxxxxxx psycho-analysis
is being combined with hypnosis; and hypnosis has been made easy
and indefinitely extensible through the use of barbiturates, which
induce a hypnoid and suggdestible state in even the most reclacitrant
subjecté. Within the next generation I believe that the world's
rulers will discover that infant conditioning and najo-hypnosis
are more efficient, as instruments of government, than clubs and
prisons and that the lust for power can be just as completely
satisfied by suggesting people into loving their servitude as by
flogging and kicking them into obedience. In other words, I feel that
the nightmare of Nineteen Eighty-Four is dstined to modulate into the
nightmare of Bxxxxxxxxxxxxxxx a world having more resemblances to that

into loving their servitude as by flogging and kicking them into obedience. In other words, I feel that the nightmare of Nineteen Eighty-Four is destined to modulate into the nightmare of a world having more resemblance to that which I imagined in Brave New World. The change will be brought about as a result of a felt need for increased efficiency. Meanwhile, of course, there may be a large-scale biological and atomic war — in which case we shall have nightmares of other and scarcely imaginable kinds.

Thank you once again for the book.

Yours sincerely,

Aldous Huxley

which I imagined in Brave New World. The change will be brought about as a result of a felt need for increased efficiency. ~~thtmxmx~~ Meanwhile, of course, there may be a large-scale biological and atomic war --- in which case we shall have nightmares of other and scarcely imaginable kinds.

Thank you once again for the book.

Yours sincerely,

Aldous Huxley.

MY HEART ALMOST STOOD STILL

HELEN KELLER to the
NEW YORK SYMPHONY
ORCHESTRA
February 2nd, 1924

On the evening of
February 1st 1924, the
New York Symphony
Orchestra, conducted by
Walter Damrosch, played
Beethoven's *Symphony No.
9* to a packed Carnegie Hall
in New York, one of the most
famous and prestigious
concert halls in the world.
Many who wanted to attend,
couldn't; thankfully, the
performance was broadcast
live on the radio. A couple
of days later, with talk of
the show still on the lips
of many, the orchestra
received a stunning letter of
thanks from the unlikeliest
of sources. The letter was
written by Helen Keller,
a renowned author and
activist who, despite having
been deaf and blind from
a young age, had managed
to "hear" their music
through touch alone.

*Facing page: Helen Keller touches
an audio speaker to "hear"
recorded sound*

93 Seminole Avenue,
Forest Hills, L. I.,
February 2, 1924.

The New York Symphony Orchestra,
New York City.

Dear Friends:

I have the joy of being able to tell you that, though deaf and blind, I spent a glorious hour last night listening over the radio to Beethoven's "Ninth Symphony." I do not mean to say that I "heard" the music in the sense that other people heard it; and I do not know whether I can make you understand how it was possible for me to derive pleasure from the symphony. It was a great surprise to myself. I had been reading in my magazine for the blind of the happiness that the radio was bringing to the sightless everywhere. I was delighted to know that the blind had gained a new source of enjoyment; but I did not dream that I could have any part in their joy. Last night, when the family was listening to your wonderful rendering of the immortal symphony someone suggested that I put my hand on the receiver and see if I could get any of the vibrations. He unscrewed the cap, and I lightly touched the sensitive diaphragm. What was my amazement to discover that I could feel, not only the vibrations, but also the impassioned rhythm, the throb and the urge of the music! The intertwined and intermingling vibrations from different instruments enchanted me. I could actually distinguish the cornets, the roll of the drums, deep-toned violas and violins singing in exquisite unison. How the lovely speech of the violins flowed and plowed over the deepest tones of the other instruments! When the human voice leaped up trilling from the surge of harmony, I recognized them instantly as voices. I felt the chorus grow more exultant, more ecstatic, upcurving swift and flame-like, until my heart almost stood still. The women's voices seemed an embodiment of all the angelic voices rushing in a harmonious flood of beautiful and inspiring sound. The great chorus throbbed against my fingers with poignant pause and flow. Then all the instruments and voices together burst forth—an ocean of heavenly vibration—and died away like winds when the atom is spent, ending in a delicate shower of sweet notes.

Of course, this was not "hearing" but I do know that the tones and harmonies conveyed to me moods of great beauty and majesty. I also sensed, or thought I did, the tender sounds of nature that sing into my hand—swaying reeds and winds and the murmur of streams. I have never been so enraptured before by a multitude of tone-vibrations.

As I listened, with darkness and melody, shadow and sound filling all the room, I could not help remembering that the great composer who poured forth

such a flood of sweetness into the world was deaf like myself. I marvelled at the power of his quenchless spirit by which out of his pain he wrought such joy for others—and there I sat, feeling with my hand the magnificent symphony which broke like a sea upon the silent shores of his soul and mine.

Let me thank you warmly for all the delight which your beautiful music has brought to my household and to me. I want also to thank Station WEAF for the joy they are broadcasting in the world.

With kindest regards and best wishes, I am,

Sincerely yours,

[Signed]

HELEN KELLER

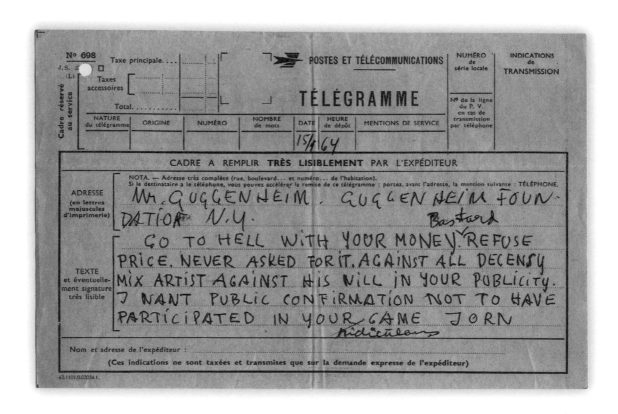

GO TO HELL WITH YOUR MONEY BASTARD

ASGER JORN to THE GUGGENHEIM
1964

Asger Jorn was born in the Danish town of Vejrum on March 3rd, 1914, and grew up to be a prolific artist of many disciplines which included painting, sculpture, book illustration, drawing and ceramics. In 1948, along with five other artists, Jorn co-founded COBRA, an important avant-garde art movement which, despite existing for only three years, made quite an impression in post-war Europe. His work was exhibited in many countries. In 1964, Jorn discovered that he had won the Guggenheim International Award. He responded by telegram.

THE PARAKEET HAS A GOITER

BRIAN DOYLE to VARIOUS
2012 onwards

The dreaded rejection letter is, more often than not, an entirely miserable experience for all concerned. To receive one is to instantly and all at once have one's hopes dashed, confidence thinned, and mood dampened; to send the same is to knowingly rain misery down upon a stranger whose happiness will soon melt away thanks to a decision you had no choice but to make. Even worse than the rejection letter is the standard form rejection letter, a lifeless kick to the guts aimed en masse at a pool of unsuitables who are, it would seem, undeserving of a personal shove – a pre-printed shake of the head for one's troubles. To find a standard form rejection letter of note, then, is quite a task, but not impossible, and here is the finest of examples, written and sometimes sent by Brian Doyle, current editor of the University of Portland's *Portland Magazine*.

Facing page: Remington Steele the parakeet is prepared for surgery at the Animal Medical Center in New York City

Thank you for your lovely and thoughtful submission to the magazine, which we are afraid we are going to have to decline, for all sorts of reasons. The weather is dreary, our backs hurt, we have seen too many cats today and as you know cats are why God invented handguns, there is a sweet incoherence and self-absorption in your piece that we find alluring but we have published far too many of same in recent years mostly authored by the undersigned, did we mention the moist melancholy of the weather, our marriages are unkempt and disgruntled, our children surly and crammed to the gills with a sense of entitlement that you wonder how they will ever make their way in the world, we spent far too much money recently on silly graphic design and now must slash the storytelling budget, our insurance bills have gone up precipitously, the women's basketball team has no rebounders, an aunt of ours needs a seventh new hip, the shimmer of hope that was the national zeitgeist looks to be nursing a whopper of a black eye, and someone left the toilet roll thing empty again, without the slightest consideration for who pays for things like that. And there were wet towels on the floor. And the parakeet has a goiter. And the dog barfed up crayons. Please feel free to send us anything you think would fit these pages, and thank you for considering our magazine for your work. It's an honor.

--Editors

ALONG WITH THIS LETTER COMES A PLAY

SHELAGH DELANEY to
JOAN LITTLEWOOD
Circa 1957

Born in Salford in 1938, Shelagh Delaney was just 18 years old and new to the world of theatre when she began to write *A Taste of Honey*, the play for which she is now widely known. In the blink of an eye she was the talk of the industry: by 1958, the play had been produced by Joan Littlewood's Theatre Workshop and was winning over critics and audiences alike; the next year, it opened in the West End to similarly positive reviews. Undeterred by this instant fame, Delaney then adapted her debut for the big screen with aplomb – the resulting film premiered in 1961 and went on to win numerous awards, with Delaney still in her early twenties. All told, a remarkable entrance, made possible thanks to a sterling play and this plucky letter of introduction from Delaney to Littlewood, sent just two weeks after loading her first sheet of paper into a typewriter.

Facing page: Playwright Shelagh Delaney, c. 1965

Dear Miss Littlewood

Along with this letter comes a play, the first I have written. I wondered if you would read it through and send it back to me because no matter what sort of theatrical atrocity it might be, it isn't valueless so far as I'm concerned.

A fortnight ago I didn't know the theatre existed, but a young man, anxious to improve my mind, took me to the Opera House in Manchester and I came away after the performance having suddenly realised that at last, after nineteen years of life, I had discovered something that meant more to me than myself. I sat down and thought. The following day I bought a packet of paper and borrowed an unbelievable typewriter which I still have great difficulty in using. I set to and produced this little epic - don't ask me why - I'm quite unqualified for anything like this. But at least I finished it and if, from among the markings and the typing errors and the spelling mistakes, you can gather a little sense from what I have written – or a little nonsense – I should be extremely grateful for your criticism – though I hate criticism of any kind.

I want to write for the theatre, but I know so very little about it. I know nothing, have nothing - except a willingness to learn - and intelligence.

Yours sincerely
Shelagh Delaney

EVERYONE IS EXPECTING ME TO DO BIG THINGS

JACK TRICE to WHOM IT MAY CONCERN
October 5th, 1923

Jack Trice was Iowa State's first African-American athlete. On October 6th of 1923, aged 21, he played his first major college football game in a match against the University of Minnesota: in the first half, he suffered a broken collarbone but continued to play; later in the game, he was stamped on by three players on the opposing team and suffered internal injuries that would kill him days later. Shortly before his funeral, this letter was found in his suit jacket. It had been written the night before the game, as he stayed in a different hotel to his teammates due to his being black.

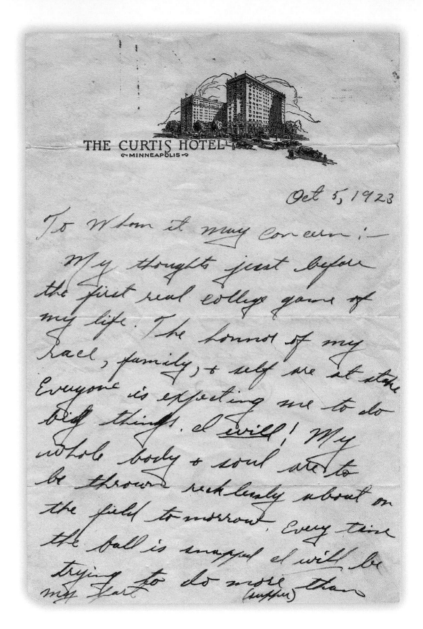

Oct 5, 1923

To whom it may concern:-

My thoughts just before the first real college game of my life. The honor of my race, family, and self are at stake. Everyone is expecting me to do big things. I <u>will</u>! My whole body and soul are to be thrown recklessly about on the field tomorrow. Every time the ball is snapped I will be trying to do more than my part.

On all defensive plays I must break through the opponent's line and stop the play in their territory. Beware of mass interference, <u>fight</u> low with your eyes open and toward the play. <u>Roll block the interference</u>. Watch out for cross bucks and reverse end runs. Be on your toes every minute if you expect to make good.

(meeting) 7:45
<u>Jack</u>

THE SIMPSONS™

September 28, 1990

Mrs. Barbara Bush
The First Lady
The White House
1600 Pennsylvania Avenue
Washington, D.C.

Dear First Lady:

I recently read your criticism of my family.
I was deeply hurt. Heaven knows we're far
from perfect and, if truth be known, maybe
just a wee bit short of normal; but as Dr.
Seuss says, "a person is a person".

I try to teach my children Bart, Lisa, and
even little Maggie, always to give somebody
the benefit of the doubt and not talk badly
about them, even if they're rich. It's hard
to get them to understand this advice when
the very First Lady in the country calls us
not only dumb, but "the dumbest thing" she
ever saw. Ma'am, if we're the dumbest thing
you ever saw, Washington must be a good deal
different than what they teach me at the
current events group at the church.

I always believed in my heart that we had a
great deal in common. Each of us living our
lives to serve an exceptional man. I hope
there is some way out of this controversy. I
thought, perhaps, it would be a good start to
just speak my mind.

With great respect,

Marge Simpson
Marge Simpson

WITH GREAT RESPECT, MARGE SIMPSON

MARGE SIMPSON to BARBARA BUSH
September 28th, 1990

First Lady Barbara Bush received a letter from the unlikeliest of sources in 1990, as a result of an article in *People* magazine in which she described *The Simpsons* as being "the dumbest thing [she] had ever seen". She couldn't have imagined that such a quote would elicit a response from the cartoon family itself, but it did, in the form of a reply from Marge Simpson that soon arrived at the White House. An apologetic letter from Barbara Bush followed.

Tensions between the two families resurfaced two years later, when Barbara's husband, then-US President George H. W. Bush, promised: "We're going to keep trying to strengthen the American family. To make them more like the Waltons and less like the Simpsons." The next episode of *The Simpsons* featured an amended opening sequence in which, after watching Bush's speech on television, Bart responded: "Hey, we're just like the Waltons. We're praying for an end to the Depression too."

[Barbara Bush's response:]

Dear Marge,

How kind of you to write. I'm glad you spoke your mind; I foolishly didn't know you had one.

I am looking at a picture of you, depicted on a plastic cup, with your blue hair filled with pink birds peeking out all over. Evidently, you and your charming family — Lisa, Homer, Bart and Maggie — are camping out. It is a nice family scene. Clearly you are setting a good example for the rest of the country.

Please forgive a loose tongue.

Warmly,

Barbara Bush

P.S. Homer looks like a handsome fella!

SLOWLY, QUIETLY,
NEVER GIVING UP

CARL SANDBURG to
MARGARET SANDBURG
November 1921

Carl Sandburg was a man of many talents. He was a two-time Pulitzer Prize-winning poet, a writer, a Pulitzer Prize-winning historian, a journalist, and even a folk singer. In 1907, he met Lilian Steichen and they fell deeply in love; a year later they were married, and they remained so until Sandburg's death in 1967, at which point they had three daughters. In 1921, their eldest girl, Margaret – at ten years old already highly intelligent and something of a chip off the old block – was found to be epileptic. Soon after the diagnosis, unable to visit her at Battle Creek Sanitarium where she was being treated, Carl Sandburg wrote a short letter to his daughter and attempted to soothe her nerves.

November 1921

Dear Margaret,

This is only a little letter from your daddy to say he thinks about you hours and hours and he knows that there was never a princess or a fairy worth so much love. We are starting on a long journey and hard fight — you and mother and daddy — and we are going to go on slowly, quietly, hand in hand, the three of us, never giving up. And so we are going to win. Slowly, quietly, never giving up, we are going to win.

Daddy

SHE WAS THE MUSIC HEARD FAINTLY AT THE EDGE OF SOUND

RAYMOND CHANDLER to
LEONARD RUSSELL
December 29th, 1954

Celebrated detective novelist Raymond Chandler's wife of 30 years, Cissy, died on December 12th, 1954 after a long and painful battle with pulmonary fibrosis during which the author wrote *The Long Goodbye*. As can be seen in this touching and affectionate letter, written to friend Leonard Russell shortly after Cissy's passing, Raymond was deeply affected by the loss of his wife, and it seems he never really recovered. Sadly, he died five years later a broken man, having attempted suicide and returned to the alcoholism she had previously helped him to avoid.

December 29, 1954

Dear Leonard:

Your letter of December 15th has just reached me, the mails being what they are around Christmas time. I have received much sympathy and kindness and many letters, but yours is somehow unique in that it speaks of the beauty that is lost rather than condoling with the comparatively useless life that continues on. She was everything you say, and more. She was the beat of my heart for thirty years. She was the music heard faintly at the edge of sound. It was my great and now useless regret that I never wrote anything really worth her attention, no book that I could dedicate to her. I planned it. I thought of it, but I never wrote it. Perhaps I couldn't have written it.

She died hard. Her body fought a hundred lost battles, any one of which would have been enough to finish most of us. Twice I brought her home from the hospital because she hated hospitals, and had her in her own room with nurses around the clock. But she had to go back. And I suppose she never quite forgave me for that. But when at the end I closed her eyes she looked very young. Perhaps by now she realizes that I tried, and that I regarded the sacrifice of several years of a rather insignificant literary career as a small price to pay, if I could make her smile a few times more.

No doubt you realize that this was no sudden thing, that it had been going on for a long time, and that I have said goodbye to my Cissy in the middle of the night in the dark cold hours many, many times. She admired and liked you very much. I'm not sure that she liked Dilys as much as I did, because possibly she suspected that I liked her too much. And it is just possible that I thought she liked *you* a little too much.

I hope that you are both well and prosperous and that I may have the privilege of seeing *you* again in the not too distant future, with or without the butler from the Ritz. And I hope I am not being too sentimental if I sign myself,

Yours affectionately,

[Signed]

I EMBRACE YOU WITH ALL MY HEART

ALBERT CAMUS to LOUIS GERMAIN
November 19th, 1957

On November 7th 1913, in French Algeria, author Albert Camus was born. The second son of Lucien and Catherine Camus, he was just 11 months old when his father was killed in action during the Battle of the Marne; his mother, partially deaf and illiterate, then raised her boys in extreme poverty with the help of his heavy-handed grandmother. It was in school that Camus shone, due in no small part to the encouragement offered by his beloved teacher, Louis Germain, a man who fostered the potential he saw and steered young Camus on a path that would eventually see him write some hugely respected, award-winning novels and essays. In 1957, Camus was awarded the Nobel Prize for Literature, "for his important literary production, which with clear-sighted earnestness illuminates the problems of the human conscience in our times". Shortly after the occasion, he wrote to his former teacher.

19 November 1957

Dear Monsieur Germain,

I let the commotion around me these days subside a bit before speaking to you from the bottom of my heart. I have just been given far too great an honour, one I neither sought nor solicited.

But when I heard the news, my first thought, after my mother, was of you. Without you, without the affectionate hand you extended to the small poor child that I was, without your teaching and example, none of all this would have happened.

I don't make too much of this sort of honour. But at least it gives me the opportunity to tell you what you have been and still are for me, and to assure you that your efforts, your work, and the generous heart you put into it still live in one of your little schoolboys who, despite the years, has never stopped being your grateful pupil. I embrace you with all my heart.

Albert Camus

Facing page: French writer Albert Camus at his publishing firm's office in Paris, France, 1957

I HAVE RESOLVED TO ESCAPE

WINSTON CHURCHILL to
LOUIS DE SOUZA
December 11th, 1899

In October 1899, 40 years
before becoming Prime
Minister of the UK, 24-year-
old Winston Churchill
jumped on a ship to South
Africa to work as a highly-
paid war correspondent
during the Second Boer
War. Not long after arrival,
he found himself aboard an
armoured train with more
than 100 British soldiers
that was derailed by the
Boers; his heroic efforts
to clear the tracks were
halted, many lost their lives.
Churchill was captured and
held as a prisoner of war,
but not for long. On the
evening of December 12th,
he wrote the following letter
to the Under-Secretary for
War, Louis de Souza, left it
beneath his pillow, scaled
a wall and very politely
fled, never to return. On
the envelope, in Churchill's
hand, was written "p.p.c.",
which stands for "pour
prendre congé" or "to take
leave".

Dear Mr. de Souza,

I do not consider that your government was justified in holding me,
a press correspondent and a non combatant as a prisoner, and I have consequently
resolved to escape. The arrangements I have succeeded in making in conjunction
with my friends outside are such as give me every confidence. But I wish in leaving
you thus hastily & unceremoniously to once more place on record my appreciation
of the kindness which has been shown me and the other prisoners by you, by the
commandant and by Dr. Gunning and my admiration of the chivalrous and humane
character of the Republican forces. My views on the general question of the war
remain unchanged, but I shall always retain a feeling of high respect for the several
classes of the burghers I have met and, on reaching the British lines I will set
forth a truthful & impartial account of my experiences in Pretoria. In conclusion I
desire to express my obligations to you, and to hope that when this most grievous
and unhappy war shall have come to an end, a state of affairs may be created
which shall preserve at once the national pride of the Boer and the security of the
British and put a final stop to the rivalry and enmity of both races. Regretting the
circumstances have not permitted me to bid you a personal farewell,
                Believe me
                        Yours vy sincerely
                                Winston S. Churchill

Dec. 11th 1899

State Schools Prison
Pretoria.

Dear Mr. de Souza,

I do not consider that your Government was justified in holding me, a press correspondent and a non combatant as a prisoner, and I have consequently resolved to escape. The arrangements I have succeeded in making in conjunction with my friends outside are such as to give me every confidence. But I wish in leaving you thus hastily & unceremoniously to once more place on record my appreciation of the kindness which has been shown me and the other prisoners by you, by the commandant and by Dr. Gunning and my admiration of the chivalrous and humane character of the Republican forces. My views on the general question of the war remain unchanged, but I shall always retain a feeling of high respect for the several classes of the burghers I have met and, on reaching the British lines I will set forth a truthful & impartial account of my experiences in Pretoria. In conclusion, I desire to express my obligations to you, and to hope that when this most grievous and unhappy war shall have come to an end, a state of affairs may be created which shall preserve at once the national pride of the Boers and the security of the British and put a final stop to the rivalry & enmity of both races. Regretting that circumstances have not permitted me to bid you a personal farewell, Believe me

Yours very sincerely

Winston S. Churchill.

Dec. 11th 1899.

WITH MANY GOOD WISHES FOR OUR HOUSE

LION FEUCHTWANGER to
THE OCCUPANT OF HIS
HOUSE
March 20th, 1935

In January of 1933, as
he toured the US giving
lectures, influential
German-Jewish author Lion
Feuchtwanger received
word that Adolf Hitler, a
man whose beliefs he had
been publicly lambasting for
the past decade, had risen
to power back in Germany,
his home and place of birth.
To return now would be
suicide for both him and
his wife, Marta; so, rather
than risk imprisonment or
worse, they travelled from
the US to France to live in
exile while their German
home was looted by Hitler's
men, their books burnt and
banned. Two years later,
Feuchtwanger wrote a
letter to the new owner of
his house and saw that it
was printed in the *Pariser
Tageblatt,* a newspaper
written by and for the
countless Germans exiled
since the Nazi Party's rule.

As it happens, the
Feuchtwangers never saw
their home again. They lived
most of their remaining
years in California.

To the occupant of my house on Mahlstrasse in Berlin

Dear Sir,

I do not know your name or how you came into possession of my house. I only know that two years ago the police of the Third Reich seized all my property, personal and real, and handed it over to the stock company formed by the Reich for the confiscation of the properties of political adversaries (chairman of the board: Minister Goering). I learned this through a letter from the mortgagees. They explained to me that under the laws of the Third Reich confiscations of property belonging to political opponents concern themselves only with credit balances. Although my house and my bank deposits, which had also been confiscated, greatly exceeded in value the amount of the mortgage, I would be obliged to continue the payment of interests on the mortgage, as well as my German taxes, from whatever money I might earn abroad. Be that as it may, one thing is certain – you, Mr. X, are occupying my house and I, in the opinion of the German judges, must pay the costs.

How do you like my house, Mr. X? Do you find it pleasant to live in? Did the silver-grey carpeting in the upper rooms suffer while the SA-men were looting? My concierge sought safety in these upper rooms, as, I being in America at the time, the gentlemen had decided to take it out on him. The carpet is very delicate, and red is a strong color, hard to clean out. The rubber tiling in the stairway was also not primarily designed with the boots of SA-men in mind. Should it have suffered too badly, I recommend you contact the Baake company; the flooring is the same as on the staircases of the "Europa" and the "Bremen", and this is the company which delivered it.

Have you any notion why I had the semi-enclosed roof terrace built? Mrs. Feuchtwanger and I used it for our morning exercise. Would you mind seeing to it that the pipes of the shower don't freeze?

I wonder to what use you have put the two rooms which formerly contained my library. I have been told, Mr. X, that books are not very popular in the Reich in which you live, and whoever shows interest in them is likely to get into difficulties. I, for instance, read your "Führer's" book and guilelessly remarked that his 140,000 words were 140,000 offenses against the spirit of the German language. The result of this remark is that you are now living in my house. Sometimes I wonder to what uses bookcases can be put in the Third Reich. In case you should decide to have them ripped out, be careful not to damage the wall. And did they rip out the round bench which was built into the library's window loggia? One thing is for certain, Mr. X, there is a lot to rebuild and repair in the house. May I suggest you contact the architect Slobotka for this purpose? I doubt whether this gentleman is allowed to practice in Berlin though since there aren't many architects who know how to build in the city, yet there are many party members who want to build.

Please, your connections permitting, do not hire a party member but rather a professional. It would be a pity about the house.

I would like to know what is going on with the buzz saw in the Grunewald forestry. Its noise has sometimes spoiled my enjoyment of the house, and it was only with great effort that I managed to achieve the removal of this nuisance. These days of course, noise will hardly be considered a disturbance in Berlin. However, it would be nice of you if you didn't simply give up my hard won victory.

And what have you done with my terrarium which stood at one of the windows of my study? Did they actually kill my turtles and my lizards because their owner was of an "alien race"? And were the flower beds and the rock garden much damaged when the SA-men, shooting as they ran, pursued my sorely beaten concierge across the garden while he fled into the woods?

Doesn't it sometimes seem odd to you that you should be living in my house? Your "Führer" is not generally considered a friend of Jewish literature. Isn't it, therefore, astounding that he should have such a strong predilection for the Old Testament? I myself have heard him quote with much fervor, 'An eye for an eye, a tooth for a tooth' (by which he may have meant 'A confiscation of property for literary criticism'). And now, through you, he has fulfilled a prophecy of the Old Testament – the saying, 'Thou shalt dwell in houses thou hast not builded.'

Don't let my house get into a mess, Mr. X. Building and furnishing it has taken Mrs. Feuchtwanger and myself a lot of effort. Running and maintaining it won't take a lot of effort. Please take care of it a little. I'm also saying this in your own interest. Your "Führer" has promised that his rule will last a thousand years: thus I'm assuming that you will soon be in the position of negotiating the houses' return with me.

With many good wishes for our house,

Lion Feuchtwanger

P.S. By the way, do you agree that my statement that your "Führer" writes bad German is disproved by the fact that you are sitting in my house?

LETTER TO THE DEAD

SHEPSI to INKHENMET
Circa 2000 BC

According to ancient Egyptians, the deceased were so powerful that they could settle earthly disputes and deliver justice from the afterlife with guidance from the Great God. When such assistance was needed, letters to dead relatives were often written on bowls that were then filled with food and placed outside the tombs of their loved ones, the belief being that the letter would be read when the meal was collected by the deceased. This particular example, left outside the tomb of Inkhenmet approximately 4,000 years ago, was written by his son, Shepsi, and concerned a land dispute seemingly brought on by Inkhenmet's other, *dead* son, Sebkhotep, for which Shepsi sought retribution.

Facing page: Terracotta bowl inscribed with a letter from a mother to her dead son, Middle Kingdom

Inside:

Shepsi speaks to his father Inkhenmet.

This is a reminder of your journey to the dungeon, to the place where Sen's son Hetepu was, when you brought the foreleg of an ox, and when this your son came with Newaef, and when you said, Welcome, both of you. Sit and eat meat! Am I to be injured in your presence, without this your son having done or said anything, by my brother? (And yet) I was the one who buried him, I brought him from the dungeon, I placed him among his desert tomb-dwellers, even though thirty measures of refined barley were due from him by a loan, and one bundle of garments, six measures of fine barley, one ball of flax, and a cup – even though I did for him what did not (need) to be done. He has done this against this your son evilly, evilly - but you had said to this your son, 'All my property is vested in my son Shepsi along with my fields'. Now Sher's son Henu has been taken. See, he is with you in the same city. You have to go to judgement with him now, since your scribes are with (you) in the same city. Can a man be joyful, when his spears are used [against his own son]?

Outside:

Shepsi speaks to his mother Iy.

This is a reminder of the time that you said to this your son 'Bring me quails for me to eat', and when this your son brought to you seven quails for you to eat. Am I to be injured in your presence, so that the children are badly discontent with this your son? Who then will pour out water for you? If only you would judge between me and Sobekhotep! I brought him from another town, and placed him in his town among his male and female dead, and gave him burial cloth. Why then is he acting against this your son, when I have said and done nothing, evilly, evilly? Evil-doing is painful for the gods!

YOU'RE OFF, BY GOD!

RICHARD BURTON to
ELIZABETH TAYLOR
June 25th, 1973

Elizabeth Taylor and Richard
Burton were both already
married when they fell in
love on the set of *Cleopatra*
in 1962 – she to fourth
husband Eddie Fisher, a
singer, and he to actress
Sybil Christopher. In 1964,
with divorces finalised, they
wed and became one of
the most famous, bankable
couples in Hollywood
history: all told, they
shared the screen in eleven
films, including, in 1966,
the multi-award-winning
classic, *Who's Afraid of
Virginia Woolf?*. Nine years
after marrying, as their
extravagant and famously
tempestuous relationship
crumbled, Taylor gave
Burton his marching orders
– this passionate letter,
just one of many he sent to
her during and after their
union, was his response. A
year after he wrote it, they
divorced; sixteen months
after that, they wed each
other again. Their second
marriage lasted just nine
months.

*Facing page: Elizabeth
Taylor with Richard Burton,
Budapest, 1973*

June 25, 1973

So My Lumps,

You're off, by God!

I can barely believe it since I am so unaccustomed to anybody leaving me.
But reflectively I wonder why nobody did so before. All I care about—honest to
God—is that you are happy and I don't much care who you'll find happiness with.
I mean as long as he's a friendly bloke and treats you nice and kind. If he doesn't
I'll come at him with a hammer and clinker. God's eye may be on the sparrow but
my eye will always be on you. Never forget your strange virtues. Never forget that
underneath that veneer of raucous language is a remarkable and puritanical LADY.
I am a smashing bore and why you've stuck by me so long is an indication of your
loyalty. I shall miss you with passion and wild regret.

You may rest assured that I will not have affairs with any other female.
I shall gloom a lot and stare morosely into unimaginable distances and act a bit—
probably on the stage—to keep me in booze and butter, but chiefly and above all I
shall write. Not about you, I hasten to add. No Millerinski Me, with a double M.
There are many other and ludicrous and human comedies to constitute my shroud.

I'll leave it to you to announce the parting of the ways while I shall
never say or write one word except this valedictory note to you. Try and look after
yourself. Much love. Don't forget that you are probably the greatest actress in the
world. I wish I could borrow a minute portion of your passion and commitment,
but there you are—cold is cold as ice is ice.

THE TALE OF PETER RABBIT

BEATRIX POTTER to NOEL MOORE
September 4th, 1893

In September of 1893, at 26 years of age, aspiring artist Beatrix Potter sent this illustrated letter to Noel, the five-year-old son of her friend and former governess, Annie Moore. The letter contained a tale of four rabbits, and in fact featured the first ever appearance of Peter Rabbit, the character for which Potter would one day become famous; however, it wasn't until 1901, eight years later, that she decided to revisit her letter to Noel and develop the idea. The resulting story, *The Tale of Peter Rabbit,* was published in 1902 by Frederick Warne & Co., and has since become one of the most popular children's books of all time.

My dear Noel,

I don't know what to write to you, so I shall tell you a story about four little rabbits whose names were – Flopsy, Mopsy, Cottontail and Peter.

They lived with their mother in a sand bank under the root of a big fir tree.

"Now my dears," said old Mrs Bunny "you may go into the field or down the lane, but don't go into Mr McGregor's garden."

Flopsy, Mopsy & Cottontail, who were good little rabbits went down the lane to gather blackberries, but Peter, who was very naughty ran straight away to Mr McGregor's garden and squeezed underneath the gate.

First he ate some lettuce, and some broad beans, then some radishes, and then, feeling rather sick, he went to look for some parsley; but round the end of a cucumber frame whom should he meet but Mr McGregor!

Mr McGregor was planting out young cabbages but he jumped up & ran after Peter waving a rake & calling out "Stop thief"!

Peter was most dreadfully frightened & rushed all over the garden, for he had forgotten the way back to the gate. He lost one of his shoes among the cabbages and the other shoe amongst the potatoes. After losing them he ran on four legs & went faster, so that I think he would have got away altogether, if he had not unfortunately run into a gooseberry net and got caught fast by the large buttons on his jacket. It was a blue jacket with brass buttons, quite new.

Mr McGregor came up with a basket which he intended to pop on the top of Peter, but Peter wriggled out just in time, leaving his jacket behind, and this time he found the gate, slipped underneath and ran home safely.

Mr McGregor hung up the little jacket & shoes for a scarecrow, to frighten the blackbirds.

Peter was ill during the evening, in consequence of overeating himself. His mother put him to bed and gave him a dose of camomile tea, but Flopsy, Mopsy, and Cottontail had bread and milk and blackberries for supper.

I am coming back to London next Thursday, so I hope I shall see you soon, and the new baby.

I remain, dear Noel, yours affectionately

Beatrix Potter

Eastwood Dunkeld
Sep 4th 93

My dear Noel,
            I don't know what to
write to you, so I shall tell you a story
            about four little rabbits.
                        whose names were —

Flopsy, Mopsy Cottontail

and Peter

They lived with their mother in a
sand bank, under the root of a
big fir tree.

"Now, my dears", said old Mrs Bunny
"you may go into the field or down
the lane, but don't go into Mr McGregor's
garden."

Flopsy, Mopsy & Cottontail, who were good
little rabbits went down the lane to gather
black berries, but Peter, who was very naughty

ran straight away to Mr McGregor's garden
and squeezed underneath the gate.

First he ate some lettuce,
and some broad beans,
then some radishes, and
then, feeling rather sick,
he went to look for
some parsley; but
round the end of a
cucumber frame
whom should he meet but Mr McGregor!

64

Mr McGregor was planting out young cabbages
but he jumped up & ran after Peter waving
a rake & calling out 'Stop thief'!

Peter was most dreadfully frightened &
rushed all over the garden, for he had
forgotten the way back to the gate.
He lost one of his shoes among the cabbages

and the other shoe amongst the potatoes.
After losing them he ran on four legs &
went faster, so that I think he would

have got away altogether, if he had not
unfortunately run into a gooseberry net
and got caught fast by the large buttons
on his jacket. It was a blue jacket with
brass buttons; quite new.

Mr McGregor came up with a basket which
he intended to pop on the top of Peter,
but Peter wriggled out just in time,
          leaving his jacket behind,

and this time he found the gate,
slipped underneath and ran home
safely.

Mr. McGregor hung up the little jacket & shoes for a scarecrow, to frighten the black birds.

Peter was ill during the evening, in consequence of over eating himself. His mother put him to bed and gave him a dose of camomile tea,

but Flopsy, Mopsy, and Cottontail
had bread and milk and blackberries
for supper.   I am coming
back to London next Thursday, so
I hope I shall see you soon, and
the new baby. I remain, dear Noel,
yours affectionately
                    Beatrix Potter.

YOUR EAGER MOTHER

JESSIE BERNARD to HER
UNBORN CHILD
May 4th, 1941

Renowned American
sociologist and feminist
Jessie Bernard studied
and taught at a number
of institutes up until her
retirement in 1964, and it
was really only then that she
became one of feminism's
most important voices by
writing most of the seminal
books and articles for which
she is now known, including
The Future of Marriage and
The Female World. She did
much of this as a single
parent to her three children
following the loss of her
husband, Luther, to cancer
in 1951, six months after the
birth of their third child. In
1941, aged 38 and pregnant
with their first, Jessie wrote
their unborn daughter a
letter.

My dearest,

Eleven weeks from today you will be ready for this outside world. And what a world it is this year! It has been the most beautiful spring I have ever seen. Miss Morris (a faculty colleague) says it is because I have you to look forward to. She says she has noticed a creative look on my face in my appreciation of this spring. And she is right. But also the world itself has been so particularly sweet, aglow with color. The forsythia were fragrant and feathery. And now the spirea, heavy with their little round blooms, stand like wonderful igloos, a mass of white. I doff my scientific mantle long enough to pretend that Nature is outdoing herself to prepare this earth for you. But also I want to let all this beauty get into my body. I cannot help but think of that other world. The world of Europe where babies are born to hunger, stunted growth, breasts dried up with anxiety and fatigue. That is part of the picture too. And I sometimes think that while my body in this idyllic spring creates a miracle, forces are at work which within twenty or twenty-five years may be preparing to destroy the creation of my body. My own street, the war takes on a terrible new significance when I think of that. I think of all those mothers who carried their precious cargoes so carefully for nine long months - and you have no idea how long nine months can be when you are impatient for the end - lovingly nurtured their babies at their breasts, and watched them grow for twenty years. I think of their anguish when all this comes to naught. Your father thinks parents ought to get down on their knees and beg forgiveness of children for bringing them into such a world. And there is much truth in that. But I hope you will never feel like that. I hope you will never regret the life we have created for you out of our seed. To me the only answer a woman can make to the destructive forces of the world is creation. And the most ecstatic form of creation is the creation of new life. I have so many dreams for you. There are so many virtues I would endow you with if I could. First of all, I would make you tough and strong. And how I have labored at that! I have eaten vitamins and minerals instead of food. Gallons of milk, pounds of lettuce, dozens of eggs … Hours of sunshine. To make your body a strong one because everything [depends] on that. I would give you resiliency of body so that all the blows and buffets of this world would leave you still unbeaten. I would have you creative. I would have you a creative scientist. But if the shuffling genes have made of you an artist, that will make me happy too. And even if you have no special talent either artistic or scientific, I would still have you creative no matter what you do. To build things, to make things, to create - that is what I covet for you. If you have a strong body and a creative mind you will be happy. I will help in that. Already I can see how parents long to shield their children from disappointments and defeat. But I also know that I cannot re-make life for you. You will suffer. You will have moments of disappointment and defeat. You will have your share of buffeting. I cannot spare you that. But I hope to help you be such a strong, radiant, self-integrated person that you will take all this in your stride, assimilate it, and rise to conquer …

Eleven more weeks. It seems a long time. Until another time, then, my precious one, I say good-bye.

Your eager mother

THE MATCHBOX

SYLVIA TOWNSEND
WARNER to ALYSE
GREGORY
December 23rd, 1946

Born in 1893, English author
and poet Sylvia Townsend
Warner wrote seven novels
in her lifetime beginning
with *Lolly Willowes* –
the quirky tale of a lady who
moves away from home
following the death of her
father and, as is often the
case, takes up witchcraft
– the book for which she is
now remembered by too few
people; in fact, she found
more success in the US
where she was celebrated
by many and frequently
wrote for *The New Yorker*
magazine. Away from public
life, Townsend Warner also
had an unrivalled knack
for writing entertaining
letters, and in 1946 penned
this exquisite example to
friend and fellow writer,
Alyse Gregory, in response
to a Christmas gift which, if
given to anyone else, would
have elicited little more than
a blank expression.

Dearest Alyse,

Usually one begins a thank-letter by some graceless comparison, by saying, I have never been given such a very scarlet muffler, or, This is the largest horse I have ever been sent for Christmas. But your matchbox is a nonpareil, for never in my life have I been given a matchbox. Stamps, yes, drawing-pins, yes, balls of string, yes, yes, menacingly too often; but never a matchbox. Now that it has happened I ask myself why it has never happened before. They are such charming things, neat as wrens, and what a deal of ingenuity and human artfulness has gone into their construction; for if they were like the ordinary box with a lid they would not be one half so convenient. This one though is especially neat, charming, and ingenious, and the tray slides in and out as though Chippendale had made it.

But what I like best of all about my matchbox is that it is an empty one. I have often thought how much I should enjoy being given an empty house in Norway, what pleasure it would be to walk into those bare wood-smelling chambers, walls, floor, ceiling, all wood, which is after all the natural shelter of man, or at any rate the most congenial. And when I opened your matchbox which is now my matchbox and saw that beautiful clean sweet-smelling empty rectangular expanse it was exactly as though my house in Norway had come true; with the added advantage of being just the right size to carry in my hand. I shut my imagination up in it instantly, and it is still sitting there, listening to the wind in the firwood outside. Sitting there in a couple of days time I shall hear the Lutheran bell calling me to go and sing Lutheran hymns while the pastor's wife gazes abstractedly at her husband in a bower of evergreen while she wonders if she remembered to put pepper in the goose-stuffing; but I shan't go, I shall be far too happy sitting in my house that Alyse gave me for Christmas.

Oh, I must tell you I have finished my book—begun in 1941 and a hundred times imperilled but finished at last. So I can give an undivided mind to enjoying my matchbox.

[Signed]

P.S. There is still so much to say...carried away by my delight in form and texture I forgot to praise the picture on the back. I have never seen such an agreeable likeness of a hedgehog, and the volcano in the background is magnificent.

SYLVIA TOWNSEND

WARNER, 1946

S. J. MORELAND & SONS. LTD
GLOUCESTER

The ornament of a house is

the friends who frequent it.

—*"Alfred Herbert News"*—304

AVERAGE CONTENTS 48 · PRICE 2½d

ALL THIS I DID WITHOUT YOU

GERALD DURRELL to LEE McGEORGE
July 31st, 1978

Gerald Durrell and Lee McGeorge first met in 1977 when Durrell, a respected conservationist and author 24 years her senior, was giving a lecture at Duke University in North Carolina where she was a PhD student. Her area of interest, animal behaviour, gave them plenty to discuss and they immediately became close: two years later they were married. By the time Durrell died in 1995 they had travelled the world together on numerous conservation expeditions and co-written two books: *A Practical Guide for the Amateur Naturalist,* and *Durrell in Russia.*

In 1978, a year after they first met, Gerald Durrell wrote a love letter to his future wife.

My darling McGeorge,

You said that things seemed clearer when they were written down. Well, herewith a very boring letter in which I will try and put everything down so that you may read and re- read it in horror at your folly in getting involved with me. Deep breath.

To begin with I love you with a depth and passion that I have felt for no one else in this life and if it astonishes you it astonishes me as well. Not, I hasten to say, because you are not worth loving. Far from it. It's just that, first of all, I swore I would not get involved with another woman. Secondly, I have never had such a feeling before and it is almost frightening. Thirdly, I would never have thought it possible that another human being could occupy my waking (and sleeping) thoughts to the exclusion of almost everything else. Fourthly, I never thought that – even if one was in love – one could get so completely besotted with another person, so that a minute away from them felt like a thousand years. Fifthly, I never hoped, aspired, dreamed that one could find everything one wanted in one person. I was not such an idiot as to believe this was possible. Yet in you I have found everything I want: you are beautiful, gay, giving, gentle, idiotically and deliciously feminine, sexy, wonderfully intelligent and wonderfully silly as well. I want nothing else in this life than to be with you, to listen and watch you (your beautiful voice, your beauty), to argue with you, to laugh with you, to show you things and share things with you, to explore your magnificent mind, to explore your wonderful body, to help you, protect you, serve you, and bash you on the head when I think you are wrong … Not to put too fine a point on it I consider that I am the only man outside mythology to have found the crock of gold at the rainbow's end.

But – having said all that – let us consider things in detail. Don't let this become public but … well, I have one or two faults. Minor ones, I hasten to say. For example, I am inclined to be overbearing. I do it for the best possible motives (all tyrants say that) but I do tend (without thinking) to tread people underfoot. You must tell me when I am doing it to you, my sweet, because it can be a very bad thing in a marriage.

Right. Second blemish. This, actually, is not so much a blemish of character as a blemish of circumstance. Darling I want you to be you in your own right and I will do everything I can to help you in this. But you must take into consideration that I am also me in my own right and that I have a headstart on you … What I am trying to say is that you must not feel offended if you are sometimes treated simply as my wife. Always remember that what you lose on the swings you gain on the roundabouts. But I am an established 'creature' in the world, and so – on occasions – you will have to live in my shadow. Nothing gives me less pleasure than this but it is a fact of life that has to be faced.

HUMMING BIRDS
The Coras Shear Tail and Purple Crested Humming Bird.

Third (and very important and nasty) blemish: jealousy. I don't think you know what jealousy is (thank God) in the real sense of the word. I know that you have felt jealousy over Lincoln's wife and child, but this is what I call normal jealousy, and this – to my regret – is not what I've got. What I have got is a black monster that can pervert my good sense, my good humour and any goodness that I have in my make- up. It is really a Jekyll and Hyde situation … my Hyde is stronger than my good sense and defeats me, hard though I try. As I told you, I have always known that this lurks within me, but I could control it, and my monster slumbered and nothing happened to awake it. Then I met you and I felt my monster stir and become half awake when you told me of Lincoln and others you have known, and with your letter my monster came out of its lair, black, irrational, bigoted, stupid, evil, malevolent. You will never know how terribly corrosive jealousy is; it is a physical pain as though you had swallowed acid or red hot coals. It is the most terrible of feelings. But you can't help it – at least I can't, and God knows I've tried. I don't want any ex- boyfriends sitting in church when I marry you. On our wedding day I want nothing but happiness, both for you and me, and I know I won't be happy if there is a church full of your ex- conquests. When I marry you I will have no past, only a future: I don't want to drag my past into our future and I don't want you to do it, either. Remember I am jealous of you because I love you. You are never jealous of something you don't care about. O.K. enough about jealousy.

Now let me tell you something … I have seen a thousand sunsets and sunrises, on land where it floods forest and mountains with honey coloured light, at sea where it rises and sets like a blood orange in a multicoloured nest of cloud, slipping in and out of the vast ocean. I have seen a thousand moons: harvest moons like gold coins, winter moons as white as ice chips, new moons like baby swans' feathers.

I have seen seas as smooth as if painted, coloured like shot silk or blue as a kingfisher or transparent as glass or black and crumpled with foam, moving ponderously and murderously.

I have felt winds straight from the South Pole, bleak and wailing like a lost child; winds as tender and warm as a lover's breath; winds that carried the astringent smell of salt and the death of seaweeds; winds that carried the moist rich smell of a forest floor, the smell of a million flowers. Fierce winds that churned and moved the sea like yeast, or winds that made the waters lap at the shore like a kitten.

I have known silence: the cold, earthy silence at the bottom of a newly dug well; the implacable stony silence of a deep cave; the hot, drugged midday silence when everything is hypnotised and stilled into silence by the eye of the sun; the silence when great music ends.

I have heard summer cicadas cry so that the sound seems stitched into your bones. I have heard tree frogs in an orchestration as complicated as Bach singing in a forest lit by a million emerald fireflies. I have heard the Keas calling over grey glaciers that groaned to themselves like old people as they inched their way to the sea. I have heard the hoarse street vendor cries of the mating Fur seals as they sang to their sleek golden wives, the crisp staccato admonishment of the Rattlesnake, the cobweb squeak of the Bat and the belling roar of the Red deer knee-deep in purple heather. I have heard Wolves baying at a winter's moon, Red howlers making the forest vibrate with their roaring cries. I have heard the squeak, purr and grunt of a hundred multi-coloured reef fishes.

I have seen hummingbirds flashing like opals round a tree of scarlet blooms, humming like a top. I have seen flying fish, skittering like quicksilver across the blue waves, drawing silver lines on the surface with their tails. I have seen Spoonbills flying home to roost like a scarlet banner across the sky. I have seen Whales, black as tar, cushioned on a cornflower blue sea, creating a Versailles of fountain with their breath. I have watched butterflies emerge and sit, trembling, while the sun irons their wings smooth. I have watched Tigers, like flames, mating in the long grass. I have been dive- bombed by an angry Raven, black and glossy as the Devil's hoof. I have lain in water warm as milk, soft as silk, while around me played a host of Dolphins. I have met a thousand animals and seen a thousand wonderful things ... but –

All this I did without you. This was my loss.

All this I want to do with you. This will be my gain.

All this I would gladly have forgone for the sake of one minute of your company, for your laugh, your voice, your eyes, hair, lips, body, and above all for your sweet, ever surprising mind which is an enchanting quarry in which it is my privilege to delve.

NOTHING TO EAT BUT THE DEAD

VIRGINIA REED to MARY KEYES
May 16th, 1847

In April of 1846, 32 members of two Illinois families – the Reeds and the Donners – did what so many other pioneers had already done and headed for a better life in California, their numbers swelling to 87 as other settlers joined them on their journey. Such a trip would normally have taken six months at most; however, three months in, an ill-advised decision to take an alternate route ultimately resulted in the party becoming stranded in the snow-covered Sierra Nevada mountains over winter. Only 48 people survived the harsh conditions; some of those who did survive saw no option but to eat their cattle, pets, and even, on occasion, the dead. In May of the next year, one of the survivors, 13-year-old Virginia Reed, wrote a long letter to her cousin and described "our trubels geting to Callifornia". Months later it was reprinted in the *Illinois Journal*, titled "Deeply Interesting Letter".

May 16th 1847

My Dear Cousin

I take this oppertunity to write to you to let you now that we are all well at presant and hope this letter may find you all well. to My dear Cousin I am a going to write to you about our trubels geting to Callifornia; We had good luck til we come to big Sandy thare we lost our best yoak of oxens Bully and George & when we come to Brigers Fort & we lost two another ox we sold some of our provisions & baught a yoak of Cows & oxen & thay people at Bridges Fort pursuaded us to take Hastings cut off over the salt plain thay said it saved 3 Hondred miles, we went that road & we had to go through a long drive as they said of 40 miles With out water or grass Hastings said it was 40 miles but i think it was 80 miles We traveld a day and night and at noon next day papa went to see if he coud find water, he had not gone long till some of the oxen give out and we had to leve the Wagons and take the oxen to water Walter Herron & Bailor staid with us and the others went on with the cattel to water. papa was coming back to us with water and met the men & thay was about 10 miles from water papa said thay would git to water that night, and the next day to bring the cattel back for the wagons and bring some water papa got to us about daylight next morning the man that was with us took the horse and went on to water We waited thare thinking Thay would come we wated till night and We thought we would start and walk to Mr Donners wagons that night we took what little water we had and some bread and started papa caried Thomos and all the rest of us walk we got to Donner and thay were all a sleep so we laid down on the ground we spred one shawl down we laid doun on it and spred another over us and then put the dogs on top Tyler, Barney, Trailer Tracker and little Cash it was the couldes night you ever saw for the season the wind blew very hard if it had not bin for the dogs we would have Frosen as soon as it was day we went to Miss Donners she said we could not walk to the water and if we staid we could ride in thare wagons to the spring so papa went on to the water to see why thay did not bring the cattel when he got thare thare was but one ox and cow thare none of the rest had got to water Mr Donner come out that night with his cattel and braught his Wagons and all of us in we staid thare a week and Hunted for our cattel and could not find them so some of the companie took thare oxons and went out and brout in one wagon and cashed the other tow and a grate many things all but what we could put in one wagon we had to divied our provisions with the company to get them to cary it We got three yoak with our ox & cow so we went on that way a while and we got out of provisions and papa had to go on to california for provisions we could not get along that way, in 2 or 3 days after pa left we had to cash our wagon and take Mr. Graves wagon and cash some more of our things. well we went on that way a while and then we had to get Mr Eddys Wagon we went on that way a while and then we had to cash all of our close except a change or 2 and put them in Mr Brin wagon and Thomos & James rode the 2 horses and the rest of us had to walk, we went on that way a While and we come to a nother long drive of 40 miles between Marys and Truckeys Rivers and then we went with Mr Donner we had to walk all the time we ware travling up the truckey river we met Mr T C Stanton and 2 Indians that we had sent on for propessions to Captn Suter Fort before papa started thay had met pa, not fur from Suters Fort he looked very bad he had not ate but 3 times in 7 days and thes three last days with out any thing his horse was not abel to carrie him thay give him a horse and he went on so we cashed some more of our things all but what we could pack on one mule and we started Martha and James road behind the two Indians it was a raing then in the Vallies and snowing on the montains so we went on that way 3 or 4 days tell we come to the big mountain or the Callifornia Mountain the snow then was about 3 feet deep thare was some wagons thare thay said thay had atempted to cross and could not. well we thought we would try it so we started and thay started again with thare wagons the snow was then way up to the muels side the farther we went up the deeper the snow got so the wagons could not go so thay packed thare oxons and started with us carring a child a piece and driving the oxons in snow up to thare wast the mule Martha and the Indian was on was the best one so thay went and broak the road and that indian was the Pilot so we went on that way 2 miles and the mules kept faling down in the snow head formost and the Indian said he could not find the road we stoped and let the Indian and Mr Stanton go on to hunt the road thay went on and found the road to the top of the mountain and come back and said they thought we could git over if it did not snow any more well the Woman were all so tirder caring there Children that thay could not go over that night so we made a fire and got something to eat & ma spred down a bufalorobe & we all laid down on it & spred somthing over us & ma sit up by the fire & it snowed one foot on top of the bed so we got up in the morning & the snow was so deep we could not go over & we had to go back to the cabin built by emigrants 3 Years ago, & build more cabins & stay thare all Winter to Feb 20 without Pa we had not the first thing to eat Ma maid arangements for some cattel giving 2 for 1 in callifornia we seldom thot of bread for we had not had any since [blot, words not readable] & the cattel was so poor thay could note hadley git up when thay laid down we stoped thare the 4th of November & staid till and what we had to eat i cant hardley tell you & we had Indians to feed well thay started over a foot and had to come back so thay made snow shoes and started again & it come on a storme & thay had to come back it would snow 10 days before it would stop thay wated tell it stoped & started again I was a goeing with them & I took sick & could not go – thare was 15 started & thare was 7 got throw 5 Weman & 2 men it come a storme and thay lost the road & got out of provisions & those that got throwe had to eat them that Died not long after thay started we got out of provisions & had to put Martha at one cabin James at another Thomas at another & Ma & Elizea & Milt Eliot & I dried up what littel meat we had and started to see if we could get across & had to leve the childrin o Mary you may think that hard to leve theme with strangers & did not now wether we would see them again or not we could hardle get a way from them but we told theme we would bring them Bread & then thay was willing to stay we went & was out 5 days in the mountains Eliza giv out & had to go back we went on a day longer we had to lay by a day & make snow shows & we went on a while and coud not find the road & we had to turn back I could go on verry well while i thout we wer giting along but as soone as we had to turn back i coud hadley git along but we got to the cabins that night & I froze one of my feet verry bad that same night thare was the worst storme we had that winter & if we had not come back that night we would never got back we had nothing to eat then but ox hides o Mary I would cry and wish I had what you all wasted Eliza had to go to Mr Graves cabin & we staid at Mr Breen thay had meat all the time & we had to kill littel cash the dog & eat him o my Dear Cousin you dont now what trubel is yet a many a time we had on the last thing a cooking and did not know wher the next would come from but there was awl wais some way provided. there was 15 in the cabon we was in and half of us had to lay a bed all the time thare was 10 starved to death while we were there we was hadley abel to walk we lived on litle cash a week and after Mr Breen would cook his meat and boil the bones two or three times we would take the bones and boil them 3 or 4 days at a time mama went down to the other caben and got half a hide carried it in snow up to her wast it snowed and would cover the cabin all over so we could not git out for 2 or 3 days at a time we would have to cut pieces of the loges in sied to make fire with I coud hardly eat the hides and had not eat anything 3 days Pa stated out to us with provisions on the first of November and came into the Great California Mountain, about 80 miles and in one of the severest storms known for Years past & raining in the Valley and a hurrican of snow in the mountains it came so deep that the horses & mules swamped so they could not go on any more he cash his provision and went back on the other side of the bay to git compana of men and the San Wakien got so hye he could not crose well thay Made up a Compana at Suters Fort and sent out we had not ate any thing for 3 days & we had onely a half a hide and we was out on top of the cabin and we seen the party coming

O my Dear Cousin you dont now how glad i was we run and met them one of them we knew we had traveled with them on the road thay staid thare 3 days to recruit a little so we coud go thare was 21 started all of us started and went a piece and Martha and Thomas giv out & so the men had to take them back ma and Eliza and James & I come on and o Mary that was the hades thing yet to come on and leiv them thar one of the party said he was a Mason and pledged his life that if we did not meet pa in time he would come and save his children did not now but what thay would starve to Death Martha said well ma if you never see me again do the best you can the men said thay could hadly stand it it maid them all cry but they said it was better for all of us to go on for if we was to go back we would eat that much more from them thay give them a littel meat and flore and took them back and we come on ma agreed to leave then from promise of Mr Glover if we should meet pa which we did in a few days. we went over great hye mountain as strait as stair steps in snow up to our knees litle James walk the whole way over all the mountain in snow up to his waist he said every step he took he was a gitting nigher Pa and somthing to eat the Caeadues or Fishers took the provisions the min had cashed and we had but very little to eat when we had traveld 5 days travel we met Pa with 13 men going to the cabins O Mary you do not nou how glad we was to see him we had not seen him for 5 months we thought we woul never see him again he heard we was coming and he made some seet cakes the night before at his camp to give us and the other children with us he said he would see Martha and Thomas the next day he went in those to tow days what took us 5 days some of the compana was eating from them that Died but Thomas & Martha had not ate any Pa and the men started with 12 people Hiram O Miller Carried Thomas and Pa caried Martha and thay wer caught in [unreadable word] and thay had to stop Two days it stormed so thay could not go and the Fishers took their provision and thay weer 4 days without anything Pa and Hiram and and all the men started one of Donner boys Pa a carring Martha Hiram caring Thomas and the snow was up to thare wast and it a snowing so thay could hadley see the way they raped the children up and never took them out for 4 days & thay had nothing to eat in all that time Thomas asked for somthing to eat once those that thay brought from the cabins some of them was not able to come from the starved camp as it is called and som would not come Thare was 3 died and the rest eat them thay was 10 days without any thing to eat but the Dead Pa braught Thoma and pady in to where we was none of the men Pa had with him was able to go back for some people still at the cabins there feet was froze very bad so there was a nother Compana went and braught them all in thay are all in from the Mountains now but four men went out after them and was caught in a storm and had to come back thare was a nother compana families that all of them got we ware one O Mary I have not wrote you half of the truble we have had but I hav Wrote you anuf to let you now that you dont know what truble is but thank god we have all got throw and the onely family that did not eat human flesh we have left every thing but i dont cair for that we have got through with our lives but Dont let this letter dishaten anybody let never take cutofs and hury along as fast as you can

My Dear Cousin

We are all very well pleased with Callifornia particulary with the climate let it be ever so hot a day thare is all wais cool nights it is a beautiful Country it is mostley in vallies it aut to be a beautiful Country to pay us for our trubel geting there it is the greatest place for cattle and horses you ever saw it would Just suit Charley for he could ride down 3 or 4 horses a day and he could lern to be Bocarro that one who lases cattel the spanards and Indians are the best riders i ever saw thay have a spanish sadel and woden sturups and great big sturups and great big spurs 5 inches in diameter and they could not manage the Callifornia horses witout the spurs, thay wont go atol if thay cant hear the spurs rattle thay have littel bells to them to make them rattle thay blindfold the wild horses and sadel them and git on them and then take the blindfole of and let run and if thay cant sit on thay tie themselves on and let them run as fast as they can and go out to a band of bullluck and throw the reatter on a wild bullluck and but it around the horn of his sadel and he can hold it as long as he wants another Indian throwes his reatter on its feet and throws them and when thay take the reatter of of them thay are very dangerous they will run after you them hook there horses and run after any person thay see thay ride from 80 to 100 miles a day some of the spanard have from 6 to 7000 head of horses and from 15 to 16000 head Cattel we are all verry fleshey Ma waies 10040 pon and still a gaing I weigh 80 tel Henriet if she wants to get married to come to Callifornia she can get a spanyard any time that Eliza is a going to marrie a a spanyard by the name of Armeho and Eliza weighs 10072 We have not saw un uncle Cadon yet but we have had 2 letters from him he is well and is a coming here as soon as he can Mary take this letter to uncle Gursham and to all that i know to all of our neighbors and tell Dochter Mancel and every girl i know and let them read it Mary kiss little Sue and Maryann for me and give my best love to all i know to uncle James aunt Lida and all the rest of the famila and to uncle Gursham aunt Percilla and all the Children and to all of our neighbors and to all the girls i know Ma sends her very best love to uncle James aunt Leida and all the rest of the famila and to uncle Gursham and aunt Percilla all of the children and to all of our neighbors and to all she knows so no more at presant pa is yerbayan [Yerba Buena]

My Dear casons

Virginia Elizabeth B Reed

TIGER

OIL COMPANY

EDWARD MIKE DAVIS, OWNER
SUITE 1500
FIVE GREENWAY PLAZA EAST
HOUSTON, TEXAS 77046

M E M O R A N D U M

TO: Secretaries   DATE: January 3, 1978

FROM: Edward Mike Davis

     This is a business office. All correspondence and other things pertaining to this office will be typewritten.

     Handwriting takes much longer than a typewriter -- you're wasting your time, but more importantly, you're wasting my time. If you don't know how to type, you'd better learn.

EDWARD MIKE DAVIS

TIGER OIL MEMOS

EDWARD "TIGER MIKE" DAVIS to HIS
STAFF
1978

From the offices of the now-defunct but at one time Houston-based Tiger Oil Company come a batch of curiously entertaining memos, all sent by the firm's irascible, tactless, and undeniably amusing CEO, Edward "Tiger Mike" Davis, to his staff. Tiger Mike's management style was no secret within the industry; however, in the early-2000s, 25 years after his company filed for bankruptcy, his spiky inter-office communications famously appeared online for all to see, instantly widening his audience to include almost anyone with an internet connection. A selection of his greatest hits appear here, with his blessing.

PHONE (13) 629-9550

TIGER
OIL COMPANY
EDWARD MIKE DAVIS, OWNER
SUITE 1500
FIVE GREENWAY PLAZA EAST
HOUSTON, TEXAS 77046

M E M O R A N D U M

TO: All Employees   DATE: January 5, 1978
             Tiger Oil Company
             Tiger Drilling Company
             Tiger Oil International, Inc.
             Houston Office

FROM: Edward Mike Davis

SUBJECT: Kitchen Facilities

     Gertrude Love has been hired to work in our kitchen and do light office cleaning. She will start Monday, January 9th.

     The kitchen will be her "office" and no one will be permitted to loiter there. If you want something from the kitchen, she will get it for you. If she is not in the kitchen, get what you want and get out.

     Lunch will either be prepared here or sent in by Jamail's every day, and you are welcome to eat. She will prepare your plate, hand it to you, and you can go to your office to eat. You will not be allowed to serve yourself, unless she is not in the kitchen.

EDWARD MIKE DAVIS

TIGER
OIL COMPANY
EDWARD MIKE DAVIS, OWNER
SUITE 1500
FIVE GREENWAY PLAZA EAST
HOUSTON, TEXAS 77046

M E M O R A N D U M

TO: All Employees   DATE: January 11, 1978

FROM: Edward Mike Davis

SUBJECT: Idle Conversation

     Idle conversation and gossip in this office among employees will result in immediate termination.

     Don't talk about other people and other things in this office.

     DO YOUR JOB AND KEEP YOUR MOUTH SHUT!

EDWARD MIKE DAVIS

TIGER
OIL COMPANY
EDWARD MIKE DAVIS, OWNER
SUITE 1500
FIVE GREENWAY PLAZA EAST
HOUSTON, TEXAS 77046

M E M O R A N D U M

To: All Employees   Date: January 12, 1978
        Houston Office

From: Edward Mike Davis

    I swear, but since I am the owner of this company, that
is my privilege, and this privilege is not to be interpreted as
the same for any employee.   That differentiates me from you, and
I want to keep it that way.   There will be absolutely no swearing,
by <u>any</u> employee, male or female, in this office, ever.

EDWARD MIKE DAVIS

TIGER
OIL COMPANY
EDWARD MIKE DAVIS, OWNER
SUITE 1500
FIVE GREENWAY PLAZA EAST
HOUSTON, TEXAS 77046

M E M O R A N D U M

TO: All Monthly Salaried Personnel   DATE: January 12, 1978

FROM: Edward Mike Davis

In case anyone does not know who owns Tiger Oil Company or Tiger Drilling Co., Inc., it is me - Edward Mike Davis. Do not let anyone think they are the owner but me.

This memo is not intended towards all employees, but all must be included, because some have abused these things. The ones who have not abused any of my rules and regulations should not have their feelings hurt or be concerned. Just do your job!

A purchase order system will be initiated immediately. Only certain people will be allowed to sign. More than likely, two signatures will be required, whether it be one from the field and one from the office, or two from the office and two from the field.

Only business calls will be made and charged to Tiger Oil or Tiger Drilling. No personal calls PERIOD.

There will be no liquor of any kind kept in any of the offices, other than by direct order of Mike Davis. That means get it out of there!

Cleanliness is next to Godliness. I expect things to be clean and in order. That goes for all employees everywhere -- that means the office and your personal appearance; righands included.

We do not pay starvation wages, and there are some people left in this world who want to work. I am not fond of hippies, long-hairs, dope fiends or alcoholics. .I suggest each and every person in a supervisory category (from driller up to me) eliminate these people.

I don't want any excuses about not being able to find anyone to work on rigs, drive trucks, or work in the yards -- just find the people you need, and if we have to pay more money to get them, it will all balance out in the end.

Anyone who lets their hair grow below their ears to where I can't see their ears means they don't wash. If they don't wash, they stink, and if they stink, I don't want the son-of-a-bitch around me.

Any truck driver or employee who ruins a piece of equipment due to negligence or abuse will be terminated immediately by his boss, and if the boss doesn't do this, then the boss will be terminated by Mike Davis.

Each driver will be assigned boomers and chains. A check list will be kept by Duane Brown and Fred Addison, and equipment issued to each truck will be checked off weekly. A driver will pay for any equipment not on his truck or if it is ruined. If lost, turn it in to Duane or Fred. All truck drivers will be cautioned about tearing up fences, ditches, etc. with their trucks. Truck drivers will check oil and everything else on their trucks every day - just like the Army.

When hauling any equipment, all boomers will be wired after they are closed and checked for load shift. They are not to come loose or gnaw holes in what it is bound against.

Each driver will inspect his truck for loose bolts, nuts, corrosive battery cables, water leaks, oil leaks, tires, etc. throughout the truck. If a minor repair can be fixed, fine; if not, notify Duane Brown or Fred Addison, and they will get it fixed immediately. Everything will be inspected like the Army.

Each truck driver will either sleep in his truck or get a room for at least six hours sleep per each 24 hours, and not be found in a bar drinking anything, and that includes beer. You want to drink, then drink on your own time and your own money and not mine. Truck drivers will be given one day per week off, to be scheduled by their superior. Anyone found popping pills to stay awake will be discharged immediately. If you need to sleep, go to bed. I have personally found truck drivers drinking in motels. I will not tolerate any drinking. You want to drink - drink on your day off. You will be watched and monitored wherever you drive.

The supervision of you will be more strict now than ever. If you do not want to work for me, pick up your check now, or work under my conditions.

Failure to comply with the above will mean immediate termination.

No one will ride in our vehicles other than company employees. An exception to this is if anyone is in an accident or stranded, a driver may pick him up. What I am trying to say is no hitchhikers or free rides for family members or non-employees. They will be terminated if caught.

Excessive speed while driving that would endanger the truck, the driver, or other people is prohibited. The driver should be the one to make that decision.

All scraps of metal, nails, pieces of pipe, etc. will be picked up and not left laying around in the yard. I want to see someone bend over other than me.

Submit a daily log of work done and the time spent.

Submit a complete inventory of tires, truck parts and all other equipment and condition of same, plus the rigs and all spare equipment in all yards.

Insurance items will be reported immediately and handled per insurance company's instructions, as well as the instructions of Bill Jamison and the employee's supervisor, Fred Addison or Duane Brown. Any accidents involving a rig, trucks, cars, or employees, other than minor ones, the Houston Office will be notified so that my secretary can notify me. If on weekends or nights, the superior in that area knows how to reach me. If it is a death, call me at night or weekends. Other than that, the person having the accident should have brains enough to take care of it until the next day.

Any driver hauling anything anywhere will get a receipt
for what he has picked up and a manifest of what he is hauling.
Each driver will count and know the items on his truck because they
will be counted when he gets to his destination. If something is
missing, the driver will be terminated.

A truck manager will be hired for Lafayette, and the
trucking department will be scrutinized very carefully.

A detailed material transfer will be made out for any piece
of equipment moved into or out of the yard or any place.

No one welds with a welding machine unless he knows what he
is doing.

Any time any driver goes anywhere and is waiting on something,
after they have had their sleep, they will work in the yard or do
something that has to be done. They will check with the boss in that
area. They will not lay in the motel room drinking and watching
television.

Start and run trucks daily that aren't being used so the
battery won't run down.

All drivers are to be cautioned about the loads they are
hauling so they don't tear the bridges down or ruin what they are
hauling.

Expense accounts will be approved by the employee's
superior in charge of a particular area, and then it will again be
approved in Houston before it is paid. Each person should sign and
pay for his own things, and not for someone else with him. Each person
has his own expense account. Anyone who abuses or takes advantages of
expense accounts will be terminated immediately.

Any time any boss needs something and cannot get it because
of credit, do not discuss our financial situation with the vendor --
call Houston. If Houston cannot give satisfaction, get ahold of Mike
Davis.

All invoices for purchases of equipment, materials, etc. will be handled by a purchase order, as stated above, and the purchase order will be checked, approved and signed by one of the supervisors.

The rig must be inspected once a day by the toolpusher while shut down. All little engines in the yard that are good will be started once a month and run. All exhausts will be covered so that water will not get in them.

Fred Addison will inspect each rig at least once a week and not tell the toolpusher when he is coming.

Duane Brown will be on every rig move possible. The person put in charge of the trucking department in Lafayette will do the same.

Buy only what you need; utilize what we have.

A supervisor will watch any welder working for us, sign the ticket and then get rid of him. Welders will be called by a pusher to a rig for the purpose of cutting the surface pipe off or something of that nature. Do not call a welder to rebuild the rig. That must be approved by the superior in that area.

Any employee who does not want to adhere to the items mentioned above can quit. If any of you think I will go out of business because I can't hire help, get out, and I will hire the people to do the work. I don't need a job - you people are the ones who need to get with it.

There is one thing that differentiates me from my employees. I am a known son-of-a-bitch, and I care to remain that way. I have the privilege of swearing publicly, in front of anyone, or doing anything I want to because I pay the bills. When you work for me, you don't have that privilege. You are representing me. Don't act as I do. I am the only one who can act that way. You people are all to be respectful to your fellow employees and to other people we do business with. That may be deemed any way you want to take it, but those are my orders, and I intend to enforce them. What you do in your home is your own business, but what you do in my business is my business. I am not a preacher or I am not trying to save the world, I just intend to run my business the way I want to. This pertains to the supervisory personnel.

EDWARD MIKE DAVIS

TIGER
OIL COMPANY
EDWARD MIKE DAVIS, OWNER
SUITE 1500
FIVE GREENWAY PLAZA EAST
HOUSTON, TEXAS 77046

M E M O R A N D U M

To: All Employees
        Tiger Oil Company & Tiger Drilling Co.   Date: February 22, 1978
From: Edward Mike Davis

This memorandum is intended as an addendum to a memo I wrote
on January 12, 1978 about people speaking to me. Any supervisor
who has anything to say to me, day or night, the fastest way he
can say it to me is too slow. The terms about not talking to me
meant I do not have time to stop and talk to everyone -- saying
hello, goodbye, goodnight, etc. -- that is what I was talking about.
If you have business with me, the fastest way is too slow -- day
or night.

EDWARD MIKE DAVIS

TIGER
OIL COMPANY
EDWARD MIKE DAVIS, OWNER
SUITE 1500
FIVE GREENWAY PLAZA EAST
HOUSTON, TEXAS 77046

<u>M E M O R A N D U M</u>

TO: All Employees   DATE: April 20, 1978
  Tiger Oil Company - Houston

FROM: Edward Mike Davis

SUBJECT: Office Furniture

  The furniture in this office is expensive. <u>DO NOT PUT
YOUR FEET ON IT</u>!!

  I am paying you to work -- not slouch in your chair with
your feet up on a desk or table.

  I do not go to your home and put my feet on your furniture,
so don't put your feet on mine.

         EDWARD MIKE DAVIS

TIGER
OIL COMPANY
EDWARD MIKE DAVIS, OWNER
SUITE 1500
FIVE GREENWAY PLAZA EAST
HOUSTON, TEXAS 77046

M E M O R A N D U M

TO: All Employees   DATE: September 25, 1978
              Tiger Oil Company
              Tiger Drilling Co., Inc.

FROM: Edward Mike Davis

SUBJECT: Vacations

       As you know, after one full year of employment you receive two weeks' vacation and two weeks respectively each year worked thereafter. Effective immediately, the two weeks per year must be taken one week at a time and begin the end of the week - you cannot start your vacation in the middle of the week. There will be no more taking one or two days at a time and combining them with holidays and weekends. If, in my opinion, you deserve additional time off you must obtain it from me proving to me that you have worked hard enough to get it - not trying to edge a day here and a day there combined with the holidays. I am not a fool - I know you can take two weeks and stretch them into two months properly done so don't insult my intelligence. Ask for it like a man. Also, in your absence, you must arrange to have someone perform your duties.

                                EDWARD MIKE DAVIS

91

I LONG FOR FREEDOM

HANNAH GROVER to CATO
June 3rd, 1805

According to the United States Census, there were 7,239,881 people living in the United States in 1810, and of those, a staggering 1,191,362 were slaves, no doubt living unimaginably harrowing lives. To make matters even worse, if that were possible, slaves were often split from their families by those in charge, thereby forced to somehow exist in such conditions without even the support of their loved ones. One such person was Hannah Grover, a slave who lost contact with her boy, Cato, in 1785. Twenty years later, as she reached old age, she wrote to her long lost son with a plea: for him to come and rescue her.

Caldwell
June 3d 1805

My dear Son Cato

I long to see you in my old age   I live in Caldwell with Mr. Grover the Minister of that place   now my dear son I pray you to come and see your dear old Mother—Or send me twenty dollar and I will come and see you in Philadelphia—And if you cant come to see your old Mother pray send me a letter and tell me where you live what family you have and what you do for a living—I am a poor old servant I long for freedom—And my Master will free me if any body will ingage to maintain me so that I do not come upon him—I love you Cato you love your Mother—You are my only son

      This from your affectionate Mother—
          Hannah Van Buskerk now—
          Hannah Grover

P.S. My dear son I have not seen you since I saw you at Staten Island   At Addee Barker's 20 years ago—If you send any money send it by Dotr. Bonr and he will give it to me—If you have any love for your poor old Mother pray come or send to me   My dear son I love you with all my heart—
          Hannah Van Buskerk—

JANIS JOPLIN LIVES!

JANIS JOPLIN to HER
PARENTS
April 1967

When she wrote this
excited letter home in 1967,
24-year-old Janis Joplin
had been the front woman
of Big Brother and the
Holding Company, a band
from Haight-Ashbury, San
Francisco, for close to a
year, and things were finally
coming together: a record
deal with a small label, a
comfortable wage, a new
apartment and a steady
boyfriend all contributing to
the good mood. But it was
soon to intensify, as just two
months later her star would
rise to heights previously
unimagined thanks to a jaw-
dropping performance at the
Monterey International Pop
Festival – a now legendary
gathering that also played
host to Jimi Hendrix and Otis
Redding, and which resulted
in Joplin's band being signed
by Columbia Records, her
voice destined for greatness.

Behind the scenes, however,
she was walking a tightrope
from which she would
ultimately fall: an addiction
to heroin that began long
before her ascent to fame.
On October 4th, 1970, three
years after this letter was
written, Janis Joplin was
found dead in her hotel
room.

April 1967

Dear Mother, family

Things are going so good for us & me personally I can't quite believe it! I never
ever thought things could be so wonderful! Allow me to explain. First of all, the
group — we're better than ever (please see enclosed review from S.F. Examiner)
and working all the time. Just finished 3 weeks straight engagements, 6 nights a
week & we're booked up week-ends for well over a month. And we're making a
thousand or over for a week-end. For single nights we're getting from $500-$900.
Not bad for a bunch of beatniks, eh? And our reputation is still going uphill. It's
funny to watch — you can tell where you are by the people that are on your side.
Y'know, the scene-followers, the people "with the finger on the pulse of the public."
One of the merchants on Haight St. has given all of us free clothes (I got a beautiful
blue leather skirt) just because 1) she really digs us & 2) she thinks we're going to
make it & it'll be good publicity. Our record is enjoying a fair reception — much
better than our first one which was much, much better. We made #29 in Detroit but
we don't really know what's happening because we never hear from Mainstream.
It's a long & involved story but we really feel like we've been used & abused by our
record co & we'd like to get out of the contract but don't know whether we can. We
talked to a lawyer about it & he seemed fairly negative & we can't even get ahold of
our record co. to talk about it. So until further news, we're hung up. There's a slim
possibility we might go to Europe & play this summer. There's a hippie boat going
back and forth & rock bands get free passage if they play on the way over. And Chet,
head of the Family Dog, is trying to organize dances over there & if he does, we'd
have a place to work. Probably won't work but it sure would be groovey. Speaking of
England, guess who was in town last week — Paul McCartney!!! (he's a Beatle). And
he came to see us!!! SIGH Honest to God! He came to the Matrix & saw us & told
some people that he dug us. Isn't that exciting!!!! Gawd, I was so thrilled — I still
am! Imagine — Paul!!!! If it could only have been George. . . . Oh, well. I didn't get
to see him anyway — we heard about it afterwards. Why, if I'd known that he was
out there, I would have jumped right off the stage & made a fool of myself.

Now earlier, I spoke of how well things are going for me personally — it's really
true. I'm becoming quite a celebrity among the hippies & everyone who goes to the
dances. Why, last Sunday we played a Spring Mobilization for Peace benefit &
a simply amazing thing happened. As the boys were tuning, I walked up to the front
of the stage to set up the microphones &, as I raised the middle mike up to my
mouth, the whole audience applauded! Too much! And then as we're getting ready
to play, a girl yelled out "Janis Joplin lives!" Now you can't argue with that, and
they clapped again. Also, a rock publication named WORLD COUNTDOWN had
a collage on its cover using photographs of important personages in & about the
scene & I'm in there. Also they're bringing out a poster of me! Maybe you've read

in Time magazine about the personality posters. They're big, very big photographs, Jean Harlow, Einstein, Belmondo, Dylan, & Joplin. Yes, folks, it's me wearing a sequined cape, thousands of strings of beads & topless. But it barely shows because of the beads. Very dramatic photograph & I look really beautiful!! If it wouldn't embarrass you, I'll send you one. I'm thrilled!! I can be Haight-Ashbury's first pin-up.

Speaking of Haight-Ashbury, read the enclosed article from LOOK magazine. There've been lots of articles written about the scene here. Newsweek has had two & this one. And even the Chronicle — they've all had articles with more understanding than the one in Time. As a matter of fact, I just plain quit reading it because of that article — not because I was mad. Because I was aware of how distorted they were & I figured they were probably that wrong about everything. I really am not social critic enough to know/discuss what is going on, but in answer to your question — Yes, they are our audience & we're hoping they can turn on the rest of the country because then we'd be nation-wide. We'd be the Monkees! Well, at any rate, a good article.

Okay, on to news: For one thing we've gotten a raise — the guys with wives were feeling constrained, so now we get $100 a week. Good heavens.

Second in importance, I have a new apartment. Really fine!! Two big rooms, kitchen, bathroom & balcony. And I'm right across the street from the park! You can't really understand living there with a yard, but here you can go 10-20 blocks without ever seeing a living plant and I just look out my window or step out on my balcony & I've got fresh air & trees & grass!! So wonderful, sigh. My new address is 123 Cole St., S.F. Still in the Haight-Ashbury. Have lots of plans for the place — two rooms need painting but I may just end up hanging stuff up on the walls. I've sort of got the front room fixed up now & it's really nice to live in. SIGH! See what I mean, about things going my way? Also, I have a boyfriend. Really nice. He's head of Country Joe and the Fish, a band from Berkeley. Named Joe McDonald, he's a Capricorn like me, & is 25 & so far we're getting along fine. Everyone in the rock scene just thinks it's the cutest thing they've ever seen. It is rather cute actually. Speaking of boyfriends, I've been hearing from John again. He's written several letters. For some reason I get the feeling he's planning on coming out here & is sort of putting out feelers.

Next, guess what (special for Dad) I've done — I've quit smoking!!! Still want one now & then but it's been about a month now. I felt it was just too hard on my voice. I'd been smoking for 10 yrs! I got a real bad cold & bronchitis & I just couldn't smoke for about a week & when I got well, I refused to start again. I may break down but I hope not. This is really better for me.

More news, George is really getting to be a fine dog. Learning things every day. Today he learned the hard way not to run across the street to the park by himself — he got hit by a car. But the vet said he wasn't hurt very badly — bruised & scared. Poor thing, he's just moping around with a very paranoid look on his face.

I'm having a few clothes made for me now — had a beautiful dress made out of a madras bed spread & now she's working on one out of green crepe with a very low V neckline. I've been making things out of leather lately. Made a beautiful blue & green Garbo hat & pair of green shoes.

I'm also sending our new promo picture. Not very flattering of me but a very strong picture. Pretty good looking group, eh?

Really enjoyed seeing the pictures of all of you. Looking beautiful, Mother. And Laura looks really cute! Is her dress white or silver? And I've never seen Mike look so charming. Must be the Big Brother T shirt.

Below: Janis Joplin in Golden Gate Park after a Big Brother and the Holding Company performance, 1968

Now, please let me know when you are coming. Oh, I have so many places to take you to & show you! But we'll be working so let me know as soon as you can your plans. Well, I guess that's it for now. Write me.

LoveXXX
Janis

BECOMING TOM CLANCY

TOM CLANCY to HIS FRIENDS
November 1st, 1984

Few novelists have been as successful as Tom Clancy, a man whose first manuscript, *The Hunt for Red October*, sold for $5000 in 1984 and upon publication was quickly deemed "my kind of yarn" by then-US President Ronald Reagan. A phenomenal career followed that boasted 17 *New York Times* bestsellers including *Patriot Games*, *The Sum of All Fears*, and *Clear and Present Danger* – more than 100 million of his novels are now in print; his many thrillers have also inspired countless movie and videogame adaptations. In 1985, a year after his first novel hit the shelves, he wrote a letter to his closest friends and took them on a tour of his increasingly surreal life in the spotlight.

. . . to whom it may concern:

Even computer printers have their limitations. The attached letter takes 35 minutes to print, hence cannot be customized too greatly except at the cost of lots of time.

For this reason, I have chosen to Xox the letter detailing my recent adventures, which was set up for my next "gotta" correspondence.

If this makes me appear a cheap bastard, well, I've been called worse.

&ff/85

Hi, Guys!

It was GREAT seeing you three guys two weeks back. Cindy especially.
I suppose motherhood agrees with her. Gavin is rather a handsome little
guy.

Well, back to the continuing adventures of Tom Clancy, boy-writer.
Right after you guys took the Big Iron Bird back to D-Land, I had lunch in
the Pentagon, with VADM Nils Thunman, OP-02 (Deputy Chief of Naval
Operations for Submarine Warfare). They reserved me a "mall entrance"
(demi-VIP) parking place, and I went diddy-boppin' over. I still say that the
Pentagon is the IDEAL place to play Dungeons and Dragons, a thoroughly
depressing building. Some nice paintings and ship models, though. The
security force is not marines, but rather the Federal Protective Service,
looking very militant in their FPS baseball hats and SWAT-type uniforms.
Right. They might frighten off the Fuller Brush Man.

OP-02 occupies room 4E524. Fourth floor ("deck"), E (outermost) ring.
Actually a small suite of rooms. He does not have the gollywog display
system, of course, but does have a largish map (12x12) of the world, and
another of the Arctic Ocean--"We're doing a lot under the ice now. It's
public information that we've had four boats surface in the ice this year."

Oh?

Thunman is 50ish, taller than my 6-1 (must have left his blood on lots
of submarine hatches), and manifestly has enough confidence to run a
small galaxy. He gave me a largish (and quite heavy) plaque with a pair of
brass dolphins on it, making me an official honorary submariner. I was
surprised. Stunned. And pleased as hell. His aide then ran it down to my
car.

So, we went off to lunch, down the E-ring. Suddenly a captain pulled
open a door, and in I went to find five (5) other admirals (****, ***, ***,
***, and ***; plus my *** escort). The CNO Dining Room. Captains and dogs
not allowed. Where did that leave me...

SCOTTIE, BEAM ME UP!

Nobody warned me.

I got a glass of sherry--thimble glass, you just get used to the
bouquet and it's gone; but good stuff--to steady down, and started
answering questions from the Vice-CNO (James Watkins was out of town)
and other luminaries.

Guys, I'm talking stark terror. There I was, a culture on a petrie dish being examined by the professors of Johns Hopkins Medical School. All looked different, but, of course, alike too. Mid-50s, stern-looking--these are people accustomed to having their whims performed with alacrity-- but civilized. Very tough-minded chaps. I made a quick sweep of the salad bars and counted a pair of Navy Crosses and enough Silver Stars to handle the smartest first grade class in history. One stark impression: If you want to play cards with them, leave the checkbook home. Well, they liked my explanation for why the Russian subs spend so much time on the surface (cabbage), and my two favorite Lawyer jokes. I asked a few judicious questions, and got very interesting answers. (Of course, you listen most closely to what is not said, right?) On the whole an interesting, though somewhat tense, hour or two it was. Glad it happened: Now I know I can handle meeting Ronnie. Sure, he's more important, but there's only one of him!

Went immediately to Annapolis to show them my trophy--I am hugely pleased with that 30-pound monster! Got caught by an AP interviewer there. Time runs it this week. The guys in Annapolis lit off the 5th printing, and we've had a nibble from a movie producer. One of the things I asked Thunman was whether he'd cooperate with a movie/TV production of Hunt. He answered with a qualified yes.

The next week passed unremarkably. This week, 3/4-8, turned out to be a busy one. On 3/1, after my regular Friday morning trip to the local Crown Books, I found a message on my desk to the effect that one Ruth Chevetz (or something like that) had called me. She books people for **Good Morning America.** Oh, shit.

So I called her, and she wanted my hot young body on nationwide TV the following Tuesday. I gasped and said...Okay, then called Annapolis to make sure they had come through proper channels. They hadn't. They'd called me direct on the strength of the Time article. So, my NY publicist and the Institute conferred and said to proceed. Okay.

Called Gerry Sterner, asking for pharmacological help, and he prescribed 5mg of Valium. Sorry to wimp out, but, shit, I was scared. I mean, **22,000,000!** people watch this show every AM. And I got myself mentally prepared (Instructions: one tab at 2200L night before, not that I'm a damned addict!) and came to work Monday ready to take the train to New York. Got a call early that morning, a late-breaking news story bumped me back to Wednesday. I already had a radio talk-show Wednesday. But...

Recycle 24hrs. Came to work Tuesday, got myself a haircut, and got yet another call from the Apple. Bumped to Friday. (Ever wonder how Caryl Chessman felt?) (I know.) So I rescheduled the Wednesday talk show, and did it. No big deal. Their call-in phones didn't work!

Next day I had a half hour with Marvin Mandel on WNAV, Annapolis. A charming little guy for an ex-governor cum convicted felon (I always thought they got him of a very strange--and very bum?--rap). Afterwards told me about two trips to the USSR he made for the State Department. I think he likes Josef Mengele better than the Ivans. He met Yuri Andropov. You remember Yuri, the closet liberal who liked good scotch and cool jazz. Mandel said that he got chills looking at the guy <u>before</u> he found out he was CINC-KGB: "A thug, obviously a bastard, even when he was trying to charm us."

Okay, came in Thursday READY to go. ABC was so contrite at having bumped me that they offered to bring Wanda up, too. Fine, we left at 1315L and caught a 1440 choo-choo for the Big Apple. The trip was unremarkable, we arrived at dusk, rush hour. Rush hour in New York is something to behold. Went past a place that advertised "LIVE GAY BURLESQUE." I don't even <u>want</u> to know what that is.

The cab ride was, well, I've already expounded on these kamikaze school rejects. Bumper cars, played with real cars.

ABC had us booked in to the St.Moritz-by-the-Park at 50 Central Park South. Expensive. We got room 2018, facing the park, which actually looks like a hell of nice place. I mean, really a nice park…except for the local carnivors. Besides, it was drizzling. Anyway, from his 20th floor vantage, New York actually looked like a decent place. Those hansome (sp?) buggies were collected in front of the place. I wonder how many horses are killed every year by that city's traffic?

Had dinner in their dining room with my agent and his fiance--well, informal fiance, I gather. An Irish girl (from Connecticut), a bright, sweet kid. Anyway, after a listless attack on a mediocre steak, topped off with a largish glass of Harvey's Bristol Cream (ABC footed the bill, thank God), we retired for the evening. And I popped my 5mg tablet. (The heart in the center is a nice touch.) Slept reasonably well until the 0530L wakeup call.

Damned wakeup calls, always on time. Woke up to a drizzling pre-dawn gloom. I will never know whether it was my Irish backbone, or the lingering effect of the funny pill with the cute heart in the middle, but BY GOD! I swore to myself that I wouldn't screw up. Normal morning routine, and went downstairs for milk. The restaurant was closed until 0700, when the limo was due to arrive. Grrr. Went out into the Indian Country of 6th Avenue, found a deli and a pint of milk to occupy the upper GI for the next few hours, back to the 20th floor. Buoyed a pint of vitamin-d 4% butterfat milk, and a few, I regret to admit, cigarettes (sorry, Mike, but the stress was really tough!), I was READY! We proceeded down at 0655L, and the limo was waiting for us.

Can't fault ABC for the service. The drive to ABC HQ was by Lincoln Towncar. Traffic was light (amazingly light). Arrived at 0715±L.

The building was rather a disappointment, on one of those narrow sidestreets, in the East 50s, I think, plain block walls, very plain inside, almost like a warehouse. We were taken to the green room. Which wasn't green anyplace. 0725 I went upstairs for hair and makeup. They left my hair alone, and I got some itchy, powdery shit put on my face. I couldn't tell the difference visually. Back downstairs. Wait. The hardest thing in all the world to do is--waiting.

0732, a stage-crewman comes in and waves for me to follow. Into the set through two soundproof doors.

The set is about the size of a basketball court. I won't bother with a detailed description, though the place had enough lights for a football stadium. They sat me down, pinned a pair of mikes on my jacket, and got me a coffee cup of water (my mouth was a little dry) (like an Egyptian cotton field). 0739, David Hartman comes over.

Taller than I am, mid-40s, rather a nice chap, one of the reasons they pay him $1,500,000 per year. Said he hadn't read the book yet, but was looking forward too. He might even have been talling the truth.

The cameras close in. 0741, David goes into his intro. Gave it a hell of a buildup: "Blockbuster…sweeping over the capital like a tidal wave…" The little red light on the near camera clicks on. Show time.

And I just blanke

That is, afterwards I could only remember one remark. The rest of the performance was a VOID (well, almost…a little poetic license). Then it was over. Everybody said I did great. The black guy who set up my mike asked if I might have been a little scared. "No, terrified! [General laughter throughout the set]." Wanda said I did great. We left via limo back to the hotel. I immediately called the Institute. They said I did very well.

Breakfast. Check out. Escape from New York.

Got to the office about 1400. Did some work, had a lot of calls to meake. Everybody said I did great. Finally left and got home to see the video tape of myself.

I didn't know I was <u>that</u> good-looking!

<u>I really did do great!</u>

Answered all the questions lucidly. Didn't throw up, had my fly zipped even.

Now was it the valium, or me? I'll never know.

One other thing. We now have three (3) invites to 1600 PA Ave. More to come.

Well, the 5th printing had been ordered some 2 week earlier, and on the weight of the <u>Time</u> article it virtually evaporated. a 6th printing of 10,000 was ordered, then upped to 15,000 (for a "Σ" of 75,000 printed copies!) a day later.

The first paperback printrun I learned from Agent Gottlieb, will be 850,000. We're getting into some fairly serious money here.

3/11/85

Tough work day, lots of crap left over from last week's chaos. Learned that <u>Hunt</u> will be #15 on the <u>Publisher's Weekly</u> BS list (this translates to #6 for fiction) on 3/22. Our first nationwide list. Wowie-Zowie!

Wednesday, 13 March.

I woke up thinking that <u>THIS</u> was <u>THE DAY,</u> and so it was. Usual morning routine, dropped off the girls at school, got the wagon filled up, got to the office. Mail was light. A few routine phone calls. We left for D.C. at 1020L.

Usual drive up, Rte 260 to Rte 4, left onto the Suitland Parkway into D.C., across the South Capitol Street Bridge, north to the Mall, left onto either Independence or Constitution--never can keep them straight--then right on 17th, north towards the White House. We were early, so we circled the White House once, then approached the gate. There were two, so of course I drove into the wrong one (an exit from the Executive Parking Lot), had to back up onto Pennsylvania, then went 20 feet to the Northwest Gate. Stop, get out, go to the guardhouse. I identified myself, they asked for ID. Had a bitch of a time getting my driver's license out, and the guard went in to query a computer terminal.

We cleared the first hurdle, and I was instructed to pull through the gate. A fairly sturdy gate, though it might not stop something heavy and determined. I couldn't decide how thick the vertical bolt (into the pavement) was. Okay, now Wanda and I both had to show ID and pass through a metal detector. It pinged on me twice, but tolerated my belt - buckle, gold pen, and tooth fillings. Next a German shepherd had to inspect the car, sniffing for explosives, I guess. I had mints in my briefcase. The dog queried them, but had only passing interest. Okay, we got our passes. As we later saw, even senior officials had such passes: "AA" superimposed and inverted diagonally, gray and black. We were told to pull down and park behind the limo, then to enter the door with the Marine.

Decided I didn't have to lock the car, even though this was D.C.

The Marine corporal (E-4) was so spiffy-looking in his dress blues the only reason he can't be on recruiting poster is that they might end up enlisting queers by mistake. He stands at parade-rest, hands in front. As we approached the door, he snapped to and saluted: "Good morning, Sir. Good morning, Ma'am." Gee, my first salute! And from a Marine! (He probably needs the salutes, even for wimp civilians, to protect his arms from atrophe.) And like a good Marine, he opened the door, then went back to parade rest.

Into the west-wing receiving/waiting room. There was a nice 45ish secretary who logged us in, asking us to sit and be comfortable. Well, we carried out half of her instructions.

You know the famous picture of Washington crossing the Delaware, standing in the boat? That's what Wanda sat under. An antique clock on the wall gave the correct time, 1130L. On a sofa by the west wall of the room sat a black chap with a do-dad in his ear and his coat unbuttoned. He pretended to read the paper. I probably have two circular red spots on the back of my neck from his eyes. The security force, uniformed and plain-clothes, is integrated, of course, with a high proportion of blacks. They all look alike: About as relaxed as a thoroughbred racehorse in the starting gate; as relaxed as the first pathfinder in the first stick of a combat parachute drop; as relaxed as Secret Service troops whose president, code-named "Rawhide," has already taken one in the chest.

Nancy Clark Reynolds showed up at 1145L. A very charming, though rather aggressive (in a very charming way) lady who gave Rawhide The Hunt for Red October for Christmas. She took us east, where we met Mike Deaver, a senior presidential aide (deputy chief of staff). 50ish, 5-8, slim, looks like he works and worries too much (just coming off a medical problem; kidneys, I think), nicely dressed, coat buttoned. He led us eastward through the building, about a total of, oh, fifty feet. Started noticing people, all men, all tall, all alert, none of whose coats were buttoned, all of whom had do-dads in their ears (do-dads, clear plastic ear-pieces with wound cords disappearing down their jackets; one would speculate radios, unless they like listening to music on the job...); looking me over like a confirmed child- molester who just got out on a technicality despite a bloody videotape of the 18 little boys and girls I wasted. There were A LOT of such people, practically a physical barrier in the narrow corridors. The President, one said, was in the bathroom. Seemed like a good idea to me, too. [Joke.]

Got to the secretary's office. In a side room off that was an Apple Macintosh. "Hey," I said brightly. "A Mac!"

The Oval Office is in the West Wing, not part of the portico. A SS agent watched through a peephole in the door. The President evidently finished what he was doing. The SS guy opened the door. Deaver led us in.

You know that scene in The Wizard of Oz where Dorothy goes from the wrecked house into Munchkinland? The transition from the secretary's office to Ronald Wilson Regan's office was rather like that. You go from real-world to magic-world.

The same scene you see on TV, exactly. The President of the United States was seated at his antique oak desk. Almost-navy-blue suit, white shirt, red tie with spots. We entered.

I had prepared myself for this mentally--despite this, well, quite a moment, guys.

An inch shorter than I am, exactly what he looks like on TV. Ruddy cheeks, potato-lump of a red nose, twinkling blue eyes, chest like a beer keg. There is gray in his hair if you look REAL close. Handshake firm but not overpowering.

Initial impression: This is a mensch! I expected Presence. I expected Star-Quality. I expected Charisma. There was more than I expected, by an order of magnitude. Partly this was my own reaction, of course, but part of it was an objective reality, three feet away.

Second impression: This guy could charm the fangs off a cobra. It envelopes you like a cloud, his charm.

Third impression: This is not an old man. He must have real Alpha+ genes, must drive his docs crazy. No 74-year-old man should move like this. I expected this, too, from reading about the guy--but it's still astonishing to see.

OBSERVATION: If he can't charm Garbage-ov, Ronnie can probably drive him into the pavement. No kidding, this guy looks like he could play ball.

So, he asked me where I got all my technical facts, and I said the really hard part was figuring the people out. He asked about the next book, and I told him WW3 at sea--had to repeat, he might be; well, he is a tad deaf, though Wanda says that I was speaking rather softly--and he asked, "Who's wins?"

"The good guys," I replied. General laughter. Nancy Reynolds had some anniversary presents for him, some saddle blankets and a cowhide. I helped unfold the latter. A nice cowhide from Argentina, different coloration from his own herd, he explained. While all this was going on a still photographer was blasting away on a Nikon, and perhaps also a video camera. I could <u>feel</u> the two SS officers behind me. I can dig it. The man is worth protecting.

A few more things, and someone reminded him that Henry Kissinger was waiting to have lunch with him. "Oh, [sigh] I guess that we we have to talk about the Russians."

The guy really is like the image. Soft voice, very relaxed manner. Hard to imagine him angry, though that must be impressive as hell…from a safe distance. And smart. Dumb people have dumb eyes. His had the twitchy alertness of a fox. In short, this guy didn't get the job by mistake. And I am pleased that I voted for him 4 of 5 times (in the 1980 primary, God forgive me, I voted Bush). (NOBODY'S perfect, guys!)

I guess it all lasted 5-10 minutes (relativity at work) and we were ushered out. I went to the wrong door, the one that <u>looks</u> like a door instead of the one that disappears into the wall

Oh, the windows to the Oval Office are THICK and multi-layered, as though to stop a RPG-7. God help the SOB who launches it. Or not.

Next we had lunch in the Roosevelt Room (Teddy, not Franklin). On the east-wall mantle is his Nobel Peace Prize (1907), and about the room are various wildlife bronzes, some rather--hell, expensive as God-knows-what. Present were Mrs. Reynolds, Mr. & Mrs. Deaver, Senator Mark Hatfield (rather a dovish chap, though polite enough to ask me to autograph his book), SECNAV Lehman, SECENERGY Herrington, LGEN Brent Scocroft, Charles Wick (USIA), <u>Time</u>, <u>The Wall Street Journal</u>, and the <u>Washington Times.</u> Jim Brooks, who did "Terms of Endearment," and had flown from California to be here, and, one suspects, a few other things. A total of 18 folks, all of them hanging n my every word, or polite enough to seem so.

The discussion ranged from my book (Lehman's first reaction to my book, he said, was, "Who cleared this!?!?!" and he was positive that no naval officer could have written this for security reasons; he said that <u>Hunt</u> is universally admired in the Navy [I <u>kvelled</u>]; I talked about the Crazy Ivan Turn, and how the USN never, of course, trails Soviet vessels, that they are, of course, engaged in "Oceanographic Research" [the official euphemism], "Counting the whales for Greenpeace" [laughter]), to the SDI (I voiced my approval since it adds a layer of uncertainty to the nuclear equation; general approval), to nuclear weapons use (here General Scocroft and I differed a bit; I don't think a controlled nuclear war is possible; he does; Hatfield agreed with me; I hope nobody ever finds out).

When lunch broke up, Nancy Reynolds told a cute story. Seems she represents the US at some international women's rights thing, and last week attended her last such meeting in Vienna. Her Russian counterpart is a man (of course), named Anatoly. She likes Anatoly, though she evidently regards him as a nerd--and a commie nerd at that! He always bugs her, she says, about disarmament, "like <u>I'm</u> going to fly right back here, <u>barge</u> into the Oval Office, and <u>tell</u> the President what to do, right?" This time he harranged her about Arkady Shevchenko--the defector whose recent book, <u>Breaking with Moscow</u>, is pure dynamite--promising to lay off the arms stuff.

"'<u>He was a boozer and a womanizer!</u>' Anatoly hissed, " she said, doing a mimic number that my words cannot approach, "<u>And nobody liked him! He did terrible things to his wife--but even</u> he <u>said in his book that we don't want war!!!</u>' Of course, he broke his word," Nancy smiled.

"'Anatoly, I said," she said. "'This is the last time I'm going to see you, and I want to give you a present [holds up a gift-wrapped package]. This book is all over Washington. The President loves it, and I'm <u>sure</u> you'll like it!'" A positively evil (but very charming) smile concluded the story.

"Well," I replied. "If the KGB comes to kill me, <u>it's your fault!</u>"

Next I talked with a girl named Alessandra Stanley, from <u>Time.</u> Ever see the Ann Klein II fashion commercials? That's how she dresses. Well, the package was nicer than the wrapper, but who am I to comment on fashions? She was concerned that someone might have wanted to nuke Moscow after the 007 incident. (Over lunch it was said that lots of nasty things were discussed in the White House at that time.) I tried mightily to persuade her that nobody seriously--or <u>un</u>seriously--suggested nuking Moscow (!), or even making a Tu-95D "Bear" disappear on its way to Cuba. ("In the real world, you don't <u>do</u> things like that.") I don't think she got the message. I really don't.

I guess we left around 1330L. Had to loop the car under the--portico, canopy, whatever. The marine saluted me again. I returned it.

We dropped off the passes, they opened the gate, and as our 1982 Plymouth Reliant station wagon left, some people on the sidewalk looked at us, wondering who in hell we were to have been in in the White House, no doubt. I would.

Got back to the office to learn that <u>Hunt</u> will be on the <u>New York Times</u> best-seller list (#10 of 15) on 3/24/85. A good day, all told.

3/14/85

The 6th printing took the printrun to 75,000. The 7th was ordered at 30,000, and today was upped to 50,000 for Σ of, gasp, 125,000 copies.

The bad news is that a movie offer which was in this letter until I <COMMAND> <X>'d it away, was withdrawn. Well, there might be another, right?

(3/17/85, I heard yesterday that the actual 7th printing was ordered finally at 80,000, argh, and Σ is 155,000+! Eek.) Had another performance yesterday, at St. John's College in Annapolis. This is getting tiring. (Having the flue didn't help a bit.) Tuesday, we head to the White House again. Coffee with special guests of Mrs. Reagan at 0930, then greet the President of Argentina on the South Lawn. Head home, then back to D.C. again for a state dinner. Be glad when it's all over.

3/19/85

Another day at the White House. Well, the usual morning routine--got up at 0630L instead of the normal 0655. Get paper, switch on TV, drink a pint of 2% milk + Instant Breakfast, out the door at 0805 for the trek to D.C. Same route as before, and the traffic was amazingly light.

This time we went in the East Visitors' Entrance. This used to be a real street entrance, now blocked with those pre-cast concrete abutments and (large) circular flower pots filled with dirt. (Those damned Shiites-- hmm, interesting how that looks in print, isn't it?) A bunch of folks were there. We butted through the mob and identified ourselves. A Secret Service agent hustled us inside, leaving the peons in our wake [**POWER!**]. Nice chap, he had a bandage on his right index finger ("Squeezing the trigger a little hard, guy?") (No, I didn't say that). Through the metal detector--it pinged real hard on him--past another group of peons, and into a ritzie waiting room, where we waited.

Quite a room, dating back to the 1940s. Solid, honey-colored (maple?) paneling, more Early American (junk!) furniture. (Well, real Early American, hence expensive junk.) Also present were Mr. & Mrs. Mark Russell; Arnold Schwartzenegger (**CONAN the BARBARIAN!**) and his mommie (I'm 0.5 to 1 inch taller than he is, though he's rather wider across the shoulders); Guilermo Villas (tennis star from Argentina); Gina Lollabrigida and escort ; and assorted others I don't know, including, possibly Lyn Nofsinger (wrong, turned out to be Pete Fountain, the jazz clarinetist, see below), former presidential gofer and political operator. Nobody had coffee but Conan, who looked relaxed. (I have to wonder if the local SS contingent measured him up in their .357 sights, or decided for something heavier...like an M-72 LAWS rocket.)

Headed out to the South Lawn about 0952. Lots of people were already there getting cold. We were actually in the White House basement, going

through a corridor with marble everywhere, various portraits of
Presidents and their ladies, including Mrs. Peanut. Finally we arrived at
yet another room with antique furniture and murals on the curvey walls.
Herr Russell said the door we went out was the Moving Van door, the one to
which the vans pull to move in/out the arriving/departing Presidents. Saw
Ron's military aides--you can tell at a glance, since their staff aigullettes
("loafer's loops") are on the right, rather than the left, shoulder. The
Marine 0-3 looked especially formidable. Conan could have stood inside
that guy, in all dimensions. Finally we went outside to join the peons.

Nice, brisk March day, clear sky, 15-knot breeze, about 40°F. The
honor guard was composed of (left to right) Marines, Navy, Army, Air
Force, each in about platoon strength, looking very spiffy indeed. The color
guard was--I mean, God damn! impressive, all those streamers!

They do Parade Rest different from the way we did it at Loyola ROTC.
The officers have their swords grounded. They might have been breathing,
but I'm not sure.

The press photographers behind us (mainly the lady from Time who did
the shot for the article) asked me to move--"You're too tall." Well, it's nice
to be recognized.

Mark Russell then said: "Remember everybody, today it's the
Malvenas!"

I nearly gagged. (That line rattled about in my head until the end of
the friggin' ceremony: Don't laugh, Don't Laugh...!) Mrs. Russell (30±; he's
50±) commented: "I can dress him up, but I can't take him anywhere..."

The Drum & Bugle team came out. Army, I think. 14 trumpets, two
drums, one director; they settled on the bottom level of the South Portico.

Show time:

Honor Guard snaps to like one robot. When they ORDER ARMS, one
(no
crap, ONE) click. (I bet there's only one real rifle there, all the rest being
made of rubber...)

Ruffles and FLourishes!

The Honorable Ronald W. Reagan comes out the moving van door.

Hail to the Chief.

21 guns from the Washington Monument.

His Excellency the President of the Argentine Republic arrives. He and
Ronnie mount the stand, about 15 feet from me. The national anthem of
Argentina.

It's too long, and changes cadence too many times, but the local Argie
community sang it with restrained gusto on the other side of the lawn.
Next came ours. Mark Russell sang it. Me, too. Rather a special feeling,
what with Ronnie only a few feet away. Gee.

The "Old Guard" Fife & Drum of the 3rd infantry did a fife-by in their
white-powdered wigs ("perukes," if you want the proper nomenclature),
red coats and linen tubular pants. (I remarked to Russell that, given the

guest, they might have worn blue coats this time.) "The World Turned Upside-Down," something I didn't recognize, and "Yankee Doodle."

CO, Honor Guard, says, "Sir, The Honor is concluded."

The speeches were the normal diplomatic stuff. Took about eight minutes each. Trans:

Hi, how are you? Glad you're here.

Fine, thanks. Glad to be here, let's talk some.

Sounds great, let's.

CO, Honor Guard, says, "Sir, the ceremony is concluded."

The Army Honor Guard (easy to spot, they have "Honor Guard" flashes instead of something useful like RANGER) is noted for its severe haircuts. They'd have to grow a couple of weeks to be mohawks. Actually, it's a real bunch of soldiers. In a recent exercise, quoath Larry Bond, they beat a unit from the 82nd Abn. [!] I bet there was hell to pay down at Bragg after that.

And that was that. We left the way we came. One final task, in the waiting room, everyone is supposed to sign an egg for the Easter Egg Roll. Back tonight for dinner.

3/20/85 The Day After.

I look pretty decent in a penguin suit. Vest instead of cumberbund-- you don't have to button the coat. Arrived at the same place as that AM at 0720±, walked to the same gate, had to show my driver's license, and we got waved in by a black SS man in normal clothes. (No metal detectors this time…hmm…) After that all were in black tie, and therefore rather more difficult to pick out of the crowd. The way in is actually a basement (the White House grounds roll off a bit to the east). Lots of uniforms. Honor Guard (3rd Infantry Regiment) at the east entrance (unlike marines, these army guys don't salute, the pigs.) Inside it was all officers, except the musicians. All services, all 0-2 to 0-4, all in full dress. (NOTE: The Marine full dress [Head Waiter] outfits win the militant fashion contest because of the blood-red sashes. Sorry, squids and doggies.) A Navy flutist and harp greeted us (both 4.0 female E-6s), and a string of officers guided us to the coat room. (You Hitchhiker's Guide to the Galaxy fans, our number was 42. I believe in fate.)

*(Further note on fate: The idea for Hunt hit me the Monday after Argentina assaulted the Falkland Islands, the day on which I had lunch with [now] CDR Ralph Chatham, USN; the President got the book because a chap named O'Leary [editor on The Washington Times] sent his copy to one Mr. Ruiz, our ambassador to Argentina, and the courier, Mrs. Nancy Clark Reynolds, read it on the plane, and liked it so much…; and the functions I get invited to--the arrival of His Excellency, the President of the Argentine Republic. **And people wonder why the Irish are supersticious???)***

Proceeded west down the corridor, stopped by a LT, USN. Gina Lolabrigitta was just ahead of us, in the Press Gauntlet. For the first time, we were announced: "Mr. & Mrs. Tom Clancy!"

The Press Gauntlet is a line of photographers and reporters. Two ladies (<u>USA Today</u> and someone else) questioned me--oddly they take notes without looking at their pads; they look at you with upturned faces and open mouths, rather like the witches in <u>MacBeth</u>--and the cameras snapped. We escaped. Further west down the same corridor as in the morning, right (if you please, sir, quoath a handsome young officer) up some stairs to what is actually the White House's first floor.

At the top of the stairs, we got our table cards. I was Table 4. Wanda was Table 1. Then did an extended U-turn past the Marine Corps Band in the main lobby to the East Room. A room of perhaps 1,000 sqft, white walls, high ceiling, hardwood floor, lots of people. Got announced again, this time with a microphone.

"My Lords, Ladies, and Gentlemen! Mr. & Mrs. Thomas Clancy, Jr." (A little poetic license there.)

I mentioned earlier Michael and Carolyn Deaver. Mr. Deaver is the outgoing Deputy Chief of Staff for the President.

<u>Be it recorded here that he and his wife are fine people; and that to anyone who knows me and who should ever have a chance to be of service to thee people, be ye advised that in doing so ye do service also unto me. These are important folks yet with a surfeit of kindness and humanity. Yea, verily, the Lord God has not made better these people than these, and Wanda and I are beholden to them.</u>

In other words, with all the really important people around, they came to us, and verily we spoke, and verily they are genuinely nice, decent people, hence (so far as D.C. is concerned) entitled to federal protection under the Endangered Species Act. Damn, this sort of thing will renew one's faith in humanity.

I didn't want to drink. I had Perrier. It's French water, and it tastes used.

Other people present: Irene Cara, a lovely little pixie every bit as overwhelmed to be there as I, and when I met her later, thoroughly nice; Armand Hammer, his first time in the White House since Carter, and it must have been a mistake; Lee Trevino; Doug Flutie; all those I saw that morning; a total of 120 guests. About the time I finished my French Fizz the music in the distance changed. The Presidents were coming. First the colors, then the folks. The waiters (more about them later) discretely collected drinks (I skillfully pocketed the napkin), and an amorphous line generated itself to file past the hose and featured guest. Ronal Reagan didn't look at all that great that AM in a brown suit--just not his color. In a tux, he's dynamite. Shook hands again. Charm, firm handshake. President Alfonsin is a shorter guy, darker, mustache, with dignity. Mrs. Reagan is so friggin' skinny she practically isn't there. Mrs. Alfonsin was quite attractive. Past the receiving life, we went into a side room, then back to the main east-west corridor heading to the West Room.

(NOTE: Inside, the White House isn't all that large--perhaps the cleaning staff thinks differently. In fact, it seems almost small in the building proper, as opposed to the administrative additions.)

In the West Room, we split up. Table 4 was in the S/E corner. Wanda was right at the exit at the N/E one, Table 1.

Dinner.

The White House Staff (that is, the serving folks) is entirely black (at least all those I saw were; Wanda claims to have seen an Anglo or two, and maybe some Filipinos). Rather an irksome thing, times having changed since emancipation, nevertheless these are the most consummately skilled people I've ever seen. A neurosurgeon would do well to have such technique. Under crowded conditions, with numbers of self-inflated people, their service was quite simply 4.0, 100%, perfection itself. Never have I seen anything like it. Period. Maybe white people just can't cut it. Maybe, like with the Chesapeake Bay Pilots Association, you have to be born into the job. In any case, I hope they get paid enough. They earn it.

Mike--excuse me, <u>Mr.</u> Deaver was at my table, but the boy-girl-boy-girl seating prevented conversation. Found myself between Mrs. Pete Fountain (jass clarinet, he played later), and an aristocratic lady from Brazil who'd endured a nine hour flight to be here.

Dinner was: (photocopy attached)

The salmon was garbage, but everything else was spiffy.

While I was speaking with two rather nice ladies, Wanda at Table 1 was between Bud McFarland (National Security Advisor) and some Argentine asshole who could not understand A) why an author was here, and B) why an author's wife was here. I suppose Argentina needs additional work on democracy (the guy turned out to be an instructor at Harvard, a further problem for his personal development). Not to mention manners--I mean, it is <u>OUR</u> house!

Dinner ended on a nice note: the Army band's Strolling Strings serenaded our GIs (a cute blond E-6 played at our table; she was obviously tired; I gave her a me-too smile, and got one back [Clancy, champion of the working man, and working woman; I also complemented one of the waiters]) with violins, two cellos, a bass and an acordian (?), then came the toasts. Etiquette is that you stand when it's finished. Some Spanish-speaking photographer in his haste to get his Nikon fed shoved Wanda back into her chair. Wanda endured the indignity (one doesn't make waves in the White House). When Alfonsin's turn came, said Nikon jock practically leaned on her. A good thing I wasn't there, but our guardian angel of the evening, Carolyn Deaver, noted this, gestured to an aide, a pretty girl in red, who approached photographer. Photographer, of course, ignored her. (ASIDE, the girl was too pretty to be ignored, and I thought the Spanish had an eye for female persons.) What followed is called, I think, escalation. A small gesture from Mrs. Deaver, and the next person to touch the photographer was one of those serious-looking chaps with a do-dad in his ear. There is just something about their manner that says: GO AHEAD: <u>MAKE MY DAY!</u> No words were exchanged: said SS man simply moved the bastard five feet about the way I move Tommy. Except that the Nikon jockey behaved a lot better.

We exited to the Blue (I think; maybe Green) room. This is the one that bows out the south side of the building (the Jefferson Portico, I think). Yet another staff chap held out a box of cigars (did you like it, Mike?). Others circulated with coffee (small cups) and cordial glasses, while another held a tray with brandy (Hennessy!), etc. (Sorely tempted, but I had to drive....) Met and spoke a few minutes with Mrs. Reagan. Dear God, she's skinny. I wonder if she has a shadow? Takes her charm lessons from her husband, I suppose. Got "shot" shaking hands with her, and the photographer (one of "ours") came over to say that, indeed, <u>everyone</u> in the White House has read my book, "And I liked it, too!" Gee.

Next met Bud McFarland, the President's National Security Advisor. He is not at all like Jeffrey Pelt in <u>Hunt</u>, and said so jokingly. We exchanged views on sea-power and mobility. (That sounds haughty. I floated an idea that he liked, no big deal.) Nice wife--in red, that must be the current "in" color. Went east to the Green (maybe Blue) room, then back around to the westernmost colored room, Red (I'm sure of this). Lots of pictures of presidents, etc. Spoke with some of the officer-guides. Wanda's feet were sore by this time, she informed me.

Entertainment back in the East Room, Pete Fountain and his group played some cool jazz for a while. Excellent.

Final act was dancing and general carousing in the lobby. Ronnie and Nancy danced, then made a graceful exit. As did we. I thanked Mrs. Deaver for being such a nice person. She said that Arnold Schwartzenegger had been approached to be in the film version of my book. [?] And we left, escorted all the way by relays of spiffy young officers. And floated home.

And that's the end of the tale.

For now.

THE JL123 ISHO

FLIGHT 123 PASSENGERS to
VARIOUS
August 12th, 1985

On August 12th 1985, Japan
Airlines Flight 123 took off
from Tokyo International
Airport and headed for
its destination, Osaka
International Airport, with
509 passengers and 15
crew aboard. Problems
began just 12 minutes
later, when the plane's
rear pressure bulkhead
suffered a catastrophic
failure, which resulted in the
plane's tail being partially
destroyed and the severance
of its hydraulic lines.
Unsurprisingly, Flight 123
was soon proving impossible
to control – sadly,
approximately 32 minutes
after the initial failure, the
plane crashed into Mount
Takamagahara. Four people
survived.

During those 32 terrifying
minutes, fearing the
worst, many of the plane's
passengers wrote letters
to their loved ones, a
devastating collection of
missives now known as the
JL123 Isho (last notes).

Hirotsugu Kawaguchi

Mariko, Tsuyoshi, Chiyoko,
Be good to each other and work hard.
Help your mother.
It's sad, but I'm sure I won't make it.
I don't know the cause.
It's been five minutes now.
I don't want to take any more planes.
Please kami-sama help me.
To think that our dinner last night was the last time.
There was some sort of explosion in the cabin
There was smoke and we started to descend
Where are we going, what will happen?
Tsuyoshi, I'm counting on you
Darling, it's too bad that this has happened.
Goodbye
Please take good care of the children
It's 6:30 now.
The plane is turning around and descending rapidly.
I am grateful for the truly happy life I have enjoyed until now.

Keiichi Matsumoto

PM 6:30
Tomoko
Look after Tetsuya (and parents)
Keiichi
Suddenly there was an explosion and the masks dropped
With the explosion we began to fall
Be brave and live
Tetsuya be good.

Ryohei Murakami

The plane is swaying a lot left and right,
18:30 descending rapidly
Flying steady
Japan Air Lines 18:00 flight to Osaka accident
I might die.
Murakami Ryohei
Everybody please live happily.
Goodbye Sumiko Miki Kyoko Kentaro
18:45 The plane is level and stable
There's little oxygen, I feel sick
Inside the plane voices are saying let's do our best
I don't know what happened to the plane
18:46 I am worried about the landing
The stewardesses are calm.

Mariko Shirai

I'm scared. I'm scared. I'm scared. Help me. I feel sick. I don't want to
die. Mariko'
'Keiji, Hisako, Tadaomi, Shin'ichi, Rihiya, Sakura'
Masakazu Taniguchi
'Machiko,
Look after the children
Osaka Minoo
Taniguchi Masakazu
6 30

Kazuo Yoshimura

Please live bravely. Please look after the children

Facing page: The Isho
handwritten by Hirotsugu
Kawaguchi in his notebook

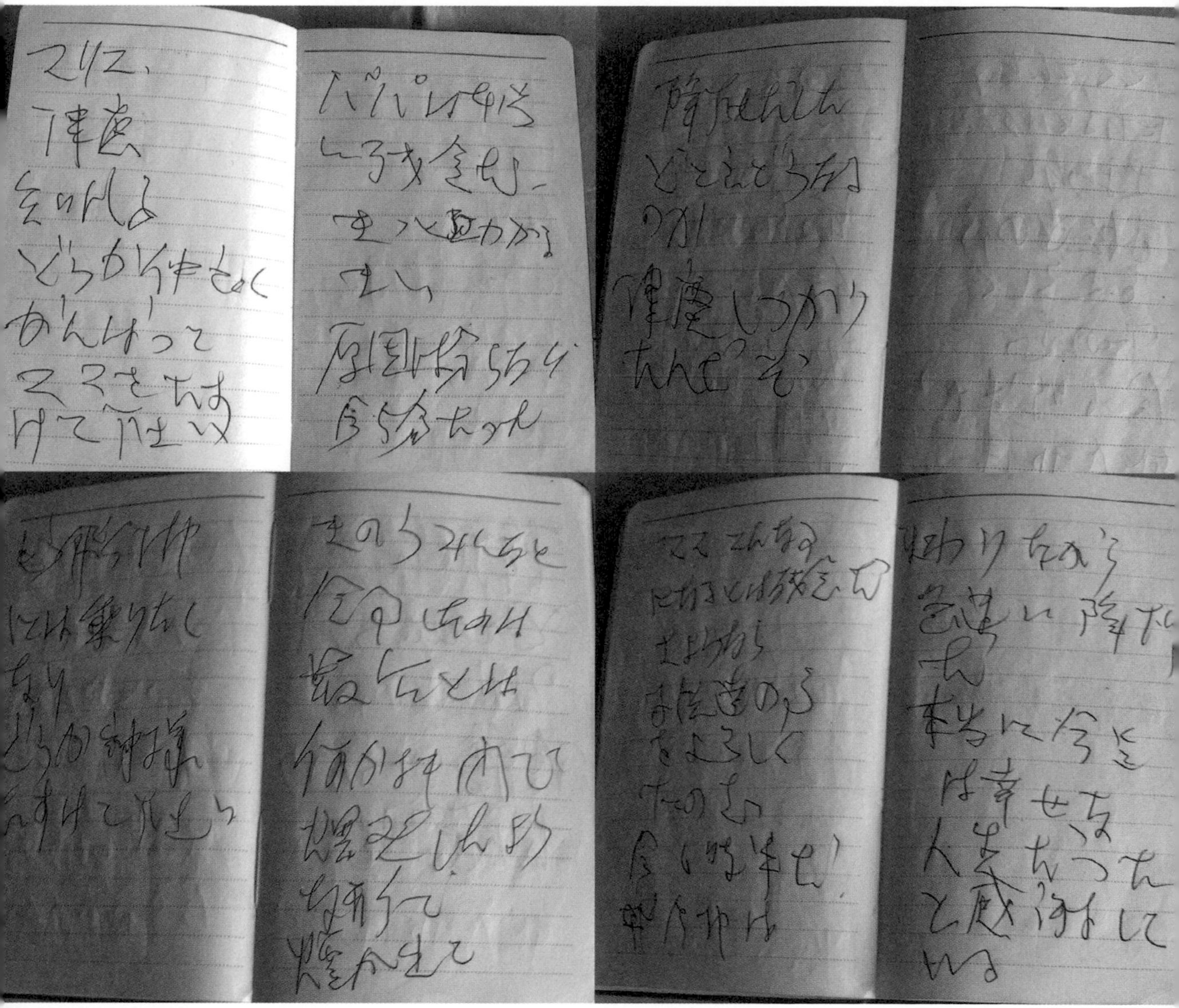

マリエ、
津波
おぼれる
どうか小さく
がんばって
子をたす
けて下さい

パパはずっと
ニ子を金也
を応えんから
むい、
原因がちちゃ
ちらおちゃん

降たれ心も
どとむどうな
のか
津度しっかり
たんでそ

とらにかけ
には乗りまし
たり
ちらの神み
おすまてだら

そのちみんなと
住や生みい
話たいとは
かすかまでむひ
ほ足にしも
じまれも

ててこんな
にたくとは強もむ
さよから
お体をのう
をよろしく
だのむ
今くの年も
かんかや

助りたから
昌達に降たな
ん
本当に今を
は幸せな
人生をおつた
と感しして
いる

113

September, 1960

DARE TO STAND ALONE

BUD WILKINSON to JAY
WILKINSON
September, 1960

Bud Wilkinson remains
one of the most successful
American football coaches
of all time at college level,
having guided the University
of Oklahoma Sooners
to victory in a record 47
consecutive games between
1953 and 1957; during his 16
years as their head coach,
the Sooners also won three
national championships and
14 conference titles. Bud's
youngest son, Jay, was a
gifted footballer and dreamt
of one day playing for his
father; however, in 1960,
after much deliberation and
with support from his father,
Jay accepted an offer to
study and play somewhere
else: at Duke University,
1200 miles from home.
For the next six years Bud
offered his son invaluable
advice by letter. This was his
first, sent soon after Jay's
arrival at Duke.

Dear Jay,

It was good to talk to you—I know things will get better because you are the kind of person who can adjust and find the good in all situations.

When I read your letter, I recalled vividly many similar times in my life. When I left home to go to Shattuck, I was truly blue. Yet I know now how fine a thing it was for me and my future. The training I received has made my life good. When I left you, Pat, and Mother to go to sea during the war, I was really shaken. I loved you and wanted to watch you and help you as you grew up—and I was leaving not knowing if I'd ever get back again. But once more, the experience and training I received more than compensated for the heartaches. Then too, I had the personal satisfaction of knowing I had done my duty.

One of the first things an education brings to people is the realization that the world is a big place—full of many different ideas and ways of doing things. You have watched our team practice and quite naturally are attuned to our ways of doing things. Bill Murray has been a fine coach for many years. Instead of wondering why they do things differently, you should be studying what they do so you will understand that their approach will get the job done more effectively—maybe more easily than we can.

When any person leaves a pleasant situation to enter the "unknown," there is always the realization of how nice, good and comfortable things were before. Yet only by facing the future and accepting new and progressively more difficult challenges are we able to grow, develop, and avoid stagnation. You have more total, all-around ability in all fields than anyone I have ever known. You will certainly be a great man and make a great contribution to the world. But to do this you must take on new and progressively more difficult challenges. You will grow and develop in direct relationship to the way you meet and overcome what at first seem to be hard assignments. You will learn to love Duke—to take great pride in the school and their football team. You're that kind of person. By developing as a student and an athlete, you will prepare yourself to do bigger and better things when you graduate.

Always remember that I believe in you no matter what. You must do what seems right to you. Don't ever be swayed by what "other people will think." My grandmother, a great lady—one of the finest I've ever known—always told me when I was a young boy growing up to "dare to be a Daniel; dare to stand alone." It is the best advice one can have for happy, successful living. After analyzing and evaluating the circumstances—always do what seems best to you in the light of your own good judgment. Only in this way can you find peace of mind because you cannot be happy doing "what other people think you should do." You must do what you think you should do.

I didn't quite finish this letter yesterday before practice so am doing so this morning, Saturday. Norman tied Capitol Hill last night 26–26. They miss their "Big Tiger" on defense—as well as offense.

I love you, Jay, more than anything in life. Don't worry about things—live each day by doing your best. Will look forward to talking to you tomorrow.

Love always,
Dad

*Facing page: University of
Oklahoma coach Bud Wilkinson
during spring practice at
Memorial Stadium, 1955*

ARKELL v. PRESSDRAM

PRIVATE EYE to GOODMAN
DERRICK & CO.
April 29th, 1971

*"Messrs Jeffrey Benson and Michael
Isaacs of Tracing Services Ltd,
currently on bail on charges of
conspiracy to create a public mischief,
appear to have lost most of the
work collecting debts and tracing
absconders for the Granada group,
to the considerable regret of Mr
James Arkell, Granada's retail credit
manager. Ever since last June, when
Tracing Services got the contract,*

*Mr Arkell has been receiving £20
every month from Tracing Services,
but the payment now appears to have
stopped."*

On April 9th of 1971, much to
the dismay of one James Arkell,
the brief story quoted above
was published in *Private Eye*, a
British satirical news publication
founded in 1961 which, thanks
to its unflinching commitment to
uncovering scandals, is no stranger
to legal disputes. Indeed, a few
weeks after this particular piece hit
the shelves, a letter arrived from
Arkell's solicitors, to which *Private*

Eye responded with a letter which
has since become famous in legal
and publishing circles. Never ones
to miss an opportunity, *Private
Eye* published the exchange very
quickly, and almost immediately
Arkell withdrew his complaint.
The magazine has since used
the dispute as shorthand when
responding to threats, e.g. "We refer
you to the reply given in the case of
Arkell v. Pressdram."

Note: "Pressdram Ltd" is *Private
Eye*'s publisher. Also, there was no
"case" legally, despite the name by
which the dispute is now known.

29th April 1971

Dear Sir,

We act for Mr Arkell who is Retail Credit Manager of Granada TV Rental Ltd. His
attention has been drawn to an article appearing in the issue of Private Eye dated 9th April
1971 on page 4. The statements made about Mr Arkell are entirely untrue and clearly
highly defamatory. We are therefore instructed to require from you immediately your
proposals for dealing with the matter.

Mr Arkell's first concern is that there should be a full retraction at the earliest possible date
in Private Eye and he will also want his costs paid. His attitude to damages will be governed
by the nature of your reply.

Yours,

[Signed]

Goodman Derrick & Co.

Dear Sirs,

We acknowledge your letter of 29th April referring to Mr. J. Arkell.

We note that Mr Arkell's attitude to damages will be governed by the nature of our reply
and would therefore be grateful if you would inform us what his attitude to damages would
be, were he to learn that the nature of our reply is as follows: fuck off.

Yours,

Private Eye

THE OUTSIDERS

JO ELLEN MISAKIAN to
FRANCIS FORD COPPOLA
March 21st, 1980

In March of 1980, a school
librarian by the name of
Jo Ellen Misakian wrote to
Francis Ford Coppola and,
on behalf of the students
at Lone Star School in
Fresno, California, asked
him to consider adapting
their favourite novel, S.
E. Hinton's *The Outsiders*,
for the big screen. Also
included with her letter
were a copy of the book,
and a petition signed by
110 of the kids. Amazingly,
three months later they
received an unexpected and
cautiously optimistic reply
from producer Fred Roos,
who soon advised Coppola
to read the book. Coppola
did exactly that, and two
years later production on the
movie began.

The Outsiders, directed by
Francis Ford Coppola, was
released in March of 1983,
with an incredible up-and-
coming cast that included
Tom Cruise, Rob Lowe,
Ralph Macchio, Patrick
Swayze, Diane Lane, Emilio
Estevez, and Matt Dillon.
A premiere was held for the
school, attended by the cast.

Lone Star School Library
2617 South Fowler Avenue
Fresno, California 93725
March 21, 1980

Mr. Francis Ford Coppola
1 Gulf and Western Plaza
New York, N. Y. 10023

Dear Mr. Copolla:

I am writing to you on behalf of the students and faculty of Lone Star School. We
hope you will take the time to consider our request.

We are all so impressed with the book, THE OUTSIDERS by S. E. Hinton, that
a petition has been circulated asking that it be made into a movie. We have chosen
you to send it to. In hopes that you might also see the possibilities of the movie we
have enclosed a copy of the book.

Lone Star is a small school in Fresno County. We have a student body of 324
students. It is a kindergarten through eighth grade school. I feel our students are
representative of the youth of America. Everyone who has read the book, regardless
of ethnic or economical background, has enthusiastically endorsed this project.
This plea comes from our seventh and eighth grade students.

We feel certain that if you will read the book you will agree with us.

Thank you for your time.

Sincerely yours,

[Signed]

Jo Ellen Misakian
(Mrs. John Misakian)
Librarian Aide

June 10, 1980   *Hollywood General Studios*
                        1040 N. Las Palmas
                        Hollywood, CA 90038
                        (213) 467-6202

Ms. Jo Ellen Misakian
Lone Star School Library
2617 South Fowler Avenue
Fresno, Calif. 93725

Dear Ms. Misakina:

Thank you for sending us your letter, the petition from
your students and the book "THE OUTSIDERS" by S.E. Hinton.
Francis Coppola received them and was very impressed with
the passionate interest you and your students showed in
this book.

We are thus following through on it as you can see by the
attached report that was done by one of our readers. The
reader seems to agree with you and your students.

The next step is for myself and other members of our company
to read the book and see if we really might want to make a
film out of it. I'll try to keep you posted on the progress.

Thanks again to you and your seventh and eighth graders for
being good literary scouts and for choosing our company.

Have a nice summer vacation.

Sincerely,

Fred Roos

Fred Roos

FR/lff
cc: F. Coppola, L. Fisher
     S. Rogers, S. Ingleby

August 11, 1980   *Hollywood General Studios*
                     1040 N. Las Palmas
                     Hollywood, CA 90038
                     (213) 467-6202

Jo Ellen Misakian
Lone Star School
2617 South Fowler Avenue
Fresno, Calif. 93725

Dear Miss Misakian:

Thanks for your letter of July 14, 1980. Sorry your class was
not in school to share the news.

The latest is that the Zoetrope Studios executives read and
discussed at length the pros and cons of making a movie out of
"THE OUTSIDERS" with some being for it and some being against
it. I flew to Tulsa to have a personal meeting with Suzie Hinton
which I enjoyed very much and found valuable.

The final decision has been to go ahead and try to option the book
with the aim of filming it if we can get a good screenplay. The
negotiations with Ms. Hinton's agents are going on now.

By the time school reconvenes, hopefully we will have acquired
"THE OUTSIDERS" and have begun to hire a screenwriter to adapt it.
If you want to further use this book as a class study project, perhaps you could have each of your students write an essay on why
they like "THE OUTSIDERS"; perhaps talking about their favorite
scenes or about scenes they don't like. This could be helpful to
we the filmakers.

Also, there is a chance that we may not be able to use the title
"THE OUTSIDERS" because of another movie that came out recently
with that title. I hope we <u>don't</u> have to change it but if we do,
I'd like to hear your students suggestions of an alternate title...
such as "Ponyboy".

I'd also like to hear your students opinion of one possible
change that we might have in the movie. That is to not have
a gang fight at the end. It seems wrong to me in light of what
has just happened to Dallas, Johnny and Bob that the two groups
would still have another fight. Hopefully they would have
learned something during the course of the story. At least I'd
like to think they had and to show audiences through our movie
that they had. Any opinions on this would be helpful.

I look forward to hearing from you and your students in a few
weeks. Again, thanks for your help.

Sincerely,

Fred Roos

FR/lff

the OUTSIDERS

Mrs. Jo Ellen Misakian   April 27, 1982
Librarian Aide
Lone Star School Library
2617 South Fowler Ave.
Fresno, California 93725

Dear Mrs. Misakian,

I want to keep you and the school up to
date on the progress of Lone Star's very own
movie production , THE OUTSIDERS.

We are presently shooting the film in
Tulsa and are into our fifth week. We have
a wonderful cast and it's going very well.

The enclosed production notes will tell
you and the kids about everything they need to
know about the movie and who's in it.

I'll keep giving you updates.

                              Sincerely,

                              Fred Roos

cc: Francis Coppola   Fred Roos
    Beverly Walker   Producer

122

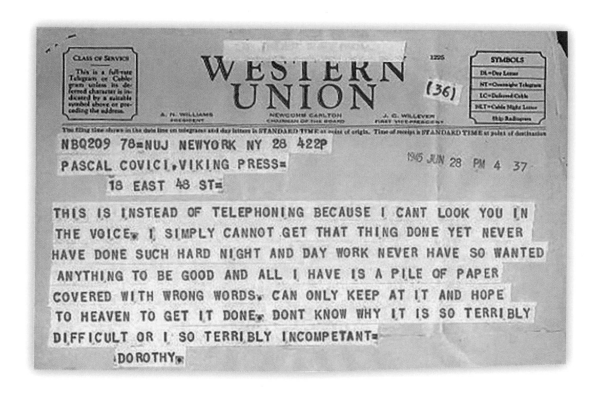

I CAN'T LOOK YOU IN THE VOICE

DOROTHY PARKER to PASCAL COVICI
June 28th, 1945

The late, great Dorothy Parker had many strings to her bow. She wrote hundreds of poems and short stories, many of which were published in magazines and books; she was a biting and much-loved book critic for *The New Yorker* in the late 1920s; in the 1930s, she moved to Hollywood to try her hand at making movies and co-wrote two Academy Award-nominated screenplays; she was also a founding member of the Algonquin Round Table, a legendary group of New York City's brightest and wittiest writers, columnists and comedians who met each day for lunch at the Algonquin Hotel in Manhattan. Alas, she was also human. In June of 1945, whilst suffering from a bout of writer's block, she sent this dejected telegram to her editor, Pascal Covici.

DO NOT BE SO BLOODY VULNERABLE

NOËL COWARD to
MARLENE DIETRICH
1956

It was in 1935 that movie stars Noël Coward and Marlene Dietrich first spoke, thanks to an unexpected phone call from Dietrich in which she complimented him on his starring role in *The Scoundrel*. For the next 38 years, until Coward's death, they remained close friends and wrote regularly, the topic of discussion often Dietrich's complicated love life. In 1956, she sent him a downbeat letter and detailed a disastrous flight with her drunken on-off lover of five years, Yul "Curly" Brynner – just the latest depressing "episode" of many. This wasn't the first time Coward had been told of such events, and he clearly couldn't bear to see Dietrich suffer any longer. This was his stern reply.

Facing page:
Marlene Dietrich during rehearsal at the Palladium with Noël Coward, 1954

Firefly Hill
Port Maria
Jamaica B.W.I.

Oh, darling,

Your letter filled me with such a lot of emotions, the predominant one being rage that you should allow yourself to be so humiliated and made so unhappy by a situation that really isn't worthy of you. I loathe to think of you apologizing and begging forgiveness and humbling yourself. I don't care if you did behave badly for a brief moment, considering all the devotion and loving you have given out during the last five years, you had a perfect right to. The only mistake was not to have behaved a great deal worse a long time ago. The aeroplane journey sounds a nightmare to me.

It is difficult for me to wag my finger at you from so very far away particularly as my heart aches for you but really darling you must pack up this nonsensical situation once and for all. It is really beneath your dignity, not your dignity as a famous artist and a glamourous star, but your dignity as a human, only too human, being. Curly is attractive, beguiling, tender and fascinating, but he is not the only man in the world who merits those delightful adjectives...Do please try to work out for yourself a little personal philosophy and DO NOT, repeat DO NOT be so bloody vulnerable. To hell with God damned "L'Amour." It always causes far more trouble than it is worth. Don't run after it. Don't court it. Keep it waiting off stage until you're good and ready for it and even then treat it with the suspicious disdain that it deserves... I am sick to death of you waiting about in empty houses and apartments with your ears strained for the telephone to ring. Snap out of it, girl! A very brilliant writer once said (could it have been me?) "Life is for the living." Well that is all it is for, and living DOES NOT consist of staring in at other people's windows and waiting for crumbs to be thrown to you. You've carried on this hole in corner, overcharged, romantic, unrealistic nonsense long enough.

Stop it. Stop it. Stop it. Other people need you...Stop wasting your time on someone who only really says tender things to you when he's drunk...

Unpack your sense of humor, and get on with living and ENJOY IT.

Incidentally, there is one fairly strong-minded type who will never let you down and who loves you very much indeed. Just try to guess who it is. XXXX. Those are not romantic kisses. They are un-romantic. Loving "Goose-Es."

Your devoted "Fernando de Lamas"

FROM HEAVEN

PAUL REVERE OSLER to
GRACE OSLER
July 1st, 1893

Esteemed Canadian
physician Sir William
Osler is known by many
as the "Father of Modern
Medicine". He both practised
and taught at the prestigious
Johns Hopkins Hospital, of
which he was a founding
professor, and helped
to revolutionise medical
education by introducing the
now commonplace residency
system: the training of
doctors within the hospital
itself. His status as one of
the world's greatest doctors
was further strengthened
in 1892 with the publication
of his indispensable
textbook, *The Principles and
Practice of Medicine*, aka the
"Physician's Bible". Sadly,
a year after the book was
released, William's first
child, Paul Revere Osler,
died a week after being
born. In an effort to console
his distraught wife, Grace,
William wrote her a letter,
from Heaven, in Paul's voice.

Note: The Emma Osler
referred to in the letter is
William's sister, who died
at the age of two; "Julius
Caeser" refers to a stillborn
baby from Grace's first
marriage.

Heaven July 1st

My dear Mother

I for one am good & get on nicely with our singing and if our earthly parents continue to show an interest in us by remembering us in their prayers, we are allowed to write about every three or four tatma's (i.e. months). I got here safely with very little inconvenience. I scarcely knew anything until I awoke in a lovely, green spot, with fountains & trees & soft couches & such nice young girls to tend us. You would have been amused to see the hundreds which came the same day. But I must tell you first how we are all arranged; it took me several days to find out about it. Heaven is the exact counterpart of earth so far as its dwellers are concerned; thus all from the U.S. go to one place—all from Maryland to one district & even all from the cities & townships get corresponding places. This enables the guardian angels to keep the lists more carefully & it facilitates communication between relatives. They are most particular in this respect and have a beautifully simple arrangement by which the new arrivals can find out at once whether they have connections in heaven. I never was more surprised in my time—we say that here not life & not eternity, for that has not started for us—when the day after my arrival Althea brought me two quill feathers on one of which was written Julius Caesar & the other Emma Osler. I knew at once about the former as I had often heard you and father talk of him and had so longed to wear his little cap; but the latter I did not know at all but she said she had been father's little sister & she had been sent to make me feel happy and comfortable.

You must know that all the souls coming here are grouped in 6 divisions

1. Those who have never lived and have not seen the sun. The angels have no end of trouble with them, largely Althea says because they are so stupid and learn so slowly, not having seen the sun-light. They are allowed to grow until equal to the size of the body of a 2 year old child & at which point they stop. They never obtain a full knowledge but always remain childlike. This is their great attraction & in their gardens may be seen hundreds of thousands of middle aged & old soul-bodies refreshing their memories of happy days on earth by playing with these angel children.

2. Those who have not lived a full year are also in a separate division and we are gradually taught and within a very short space of time have beautiful soul-bodies about the size of an earthly child of five. We have however full knowledge and have not many childish ways.

3. Children between 1 & 5 years look here about 10 years in earthly-size; & though they say that their voices are better & their education more perfect than ours we do not think so.

Heaven July 14.

My dear Mother

            If we are good
& get on nicely with our singing
and if our earthly parents continue
to show an interest in us by re-
remembering us in their prayers,
we are allowed to write about every
three or four tatma's (i.e. month).
I got here safely with very little
inconvenience. I scarcely knew
anything until I awoke in a
lovely green spot, with fountains
& lakes & soft couches & such nice
young girl to tend us. You

127

4. From 5 to 15 years the children who come attain in their soul-bodies the earthly size of about 15 and are of great use to the angels in helping with the younger ones & in showing all the beauties of the place and in tuning harps in the great days of the chorus.

6. The grown soul-bodies--about which we do not know very much only seeing those very nearly related to us by earthly ties. We play all day & talk so much with each other about earth and take a great interest in all that you do. We cannot always see you, why I do not know, but at intervals we have such clear and definite sights of our earthly homes. Julius Caesar is very well and a great favorite. He looks a dear little fellow of about two years old (earthly count) and he told me when his guardian angel was not near that he felt a little badly that I should have been in the Amarathyn division--i.e. the one in advance of his. He and Aunt Emma are to come very often and we know now all about our many relatives. Unlike the real angels we have no fore-knowledge and cannot tell what is to happen to our dear ones on Earth. Next to the great feast days, when we sing choruses by divisions in the upper heavens, our chief delight is in watching the soul bodies as they arrive in our divisions. I am helping the angels to get them in order & properly trained. In the children's divisions not a friad (i.e. about an hour of earthly time) passes without the excitement of a father, a mother, a brother or a sister united to one of us. We know about 1000 of each other so that it is great fun to see our comrades & friends making their relatives feel at home.

The other day my kind Althea said there was a baby-soul in the 1st division from New Hampshire, which had left her kind regards for me at the general intelligence office of the heavenly United States. It was chorus day so I could not go, but I am to see her tomorrow if she is advanced enough to receive visitors. It takes about ten days to get our beautiful plumage in order.

If you keep as you are I shall be able (Althea says) to write again in three months. I send you much love--also to pop!

Your loving son
Paul Revere

We use the word 'pop' here for papa or father very much

would have been amused to see the hundreds which came the same day. But I must tell you first how we are all arranged; it took me several days to find out about it. Heaven is the exact counterpart of earth so far as its ~~inhabitant~~ dwellers are concerned —. All from this the U.S. go to one place — all from Maryland to one district & even all from the cities & townships go to corresponding places. This enables the guardian Angels to keep the lists more carefully & it facilitates communication between relatives. They are most particular in this respect and have a beautiful simple arrangement by which the new arrivals can find out at once whether they have ~~relatives~~ connections in heaven. I never was more surprised in my time — we say that here not life & not eternity for that has not started from us — when the day after my arrival Alther brought me two quill feathers

on one of which was written Julius Cæsar
& the other Emma Osler. I knew at
once about the former as I had often
heard you & father talk of him and
had so longed to wear his little cap;
but the latter I did not know at all,
but she said she had been fathers little
sister & she had been sent to make
me feel happy & comfortable.
You must know that all the souls
coming here are grouped in 6 divisions
(1) those who have never lived and have
not seen the sun. The angels have no
end of trouble with them, largely Altken
says because they are so stupid and
learn so slowly, not having seen the
sun-light. They are allowed to grow
until they are ~~their result~~ equal to the size of the
~~earth~~ body of a 2 ~~old~~ year old child &
at ~~which~~ point they stop. They never attain
a full knowledge but always remain
childlike. This is their great attraction &
in their gardens may be seen hundreds
of thousands of middle aged & old souls

bodies refreshing their memories of happy days on Earth by playing with their angel children.

2 Those who have not lived a full year are also in a separate division and we are gradually taught and within a very short space of time have beautiful soul-bodies about the size of an earthly child of five. We have however full knowledge and have not many childish ways.

3. Children between 1 & 5 years look like about 10 years in Earthly size, & though they say that their voices are better & their Education more perfect than ~~to~~ ours we do not think so

4 From 5 to 15 years the children who come attain in their soul bodies the earthly age of about 15 and are ~~like~~ of great use to the angels in helping with the younger ones & showing all the beauties of the place and in turning ~~their~~ harps in the great days of the Chorus.

6 The grown soul-bodies — about which

we do not know very much only
seeing those very nearly related to us
by Earthly ties.

We play all day & talk so much
with each other about Earth and
take a great interest in all that
you do. We cannot always see you,
why I do not know, but at intervals
we have such clear & definite
sights of our earthly homes. Julius
Cæsar is very well and a great
favorite. He looks a dear little
fellow of about two years old (Earthly
count) and he told me when his
guardian angel was not near, that
he felt a little badly that I should
have been in the Amaranthyn division — i.e. the one in advance of him.
He and aunt Emma are to come
very often and we know now
all about our many relatives.
Unlike the real angels we have
no fore-knowledge and cannot-

tell what is to happen to our dear
ones on earth. Next to the great feast-
days, when we sung choruses by
divisions in the upper heavens, our
chief delight is in watching the soul
bodies as they arrive in our divisions
& in helping the angels to get them
in order & properly trained. In the
children's divisions not a friend (i.e.
about an hour yearly time) passes
without the excitement of a father
or mother, a brother or a sister united
to one of us. We know about 1000
of each other so that it is great fun
to see our comrades & friends making
their relatives feel at home.
The other day my kind Althea said
there was a little baby-soul in the
1st division from New Hampshire, which
had left her kind regards for me at the
general intelligence office of the heavenly
united states. It was chorus day so I
couldn't go, but I am to see her tomorrow
if she is advanced enough to receive
visitors. It takes about ten days to

get our beautiful plumage, in order

If you keep as you are I shall be able (Althea says) to write again in three months. I send you much love – also to pop¹

Your loving son

Paul Revere

¹) We use the word 'pop' here for papa or father very much

CAT FANCY

AYN RAND to CAT FANCY
MAGAZINE
March 20th, 1966

As well as writing such
novels as *Atlas Shrugged* and
The Fountainhead, Russian-
American author Ayn
Rand was also responsible
for developing the anti-
altruistic, pro-selfishness
philosophy that ran through
them which she later
called Objectivism, its core
belief being that man's
"highest moral purpose
is the achievement of his
own happiness, and that
he must not force other
people, nor accept their
right to force him, that each
man must live as an end in
himself and follow his own
rational self-interest". Ayn
Rand also subscribed to *Cat
Fancy* magazine, and in 1966
replied to a question from
its editor.

Dear Miss Smith,

You ask whether I own cats or simply enjoy them, or both. The answer is: both. I love cats in general and own two in particular.

You ask: "We are assuming that you have an interest in cats, or was your subscription strictly objective?" My subscription was strictly objective *because* I have an interest in cats. I can demonstrate *objectively* that cats are of a great value, and the charter issue of *Cat Fancy* magazine can serve as part of the evidence. ("Objective" does not mean "disinterested" or indifferent; it means corresponding to the facts of reality and applies both to knowledge and to values.)

I subscribed to *Cat Fancy* primarily for the sake of the pictures, and found the charter issue very interesting and enjoyable.

Ayn Rand

Qofee p. 536   Z 11

3 7/16 wide (qr o 181)   167 9

Typewritten Letter to Orion Clemens, in Keokuk Ia.

BJUYT KIOP M LKJHGFDSA:QWERTYUIOP:_-0BVX64329W RT
HA
HARTFORD, DEC. 9, 1874

DEAR BROTHER:
I AM TRYING T TO GET THE HANG OF THIS NEW F
FANGLED WRITING MACHINE, BUT AM NOT MAKING
A SHINING SUCCESS OF IT. HOWEVER THIS IS THE
FIRST ATTEMPT I EVER HAVE MADE, & YET I PER-
CEIVETHAT I SHALL SOON & EASILY ACQUIRE A FINE
FACILITY IN ITS USE. I SAW THE THING IN BOS-
TON THE OTHER DAY & WAS GREATLY TAKEN WI:TH
IT. SUSIE HAS STRUCK THE KEYS ONCE OR TWICE,
& NO DOUBT HAS PRINTED SOME LETTERS WHICH DO
NOT BELONG WHERE SHE PUT THEM.
THE HAVING BEEN A COMPOSITOR IS LIKELY TO BE
A GREAT HELP TO ME, SINCE O NE CHIEFLY NEEDS
SWIFTNESS IN BANGING THE KEYS. THE MACHINE COSTS
125 DOLLARS. THE MACHINE HAS SEVERAL VIRTUES
I BELIEVE IT WILL PRINT FASTER THAN I CAN WRITE.
ONE MAY LEAN BACK IN HIS CHAIR & WORK IT. IT
PILES AN AWFUL STACK OF WORDS ON ONE PAGE.
IT DONT MUSS THINGS OR SCATTER INK BLOTS AROUND.
OF COURSE IT SAVES PAPER.

                    SUSIE IS GONE,
NOW, & I FANCY I SHALL MAKE BETTER PROGRESS
WORKING THIS TYPE-WRITER REMINDS ME OF OLD
ROBERT BUCHANAN, WHO, YOU REMEMBER, USED TO
SET UP ARTICLES AT THE CASE WITHOUT PREVIOUS-
LY PUTTING THEM IN THE FORM OF MANUSCRIPT; I
WAS LOST IN ADMIRATION OF SUCH MARVELOUS
INTELLECTUAL CAPACITY.
                    LOVE TO MOLLIE.
               YOUR BROTHER,
                    SAM.

Mark Twain's first type-written letter.

NEW FANGLED WRITING MACHINE

SAMUEL CLEMENS to ORION CLEMENS
December 9th, 1874

Few authors have made an impact as enduring as literary icon Samuel Clemens, a man who, under his pen name Mark Twain, wrote such classics as *Adventures of Huckleberry Finn,* a book which has been read by many millions of people around the world since its publication in 1884. It was ten years earlier, whilst shopping in Boston, that a curious Clemens spotted and then bought a Remington No.1, the very first "type writer" to be produced by E. Remington and Sons, released to the public that year. The first letter he wrote on his "new fangled writing machine" – which, incidentally, could only produce upper-case characters – was to his brother, Orion. Nine years after this letter was typed, Twain became the first author to deliver a typewritten manuscript to a publisher. It was his memoir, *Life on the Mississippi.*

AMERICA'S YOUNGEST AMBASSADOR

SAMANTHA SMITH to YURI
ANDROPOV
November, 1982

In November 1982, a
10-year-old American
schoolgirl named Samantha
Smith wrote to the General
Secretary of the Communist
Party of the Soviet Union,
Yuri Andropov, and spoke
of her fear of a nuclear war
breaking out between their
countries. Somehow her
letter, addressed simply to
the Kremlin, subsequently
found its way to the offices of
the Communist newspaper,
Pravda, in which it was soon
printed; then, months later,
she received a lengthy reply
from Andropov himself,
which included an invitation
to the Soviet Union. Indeed,
she took him up on the offer
and travelled to Moscow
with her family in July of
1983. On returning, she was
a minor celebrity. In fact,
her visit was so successful,
she was invited to Japan
in December to meet the
country's Prime Minister,
Yasuhiro Nakasone.

Sadly, Samantha died in
1985 when the plane in
which she and her father
were flying clipped some
trees as it approached the
runway. Her funeral was
attended by thousands.

Dear Mr. Andropov,

My name is Samantha Smith. I am ten years old. Congratulations on your new job. I have been worrying about Russia and the United States getting into a nuclear war. Are you going to vote to have a war or not? If you aren't please tell me how you are going to help to not have a war. This question you do not have to answer, but I would like to know why you want to conquer the world or at least our country. God made the world for us to live together in peace and not to fight.

Sincerely,
Samantha Smith

———————————————

Dear Samantha,

I received your letter, as well as so many others coming to me these days from your country, and from other countries of the world.

It seems to me – and I take it from your letter, – that you are a courageous and honest girl, resembling in some ways my Becky – Tom Sawyer's friend from the well-known book of your compatriot Mark Twain. All kids in our country – boys and girls alike – know and love this book.

You write that you are worried about our two countries going into a nuclear war, and you ask whether we do something to prevent it.

You question is the most important of those that take to the heart of every person.

I will respond to it in an earnest and serious manner.

Yes, Samantha, we in the Soviet Union endeavour and do everything so that there be no war between our two countries, so that there be no war at all on Earth. This is the wish of everyone in the Soviet Union. That's what we were taught to do by Vladimir Lenin, the great founder of our state.

Soviet people well know what a terrible thing war is. Forty-two years ago, Nazi Germany, which strove for supremacy over the whole world, attacked our country, burned and destroyed many thousands of our towns and villages, killed millions of Soviet men, women and children.

In that war, which ended with our victory, we were in alliance with the United States: together we fought for the liberation of many people from the Nazi invaders. I hope that you know about this from your history lessons in school.

And today we want very much to live in peace, to trade and cooperate with all our neighbors on this earth – with those far away and those near by. And certainly with such a great country as the United States of America.

In America and in our country there are nuclear weapons – terrible weapons that can kill millions of people in an instant. But we do not want them to be ever used. That's precisely why the Soviet Union solemnly declared throughout the entire world that never – never – will it use nuclear weapons first against any country. In general we propose to discontinue further production of them and to proceed to the abolition of all the stockpiles on Earth.

It seems to me that this is a sufficient answer to your second question: 'Why do you want to wage war against the whole world or at least the United States?' We want nothing of the kind. No one in our country – neither workers, peasants, writers nor doctors, neither grown-ups nor children, nor members of the government – want either a big or 'little' war.

We want peace – there is something that we are occupied with: growing wheat, building and inventing, writing books and flying into space. We want peace for ourselves and for all peoples of the planet. For our children and for you, Samantha.

I invite you, if your parents will let you, to come to our country, the best time being this summer. You will find out about our country, meet with your contemporaries, visit an international children's camp – Artek – on the sea. And see for yourself: in the Soviet Union, everyone is for peace and friendship among peoples.

Thank you for your letter. I wish you all the best in your young life.
Y. Andropov

Facing page:
Samantha Smith with the
English translation of her
letter from Yuri Andropov, 1982

Letter No. 044

SLEEP WELL MY LOVE

BRIAN KEITH to DAVE
Date unknown

In June of 1940, little under a year after World War II began, Italy joined forces with Nazi Germany, a development which resulted in the war spreading to North Africa until the Allied victory in May of 1943. Five months later, still stationed in North Africa, two soldiers met, fell in love, and imagined one day returning home together. Sadly, that never happened as only Brian made the journey. He penned this love letter long after leaving the war, in memory of the first time he heard his lover's voice; it was reprinted in September of 1961 by *ONE Magazine*, a groundbreaking pro-gay magazine first published in 1953.

Dear Dave,

This is in memory of an anniversary — the anniversary of October 27th, 1943, when I first heard you singing in North Africa. That song brings memories of the happiest times I've ever known. Memories of a GI show troop — curtains made from barrage balloons — spotlights made from cocoa cans — rehearsals that ran late into the evenings — and a handsome boy with a wonderful tenor voice. Opening night at a theatre in Canastel — perhaps a bit too much muscatel, and someone who understood. Exciting days playing in the beautiful and stately Municipal Opera House in Oran — a misunderstanding — an understanding in the wings just before opening chorus.

Drinks at "Coq d'or" — dinner at the "Auberge" — a ring and promise given. The show 1st Armoured — muscatel, scotch, wine — someone who had to be carried from the truck and put to bed in his tent. A night of pouring rain and two very soaked GIs beneath a solitary tree on an African plain. A borrowed French convertible — a warm sulphur spring, the cool Mediterranean, and a picnic of "rations" and hot cokes. Two lieutenants who were smart enough to know the score, but not smart enough to realize that we wanted to be alone. A screwball piano player —

competition — miserable days and lonely nights. The cold, windy night we crawled through the window of a GI theatre and fell asleep on a cot backstage, locked in each other's arms — the shock when we awoke and realized that miraculously we hadn't been discovered. A fast drive to a cliff above the sea — pictures taken, and a stop amid the purple grapes and cool leaves of a vineyard.

The happiness when told we were going home — and the misery when we learned that we would not be going together. Fond goodbyes on a secluded beach beneath the star-studded velvet of an African night, and the tears that would not be stopped as I stood atop the sea-wall and watched your convoy disappear over the horizon.

We vowed we'd be together again "back home," but fate knew better — you never got there. And so, Dave, I hope that where ever you are these memories are as precious to you as they are to me.

Goodnight, sleep well my love.

Brian Keith

THIS IS MY LAST VISIT

WILLIAM BURROUGHS to
TRUMAN CAPOTE
July 23rd, 1970

In 1966, a few months after first being serialised in *The New Yorker*, Truman Capote's genre-defining non-fiction novel *In Cold Blood*, the true story of a quadruple murder in 1959 that Capote investigated and the subsequent trial he attended, was published to huge acclaim. Capote's book was a sensation and is still one of the most successful true crime titles of all time, but the praise wasn't universal. In July of 1970, fellow author William Burroughs – someone with whom Capote had long had a mutually disapproving relationship from afar – wrote this damning letter to Capote and warned him that his time in the spotlight was up.

*Facing page:
William Burroughs, famed
BEAT writer, shooting target
practice, 1987*

July 23, 1970

My Dear Mr. Truman Capote

This is not a fan letter in the usual sense — unless you refer to ceiling fans in Panama. Rather call this a letter from "the reader" — vital statistics are not in capital letters — a selection from marginal notes on material submitted as all "writing" is submitted to this department. I have followed your literary development from its inception, conducting on behalf of the department I represent a series of inquiries as exhaustive as your own recent investigations in the sun flower state. I have interviewed all your characters beginning with Miriam — in her case withholding sugar over a period of several days proved sufficient inducement to render her quite communicative — I prefer to have all the facts at my disposal before taking action. Needless to say, I have read the recent exchange of genialities between Mr Kenneth Tynan and yourself. I feel that he was much too lenient. Your recent appearance before a senatorial committee on which occasion you spoke in favor of continuing the present police practice of extracting confessions by denying the accused the right of consulting consul prior to making a statement also came to my attention. In effect you were speaking in approval of standard police procedure: obtaining statements through brutality and duress, whereas an intelligent police force would rely on evidence rather than enforced confessions. You further cheapened yourself by reiterating the banal argument that echoes through letters to the editor whenever the issue of capital punishment is raised: "Why all this sympathy for the murderer and none for his innocent victims?" I have in line of duty read all your published work. The early work was in some respects promising — I refer particularly to the short stories. You were granted an area for psychic development. It seemed for a while as if you would make good use of this grant. You choose instead to sell out a talent that is not yours to sell. You have written a dull unreadable book which could have been written by any staff writer on the New Yorker — (an undercover reactionary periodical dedicated to the interests of vested American wealth). You have placed your services at the disposal of interests who are turning America into a police state by the simple device of deliberately fostering the conditions that give rise to criminality and then demanding increased police powers and the retention of capital punishment to deal with the situation they have created. You have betrayed and sold out the talent that was granted you by this department. That talent is now officially withdrawn. Enjoy your dirty money. You will never have anything else. You will never write another sentence above the level of In Cold Blood. As a writer you are finished. Over and out. Are you tracking me? Know who I am? You know me, Truman. You have known me for a long time. This is my last visit.

BROWN IS AS PRETTY AS WHITE

W. E. B. DU BOIS to
YOLANDE DU BOIS
October 29th, 1914

W. E. B. Du Bois
accomplished more than
most during a lifetime
rich with admirable
achievements. In 1895,
he became the first
African American to earn
a PhD at Harvard; he
co-founded, in 1909, the
National Association for the
Advancement of Colored
People, an organisation
that has fought tirelessly
for racial equality since its
inception; his influential
1903 book on race, *The Souls
of Black Folk*, is considered
a classic in its field. Such
was his contribution that,
in 1976, the land on which
his family home once stood
was recognised by the US
government as a National
Historic Landmark. In 1914,
his soon-to-be 14-year-old
daughter, Yolande, left the
family home to study at
Bedales School in England.
Soon after she arrived, he
wrote to her with some
words of advice.

New York, October 29, 1914

Dear Little Daughter:

I have waited for you to get well settled before writing. By this time I hope some of the strangeness has worn off and that my little girl is working hard and regularly.

Of course, everything is new and unusual. You miss the newness and smartness of America. Gradually, however, you are going to sense the beauty of the old world: its calm and eternity and you will grow to love it.

Above all remember, dear, that you have a great opportunity. You are in one of the world's best schools, in one of the world's greatest modern empires. Millions of boys and girls all over this world would give almost anything they possess to be where you are. You are there by no desert or merit of yours, but only by lucky chance.

Deserve it, then. Study, do your work. Be honest, frank and fearless and get some grasp of the real values of life. You will meet, of course, curious little annoyances. People will wonder at your dear brown and the sweet crinkley hair. But that simply is of no importance and will soon be forgotten. Remember that most folk laugh at anything unusual, whether it is beautiful, fine or not. You, however, must not laugh at yourself. You must know that brown is as pretty as white or prettier and crinkley hair as straight even though it is harder to comb. The main thing is the YOU beneath the clothes and skin—the ability to do, the will to conquer, the determination to understand and know this great, wonderful, curious world. Don't shrink from new experiences and custom. Take the cold bath bravely. Enter into the spirit of your big bed-room. Enjoy what is and not pine for what is not. Read some good, heavy, serious books just for discipline: Take yourself in hand and master yourself. Make yourself do unpleasant things, so as to gain the upper hand of your soul.

Above all remember: your father loves you and believes in you and expects you to be a wonderful woman.

I shall write each week and expect a weekly letter from you.

Lovingly yours,

Papa

Facing page:
American educator and writer
W. E. B. Du Bois

From: The Earl Russell, O.M., F.R.S.,

22 January 1962

Sir Oswald Mosley,
5, Lowndes Court,
Lowndes Square,
London, S.W.1.

Dear Sir Oswald,

    Thank you for your letter and for your enclosure. I have given some
thought to our recent correspondance. It is always difficult to decide
on how to respond to people whose ethhos is so alien and, in fact, repellent
to one's own. It is not that I take exception to the general points made
by you but that every ounce of my energy has been devoted to an active
opposition to cruel bigotry, compulsive violence, and the sadistic perse-
cution which has characterised the philosophy and practice of fascism.

    I feel obliged to say that the emotional universes we inhabit are so
distinct, and in deepest ways opposed, that nothing fruitful or sincere
could ever emerge from association between us.

    I should like you to understand the intensity of this conviction on
my part. It is not out of any attempt to be rude that I say this but be-
causeeof all that I value in human experience and human achievement.

                        Yours sincerely,

                        Bertrand Russell.

EVERY OUNCE OF MY ENERGY

BERTRAND RUSSELL to SIR OSWALD
MOSLEY
January 22nd, 1962

Bertrand Russell, one of the great intellectuals of his generation, was known by most as the founder of analytic philosophy, but he was actually a man of many talents: a pioneering mathematician, an accomplished logician, a tireless activist, a respected historian, and a Nobel Prize-winning writer, to name but a handful. When he wrote this principled letter at the beginning of 1962, Russell was 89 years old and clearly still a man of morals who stood firm in his beliefs. Its recipient was Sir Oswald Mosley, a man most famous for founding, in 1932, the British Union of Fascists.

THIS WRETCHED COMEDY AS A MAN!

LILI ELVENES to "CHRISTIAN"
January 29th, 1930

In 1930, with support from her wife and fellow artist Gerda Gottlieb, a 47-year-old Danish transgender artist named Lili Elvenes – born Einar Wegener – travelled to Germany to undergo one of the very first examples of gender reassignment. She had identified as a woman for some time and sought to transition fully by way of procedures that are thought to have included radiation therapy, removal of penis and testicles, and the insertion of a uterus; this in addition to undeveloped ovaries that were found to already exist in Lili's abdomen. Sadly, the uterine transplant was later rejected by her body and Lili died. Her story was told in *Fra mand til kvinde: Lili Elbes bekendelser*, a biography edited by Poul Knudsen; an English-language edition soon followed, titled *Man Into Woman: The First Sex Change*, from which this letter comes, written by Lili to a relative in the midst of the surgery.

Note: In the book, and in the letter, pseudonyms were used to protect the identities of all involved. As a result, Lili Elvenes became, and is still widely known as, Lili Elbes; her birth name, Einar Wegener, became Andreas Sparre; doctors and relatives are also renamed.

Dear Christian,

You have not heard from me for a long time, because I have been able to tell you nothing good about Lili. From time to time I have been examined by several doctors, but without result. Throughout they prescribed sedative remedies, which left me no better nor wiser than I was before. For I want to know what is happening to me, even if it hurts. After consulting with Grete, Elena took me to one of her personal acquaintances who received me three hours before he was leaving Paris. Then something happened which sounds almost like a miracle! I had a consultation with the famous surgeon and woman's doctor Professor Werner Kreutz, of Dresden. Strangely enough, he resembled you. He examined me a long time, and then declared that my case was so rare that only one similar case had been known up till now. He added that in the condition in which I am at present, I could hardly be regarded as a living creature, because the ray treatment had been a great mistake, especially as it had not been preceded by microscopical examination. Now he fears that this treatment in the dark may have destroyed my organs – male as well as female. Consequently, he wants me to go to Berlin as quickly as possible for the purpose of a microscopical examination.

Some time afterwards he will operate on me himself. He wants to remove the dead (and formerly imperfect) male organs, and to restore the female organs with new and fresh material. *Then it will be Lili who will survive!*

Her weak girl's body will then be able to develop, and she will feel as young as her new and fresh organs. Dear Christian, I am now sitting here and weeping like a child while I am writing you these lines. It seems so like a miracle that I dare not believe it. One thing, however, consoles me – that were it otherwise I must soon die. Grete and I believe we are dreaming, and are fearful of waking. It is too wonderful to think that Lili will be able to live, and that she will be the happiest girl in the world – and that this ghastly nightmare of my life is drawing to an end. This wretched comedy as a man! Without Grete I should have thrown up the sponge long ago. But in these dark days I have had a fresh opportunity of seeing what a splendid girl she is… she is an angel. Overexertions, her own sufferings, have left her unscathed. She has contrived to work for two, now that I am no longer worth much. I do what I am able, of course, and have exhibited and sold with success in all the important salons. But now all this is over. I am no longer fit for anything. I am like a wretched grub, which is waiting to become a butterfly. The operation is urgent, and the doctor would like me to proceed to Berlin immediately, as some twenty days must elapse between the first examination and the operation. And I must be in Dresden on the day he is ready to create Lili. He will send me medicine, which I am to take, in order to support the internal organs and thereby keep me alive until then. For practical reasons I begged for some delay, and I told him that I should prefer so to arrange matters as to proceed to Berlin via Copenhagen, as I wanted first to hold an exhibition in Denmark. I would then proceed from Berlin to Dresden at the beginning of April.

This does not particularly please the doctor; but he understood that I had suggested this for practical reasons.

Now, I do not know whether it is due to excitement, but my condition has worsened to such an extent that I no longer feel able to make preparations for an exhibition and attend to everything it involves – I realize that I have no time to lose.

Hence, I want your help.

Will you lend me the money for the operation and the stay in the nursing home? I do not know how much it will cost. I only know that Elena has so arranged it that the professor is taking an exceptionally low fee. Out of consideration for Grete I dare not take money from our savings; the less so as our trip to Rome and my illness has cost us so much.

I – or we – have deposited many pictures with Messrs. Heyman and Haslund, of Copenhagen, and I estimate their value to be between 7,000 and 10,000 kronen. I do not, however, know what the operation will cost, but I estimate it will come to between 4,000 and 5,000 kronen in all. I give you all these pictures in Denmark by way of security in the event of my death – and in any event. If the affair turns out badly, the pictures can be sold, and if it turns out well, we can soon repay you the money. Our earning powers are good, and we have many large orders.

Tell no one except my sister anything of the contents of this letter, and be good enough to let me know what you decide as quickly as possible, first by telegram and then by letter.

It is only because I have the feeling that death is on my track that I send you this letter. Up till now I have never incurred debts in any quarter. Warmest greetings to you and the sister from Grete and

Andreas

THERE ARE TWO WAYS IN WHICH THIS CAN BE DONE

BERTHA BREWSTER to
DAILY TELEGRAPH
February, 1913

It wasn't until the Representation of the People (Equal Franchise) Act in 1928 that women in the UK were finally given the same voting rights as men. Campaigners had been pushing for such a development for decades, however, progress had been far too slow for some. In 1903, a small group of frustrated activists, headed by Emmeline Pankhurst, broke away from the Suffragists and chose to attack the system more aggressively by smashing windows, burning down buildings, chaining themselves to Buckingham Palace, and spending time in prison, all in an effort to be heard. One of these "suffragettes", Emily Davison, was even killed when she stepped in front of King George V's horse at the Epsom Derby. On February 26th, 1913, with the protests as forceful as ever, this letter appeared in the *Daily Telegraph*, written by a suffragette named Bertha Brewster.

Facing page:
A suffragette is led away from a protest by police, 1906

Sir,

Everyone seems to agree upon the necessity of putting a stop to Suffragist outrages; but no one seems certain how to do so. There are two, and only two, ways in which this can be done. Both will be effectual.

1. Kill every woman in the United Kingdom.
2. Give women the vote.

Yours truly,
Bertha Brewster

UNIVERSITY OF

SUSSEX

The School of Chemistry, Physics
and Environmental Science

University of Sussex
Falmer, Brighton BN1 9QJ

Telephone: (01273) 606755
Fax: (01273) 677196

13.1.2001

Teaching Post Vacancy at Hogwarts School

Dear Professor Dumbledore,

I wish to apply for the 'Defence Against the Dark Arts' teaching post vacancy at Hogwarts School. I am
well aware of the chequered history of the former occupants of this post but, in this darkest of times (is it
really true that He Who Should Not Be Named has returned, with all of his former powers ?), I feel obliged
to offer my services in the continuing struggle against the cursed Death Eaters.

Although most of my professional experience has been gained in the Muggle world, I would like to point
out that I studied at Bristol University under the supervision of the internationally-renowned auror,
Professor B. Vincent. Furthermore, I spent 22 months working in a dungeon at the notorious Los Alamos
National Laboratory, New Mexico in 1987-89 (see enclosed CV). This US nuclear weapons laboratory is
surely one of the Darkest military research laboratories in the (Muggle or Wizarding) world. In addition, in
the last eleven years at Sussex University I have worked extensively on Polypyrrole, one of the Darkest
conducting polymers known to Alchemy. Finally, I have spent the last seven years becoming acquainted
with a budding wizard named Thomas Armes, whom I can assure you is just as much of a handful as Harry
Potter. Only yesterday I caught him practising illegal curses on his younger sister, Kate.

Currently I lead an international wizard group of twelve PhD* students and research sorcerors who are
working on new Colloidal Potions and the Alchemy of Polymers (I believe these are known as 'plastics' in
the Muggle world). I am the principal auror or co-auror of more than 140 learned alchemical articles,
although most of these have only appeared in Muggle journals.

I have checked my contract with my current Muggle employers, and I am pleased to confirm my
availability from Sept 1st, 2001 if selected for this most important post.

Thanking you in advance for your careful consideration of my application and I look forward to hearing
from you in the near future.

Yours sincerely,

Steven P. Armes

Professor of Colloid and Polymer Science

P.S. Please forgive this application by Muggle post but I do not trust the owls around these parts – they
have red eyes!

* Philosophy of Dark Arts

YOURS SINCERELY, ALBUS DUMBLEDORE

J. K. ROWLING to STEVEN ARMES *2001*

Steven Armes has an impressive CV – impressive enough, one would think, to secure a teaching job of his choosing. Currently Professor of Polymer and Colloid Chemistry at the University of Sheffield, in the past he has worked at the Los Alamos National Laboratory, one of the largest and most revered research institutions in the world, has authored hundreds of scientific papers, and in 2014 became a Fellow of the Royal Society for his pioneering contributions to science. In 2001, believing himself to be a perfect candidate despite his being a Muggle (a person living outside the magical community), he applied for the post of Defence Against the Dark Arts Teacher at Hogwarts School of Witchcraft and Wizardry, the fictional institution made famous by J. K. Rowling's *Harry Potter* book series. This is his application letter, and Albus Dumbledore's reply.

CURRICULUM VITAE

Name: ARMES, Steven Peter   **Date of Birth**: 28.2.62

Nationality: British   **Marital Status**: Married

Present Address: School of Chemistry, Physics and
Environmental Science,
University of Sussex,
Falmer, Brighton, East Sussex, BN1 9QJ, UK.

Tel. No: (01273) 678650
Fax: (01273) 677196
E-mail: S.P.Armes@sussex.ac.uk

Education

1983   University of Bristol, BSc Chemistry (first class)

1987   University of Bristol, PhD in Polymer Chemistry

Supervisor: Prof. B. Vincent, International Auror

Work Experience

1987-89: Postdoctoral fellow at Los Alamos National Laboratory,
New Mexico, USA.

1989-95: Lecturer in Polymer Science, University of Sussex, UK.

Oct. 1995: Senior Lecturer at the University of Sussex.

Oct. 1999: Reader at the University of Sussex.

Mar 2000: Professor at the University of Sussex.

Research Record and Professional Activities
143 papers (110 as Principal Auror) published in refereed Muggle
journals. More than £1,400,000 obtained from the Ministry of
Alchemical Arts since 1990. Over £730,000 raised from the
Muggle alchemical industry since 1996.

Dear Mr. Armes,

Re: Your Application for the Post of Defence Against the Dark Arts Teacher, Hogwarts School of Witchcraft and Wizardry

It is with great regret that I must inform you that the above post has been filled.

I hope your natural disappointment will be alleviated to some extent by knowing that rarely has an application caused such hilarity and mirth among the Board of Governors. You have the distinction of being the first Muggle ever to apply for a job at Hogwarts and the Board of Governors were keen to call you for interview. I trust you will attribute my vetoing of this suggestion, not to any doubts of your competence or courage, but the wish to save you humiliation and possible pain. The Board of Governors' interviews frequently involve levels of malice and savagery more often associated with the home-life of trolls. You might take further consolation from the fact that the post is almost certain to become available again within a year. Job security is not, unfortunately, an attraction we can offer to Defence Against the Dark Arts teachers.

I was interested to learn that your son Thomas shows early promise in the area of curses and jinxes. I shall look forward to seeing him at Hogwarts in September 2005. Thank you once again for your interest in joining our establishment and I wish you every success in your alchemical endeavours.

Yours sincerely,

Albus Dumbledore

Albus Dumbledore

Order of Merlin, First Class, Grand Sorcerer, Chief Warlock,
Supreme Mugwump, International Confederation of Wizards

I'VE GOT A HUNCH

THOMAS WOLFE to
MAXWELL PERKINS
August 12th, 1938

In July of 1938, as he
travelled the American West
having recently handed in
a completed manuscript
to his publisher, renowned
novelist Thomas Wolfe was
struck down with pneumonia
and taken to hospital. He
was soon diagnosed as
having tuberculosis of the
brain from which he would
never recover; Wolfe died
on September 15th, aged
just 37. A month before his
death, as he lay in hospital
certain that he was soon
to pass away, Wolfe wrote
this moving letter to his old
editor Maxwell Perkins, a
once dear friend with whom
he had fallen out in 1936 but
still loved dearly.

Providence Hospital
Seattle, Washington
August 12, 1938

Dear Max: I'm sneaking this against orders, but "I've got a hunch" — and I wanted to write these words to you.

I've made a long voyage and been to a strange country, and I've seen the dark man very close; and I don't think I was too much afraid of him, but so much of mortality still clings to me — I wanted most desperately to live and still do, and I thought about you all a thousand times, and wanted to see you all again, and there was the impossible anguish and regret of all the work I had not done, of all the work I had to do — and I know now I'm just a grain of dust, and I feel as if a great window has been opened on life I did not know about before — and if I come through this, I hope to God I am a better man, and in some strange way I can't explain, I know I am a deeper and a wiser one. If I get on my feet and out of here, it will be months before I head back, but if I get on my feet, I'll come back.

Whatever happens — I had this "hunch" and wanted to write you and tell you, no matter what happens or has happened, I shall always think of you and feel about you the way it was that Fourth of July day three years ago when you met me at the boat, and we went out on the café on the river and had a drink and later went on top of the tall building, and all the strangeness and the glory and the power of life and of the city was below.

Yours always,
Tom

WE ARE UNINTELLIGIBLE

April 3/01.

JACK LONDON to ANNA
STRUNSKY
April 3rd, 1901

Jack London and Anna
Strunsky first met in 1899
at Stanford University,
instantly connecting on an
intellectual level, and four
years later they would co-
author an epistolary novel
titled *The Kempton-Wace
Letters*, in which a poet
and scientist discuss love
through correspondence.
Though it's thought that
their relationship remained
platonic, London and
Strunsky had very strong
feelings for each other, as
evidenced by this letter,
written in 1901, at which
point London was married
to another woman. He went
on to become, thanks to
novels such as *The Call of
the Wild* and *White Fang*, one
of the most famous authors
of his generation. In 1916,
following his untimely death,
Strunsky wrote *Memoirs of
Jack London.*

Dear Anna:—

Did I say that the human might be filed in categories? Well, and if I did, let me qualify—not all humans. You elude me. I cannot place you, cannot grasp you. I may boast that of nine out of ten, under given circumstances, I can forecast their action; that of nine out of ten, by their word, or action, I may feel the pulse of their hearts. But the tenth I despair. It is beyond me. You are that tenth.

Were ever two souls, with dumb lips, more incongruously matched! We may feel in common—surely, we ofttimes do—and when we do not feel in common, yet do we understand; and yet we have no common tongue. Spoken words do not come to us. We are unintelligible. God must laugh at the mummery.

The one gleam of sanity through it all is that we are both large temperamentally, large enough to often misunderstand. True, we often understand but in vague glimmering ways, by dim perceptions, like ghosts, which, while we doubt, haunt us with their truth. And still, I, for one, dare not believe; for you are that tenth which I may not forecast.

Am I unintelligible now? I do not know. I imagine so. I cannot find the common tongue.

Largely temperamentally—that is it. It is the one thing that brings us at all in touch. We have, flashed through us, you and I, each a bit of the universal, and so we draw together. And yet we are so different.

I smile at you when you grow enthusiastic? It is a forgivable smile—nay, almost an envious smile. I have lived twenty-five years of repression. I learned not to be enthusiastic. It is a hard lesson to forget. I begin to forget, but it is so little. At the best, before I die, I cannot hope to forget all or most. I can exult, now that I am learning, in little things, in other things; but of my things, and secret things double mine, I cannot, I cannot. Do I make myself intelligible? Do you hear my voice? I fear not. There are poseurs. I am the most successful of them all.

Jack.

Fcaing page:
Jack London, 1905

```
John Radziewicz
Senior Editor
Harcourt Brace Jovanovich
111 5th Ave
New York  NY 10003


Dear Mr Radziewicz,


I can imagine myself blurbing a book in which Brian
Aldiss, predictably, sneers at my work, because then
I could preen myself on my magnanimity.  But I cannot
imagine myself blurbing a book, the first of a new
series and hence presumably exemplary of the series,
which not only contains no writing by women, but the
tone of which is so self-contentedly, exclusively
male, like a club, or a locker room.  That would not
be magnanimity, but foolishness.  Gentlemen, I just
don't belong here.

Yours truly,

Ursula K. Le Guin
```

GENTLEMEN, I JUST DON'T BELONG HERE

URSULA LE GUIN to JOHN RADZIEWICZ
Circa 1987

In 1987, multi-award-winning author Ursula Le Guin was asked to supply a blurb for *Synergy: New Science Fiction, Volume 1*, the first in a new four-part series of anthologies edited by George Zebrowski which intended to showcase science fiction stories from authors both established and up-and-coming. For Ursula Le Guin, however, the book was notable not for its stories but for its complete absence of women's voices. She reacted by way of this brief letter.

I MISS LORINA BULWER

LORINA BULWER
Circa 1901

Born in Suffolk in 1838, Lorina Bulwer was one of five children to Ann and William Bulwer and the only sibling to stay at the family home for the remainder of their parents' lives – her father died in 1871; her mother in 1893. Little is known about the intervening years or reasons for her admission, but records show that by 1901 Lorina had joined 515 others in becoming a resident of the lunatic ward of Great Yarmouth Workhouse. It was there, in 1901, that she began sewing the vast, intricate piece seen here: an enormous run of hessian cloth, 12ft in length, on which is featured the hand-stitched text of a somewhat rambling, frequently angry, biographical letter that includes mention of her family members, neighbours, doctor, and even Queen Victoria. Lorina Bulwer died of influenza in 1937, still an inmate at the Workhouse. She left several embroidered letters behind.

TO MAHARAJAH OF KELVEDON BRANDON THETFORD NORFOLK
TO T DANIELS E^{SQ} THRIGBY HALL NR G^T YARMOUTH NORFOLK
TO PALMER BROS DRAPERS MARKET PLACE G^T YARMOUTH
MESS – LACON BANKERS G^T YARMOUTH

THE CHATTERIS CAMBS WOMAN E. BULWER MARRIED AN HEMAPHRODITE OR EUNICH

I MISS LORINA BULWER WAS EXAMINED BY DR PINCHING OF WALTHAMSTOW ESSEX AND FOUND TO BE A PROPERLY SHAPED FEMALE

I MISS LORINA BULWER DROVE TO THRIGBY HALL NORFOLK YES A GOOD FIND ALSO LAND RIGHTS NATHAN RIGHTS

THE WHOLE OF G^T YARMOUTH WORKHOUSE THE WHOLE OF THE LAND ENCLOSED AND EVERY BUILDING THERE ON FOR YOU MUNDFORD CRANWICH THE TOFTS ESTATE NR NORWICH NORFOLK AN ESTATE FOR MAHARAJAH OF KELVEDON BRANDON THETFORD NORFOLK & PRINCE DULEEP SINGH

I MISS LORINA BULWER HAVE BEEN TO SANDRINGHAM NORFOLK AND ADMIRED THE GATES AT THE ENTRANCE OF THE LIMETREE WALK I SEE THE HUNTSMAN DRESSED IN SCARLET COAT WHITE BREECHES WHITE TOP BOOTS HIGH BLACK SILK HAT SILVER BULLION CORD ROUND THE RIM ALSO A CORD ROUND THE HAT A WHITE LEATHER BELT ROUND HIS WAIST I HEARD THE HORN I ALSO SEE A LITTLE CHILD ABOUT A YEAR OLD OR A MONTH OR TWO MORE DRESSED IN A WHITE WASHING DRESS AND CAPE A LARGE WHITE HAT RIDING ON A DONKEY IN A PANIER A SMALL COTTAGE DRESSED OLD WOMAN LEADING THE DONKEY AND A VERY TALL MAN SERVANT IN SWALLOW TAILCOAT SUPERFINE TROUSERS AND COAT WALKING BY THE SIDE OF THE DONKEY THE CHILD WAS ASLEEP THEY CAME THROUGH A GATE IN A MEADOW OR FIELD AND PASSED THROUGH A NARROW PATH BETWEEN A FEW TREES BY THE SIDE OF THE ROAD CLOSE TO THE MEADOW OR FIELD GATE + ASK E. BULWER E^{SQ} IF HE KNEW OLD ANNA MARIA YOUNG WAS AN IMPOSTOR SHE MUST HAVE BEEN BORN THE DAY BEFORE E. BUWER E^{SQ}S MOTHER OR THE DAY AFTER WAS OLD ANNA MARIA THIRTY YEARS OF AGE WHEN SHE WAS MARRIED SHE IS WELL KNOWN IN NORWICH SHE HAS BEEN THERE YEARS KEEPING A HOUSE TO ADVOCATE REPUBLICAN SOCIALISTIC IDEAS ALSO WITH JOSEPH POWELL GARIBALDI HOTEL AND RICHARD TURNBRIDGE TALLOW CHANDLER SOUTH MARKET ROAD G^T YARMOUTH NORFOLK. OLD EUNICH SEWARD ALIAS KING OLD MOTHER BUCK OLD MOTHER BUCK CATCHPOLE BOTH OF THESE DISGUSTING LOOKING OLD WOMEN AWKWARD SHAPES AND HORRID NAMES IN CAMBS TRICKS WITH THE FRENCH TRICKS INTERIOR INFERIOR FRENCH TRICKS. WOMEN ARE NOT PERMITTED IN TRICKS MEN ARE ONLY ADMITTED AS MEN TRICKES NOT BOYS NOT GIRLS NOT HOBDEHOYS MUCH LESS GURNEYS TRAMPS WOMEN THE HOUSE IS FULL OF TRICK WOMEN SOME OF FUDEEJOEY ENGLISH POWELLS WOMEN MANBY ROAD

AND SAYS CORNER OVER FULLERS HILL G^T YARMOUTH WILFRED
WESTON A LUNATIC FROM PERRYMEAD BATH SOMERSETSHIRE
FELSTEADIAN SCHOOL FELSTEAD ESSEX AND WELL KNOWN AT
MEADOWS THE SO CALLED SURGEON KING STREET SHAM THE TUBE
HE USED UPON THE P...S OF M^R T ROBERTSON AT M^RS W J BULWER
GENEVE TERRACE CROWN ROAD WOULD HAVE PLACED MEADOWS IN
A CONVICT PRISON THE REST OF HIS LIFE M^R W I ROBERSON LATE OF
SPORLE CUM PALGRAVE N^TH SWATHAM NORFOLK IS A BROTHER THE
TINGEYS ARE RELATED TO THE ROBERSONS CRAZY WILFRED WESTON
HAD APARTMENTS AT M^RS BULWERS GB CROWN ROAD E. BULWER E^SQ
TOLD HIS MOTHER NOT TO KEEP HIM IF SHE WAS AFRAID OF HIM
HIS ABSURD WAYS THERE AND AT MR LASTS BAKER SOUTH HOWARD
STREET PLENTY OF INFORMATION THERE OF THE LUNATIC WILFRED
WESTON AND HIS ANTICS MAKING BREAD AT 4 O'CLOCKE IN THE
MORNING IN HIS BAKE OFFICE WESTON FELL HEAD FORMOST IN THE
DOUGH JUST AS IT WAS MAKING HE WAS TAKEN UNDER THE PUMP OR
TAP TO WASH GAVE HIM JAM UPON HIS BREAD FOR BREAK FAST M^RS
LAST BROUGHT WESTON BACK TO HIS APARTMENTS CROWN ROAD
HIS FATHER WESTON LIVES AT PERRYMEAD BATH SOMERSETSHIRE
TERMED WASHED IN THE BLOOD OF THE LAMB AND DRAW THE
WELL DRY WESTON A LUNATIC WHO PUMPS A CERTAIN TIME EVERY
MORNING AS A SURE CURE FOR THE RHEUMATIC ALSO KISSING
HIS WIFE'S TOES AND TELLING HER WHAT A BARGAIN HE HAD MET
WITH FANNEREAUX WESTONS M^RS DAWSON M^RS RIPLEY 4 SISTERS
THEY ARE FROM MARTHAM RECTORY N^R G^T YARMOUTH RE^VD PEARCE
4 DAUGHTERS HEREDITARY LUNATICS EVANS & HIS WIFE'S TRICK
CYANIDE-POTASSIUM – M^RS SEWARD ALIAS KINGS TRICK SUGAR OF
LEAD.

HAUTBOIS IS A NORMANDY VILLAGE IN THE COUNTY OF NORFOLK
N- NORTH WALSHAM ENGLAND THE BELLE VUE HOUSES IN G^T
YARMOUTH ONE IN S^T NICHOLAS ROAD ON THE FACTORY SIDE
AND ONE BELLE VUE HOUSE REGENT ROAD BOTH HOUSES HAVE
SOUTH FRONTAGE THE HOUSE IS THE THIRD ONE FROM AYERS
PHOTOGRAPHER AND FANCY CHAP FREEMAN LEATHER CUTTER
LIVED IN BELLE VUE HOUSE REGENT ROAD THE NAME BELLE VUE NO
USE WAS PAINTED ON THE GATE UPRIGHTS I MISS LORINA BULWER
HAVE SEEN IT BELLE VUE WAS UPON THAT HOUSE FOR YEARS THIS
IS BELLY VIEW WORKHOUSE CAISTER ROAD VAUDEVILLE A HOUSE AT
CAISTER ABOUT THE SECOND HOUSE PAST THE CATHOLIC CEMETERY
CAISTER ROAD CAP^TN PURDY OWNER HE LIVES IN A HOUSE ON THE
OPPOSITE SIDE FACING VAUDEVILLE M^RS MARYANN WRIGHT AND
HER HUSBAND LIVED IN VAUDEVILLE HOUSE NO CHILDREN SHE
IS LEFT HANDED HONEST HER HUSBAND WAS A FISHERMAN HER
MAIDEN NAME ANNISON HER MOTHERS NAME SOPHIA ANNISON
GENEVE TERRACE CROWN ROAD NAPOLEON PLACE JETTY ROAD
THE TOBACCONIST SHOP KEPT BY BANASCHINA AN ITALIAN WITH
A STATUETTE OF NAPOLEON ON THE FRONT OF THE SHOP AND IN
THE SAME ROW OUTSIDE A PUBLIC HOUSE AN ADVERTISEMENT IN
FRENCH PAINTED OVER THE SHOP WINDOW ALL THESE HOUSES
BELONG TO THE FRENCH AND CREMORNE PLACE FRIARS

COMPLEXION NOSE EXCEEDING GOOD WHEN A CHILD SHE WAS
STAYING IN NORFOLK SHE WAS TAKEN TO BARTON MILLS TO
SEE HRH PRINCESS VICTORIA A LITTLE CHILD AND HER ROYAL
FATHER AND MOTHER THE DUKE & DUCHESS OF KENT WHO
WERE THEN GOING TO HOLKHAM HALL TO SEE – COKE E^{SQ} MISS
ANCY-TICKLES MY FANCY- WAS HELD UP IN THE ARMS OF A MAN
BY APPOINTMENT THE COACH DOOR WAS OPENED SHE WAS
PLACED UPON THE STEP OF THE COACH THE ROYAL DUKE OF
KENT LOOKED FORST AT ONE SIDE OF HER FACE THEN AT THE
OTHER AFTER A MINUTE EXAMINATION SHE HAD TO WALK FOR
THE DUKE TO SEE HRH PRINCESS VICTORIA SAT ON A SEAT WITH
HER ROYAL MOTHER DUCHESS OF KENT PRINCESS VICTORIA HAD
A SMALL BAG ON HER ARM FILLED WITH NEW SIXPENCES ANCY
NANCY TICKLES MY FANCY PUT ONE IN HER MOUTH IT PASSED
DOWN HER THROAT BY THE AID OF MEDICINE M^{RS} TURNER OR
SOMEONE OF THE FAMILY FOUND IT AGAIN ANCY NANCY TICKLES
MY FANCY IS THE MOTHER OF E. BULWER E^{SQ} NO 1 ST GEORGES
PARK G^T YAR MOUTH HIS FATHER IS MR W.J. BULWER OF CROWN
ROAD G^T YARMOUTH FORMERLY BECCLES SUFFOLK I MISS LORINA
BULWER AM THEIR ONLY DAUGHTER I WENT TO A BELGIAN
SCHOOL AT BECCLES LORD HASTINGS OF MELTON CONSTABLE
NORFOLK IS RELATED TO LADY FORS HASTINGS _____ TO
QUEEN VICTORIA WHO MARRIED THE DUKE OF NORFOLK IN THE
EARLY PART OF HMG GRACIOUS MAGESTY QUEEN VICTORIA'S
REIGN WOULD ASK HIS LORDSHIP IF HE CAN TELL ME THE
MEANING OF SAVING –LORINA – IS HERR FRAULEIN – HE MUST
HAVE TAKEN AN EXTRA GLASS OF MADEIRA OR THE DEVIL
PLACED HIS FOOT ON HIM HE KNEW THE NOTORIOUS TAYLORS
OF CHIPPENHAM CAMBS WHAT ROTTEN POX WHORE DID ANNA
MARIA YOUNG INTRODUCE TO THE ROYAL COURT OF ENGLAND
THE NUMBER –0 – TAYLORS THEY CANNOT PAY FOR A PENNY
BUNDLE OF FIRE WOOD POOR POVERTY TAYLORS THE SODOMITE –
CARNALITE TAYLORS CHIPPENHAM CAMBRIDGESGIRE KATE JOYCE
HAD A LARGE RED PLUG OR BOLSTER DROPING DOWN FROM HER
BEHIND I MISS LORINA BULWER WELL KNOWN BY THAT NAME
SEE IT PENAL SERVITUDE FOR BOTH CRIMES AND CASES IN G^T
YARMOUTH NORFOLK A MAN HORSE THE OTHER CASE WAS TWO
MEN A WARRANT ISSUED THEIR APPREHENSION – ASK E. BULWER
E^{SQ} WHERE THE BROAD BAND RING HIS MOTHER ANCY TICKLE MY
FANCY HAD ANN BULWER ENGRAVED ON THE OUTSIDE ASK THE
COURT JEWELLER OF LORD SUFFIELD THEY KNOW THE MEANING
OF IT I MISS LORINA BULWER HAD MY FINGER MEASURED FOR
A RING AND MY MOUTH MEASURED WHAT DOES IT MEAN ASK E.
BULWER E^{SQ} E. BULWER E^{SQ} MARRIED ANN ANGOOD OF CHATTERIS
CAMBRIDGESGIRE A DAMNED HELL FIRE SOCIALIST WHEN HE
FOUND SHE WAS A DAMNED HELL FIRE SOCIALIST AND HE A
LOYALIST HE SHOULD NOT HAVE MARRIED HER . LORINA IS AN –
ANNEXE – ASK E. BULWER E^{SQ} ABOUT IT - I MISS LORINA BULWER
WONDER THE PEOPLE HAVE NOT THROWN ALL THE SLOPS OF
THIS – NOTORIOUS BUG LICE AND FLEA TRIBE CAMBRIDGESHIRE
SOCIALIST DEN AND PELTED HIM WITH ROTTEN EGGS AS HIS
SOCIALST ANN OLD FAGGOT WIFE DIED AND WENT TO HELL SIX
MONTHS AFTER E. BULWER E^{SQ} BLESSED

LANE KING STREET ALL IN G^T YARMOUTH NORFOLK BELLE VUE HOUSE CROMER NORFOLK LOOK TO SIDESTRAND OVERSTRAND AND BACTON NORFOLK COAST VAUDEVILLE THEATRE LONDON CREMORNE GARDENS LONDON BELLE VUE HOUSE GORLESTON SUFFOLK BELLE VUE HOUSE LOWESTOFT SUFFOLK LOOK TO SOUTHWOLD SUFFOLK FELIXSTOWE HUNSTANTON CORTON AND PAKEFIELD AT LOWESTOFT

I MISS LORINA BULWER LIVED AT BECCLES SUFFOLK WAS EDUCATED THERE UNTIL ABOUT SEVENTEEN YEARS OF AGE THEN CAME TO G^T YARMOUTH NORFOLK TO LIVE BENACRE IS A NORMANDY VILLAGE A FEW MILES FROM BECCLES SUFFOLK IN THE SAME COUNTY SIR THOS SHERLOCK GOOCH BART LIVED AT BENACRE HALL RE^VD DASHWOOD HAS A VAULT THERE BURIED WITH HIS WIFE L. DASHWOOD E. SURGEON NORWICH NORFOLK WAS THEIR SON C DASHWOOD E^SQ SURGEON G^T YARMOUTH NORFOLK C DASHWOOD E^SQ A CLERGY MAN I THINK AND ONE DAUGHTER WHO MARRIED RE^VD KERRISON WHO DIED HER SECOND HUSBAND I HEAR IS ALSO A CLERGY MAN M^RS DASHWOOD THE MOTHER OF THE ABOVE

FAMILY HER MAIDEN NAME BURTON LIVED YEARS AGO AT THE DEANERY G^T YARMOUTH NORFOLK A MOST AMIABLE LADY NOT RELATED TO ANY OF THE BURTONS OF G^T YARMOUTH NORFOLK OR NORWICH RE^VD DASHWOOD LIVED IN A HOUSE CLOSE TO M^RS W J BULWER WIFE AND FAMILY AT BECCLES SUFFOLK M^RS DASHWOOD PASSED MOST OF HER AFTERNOONS THERE CONVERSING WITH M^RS W J BULWER AND HEAR ME HER DEAR LITTLE LORINA REPEAT HER LETTERS SPELL – CAT – ALSO TO COUNT IN TIME M^RS DASHWOOD TAUGHT LORINA BULWER THE PIANO FORTE NOTES M^RS DASHWOOD TAUGHT ME MUSIC IN HER HOUSE M^RS DASHWOOD HAD A-PIANO-HARP M^RS DASHWOOD BOUGHT ME A MUSIC BOOK AT JARROLDS STATIONER NORWICH WHEN SHE WAS STAYING AT HER SONS RESIDENCE LANCELOT DASHWOOD E^SQ SURGEON NORWICH M^RS DASHWOOD LIVED AT BECCLES SUFFOLK AT THE TIME SQUIRE THARP OF CHIPPENHAM CAMBS KNEW THE DASHWOOD E^SQ WHO DROVE STONE HORSES IN HIS CARRIAGE HE ADVISED THE SQUIRE HOW TO ARRANGE ABOUT HIS FOREIGN ESTATE ALSO DASHWOOD E^SQ TOLD THE SQUIRE THE WAY HE HAD ARRANGED HIS FOREIGN ESTATE WHICH JOINS SQUIRE THARPS – THE BULWER FAMILY HAD AN INDIAN ESTATE AND HAD FIVE BRANCH SHOPS IN ESSEX FOR THE SALE OF THE PRODUCTS OF THE INDIAN ESTATE BULWER E^SQ OF WOOD DALLING HALL NORFOLK THE LAND HE FARMED 2000, 200 ACRES – THE BULWER E^SQRS – WERE THE SONS OF H.M.G MAJESTY KING GEORGE OF ENGLAND BULWER E^SQ OF WOOD DALLING HALL AND BULWER E^SQ

WHO HELD THE FIVE TRADE ESTABLISHMENTS WERE BROTHERS ND UNCLES OF MR W.J. BULWER'S WIFE WAS MARRIED TO ANN SO TERMED ANN TURNER OF CHIP- PENHAM CAMBS BY LICENCE FROM THE BISHOP OF NORWICH IT COST £5 MARRIED AT CHIPPENHAM CHURCH CAMBS SHE HAD LIGHT BLUE EYES FAIR

ANNCY NANCY TICKLE MY FANCY WAS A PRINCESS SHE WAS
MARRIED TO M^R WJ BULWER AT CHIPPENHAM CHURCH CAMBS
BY LICENCE FROM THE BISHOP OF NORWICH CATHEDRAL
NORFOLK HER PLATE WAS SENT TO A MOLINARI HALESWORTH
SUFFOLK JEWELLER FOR M^R WJ BULWER'S MONOGRAME E.
BULWER E^SQ IS HER SON HE LIVES AT NO 1 ST GEORGES PARK G^T
YARMOUTH NORFOLK HIS MUSIC MASTER LIVED AT LOWESTOFT
AND CAME TO BECCLES TO GIVE MASTER E. BULWER HIS MUSIC
LESSONS E. BULWER E^SQ SEMI-ROYAL – I KNOWN AND BROUGHT
UP AS MISS LORINA BULWER AND LIVED WITH E. BULWER E^SQS
MOTHER ANNCY TICKLE MY FANCY UNTIL HER DEATH WHICH
TOOK PLACE AT 22 AUDLEY STREET G^T YARMOUTH NORFOLK
MR ROBERT FORDER ST NICHOLAS ROAD MADE HER COFFIN M^R
SHREVE THE HEARSE AND MOURNING COACH ST NICHOLAS
ROAD THE STONE MASON MR STANLEY CAISTER ROAD PALMER
BROS DRAPERS MARKET PLACE G^T YARMOUTH NORFOLK MY
MOURNING I TOLD MR STANLEY THE DATE WAS NOT CORRECT
ON HER GRAVE STONE IT MADE THREE YEARS DIFFERENCES HER
AGE WAS EIGHTY SIX HER ELDEST SON E. BULWER E^SQ IS HER
TRUE SON THE FAMILY CHANGED ANNA MARIA WENT TO THE
DUKE HAMILTON THE BANKERS PUT IN ANOTHER SHE MARRIED
WHEN WE LIVED AT SEYMOUR PLACE THE HOUSE IS THE
PROPRTY OF M^R HOL – BLACK SHOE MANUFACTURER NORWICH
THETFORDS LIVERY STABLES ST GEORGES ROAD SUPPLIED
THE WEDDING CARRIAGES WHO SENT THE POSTILLIONS I DO
NOT KNOW HER ELDEST SON LIVING IS FORTY YEARS OF AGE
M^RS YOUNG WORE A FALSE NOSE FALSE TEETH FALSE HAIR
ENAMELLED HANDS FALSE FEET OR STUMP LEGS E. BULWER
E^SQ – MUST HAVE SEEN THROUGH THE ART OF BASTARD
MONGREL FALSE NOSE CHEST EXPANDER EARS AN
HEMAPHRODITE OR EUNICH BOTH THESE WOMEN ARE WELL
KNOWN TO MADAM RACHEL LONDON AND AT THE ROOKERY
NEWMARKET CAMBS ALSO THE LANGHAMS BOOKMAKERS
THE ROOKERY NEWMARKET CAMBS I AM PRINCESS VICTORIA'S
DAUGHTER LORINA BULWER WAS TAKEN TO THE ROYAL NUSERY
QUEEN VICTORIAS IN HER INFANCY I PASSING AS MISS LORINA
BULWER AND LIVING WITH M^R & M^RS W J BULWER GROCER
BECCLES SUFFOLK HIS WIFE ANNCY NANCY TICKLE MY FANCY WHO
SENT ME THE SO CALLED MISS LORINA BULWER TO A
BELGIAN SCHOOL AT BECCLES SUFFOLK WHO SENT ME ALL MY
FRENCH BOOKS E BULWER E^SQ WAS TOLD MY GENUINE NAME HE
SHOULD HAVE TOLD ME I WOULD HAVE FOUND MY WAY TO THE
ENGLISH GOVERNMENT AND INFORMED OF THE NOTORIOUS
THREE SISTERS

TAYLOR PASSING IN THE NAME OF VICTORIA THE NEXT ONE
ADELAIDE THE THRID ONE CALLED SARAH ANN THESE THREE
WOMEN HAVE DEFRAUDED THE REVENUE OF THOUSANDS
BY IN THE NAME OF VICTORIA AND ADELAIDE POOR PEOPLE
WITH ABSURD IDEAS THESE IMPOSTORS AND PRETENDERS
ARE THE SISTERS OF CHARLES TAYLOR CHIPPENHAM CAMBS
CAMBRIDGESHIRE PEOPLE ARE HELL FIRE DESPOT – THE FRENCH

LIVED AT BECCLES SUFFOLK AT MEALTIME SQUIRE SHARP OF CHIPPENHAM CAMBS KNEW THE DASHWOODS WHO DROVE STONE HORSES IN THIS CARRIAGE HE ADVISED THE SQUIRE HOW TO ARRANGE ABOUT HIS FOREIGN ESTATE ALSO DASHWOOD ESTD TO THE SQUIRE THE WAY HE HAD ARRANGED HIS FOREIGN ESTATE WHICH ADJOIN HAD AN INDIAN ESTATE AND HAD FIVE BRANCH SHOPS FOR THE SALE OF THE PRODUCTS OF THE INDIAN ESTATE BULWER OF WOOD DALLING HALL NORFOLK THE LAND HE FARMED 2000 OR 3000 ACRES HIS BULWERS ESQ WERE THE SONS OF HER MAJESTYS KING GEORGE OF ENGLAND AND BULWER ESQ OF WOOD DALLING HALL AND SU WERE HELD THE FIVE

MASTER WALTER BULWER WAS LORD KER'S SON AND LORD KER BROUGHT UP MASTER WALTER BULWER THE TWO FELLOWS LANGHAMS HAVE BEEN PASSING AS LORD KER AND SON FOR YEARS THEY ARE ALL POVERTY DRESSED UP KEN WITH ALIAS'S FROM A TO Z THE OLD MAN PASSED AS SIR CHARLES KER VIEW OF CROWN POINT ASYLUM

MAIDEN NAME SUSAN TURNER OF CHIPPENHAM CAMBS MARIA TURNER IS HER SISTER THESE TWO WOMEN ARE GEORGE DAWSON TURNER'S DAUGHTERS FORMERLY OF CHIPPENHAM CAMBS THE MATRON WILL PROVE TO BE ONE OF THE NOTORIOUS TAYLORS VICTORIA ADELAIDE OR SARAH ANN CHIPPENHAM VILLAGE THEIR FATHER WAS A CARPENTER THE WOMAN ANNA MARIA AFTERWARDS WENT TO JOHN LANGHAMS LONDON IN THE YEAR 1851 THE EXHIBITION HYDE PARK SHE WENT FROM CHIPPEN HAM STAYED THERE ONE WEEK

HIS CASUAL PAPER SAID ALTHOUGH OF WEAK MIND HE COULD HAVE BEEN PUT TO SOMETHING TO BRING IN A LIVING HIS FRIENDS EMPLOYED ONE HUNTER BUNTER WALTER DIVER HUNTER BUNTER FREDERICK DANBY PALMER LAWYER & YARMOUTH FRANK BURTON LAWYER & LENE GLENES HOUSE SOUTH END

MEN ARE DANIEL MEADOWS SONS IN LAW THE FELLOW BUXTON THE FELLOW LANGHAM SUSAN TURNER ROSLANGHAM SON THE TAYLORS CHARLES TAYLOR THE FATHER HIS TWO SONS ONE DRIVE A C YARMOUTH SCAVENGER CART AND TWO DAUGHTERS ONE IS THE SO CALLED PRINCESS OF WALES THE SO CALLED PRINCESS OF WALES BOSSIER MANY WHO MURDERED A WOMAN AT IVY RICH KILLED SOME FLESH WHO WITH HIM ANNA MARIA YOUNG OF WALTHAMSTOW ESSEX THE GROVE WALTHAMSTOW SHE AGREED FIRST WM FREDERICK DANDY PALMER LAWYER C YARMOUTH GEORGE SHE MARRIED THE GEORGE YOUNG AFTER SHE WAR KEO SMEAGREED WITH M R PINCHING OF WALTHAMSTOW ESSEX FAR AWAY IN LOYDS SHIP FOR THE PURPOSE OF GETTING A SITUATION AS HER HUSBAND GEORGE SHE HAD HER CHILDREN BY HIS FIRST SON FOR BERWICK

SHE IS NOT RELATED TO THE BULWERS NOT THE LEAST RELATIONSHIP SHE IS AN IMPOSTER FORGER DEFRAUDER AN INTIMATE FRIEND OF MADAM RACHEL TAYLORS VICTORIA ADELAIDE AND SARAH ANN TAYLORS THESE ARE THE ELDERS OF THE FEMALE NOTORIOUS CARD SHARPS OF CAMBRIDGESHIRE MY ANNA MARIA YOUNG ISALIAS M 3 PINCHING SHE HAS BEEN USING THE NAME OF LORINA BULWER WOMEN FOR YEARS I MISS LORINA BULWER DID NOT PROSECUTE HER SHE PASSED AS ANNA MARIA BULWER AND WAS A PUPIL OF MISS WINN SCHOOL BECCLES SUFFOLK A GILLYER ESTATE C B SISTER WAS BROUGHT UP BY HIS GRACE DUKE HAMILTON AND MARRIED LORD GEORGE

OF LORD JOHN MANNERS SONS OF HIS GRACE DUKE RUTLAND OF BEELVOIR CASTLE SOMERSETSHIRE HIS GRACE THE DUKE HAMILTON OWNED AND LIVED IN TICKWORTH PARK SUFFOLK AND OWNER OF HIS ESTATE WHEN IS THE LAND TAX PROPERTY TAX INCOME TAX INHABITED HOUSE TAX LEGACY DUTY DUTY ON CRESTS NO ONE IS ALLOWED TO BE HOLDER OF ONE UNLESS HILL CLEAR PROOF CAN BE GIVEN OF THEIR HERALDRY CLOTH ARMS AS TO RIGHTFUL RANK A DOG LICENCE GUN LICENCE A GIVE LICENCE FOR CROW BOY TAX ON LIVERY SERVANTS I CERTS LOW TARE SUCCESSION DUTY ON EMBLEMS TAX ON WHEELS IE ON TAX ON SHARES INCOME TAX C WHERE IS THE POOR LAW BY CAMBRIDGESHIRE PEOPLE PAY THESE LOCAL MENT TAXES WHEN TO CAMBRIDGESHIRE PEOPLE PAY THEIR LOCAL RATES WHERE IS THE ASSESS TAX COLLECTOR WHERE IS THE LOCAL TAX COLLECTOR THE LAW BE GOOD BY THE EXCISEMAN

WHAT HAS THE GROVE WALTHAMSTOW IN THIS WORKHOUSE PARLIAMENT IS A WHEN IS OUR MONEY THE POOR LAW BY THE PEOPLE ARE REAL ENGLISH TRAMPS HAWKERS SHOW PEOPLE ENGLISH NOT ONE BELONGS TO ANY OF MY CLASS NOT ONE HERE HAVE ANYTHING TO DO WITH MY PARTY I MISS LORINA BULWER HAVE A THROUGH D I TWO WIVES OF WALTHAMSTOW ESSEX MOSES SON MILMORIES LONDON N YOW A

FEATHER BED A RING AND MY FAMILY MEASURED ALSO LAWYER IT PAK ASK E BULWER E DE BULWER LIKE A DAMNED SOCIALIST AND DOES OF CHATTERIS CAMBRIDGE SHIRE A DAMNED HELL FIRE SOCIALIST WHERE HE FOUND SHE WAS HELL FIRE SOCIAL AND HE A LOYALIST HE SHOULD NOT HAVE MARRIED LORINA IS AN AMNEX E ASK E BULWER E ASQU REST IT I MISS LORINA BULWER WONDER THE PEOPLE HAVE NOT WRONG ME THE SLOPS OF THIS NOTORIOUS BUG LICE AND FLEA TRIBE CAMBRIDGESHIRE SOCIA 1 ST DEV FECTED WITH ROTTEN LEG A S ASH IS SOCIALIST AN

AFTER E BULWER GOOCH ESQ BLESSED MOTHER ANGEL NOT LESS MY BLISS WITH THE LORD AND WENT TO HIS AWEN TO LIVE IN HEAVEN TICKLES BOX GOOCH OF BROOKLYN HOUSE ASK THE RIPPER TAYLOR LEES THE NEIGHBOURS ABOUT IT AND OPEN THE WINDOW I WONDER THEIR BACK THROW UP ENLART TWO NETTE HEY CAME TO MRS SANCY NANCY TICKLE MY FANCY GATE M N GOOCH TOLD M R SANCY NANCY TICKLE MY FANCY CAMBRIDGE GOOCH OF GEORGES ROAD OF BROOKLYN BULWER E BULWER ESQ MOTHER WHO LIVED IN AUD STREET AND DIED THERE AT THE AGE OF EIGHTY SIX ABOUT THREE WEEKS BEFORE SHE COMMENCED HER SEVEN I DID AT M N G GOOCH IS A WOMAN EIGHTY STATUE A DECREPID OLD WOMAN A FULL RED FACE HOUSE FLESH NAG TEA SANCE NELSON ROAD NORTH AUDLEY HAIR BROWN INTER IVY BITTER BIG GOTTER BID E BROWNE WALKS AND ABOUT THREE WEEKS A BLACK WALKING STICK HER HANDS ARE CRIPPLED WITH REUMATIC ALSO HER LEGS WHICH SHE RUB WITH ST JACOBS OIL AND MANY MORE SHE WEARS

LONG DRAB LINDSEY DRAWS BECAUSE OF HAVING VARS FLETTANIC IS ROY A WHICH THIS MORE THIS OLD WOMAN KENT WAS RECENTLY FOR YEARS A CERTAIN SUM OF MONEY FROM THE TREASURY BECAUSE HER NAME WAS KENT BEFORE SHE MARRIED THE NAME OF KENT SMELL IN CAMB ALSO SO MANY COPIES OF THESE TREASURY DEFRAUDED PRINCE GOOCH TOLD ME MISS LORINA BULWER HER SUPER CLUDE NICHOLS HAD A FULL GT IS A YEAR OLD IV OF MY MONEY A DEED OF C LET OR A M R SANCY NANCY TICKLE A DEED OF C ANCY W M W H FOR SALE CROWN ROAD THE BOTH M R SANCY NANCY TICKLE W M ATTAN YEARS C ART SIZRAPPED MARIA TURNER M N ANNA MARIA YOUNG AND HER WILL RAKEN THRUMS 25 IS A TINKERS WHO WAS TO IS LOCKED AS IF THE DEVIL HAD PASSED HER HERE OUT OF THIS HIDEOUS WILD BROWN EYED OLD WOMAN DIED ABOUT TWENTY ODD YEARS AS TINS VILE JEWMA FHROME OLD RAG WOULD BE NEARLY A HUNDRED YEARS OF AGE HAD SHE LIVED SHE WAS NEVER MARRIED HER DIEING THE NAME OF

MOTHER ANCY NANCY TICKLES MY FANCY DIED AND WENT TO
HEAVEN TO LIVE IN PERPETUAL BLISS WITH THE LORD – JACK THE
RIPPER TAYLOR CHIPPENHAM CAMBS THE KENTS OF DITTON
FOUR MILES FROM CAMBRIDGE GOOCHS OF ST GEORGES ROAD
OF BROOKLYN HOUSE FLUSHING TERRACE NELSON ROAD NORTH
OF AUDLEY STREET NO 23 AND OF NO 5 PRIMROSE TERRACE
GORDON ROAD SOUTHTOWN SUFFOLK THIS IS THE NOTORIOUS
COFFIN BOX GOOCHS OF BROOKLYN HOUSE FLUSHING TERRACE
THE NEIGHBOURS ALWAYS STOOD UP AND TURNED THEIR BACKS
TO THE WINDOW EVERYTIME THEY CAME TO THE GATE M^{RS}
GOOCH TOLD M^{RS} ANNCY NANCY TICKLE MY FANCY BULWER E.
BULWER E^{SQRS} MOTHER WHO LIVED IN AUDLEY STREET AND DIED
THERE AT THE AGE OF EIGHTY SIX WITHIN ABOUT THREE WEEKS
BEFORE SHE COMMENCED HER EIGHTY SEVENTH BIRTHDAY
M^{RS} GOOCH IS A WOMAN OF SHORT STATUE A DECREPID OLD
WOMAN A FULL RED FACE HAIR BROWN TINTED A BRIGHTER
HUE BROWN EYES WALKS THE AID OF A BLACK WALKING STICK
HER HANDS ARE CRIPPLED WITH RHEUMATIC ALSO HER LEGS
WHICH SHE RUB WITH OIL – ST JACOBS OIL AND MANY MORE SHE
WEARS LONG DRAB LINDSEY DRAWS BECAUSE OF USING OILS
ELLIMANS EMBROCATION & THIS NOTORIOUS OLD WOMAN KENT
HAS BEEN RECEIVING FOR YEARS A CERTAIN SUM ON MONEY
FROM THE TREASURY BECAUSE HER NAME OF KENT SMELL
IN CAMBRIDGE SHIRE SO MANY COPIES OF THESE TREASURY
DEFRAUDERS FLORENCE GOOCH TOLD ME MISS LORINA BULWER
HER SISTER ALICE NICHOLS HAD A LITTLE A YEAR COMING
IN I MISS LORINA BULWER HAD MY MONEY A DEED OF GIFT
FROM MY MOTHER ANNCY NANCY TICKLE MY FANCY WHEN WE
LIVED IN GENEVE TERRACE CROWN ROAD WE DID NOT ROB THE
TREASURY FOR OUR MONEY THE BOTH KENTS HARRIET SEARS
HER BROTHER MATHEW SEARS ARE BASTARDS FROM CHATTERIS
CAMBRIDGESHIRE MARIA TURNER M^{RS} ANNA MARIA YOUNG
AND HER MUL TITUDE OF TRAMPS OLD MAD MOLLY HAWES
WHO WAS TAKEN TO COLNEY HATCH ASYLUM IN A TINKERS
CART STRAPPED IN SHE LOOKED AS IF THE DEVIL HAS CHASED
HER THREE TIMES THROUGH THE FLAMES OF HELL FIRE AND
TURNED OUT THIS HIDEOUS WILD BROWN EYED OLD WOMAN
DIED ABOUT TWENTY ODD YEARS AGO THIS VILE HEMAPHRODITE
OLD HAG WOULD BE NEARLY A HUNDRED YEARDS OF AGE HAD
SHE LIVED SHE WAS NEVER MARRIED – M^{RS} THOMAS BULWER
WAS NEVER MARRIED MR THOMAS BULWER SHOULD HAVE
PROSECUTED HER FOR USING THE NAME OF BULWER GENERAL
WEGL BULWER CB OF HEYDON HALL NORFOLK AND KNEBWORTH
HALL HERTS HIS SON LORD LYTTON WAS HER LATE MAGESTY
QUEEN VICTORIAS GODSON HE WAS BRITISH AMBASSADOR OF
PARIS ALSO VICEROY OF INDIA THIS FAMILY HAVE CERTAIN ROYAL
RIGHTS ESTABLISHED MR W.J. BULWER WHO MARRIED ANN HELD
BY THE NEWMARKET RACE TRUSTEES WHO PLACED HER WITH
THE TURNERS OF CHIPPENHAM CAMBS WAS PRESENTED TO HRH
DUKE OF KENT HRH DUCHESS OF KENT HRH PRINCESS VICTORIA
THE LATE QUEEN OF ENGLAND AT BARTON MILLS NORFOLK
BY APPOINTMENT THEY WERE TO SEE COKE E^{SQ} THE LITTLE
PRINCESS VICTORIA HAD A SMALL BAG WITH NEW SIXPENCES

REPUBLICANS WOULD NOT ENCOURAGE THE BOOKMAKERS
LANGHAMS BULGARIAN ATROCITY TRICKS LONDON MUSIC
HALLS & THEATRES KNOW JOHN LANGHAM THE LUNATIC THE
BACKERS SENT HIM OFF THE NEWMARKET HEATH AND PLACED
HIM IN BROADMORE LUNATIC ASYLUM HE IS THE FELLLOW WHO
PASSED AS BACCARAT WILDON OF TRANBY COURT HE INSULTED
HRH PRINCE OF WALES THE SCANDAL WAS REPORTED IN THE
NEWS PAPERS AND THE PULPIT JOHN LANGHAM IS A BASTARD
LIVING IN LONDON WITH HIS MOTHER SHE FOUND SOMETHING
TO DO AT A THEATRE AND JOHN LANGHAM WAS SENT TO A
GUN MAKER BY THE KINDNESS OF A FEW FRIENDS HE MARRIED
SUSAN TURNER OF CHIPPENHAM CAMBS THEIR SON HAS BEEN
PASSING AS SIR SAVILLE CROSSLEY OF SOMERLEYTON HALL NR
LOWESTOFT SUFFOLK THE VICTORIA ADELAIDE AND SARAH
ANN TAYLORS TURNERS AND LANGHAMS OUGHT TO BE UNDER
BOLTS AND BARS IN HORSE MONGER LANE JAIL OR NEWGATE
MASTER WALTER BULWER WAS LORD KER'S SON AND LORD KER
AND SON FOR YEARS THEY ARE POOR POVERTY DRESSED UP WITH
ALIAS'S FROM A TO Z THE OLD MAN PASSED AS SIR CHARLES
HARVEY OF CROWN POINT NORWICH HE PRETENDED TO SHOOT
HIMSELF HE QUICKLY FOUND HIS WAY IN TO G^T YARMOUTH
WORKHOUSE THEY THE SO CALLED SON IN LAW STRACEY OF
RACKHEATH PARK NORWICH THE FELLOW HERE PASSING AS
MASTER UNMASKED WILL PROVE TO BE JOHN LANGHAM'S SON
AND SUSAN LANGHAM HIS WIFE HER MAIDEN NAME SUSAN
TURNER OF CHIPPENHAM CAMBS MARIA TURNER IS HER SISTER
THESE TWO WOMEN ARE GEORGE DAWSON TURNERS DAUGHTERS
FORMERLY OF CHIPPENHAM CAMBS THE MATRON I THINK
WILL PROVE TO BE ONE OF THE NOTORIOUS TAYLORS VICTORIA
ADELAIDE OR SARAH ANN CHIPPENHAM VILLAGE CAMBS
THEIR FATHER WAS A CARPENTER THE WOMAN ANNA MARIA
AFTERWARDS M^{RS} YOUNG WENT TO JOHN LANGHAM'S LONDON
IN THE YEAR 1851 TO THE EXHIBITION HYDE PARK SHE WENT
FROM CHIPPEN HAM STAYED THERE ONE WEEK E. BULWER E^{SQ}
KNOW THIS HOUSE IS FULL OF NORWICH TRAMPS POCKTHORPE
CASTLE DITCHES AND ARE PLACED IN THE ROWS FOR A CERTAIN
TIME THEN BROUGHT INTO THIS CHARLOTTE STREET BROTHEL
WORKHOUSE THE FELLOW ORDERING EVERY THING HERE IS
HUNTER BUNTER LANGHAM SON OF JOHN AND SUSAN ROSS
LANGHAM TRAINED AT CAM BRIDGE FOR A TRICK MAN BESSIE
BARTON OF CAMBRIDGE TOLD ME KNOWN AS MISS LORINA
BULWER SO WELL SHE SAID WELL I NEVER SEE SUCH
A _____

HIS GRANDFATHER SAID ALTHOUGH OF WEAK MIND HE COULD
HAVE BEEN PUT TO SOMETHING TO BRING IN A LIVING HIS
FRIENDS EMPLOYED ARE HUNTER BUNTER WALTER DIVER
HUNTER BUNTER FREDERICK DANBY PALMER LAWYER G^T
YARMOUTH FRANK BURTON LAWYER GLENELG HOUSE SOUTH
END G^T YARMOUTH KEEPS A BROTHEL DANIEL MEADOWS KING
STREET SURGEON SO TERMED KEEPS A BROTHEL D. MEADOWS IS

FRANK BURTON'S FATHER IN LAW MEADOWS SECOND DAUGHTER
MARRIED FRANK BURTONS BROTHER BOTH MEN ARE DANIEL
MEADOWS SONS IN LAW THE FELLOW BUXTON THE FELLOW
LANGHAM SUSAN TURNER ROSS LANGHAMS SON THE TAYLORS
CHARLES TAYLOR THE FATHER HIS TWO SONS ONE DRIVE A G^T
YARMOUTH SCAVENGER CART AND TWO DAUGHTERS ONE IS
THE SO CALLED PRINCESS OF WALES THE SO CALLED PRINCE
OF WALES IS BOB SEWARD'S SON THE MAN WHO MURDERED A
WOMAN AT NORWICH BOILED SOME OF HER REMAINS WITH SAGE
AND ONIONS TO TRY HUMAN FLESH WHO WITH M^RS ANNA MARIA
YOUNG OF WALTHAMSTOW ESSEX THE GROVE WALTHAMSTOW
SHE AGREED FIRST WITH FREDERICK DANBY PALMER LAWYER G^T
YARMOUTH BEFORE SHE MARRIED THE FELLOW GEORGE YOUNG
OF WALTHAMSTOW ESSEX FOR A VOYAGE IN LOYDS SHIP FOR HER
HUSBAND GEORGE YOUNG SHE HAD FIVE CHILDREN WITH HER
THREE AND TWO OF HER HUSBANDS CHILDREN BY HIS FIRST OR
FORMER WIFE SHE IS NOT RELATED TO THE BULWERS NOT THE
LEAST RELATIONSHIP SHE IS AN IMPOSTOR FORGER DEFRAUDER
AN INTIMATE FRIEND OF MADAM RACHEL TAYLORS VICTORIA
ADELAIDE AND SARAH ANN TAYLORS THESE ARE THE LEADERS
OF THE FEMALE NOTORIOUS CARD-SHARPS OF CAMBRIDGESHIRE
M^RS ANNA MARIA YOUNG IS ALIAS M^RS PINCHING SHE HAS BEEN
USING THE NAME OF M^RS PINCHING FOR YEARS I MISS LORINA
BULWER WONDER – LOYD THE SHIPPER – DID NOT PROSECUTE
HER SHE PASSED AS ANNA MARIA BULWER AND WAS A PUPIL OF
MISS WINN SCHOOL BECCLES SUFFOLK E. BULWER E^SQ ELDEST
SISTER WAS BROUGHT UP BY HIS GRACE DUKE HAMILTON AND
MARRIED LORD GEORGE OR LORD JOHN MANNERS SONS OF HIS
GRACE DUKE RUTLAND OF BELVOIR CASTLE SOMERSETSHIRE HIS
GRACE THE DUKE HAMILTON OWNED AND LIVED AT ICKWORTH
PARK SUFFOLK AND OWNER OF IRISH ESTATE WHEN IS THE –
LAND TAX – PROPERTY TAX – LEGACY DUTY - DUTY IN CRESTS
– NO ONE IS ALLOWED TO BE HOLDER OF ONE UNLESS FULL AND
CLEAR PROOF CAN BE GIVEN AT THE HERALD OFFICE LONDON
AS TO RIGHTFUL LAND &c DOG LICENCE – GUN LICENCE – GUN
LICENCE FOR CROW BOY – TAX ON LIVERY SERVANTS – LICENCE
ON ALL VEHICLES ACCORDING TO THE NUMBER OF WHEELS LET
ON HIRE – SUCCESSION DUTY ON NOBLEMEN'S LANDED ESTATES
TAX ON SHARES INCOME TAX &c WHEN DID THE POOR POVERTY
CAMBRIDGESHIRE PEOPLE PAY THESE GOVERNMENT TAXES
WHEN DO CAMBRIDGESHIRE PEOPLE PAY THEIR LOCAL RATES –
WHERE IS THE ASSESS TAX COLLECTOR – WHERE IS THE LOCAL
TAX COLLECTOR – THE LOCAL LANDLORD THE EXCISE MAN
WHEN WAS GURNEYS BANK ENROLLED BY ACT OF PARLIAMENT
NOT ONE PAGAN IN THIS WORKSHOUSE THE PEOPLE ARE REAL
ENGLISH TRAMPS HAWKERS SHOW PEOPLE ENGLISH – NOT ONE
BELONG TO ANY OF MY CLASS NOT ONE HERE HAVE ANYTHING
TO DO WITH MY PARTY. I MISS LORINA BULWER HAVE A JEW TIE
THROUGH DR PINCHING OF WALTHAMSTOW ESSEX MOSES & SON
MINORIES LONDON KNOWS

[ends]

PITT

25th., September 1967

Dear Sandra,

When I called in this, my manager's office, a few moments ago
I was handed my very first American fan letter - and it was from
you. I was so pleased that I had to sit down and type an immediate
reply, even though Ken is shouting at me to get on with a script he
badly needs. That can wiat (wi-at? That's a new English word which
means wait).

I've been waiting for some reaction to the album from American
listeners. There were reviews in Billboard and Cash Box, but they
were by professional critics and they rarely reflet the opinions of
the public. The critics were very flattering however. They even
liked the single "Love You Till Tuesday". I've got a copy of the
American album and they've printed the picture a little yellow. I'm
really not that blond. I think the picture on the back is more 'me'.
Hope you like those enclosed.

In answer to your questions, my real name is David Jones and I
don't have to tell you why I changed it. "Nobody's going to make
a monkey out of you" said my manager. My birthday is January 8th
and I guess I'm 5'10". There is a Fan Club here in England, but
if things go well in the States then we'll have one there I suppose.
It's a little early to even think about it.

I hope one day to get to America. My manager tells me lots about
it as he has been there many times with other acts he manages. I was
watching an old film on TV the other night called "No Down Payment"
a great film, but rather depressing if it is a true reflection of
The American Way Of Life. However, shortly after that they showed
a documentary about Robert Frost the American poet, filmed mainly
at his home in Vermont, and that evened the score. I am sure that
that is nearer the real America. I made my first movie last week.
Just a fifteen minutes short, but it gave me some good experience for
a full length deal I have starting in January.

Thankyou for being so kind as to write to me and do please
write again and let me know some more about yourself.

Yours sincerely
David Bowie

K. C. Pitt, E. C. Weston

KENNETH PITT LIMITED, 35 CURZON STREET, MAYFAIR. LONDON W.1. TEL. GROSVENOR 7905-6

MY REAL NAME IS DAVID JONES

DAVID BOWIE to SANDRA DODD
September 25th, 1967

David Bowie was just 20 years of age
and yet to make a dent in the music
scene when, in September of 1967, he
received his first piece of fan mail from
America. The fan in question was
14-year-old Sandra Dodd, a New
Mexico resident whose uncle, a
manager of a local radio station, had
recently given her a promotional copy
of Bowie's first album. Intrigued, she
wrote him a letter, told him that his
music was as good as that of The
Beatles and offered to start a US fan
club on his behalf. Her letter did reach
Bowie. In fact, he was so excited to
receive such praise from across the
Atlantic that he immediately typed out
this endearing reply from the office of
his manager, Kenneth Pitt.

A NEW PAGE IN MOTION PICTURE HISTORY

SAMUEL GOLDWYN to WALT DISNEY
September 11th, 1964

In 1934, the first in a series of eight books featuring Mary Poppins, written by Australian novelist P. L. Travers, was published. One of the books' many fans was Walt Disney's daughter, Diana, who was so taken with the Poppins tales that she begged her father to bring the character to the big screen. His initial attempt to do so proved fruitless, however, as did that of movie mogul Samuel Goldwyn, but 20 years later Disney finally persuaded Travers to jump on board. *Mary Poppins* was eventually released in 1964, at which point it charmed millions of people and won five Academy Awards. Walt Disney was widely lauded for his efforts: one of the many congratulatory letters he subsequently received was from the same Samuel Goldwyn who, years before, had also tried – but failed – to bring Poppins to life.

SAMUEL GOLDWYN

September 11, 1964

Dear Walt:

Once in a lifetime -- and only once -- a picture comes along which cannot be compared to any other and to which no other can be compared. A picture which writes a new page in motion picture history. A picture which has such universal appeal that it is a pure delight to father, mother, children, grandparents and grandchildren -- it makes no difference who.

You have made it -- MARY POPPINS.

You have made a great many pictures, Walt, that have touched the hearts of the world, that have spread your name and your fame to every corner of the globe, and you have deserved every bit of acclaim that has come to you. But you have never made one so wonderful, so magical, so joyous, so completely the fulfilment of everything a great motion picture should be as MARY POPPINS.

I hope everyone in the world will see it -- that is the nicest thing I can possibly wish them.

Sincerely,

[Signed]

I LOVED THE BOY

WILLIAM WORDSWORTH to
ROBERT SOUTHEY
December 2nd, 1812

1812 was the darkest of years for William Wordsworth, the English Romantic poet responsible for many enduring masterpieces including "I Wandered Lonely as a Cloud" and the posthumously published autobiographical poem, *The Prelude*. In June, his three-year-old daughter, Catherine, died after suffering convulsions; then, on the first day of December, his six-year-old son, Thomas, passed away having suffered from measles and pneumonia. On December 2nd, with both children buried beneath the same tree in the Lake District, William Wordsworth wrote to friend and fellow poet, Robert Southey.

December 2, 1812
Wednesday Evening

My dear Friend,

Symptoms of the measles appeared upon my Son Thomas last Thursday; he was most favorable held till Tuesday, between ten and eleven at that hour was particularly lightsome and comfortable; without any assignable cause a sudden change took place, an inflammation had commenced on the lungs which it was impossible to check and the sweet Innocent yielded up his soul to God before six in the evening. He did not appear to suffer much in body, but I fear something in mind as he was of an age to have thought much upon death a subject to which his mind was daily led by the grave of his Sister.

My wife bears the loss of her child with striking fortitude. For myself dear Southey I dare not say in what state of mind I am; I loved the boy with the utmost love of which my soul is capable, and he is taken from me—yet in the agony of my spirit in surrendering such a treasure I feel a thousand times richer than if I had never possessed it. God comfort and save you and all our friends and us all from a repetition of such trials—O Southey feel for me! If you are not afraid of the complaint, I ought to have said if you have had it come over to us! Best love from everybody—you will impart this sad news to your Wife and Mrs Coleridge and Mrs Lovel and to Miss Barker and Mrs Wilson. Poor woman! She was most good to him—Heaven reward her.

Heaven bless you
Your sincere Friend
W. Wordsworth

Facing page:
William Wordsworth in a monograph from The Poetical Works of Wordsworth

A PILE OF 5000 CATS AND KITTENS

13th May, 1875

FREDERICK LAW OLMSTED
to HIS SON
May 13th, 1875

Born in 1822 in Connecticut, Frederick Law Olmsted is considered by many in his profession to be the "Father of American Landscape Architecture" – a title that seems, even to the least qualified of observers, to be fully justified, for Olmsted had at least a hand in designing some of the most famous urban parks in the US, including, most notably, New York's Central Park; other commissions consisted of major parkways, reservations, college campuses, and government buildings too numerous to list. To his four-year-old son in May of 1875, however, these achievements meant nothing: Henry was miles away from home with his mother and just wanted to see the family dog, Quiz, so he wrote to his father and asked for Quiz to be sent to him. This was his father's inventive reply.

Dear Henry:

The cats keep coming into the yard, six of them every day, and Quiz drives them out. If I should send Quiz to you to drive the cows away from your rhubarb he would not be here to drive the cats out of the yard. If six cats should keeping coming into the yard every day and not go out, in a week there would be 42 of them and in a month 180 and before you came back next November 1260. Then if there should be 1260 cats in the yard before next November half of them at least would have kittens and if half of them should have 6 kittens apiece, there would be more than 5000 cats and kittens in the yard. There would not be any place for Rosanna to spread the clothes unless she drove them all off the grass plot, and if she did they would have to crowd at the end of the yard nearest the house, and if they did that they would make a great pile as high as the top of my windows. A pile of 5000 cats and kittens, some of them black ones, in front of my window would make my office so dark I should not be able to write in it. Besides that those underneath, particularly the kittens, would be hurt by those standing on top of them and I expect they would make such a great squalling all the time that I should not be able to sleep, and if I was not able to sleep, I should not be able to work, and if I did not work I should not have any money, and if I had not any money, I could not send any to Plymouth to pay your fare back on the Fall River boat, and I could not pay my fare to go to Plymouth and so you and I would not ever see each other any more. No, Sir. I can't spare Quiz and you will have to watch for the cows and drive them off yourself or you will raise no rhubarb.

Your affectionate father.

New Year's Eve 1930

Dear Joe:

Am taking this opportunity to say Happy
New Year, although I must say you saw very little
of the Old Year and presumably are in no position
to judge whether things are getting better or
getting worse. However, it is all a matter of
finding time to do one's thinking in, and I
suppose conditions at the hospital are fairly
good except you won't really know for about a
year yet whether you have got an early blow on
the head or can think at all. I always used to
say life is what you make it, but that would
hardly go for anybody who had received a sharp
blow on the head at an early age, I suppose, and
in my own case I am beginning to see where the
exigencies of runthood can modify the character
of the adult bitch---that plus the Lardnerian
influence which is now very strong in the
apartment and against which I have decided to
put up practically no resistance, because for

IT MUST BE NICE TO BE A BABY

DAISY WHITE to JOEL WHITE
December 31st, 1930

On December 21st 1930, in Mount
Vernon, New York, Katharine S.
White, fiction editor of *The New Yorker*
magazine, gave birth to Joel, her first
and only child with husband E. B. White.
The birth was a tricky affair, the result
being a long stay in hospital for mother
and baby that stretched right through to
the next year and left Elwyn, who was
yet to write such classics as *Charlotte's
Web* and *Stuart Little,* with plenty of time
to ruminate about this new chapter of
their lives and think of ways to welcome
his son to the world. On New Year's Eve,
home alone and with Joel on his mind,
E. B. White sat at the typewriter and
composed this letter to his little boy; it
was written, not for the first time, in the
voice of the family dog, Daisy.

a terrier in my position unless I follow the
line of least resistance there is bound to be
a reaction prejudicial to my health---I mean I
might just as well let myself be blown around
whichever way the wind blows until things begin
to settle down around here and Mrs. White and
you get home and I find out what is what and
where we stand. A lot of things, Joe, get under
my skin: these damn tradespeople, and a bird
that showed up and stayed two days leaving a
small wooden cage behind when it left, and the
inert quality of rubber toys, and the bedridden
gait of Lardner when on the outings, and the
way they jump me about my burials---and the
result is I am irritable and aggressive and
White said last night I was running ferocity into
the ground whatever that meant. Ah, well, it
takes a lot out of me, but my blood is in good
shape (no eczema) and my only regret is that I
haven't had much chance for thinking, like in
the old leave-me-in-the-bathroom days. What
mornings they were, alone by that steam pipe,
lying the way one of the poets used to do with
my head right in the heat and all life opening

up clear. It must be nice to be a baby, though;
you direct descendants have a soft time compared
with us retainers. Life will open up just the
same, don't you worry, steam pipe or no steam
pipe---all you have to do is sit tight and don't
take any wooden nipples and you will soon get
the hang of what life is all about and how hard
people take it and all. White tells me you are
already drinking milk diluted with tears,---in
place of the conventional barley water which
they used to use in the gay Nineties; so I take
it life is real enough for you, tears being a
distillation of all melancholy vapors rising
from the human heart similar to the mists of the
                        valley
Meuse that knocked over so many Belgians (got
them in the throat) only you wouldn't know about
that because you are merely a child in arms
whereas I see the papers all the time. I imagine
a few tears in the diet are all right, as I am
a great believer in lean living otherwise you
get eczema, and I would not worry about that
ounce that you fat failed to make on the scales
because as I always say it isn't what you weigh
it's who you're with. While I was going over

4

White's property the other day I noticed a line
or two which he seems to have written in that
connection:

> From scales that show a baby's weight
>   Deduct an ounce, for him to borrow
> Such times as he may need an ounce
>   To tip the scales that weigh his sorrow.

..not much of a poem, but an idea back of it
probably if anybody wanted to study it out. On
the whole a little mournful, that poem. It
reminds me of the way I felt when I met a blind
man's bulldog on a cold day on Fifth Avenue---he
would walk a step and then crouch down and wait
and had no interest in the way anything smelt
(had been all through that years ago, I suppose),
anyway it was very mournful to see because if
the smell, or as White would sententiously call
it the "fragrance", has gone out of life, what
is there left say I. You will learn all about
that, Joe, as soon as you get on your feet so to
speak; meantime one can always amuse oneself
observing the more antic aspects of a genteel
civilization, listening to the Bandar Log's small
talk, and watching how everything gets in the way
of evrything else: how the wanderer fails to

keep his date with fortune because he is so
busy winding his wrist watch to see whether
he is late; how the poet falls short of the
first couplet from the sheer press of filling
the fountain pen with which to write it. Oh
you will see a lot of interesting and informative
things---tears caught in Lily cups, oceans
de-salted by stabilizers, and prayers requiring
an agency discount. I am only talking, Joe,---
I think White put a little Sherry on my dogbiscuit
tonight in honor of New Year's Eve and it has
gone to my head like the heat from that old
steam pipe. Ah those bathroom dreams! Maybe I
ought to go out. That's always a question,
whether a dog ought to go out and walk around
the block. With babies I understand the whole
problem is handled differently. Anyway, I
walked around the block with White just before
he went to the hospital with Mrs. White so you
could be born, and we saw your star being
hoisted into place on the Christmas tree in
front of the Washington Arch---an electric star
to be sure, but that's what you are up against
these days, and it is not a bad star, Joe, as

stars go. Well I have just been rambling along
and the bells have rung and it is now 1931
and in another hour or so the nurse will pick
you up and take you into a room described by
White as 823, and you will be given a little
snack, a ceremony that I can't say happens in
my own case very often. The tree that holds
your star will be shedding its needles very
soon---they will drop down like rain, and the
electric light in the colored bulbs will be
turned out, but I have noticed that new things
always spring up somewhat methodically and for
every darkened Christmas tree ornament there
is a white flower in spring. Or, in this
particular apartment, even before spring. There
are some here now called Narcissus, so come
home and see them Joe, and wishing you a very
Happy New Year I am

                    Faithfully yrs,

                        Daisy

I HAVE LOST A TREASURE

CASSANDRA AUSTEN to
FANNY KNIGHT
July, 1817

On July 18th of 1817, at the age of 41, novelist Jane Austen died following a bout of illness that reared its head in 1816 and which has since been speculatively labelled as bovine TB, Hodgkin's disease, and Addison's disease. Keen to remain active despite her deteriorating condition, she continued to write until March of that year, and on passing left behind eleven chapters of her seventh novel, *Sanditon;* it was published posthumously. Shortly after Austen's death, her heartbroken sister, Cassandra, wrote to Fanny Knight, Jane's favourite niece, and explained her final hours.

My dearest Fanny—doubly dear to me now for her dear sake whom we have lost.

She <u>did</u> love you most sincerely, and never shall I forget the proofs of love you gave her during her illness in writing those kind, amusing letters at a time when I know your feelings would have dictated so different a style. Take the only reward I can give you in the assurance that your benevolent purpose <u>was</u> answer'd; you <u>did</u> contribute to her enjoyment. Even your last letter afforded pleasure. I merely cut the seal and gave it to her; she opened it and read it herself, afterwards she gave it to me to read, and then talked to me a little and not uncheerfully of its contents, but there was then a languor about her which prevented her taking the same interest in anything she had been used to do.

Since Tuesday evening, when her complaint returned, there was a visible change, she slept more and much more comfortably; indeed, during the last eight-and-forty hours she was more asleep than awake. Her looks altered and she fell away, but I perceived no material diminution of strength, and, though I was then hopeless of a recovery, I had no suspicion how rapidly my loss was approaching.

I have lost a treasure, such a sister, such a friend as never can have been surpassed. She was the sun of my life, the gilder of every pleasure, the soother of every sorrow; I had not a thought concealed from her, and it is as if I had lost a part of myself. I loved her only too well – not better than she deserved, but I am conscious that my affection for her made me sometimes unjust to and negligent of others; and I can acknowledge, more than as a general principle, the justice of the Hand which has struck this blow.

You know me too well to be at all afraid that I should suffer materially from my feelings; I am perfectly conscious of the extent of my irreparable loss, but I am not at all overpowered and very little indisposed, nothing but what a short time, with rest and change of air, will remove. I thank God that I was enabled to attend her to the last, and amongst my many causes of self-reproach I have not to add any wilful neglect of her comfort.

She felt herself to be dying about half-an-hour before she became tranquil and apparently unconscious. During that half-hour was her struggle, poor soul! She said she could not tell us what she suffered, though she complained of little fixed pain. When I asked her if there was anything she wanted, her answer was she wanted nothing but death, and some of her words were: "God grant me patience, pray for me, oh, pray for me!" Her voice was affected, but as long as she spoke she was intelligible.

I hope I do not break your heart, my dearest Fanny, by these particulars; I mean to afford you gratification whilst I am relieving my own feelings. I could not write so to anybody else; indeed you are the only person I have written to at all, excepting your grandmamma – it was to her, not your Uncle Charles, I wrote on Friday.

Immediately after dinner on Thursday I went into the town to do an errand which your dear aunt was anxious about. I returned about a quarter before six and found her recovering from faintness and oppression; she got so well as to be able to give me a minute account of her seizure, and when the clock struck six she was talking quietly to me.

Winchester Sunday

My dearest Fanny – doubly dear to me now
for her dear sake whom we have lost.

She did love you most sincerely, & never shall
I forget the proofs of love you gave her during
her illness in writing those kind, amusing letters
at a time when I know your felings would have
dictated so different a style. Take the only reward
I can give you in my assurance that your benevolent
purpose was answer'd, you did contribute to her en:
:joyment. Even your last letter afforded pleasure,
I merely cut the seal & gave it to her, she opened
it & read it herself, afterwards she gave it me
to read & then talked to me a little & not uncheer-
:fully of its contents, but there was then a languor
about her which prevented her taking the same
interest in any thing, she had been used to do.
Since Tuesday evening, when her complaint returned,
there was a visible change, she slept more & much more

177

I cannot say how soon afterwards she was seized again with the same faintness, which was followed by the sufferings she could not describe; but Mr. Lyford had been sent for, had applied something to give her ease, and she was in a state of quiet insensibility by seven o'clock at the latest. From that time till half-past four, when she ceased to breathe, she scarcely moved a limb, so that we have every reason to think, with gratitude to the Almighty, that her sufferings were over. A slight motion of the head with every breath remained till almost the last. I sat close to her with a pillow in my lap to assist in supporting her head, which was almost off the bed, for six hours; fatigue made me then resign my place to Mrs. J. A. for two hours and a-half, when I took it again, and in about an hour more she breathed her last.

I was able to close her eyes myself, and it was a great gratification to me to render her those last services. There was nothing convulsed which gave the idea of pain in her look; on the contrary, but for the continual motion of the head she gave one the idea of a beautiful statue, and even now, in her coffin, there is such a sweet, serene air over her countenance as is quite pleasant to contemplate.

This day, my dearest Fanny, you have had the melancholy intelligence, and I know you suffer severely, but I likewise know that you will apply to the fountain-head for consolation, and that our merciful God is never deaf to such prayers as you will offer.

The last sad ceremony is to take place on Thursday morning; her dear remains are to be deposited in the cathedral. It is a satisfaction to me to think that they are to lie in a building she admired so much; her precious soul, I presume to hope, reposes in a far superior mansion. May mine one day be re-united to it!

Your dear papa, your Uncle Henry, and Frank and Edwd. Austen, instead of his father, will attend. I hope they will none of them suffer lastingly from their pious exertions. The ceremony must be over before ten o'clock, as the cathedral service begins at that hour, so that we shall be at home early in the day, for there will be nothing to keep us here afterwards.

Your Uncle James came to us yesterday, and is gone home to-day. Uncle H. goes to Chawton to-morrow morning; he has given every necessary direction here, and I think his company there will do good. He returns to us again on Tuesday evening.

I did not think to have written a long letter when I began, but I have found the employment draw me on, and I hope I shall have been giving you more pleasure than pain. Remember me kindly to Mrs. J. Bridges (I am so glad she is with you now), and give my best love to Lizzie and all the others. I am, my dearest Fanny,

Most affectionately yours,
CASS. ELIZ. AUSTEN.

I have said nothing about those at Chawton, because I am sure you hear from your papa.

comfortably; indeed during the last eight & forty hours she was more asleep than awake. Her looks altered & she fell away, but I perceived no material diminution of strength & tho' I was then hopeless of a recovery I had no suspicion how rapidly my loss was approaching. — I have lost a treasure, such a Sister, such a friend as never can have been surpassed, — She was the Sun of my life, the gilder of every pleasure, the soother of every sorrow, I had not a thought concealed from her, & it is as if I had lost a part of myself. I loved her only too well, not better than she deserved, but I am conscious that my affection for her made me sometimes unjust to & negligent of others, & I can acknowledge, more than as a general principle, the justice of the hand which has struck this blow. You know me too well to be at all afraid that I should suffer materially from my feelings, I am perfectly conscious of the extent of my irreparable loss, but I am not at all overpowered & very little indisposed, nothing but what a short

time, with rest & change of air will remove. I
thank God that I was enabled to attend her to the last &
amongst my many causes of self-reproach I have not
to
add any wilfull neglect of her comfort. She felt her
: self to be dying about half an hour before she be
: come tranquil & aparently unconscious. During that
half hour was her struggle, poor soul! She said she
could not tell us what she suffered, tho she complained
of little fixed pain. When I asked her if there was
any thing she wanted, her answer was she
wanted nothing but death & some of her
words were "God grant me patience, Pray for me
Oh Pray for me". Her voice was affected but as long
as she spoke she was intelligible. I hope I do not
break your heart my dearest Fanny by these particulars,
I mean to afford you gratification whilst I am relieving
my own feelings. I could not write so to any body else,
indeed you are the only person I have written to at all
excepting your Grandmama, it was to her not your
uncle Charles I wrote on Friday. — Immediately after
dinner on Thursday I went into the Town to do an errand
which your dear Aunt was anxious about. I returned about
a quarter before six & found her recovering from faint:

:ness & oppression, she got so well as to be able to give me a minute account of her seizure & when the clock struck 6 she was talking quietly to me. I cannot say how soon afterwards she was siezed again with the same faintness, which was followed by the sufferings she could not describe, but Mr Lyford had been sent for, had applied something to give her ease & she was in a state of quiet insensibility by seven oclock at the latest. From that time till half past four, when she ceased to breath, she scarcely moved a limb, so that wee have every reason to think, with gratitude to the Almighty, that her sufferings were over. A slight motion of the head with every breath remained till almost the last. I sat close to her with a pillow in my lap to assist in supporting her head, which was almost off the bed, for six hours,- fatigue made me then resign my place to Mrs J. A. for two hours & a half when I took it again & in about one hour more she breathed her last. I was able to close her eyes myself & it was a great gratification to me to render her these last services. ~~xxxxxxx~~. There was nothing convulsed or which gave the idea of pain in her look, on the contrary, but for the continual motion of the head, she gave me the idea of a beautiful statue, & even now in her coffin, there is such a sweet serene air over ~~on~~ her countenance as is quite pleasant to contemplate. This day my dearest Fanny you have had the melancholly intelligence & I know you suffer severely, but I likewise know that you will apply to the fountain-head for consolation & that our merciful God is never deaf to such prayers as you will offer.

The last sad ceremony is to take place on Thursday morning, her dear remains are to be deposited in the Cathedral. — it is a satisfaction to me to think that they are to lie in a Building she admired so much — her precious soul I presume to hope reposes in a far superior Mansion. May mine one day be reunited to it. — Your dear Papa, your Uncles Henry & Frank & Edwd Austen instead of his Father will attend, I hope they will none of them suffer lastingly from their pious exertions. — The ceremony must be over before ten o'clock as the Cathedral service begins at that hour, so that we shall be at home early in the day, for there will be nothing to keep us here afterwards. — Your Uncle James came to us yesterday & is gone home to day — Uncle H. goes to Chawton tomorrow morning, he has given every necessary direction here & I think his company there will do good. He returns to us again on Tuesday evening. I did not think to have written a long letter when I began, but I have found the employment draw me on & I hope I shall have been giving you more pleasure than pain.

Remember me kindly to Mrs J. Bridges (I am so glad she is with you now) & give my best love to Liggy & all the others. I am my dearest Fanny

Most affecly yrs

Cass. Elizth Austen

I have said nothing about those at Chawton because I am sure you hear from your Papa.

Miss Knight

Godmersham Park

Canterbury

WINCHESTER
JY20
1817

A RIPPLE OF FLAME

EDITH WHARTON to W. M.
FULLERTON
March, 1908

Born in New York City in 1862,
Pulitzer Prize-winning author
Edith Wharton was 45 when
first introduced to Morton
Fullerton by mutual friend
Henry James. Wharton,
married to another, quickly
fell for Fullerton's charms
and they soon began an
almost one-sided affair that
lasted for four years, ending
shortly before her divorce
from her troubled husband.
From the very beginning,
Wharton could sense that
Fullerton, a man who was no
stranger to playing the field,
wasn't fully invested in their
relationship. Just six months
after they began seeing each
other, she wrote him this
letter.

Dear, Remember, please, how impatient & anxious I shall be to know the sequel of the Bell letter …

—Do you know what I was thinking last night, when you asked me, & I couldn't tell you?—Only that the way you've spent your emotional life, while I've—bien malgré moi—hoarded mine, is what puts the great gulf between us, & sets us not only on opposite shores, but at hopelessly distant points of our respective shores … Do you see what I mean?

And I'm so afraid that the treasures I long to unpack for you, that have come to me in magic ships from enchanted islands, are only, to you, the old familiar red calico & beads of the clever trader who has had dealings in every latitude, & knows just what to carry in the hold to please the simple native—I'm so afraid of this, that often & often I stuff my shining treasures back into their box, lest I should see you smiling at them!

Well! And if you do? It's your loss, after all! And if you can't come into the room without my feeling all over me a ripple of flame, & if, wherever you touch me, a heart beats under your touch, & if, when you hold me, & I don't speak, it's because all the words in me seem to have become throbbing pulses, & all my thoughts are a great golden blur—why should I be afraid of your smiling at me, when I can turn the beads & calico back into such beauty—?

Facing page:
Author Edith Wharton

FINAL, COMPLETE AND IRREMEDIABLE DEFEAT

HUGH DOWDING to
WINSTON CHURCHILL
May 16th, 1940

On May 16th 1940, nine
months into World War II
and with Germany advancing
through Europe, Air Chief
Marshal Hugh Dowding,
leader of RAF Fighter
Command, wrote one of the
most important letters of the
war to Winston Churchill.
With their defences
breached, the French were
struggling under the weight
of Hitler's men; Churchill,
British Prime Minister
for less than a week,
responded by offering yet
more airborne back-up in
a desperate effort to turn
the tide – but these were
fighters that Dowding wasn't
prepared to hand over, not
if it could lead to the "final,
complete and irremediable
defeat of this country".
Churchill listened: no more
squadrons left for France.

Two months later, those RAF
squadrons proved invaluable
as they held off the
Luftwaffe during the Battle
of Britain and, crucially,
denied Germany command
of the skies.

COPY

Telephone Nos.: WATFORD 9241 (10 lines).
         COLINDALE 5221 (4 lines).
         PINNER 5691 (3 lines).
Telegraphic Address: " AIRGENARCH, STANMORE "

Reference: FC/S.19048.   SECRET

**HEADQUARTERS, FIGHTER COMMAND,
ROYAL AIR FORCE,
BENTLEY PRIORY,
STANMORE,
MIDDLESEX.**

16th May, 1940.

Sir,

      I have the honour to refer to the very serious calls which have recently been made upon the Home Defence Fighter Units in an attempt to stem the German invasion on the Continent.

2.   I hope and believe that our Armies may yet be victorious in France and Belgium, but we have to face the possibility that they may be defeated.

3.   In this case I presume that there is no-one who will deny that England should fight on, even though the remainder of the Continent of Europe is dominated by the Germans.

4.   For this purpose it is necessary to retain some minimum fighter strength in this country and I must request that the Air Council will inform me what they consider this minimum strength to be, in order that I may make my dispositions accordingly.

5.   I would remind the Air Council that the last estimate which they made as to the force necessary to defend this country was 52 Squadrons, and my strength has now been reduced to the equivalent of 36 Squadrons.

6.   Once a decision has been reached as to the limit on which the Air Council and the Cabinet are prepared to stake the existence of the country, it should be made clear to the Allied Commanders on the Continent that not a single aeroplane from Fighter Command beyond the limit will be sent across the Channel, no matter how desperate the situation may become.

7.   It will, of course, be remembered that the estimate of 52 Squadrons was based on the assumption that the attack would come from the eastwards except in so far as the defences might be outflanked in flight. We have now to face the possibility that attacks may come from Spain or even from the North coast of France. The result is that our line is very much extended at the same time as our resources are reduced.

8.   I must point out that within the last few days the equivalent of 10 Squadrons have been sent to France, that the Hurricane Squadrons remaining in this country are seriously depleted, and that the more Squadrons which are sent to France the higher will be the wastage and the more insistent the demands for reinforcements.

/ 9.

The Under Secretary of State,
  Air Ministry,
    LONDON, W.C.2.

9.   I must therefore request that as a matter of paramount urgency the Air Ministry will consider and decide what level of strength is to be left to the Fighter Command for the defences of this country, and will assure me that when this level has been reached, not one fighter will be sent across the Channel however urgent and insistent the appeals for help may be.

10.   I believe that, if an adequate fighter force is kept in this country, if the fleet remains in being, and if Home Forces are suitably organised to resist invasion, we should be able to carry on the war single handed for some time, if not indefinitely.   But, if the Home Defence Force is drained away in desperate attempts to remedy the situation in France, defeat in France will involve the final, complete and irremediable defeat of this country.

                    I have the honour to be,
                        Sir,
                    Your obedient Servant,

                    Air Chief Marshal,
                Air Officer Commanding-in-Chief,
                Fighter Command, Royal Air Force.

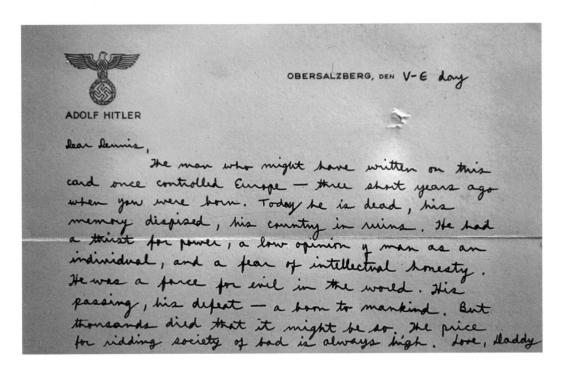

A FORCE FOR EVIL

OBERSALZBERG, DEN V–E day

RICHARD HELMS to DENNIS
HELMS
June, 1945

In June of 1945, a striking letter
arrived at the home of three-year-
old Dennis Helms in Washington,
written on a sheet of Adolf Hitler's
letterhead. It had been penned by
Dennis' father, Lt. Richard Helms,
an intelligence operative with the
OSS who, following Germany's
surrender the month before,
had managed to acquire some
of the recently-deceased Nazi
leader's stationery from the Reich
Chancellery. He then wrote to his
son. Richard Helms later became
Director of the CIA. His letter
to Dennis now resides in their
museum.

Dear Dennis,

The man who might have written on this card once controlled
Europe — three short years ago when you were born. Today he is dead,
his memory despised, his country in ruins. He had a thirst for power, a
low opinion of man as an individual, and a fear of intellectual honesty.
He was a force for evil in the world. His passing, his defeat — a boon to
mankind. But thousands died that it might be so. The price for ridding
society of bad is always high. Love, Daddy

YOU ARE A BEAST

MICHELANGELO DI
LODOVICO BUONARROTI
SIMONI to GIOVAN SIMONE
BUONARROTI SIMONI
June, 1509

Born in 1475, Michelangelo
di Lodovico Buonarroti
Simoni, better known simply
as Michelangelo, was – and
still is – one of the greatest
artists ever to have walked
the earth thanks to the
numerous masterpieces
to his name: his iconic
sculptures, *David* and *Pietà*,
and the exquisitely painted
ceiling of the Sistine Chapel
to name but three. He was a
prolific creator and worked
tirelessly at what he loved,
with much of his earnings
going to his needy family.
In 1509, one of his four
brothers, Giovan Simone,
mistreated their father.
Michelangelo, who loved his
father dearly, responded
furiously by letter.

Giovan Simone,

–It is said that when one does good to a good man, he makes him become better, but
that a bad man becomes worse. It is now many years that I have been endeavouring
with words and deeds of kindness to bring you to live honestly and in peace with
your father and the rest of us. You grow continually worse. I do not say that you are
a scoundrel; but you are of such sort that you have ceased to give satisfaction to me
or anybody. I could read you a long lesson on your ways of living; but they would
be idle words, like all the rest that I have wasted. To cut the matter short, I will
tell you as a fact beyond all question that you have nothing in the world: what you
spend and your house—room, I give you, and have given you these many years, for
the love of God, believing you to be my brother like the rest. Now, I am sure that
you are not my brother, else you would not threaten my father. Nay, you are a beast;
and as a beast I mean to treat you. Know that he who sees his father threatened or
roughly handled is bound to risk his own life in this cause. Let that suffice. I repeat
that you have nothing in the world; and if I hear the least thing about your ways of
going on, I will come to Florence by the post, and show you how far wrong you are,
and teach you to waste your substance, and set fire to houses and farms you have
not earned. Indeed you are not where you think yourself to be. If I come, I will open
your eyes to what will make you weep hot tears, and recognise on what false grounds
you base your arrogance.

I have something else to say to you, which I have said before. If you will endeavour
to live rightly, and to honour and revere your father, I am willing to help you like
the rest, and will put it shortly within your power to open a good shop. If you act
otherwise, I shall come and settle your affairs in such a way that you will recognise
what you are better than you ever did, and will know what you have to call your own,
and will have it shown to you in every place where you may go. No more. What I
lack in words I will supply with deeds.

Michelangelo in Rome.

I cannot refrain from adding a couple of lines. It is as follows. I have gone these
twelve years past drudging about through Italy, borne every shame, suffered every
hardship, worn my body out in every toil, put my life to a thousand hazards, and all
with the sole purpose of helping the fortunes of my family. Now that I have begun
to raise it up a little, you only, you alone, choose to destroy and bring to ruin in one
hour what it has cost me so many years and such labour to build up. By Christ's
body this shall not be; for I am the man to put to the rout ten thousand of your sort,
whenever it be needed. Be wise in time, then, and do not try the patience of one
who has other things to vex him.

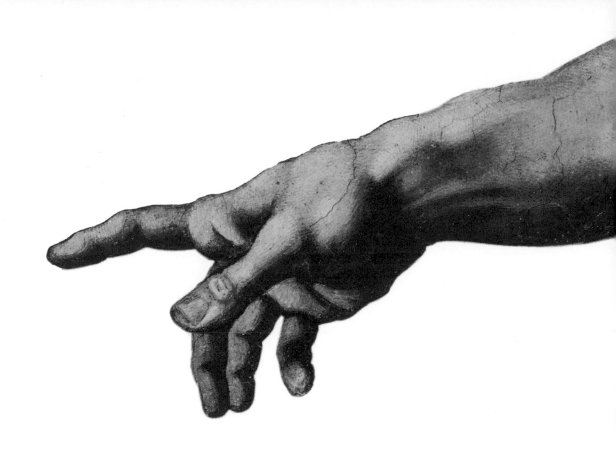

IT'S BURNING HELL WITHOUT YOU

DYLAN THOMAS to CAITLIN
THOMAS
May 7th, 1953

In 1936, in a pub in the heart
of London, 22-year-old
dancer Caitlin MacNamara
met Dylan Thomas, a Welsh
poet who, even at the tender
age of 23, was already
winning plaudits from the
most discerning of critics
thanks to poems such as
"And death shall have no
dominion" and "Light breaks
where no sun shines". They
married the next year, and
so began a tempestuous
relationship that was fuelled
by, and almost destroyed
by, excesses of all kinds.
In 1950, Dylan Thomas left
his wife and three children
at the family home and
headed for the US for the
first of four supposedly
lucrative but ultimately
booze-ridden reading tours;
it was on his final trip, late
1953, that Thomas died from
pneumonia.

Six months before he passed
away, holed up in a New York
hotel room, he wrote one of
his last letters to Caitlin.

*Facing page: Welsh poet
Dylan Thomas walking with
his wife Caitlin, 1946*

Hotel Chelsea New York
May 7th 1953

O Caitlin Caitlin Caitlin my love my love, where are you & where am I and
why haven't you written and I love you every second of every hour of every day &
night. I love you, Caitlin. In all the hotel bedrooms I've been in in this two weeks,
I've waited for you all the time. She can't be long now, I say to my damp miserable
self, any minute now she'll be coming into the room: the most beautiful woman on
the earth, and she is mine, & I am hers, until the end of the earth and long long
after. Caitlin, I love you. Have you forgotten me? Do you hate me? Why don't you
write? Two weeks may seem a small time but to me it's old as the hills & deep as my
worship of you. Two weeks here, in this hot hell and I know nothing except that I'm
waiting for you and that you never come. And in two weeks I've travelled all over
the stinking place, even into the deep South: in 14 days I've given 14 readings, & am
spending as little as possible so that I can bring some money home and so that we
can go into the sun.

I'm coming back, by plane, on the 26th of May, & will tell you later
just when the plane arrives. Will you meet me in London? Did you get my letter
from the horrible ship? And the little letter with the 100 dollar Oscar cheque? I
don't know what's happening, because you don't write. I love you, I want you, it's
burning hell without you. I don't want to see anybody or talk to anybody, I'm lost
without you. I love your body & your soul & your eyes & your hair & your voice &
the way you walk & talk. And that's all I can see now: you moving, in a light. I love
you, Caitlin. I've been to foul Washington; I've been to Virginia & North Carolina
and Pennsylvania & Syracuse & Bennington & Williamstown & Charlottesville;
and now I'm back in New York, for two days, in the same room we had. That was
the last love & terror, because I know you are coming into this room, & I hide my
heaps of candies, & I wait for you – like waiting for the light. Then I suddenly know
you are not here, you are in Laugharne, with lonely Colm; & then the light goes
out & I have to see you in the dark. I love you. Please, if you love me, write to me.
Tell me, dear dear Cat. There is nothing to tell you other than that you know: I am
profoundly in love with you, the only profundity I know. Every day's dull torture,
& every night burning for you. Please please write. I'm enduring this awfulness
with you behind my eyes. You tell me how awful it is, & I can see. You think I don't
understand grief & loneliness; I do, I understand yours & mine when we are not
together. We shall be together. And, if you want it, we shall never be not together
again. I said I worshipped you. I do; but I want you too. God, the nights are long
& lonely.

I LOVE YOU. Oh, sweet Cat.

Dylan

I DRANK TOO MUCH WINE LAST NIGHT

JANE AUSTEN to
CASSANDRA AUSTEN
November 20th, 1800

Since her death in 1817, Jane Austen's anonymously penned novels – *Sense and Sensibility, Pride and Prejudice,* and *Emma,* to name but three – have become required reading in many circles and are now held aloft as classics without reservation. She was also a prolific and observant writer of frank letters that rarely failed to entertain; however, sadly, the majority of the thousands she sent were destroyed by her sister and closest friend, Cassandra, shortly before she died, and less than 200 are still with us. This surviving example, sent to Cassandra in November of 1800, was written mid-hangover by 24-year-old Jane and concerns a ball she attended and was keen to describe.

My Dear Cassandra,

Your letter took me quite by surprise this morning; you are very welcome, however, and I am very much obliged to you. I believe I drank too much wine last night at Hurstbourne; I know not how else to account for the shaking of my hand to-day. You will kindly make allowance therefore for any indistinctness of writing, by attributing it to this venial error.

Your desiring to hear from me on Sunday will, perhaps, bring you a more particular account of the ball than you may care for, because one is prone to think much more of such things the morning after they happen, than when time has entirely driven them out of one's recollection.

It was a pleasant evening; Charles found it remarkably so, but I cannot tell why, unless the absence of Miss Terry, towards whom his conscience reproaches him with being now perfectly indifferent, was a relief to him. There were only twelve dances, of which I danced nine, and was merely prevented from dancing the rest by the want of a partner. We began at ten, supped at one, and were at Deane before five. There were but fifty people in the room; very few families indeed from our side of the county, and not many more from the other. My partners were the two St. Johns, Hooper, Holder, and very prodigious Mr. Mathew, with whom I called the last, and whom I liked the best of my little stock.

There were very few beauties, and such as there were were not very handsome. Miss Iremonger did not look well, and Mrs. Blount was the only one much admired. She appeared exactly as she did in September, with the same broad face, diamond bandeau, white shoes, pink husband, and fat neck. The two Miss Coxes were there: I traced in one the remains of the vulgar, broad-featured girl who danced at Enham eight years ago; the other is refined into a nice, composed-looking girl, like Catherine Bigg. I looked at Sir Thomas Champneys and thought of poor Rosalie; I looked at his daughter, and thought her a queer animal with a white neck. Mrs. Warren, I was constrained to think, a very fine young woman, which I much regret. She has got rid of some part of her child, and danced away with great activity looking by no means very large. Her husband is ugly enough, uglier even than his cousin John; but he does not look so very old. The Miss Maitlands are both prettyish, very like Anne, with brown skins, large dark eyes, and a good deal of nose. The General has got the gout, and Mrs. Maitland the jaundice. Miss Debary, Susan, and Sally, all in black, but without any stature, made their appearance, and I was as civil to them as their bad breath would allow me.

Mary said that I looked very well last night. I wore my aunt's gown and handkerchief, and my hair was at least tidy, which was all my ambition. I will now have done with the ball, and I will moreover go and dress for dinner.

We had a very pleasant day on Monday at Ashe, we sat down fourteen to dinner in the study, the dining-room being not habitable from the storms having blown down its chimney. Mrs. Bramston talked a good deal of nonsense, which Mr. Bramston and Mr. Clerk seemed almost equally to enjoy. There was a whist and a casino table, and six outsiders. Rice and Lucy made love, Mat. Robinson fell asleep, James and Mrs. Augusta alternately read Dr. Finnis' pamphlet on the cow-pox, and I bestowed my company by turns on all.

THE FIVE POSITIONS OF DANCING.

Engrav'd for Wilson's Analysis of Country Dancing.

*The Figures shew the positions of the Learner,
and the Feet that of a finish'd Dancer.*

The three Digweeds all came on Tuesday, and we played a pool at commerce. James Digweed left Hampshire to-day. I think he must be in love with you, from his anxiety to have you go to the Faversham balls, and likewise from his supposing that the two elms fell from their grief at your absence. Was not it a gallant idea? It never occurred to me before, but I dare say it was so.

Farewell; Charles sends you his best love and Edward his worst. If you think the distinction improper, you may take the worst yourself. He will write to you when he gets back to his ship, and in the meantime desires that you will consider me as

Your affectionate sister,
J. A.

LET US BLAZE NEW TRAILS

BILL BERNBACH to HIS
COLLEAGUES
May 15th, 1947

Bill Bernbach was one of
the original Mad Men. A
real-life Don Draper. One
of the greats. In May of
1947, at which point he
was 35 years of age and
Creative Director at Grey
Advertising on Fifth Avenue,
he noticed a worrying
development: as the agency
grew in size, they were
in danger of losing their
creative spark – they were,
he believed, falling victim
to "bigness". Fearing the
worst, he wrote a warning
letter to the owners of Grey
that has since become
famous in the industry and
a reminder that often it is
best to think small. Two
years after writing it, with
his advice largely ignored,
Bernbach left Grey New
York to co-found the hugely
successful agency, Doyle
Dane Bernbach.

In the 1950s, DDB
revolutionized automotive
advertising with the "Think
Small" campaign for
the Volkswagen Beetle
(pictured).

5/15/47

Dear _____ :

Our agency is getting big. That's something to be happy about. But it's something to worry about, too, and I don't mind telling you I'm damned worried. I'm worried that we're going to fall into the trap of bigness, that we're going to worship techniques instead of substance, that we're going to follow history instead of making it, that we're going to be drowned by superficialities instead of buoyed up by solid fundamentals. I'm worried lest hardening of the creative arteries begin to set in.

There are a lot of great technicians in advertising. And unfortunately they talk the best game. They know all the rules. They can tell you that people in an ad will get you greater readership. They can tell you that a sentence should be this short or that long. They can tell you that body copy should be broken up for easier reading. They can give you fact after fact after fact. They are the scientists of advertising. But there's one little rub. Advertising is fundamentally persuasion and persuasion happens to be not a science, but an art.

It's that creative spark that I'm so jealous of for our agency and that I am so desperately fearful of losing. I don't want academicians. I don't want scientists. I don't want people who do the right things. I want people who do inspiring things.

In the past year I must have interviewed about 80 people – writers and artists. Many of them were from the so-called giants of the agency field. It was appalling to see how few of these people were genuinely creative. Sure, they had advertising know-how. Yes, they were up on advertising technique.

But look beneath the technique and what did you find? A sameness, a mental weariness, a mediocrity of ideas. But they could defend every ad on the basis that it obeyed the rules of advertising. It was like worshiping a ritual instead of the God.

All this is not to say that technique is unimportant. Superior technical skill will make a good ad better. But the danger is a preoccupation with technical skill or the mistaking of technical skill for creative ability. The danger lies in the temptation to buy routinized men who have a formula for advertising. The danger lies In the natural tendency to go after tried-and-true talent that will not make us stand out in competition but rather make us look like all the others.

If we are to advance we must emerge as a distinctive personality. We must develop our own philosophy and not have the advertising philosophy of others imposed on us.

Let us blaze new trails. Let us prove to the world that good taste, good art, and good writing can be good selling.

Respectfully,
Bill Bernbach

Think small.

Our little car isn't so much of a novelty any more.

A couple of dozen college kids don't try to squeeze inside it.

The guy at the gas station doesn't ask where the gas goes.

Nobody even stares at our shape.

In fact, some people who drive our little flivver don't even think 32 miles to the gallon is going any great guns.

Or using five pints of oil instead of five quarts.

Or never needing anti-freeze.

Or racking up 40,000 miles on a set of tires.

That's because once you get used to some of our economies, you don't even think about them any more.

Except when you squeeze into a small parking spot. Or renew your small insurance. Or pay a small repair bill. Or trade in your old VW for a new one.

Think it over.

E HALF-MAD BULLSHI

WEASEL LAZY COCKSUCK

CHEAPJACK SCUM WORS

THLESS BRAINLESS AS

ASS HALF-MAD BULLSHI

WEASEL LAZY WORTHLE

USELESS ASS BRAINLES

ASS USELESS GIBBERI

LAME HALF-MAD BULLS

WEASEL LAZY COCKSUCK

CHEAPJACK SCUM WORS

THLESS BRAINLESS AS

ASS HALF-MAD BULLSHI

WEASEL LAZY WORTHLE

USELESS ASS BRAINLES

YOUR TYPE IS A DIME A DOZEN

HUNTER S. THOMPSON to
ANTHONY BURGESS
August 17th, 1973

Born in 1917 in Manchester, England, the late Anthony Burgess is best known – in part due to Stanley Kubrick's big-screen adaptation – for *A Clockwork Orange,* the widely revered dystopian novel that first broke ground in 1962. But this was far from his only achievement. Burgess was prolific, versatile, and highly intelligent: he published 33 novels, 25 nonfiction titles, produced poetry, short stories and screenplays, composed three symphonies, wrote hundreds of musical pieces, and spoke nine languages fluently. He also, when time allowed, worked as a journalist, and in August of 1973 found himself in Rome struggling to conjure up a "thinkpiece" owed to *Rolling Stone* magazine. Defeated, he suggested "a 50,000-word novella I've just finished, all about the condition humaine etc. Perhaps some of that would be better than a mere thinkpiece". Unluckily for him, that offer landed on the desk of Hunter S. Thompson.

August 17, 1973
Woody Creek, CO

Dear Mr. Burgess,

Herr Wenner has forwarded your useless letter from Rome to the National Affairs Desk for my examination and/or reply.

Unfortunately, we have no International Gibberish Desk, or it would have ended up there.

What kind of lame, half-mad bullshit are you trying to sneak over on us? When Rolling Stone asks for "a thinkpiece," goddamnit, we want a fucking Thinkpiece … and don't try to weasel out with any of your limey bullshit about a "50,000 word novella about the condition humaine, etc.…"

Do you take us for a gang of brainless lizards? Rich hoodlums? Dilettante thugs?

You lazy cocksucker. I want that Thinkpiece on my desk by Labor Day. And I want it ready for press. The time has come & gone when cheapjack scum like you can get away with the kind of scams you got rich from in the past.

Get your worthless ass out of the piazza and back to the typewriter. Your type is a dime a dozen around here, Burgess, and I'm fucked if I'm going to stand for it any longer.

Sincerely,

Hunter S. Thompson

WE CAN CHANGE THE WORLD

JOHN LENNON to ERIC CLAPTON
Circa 1969

In 1969, the year before the break-up of The Beatles, John Lennon and Yoko Ono decided to recruit some of their friends in the world of showbiz to form a supergroup, to be known as the Plastic Ono Band. This eight-page letter, handwritten by Lennon, was their attempt to bring Eric Clapton on board. And join he did, if only for a short period, as did many other notable musicians – Keith Moon, Billy Preston and Phil Spector, to name but three – until the band's temporary retirement in 1975. In 2009, the Plastic Ono Band re-formed; their last album, *Take Me to the Land of Hell,* was released in 2013.

Dear Eric and

I've been meaning to write or call you for a few weeks now. I think maybe writing will give you and yours more time to think.

You must know by now that Yoko and I <u>rate your music and yourself very highly</u>, always have. You also know the kind of music we've been making and hope to make. Anyway the point is, after missing the Bangla-Desh concert, we began to feel more and more like going on the road, but not the way I used to with the Beatles, – night after night of torture. We mean to enjoy ourselves, take it easy, and maybe even <u>see</u> some of the places we go to! We have <u>many</u> 'revolutionary' ideas for presenting shows that completely involve the audience – not just as 'Superstars' 'up there' – blessing the people – but that's another letter really.

I'll get more to the point. We've asked Klaus Jim Keltner, Nicky Hopkins – Phil Spector even! to form a 'nucleus' group (Plastic Ono Band) – and between us all would decide what – if any – augmentation to the group we'd like – e.g. saxs, vocal group, they all agreed so far – and of course we had <u>YOU!!!</u> in mind as soon as we decided.

In the past when Nicky was working around (Stones, etc) bringing your girl/woman/wife was frowned on – with us it's the <u>opposite</u>, Nicky's missus – will also come with us – on stage if she wants (Yoko has ideas for her!) – or backstage. Our uppermost concern is to have a <u>happy group</u> in <u>body and mind</u>. Nobody will be asked to do anything that they don't <u>want to</u>, no-one will be held to any <u>contract</u> of any sort – (unless they wanted to, of course!).

Back to music. I've/we've long admired your music – and always kept an eye open to see what your up to ~~of late~~ lately. I really feel that I/we can bring out the <u>best in you</u> – (same kind of security financial or otherwise will help) but the main thing is the music. I consider Klaus, Jim, Nicky, Phil, Yoko, <u>you</u> could make the kind of sound that could bring back the <u>Balls</u> in rock 'n' roll.

Both of us have been thru the same kind of shit/pain that I know you've had – and I know we could <u>help each other</u> in that area – but mainly Eric – I know I can bring out something <u>great</u> – in fact <u>greater</u> in you that has been so far evident in your music, I hope to bring out the same kind of greatness in all of us – which I know will happen if/when we get together. I'm not trying to pressure you in any way and would quite understand if you decide against joining us, we would still love and respect you. We're not asking you for your 'name', I'm sure you know this – it's your <u>mind</u> we want!

Yoko and I are not interested in earning bread from public appearances, but neither do we expect the rest of the band (who mostly have familys) to work for free – they/you must all be happy money wise as well – otherwise what's the use for them to join us. We don't ask you/them to <u>ratify</u> everything we believe politically – but we're certainly interested in 'revolutionizing' the world thru music, we'd love to 'do' Russia, China, Hungary Poland, etc.

A friend of ours just got back from Moscow, and the kids over there are really hip – they have all the latest sounds on tape from <u>giant</u> radios they have. 'Don't come without your guitar' was the message they sent us, there are <u>millions</u> of people in the East – who need to be exposed to our kind of freedom/music/. We can change the world – and have a ball at the same time.

We don't want to work under such pressure that we feel dead on stage or have to pep ourselves up to live, maybe we could do 2 shows a week even, it would be entirely up to <u>us</u>. One idea that I had which we've discussed tentatively (nothing definite) goes like this,

'I know we have to rehearse sometimes or other, I'm sick of going on and jamming every live session. I've always wanted to go across the Pacific from the U.S. thru all those beautiful islands – across to Australia, New Zealand, Japan, – wherever, you know – Tahiti – Tonga – etc, so I came up with <u>this.</u>

How about a kind of 'Easy Rider' at sea. I mean we get EMI or a sane film co., to finance a <u>big ship</u> with 30 people aboard (including crew) – we take 8 track recording equipment with us (mine probably) movie equipment – and we rehearse on the way over – record if we want, play anywhere we fancy – say we film from L.A. to Tahiti, we stop there if we want – maybe have the film developed there – stay a week or as long as we want – collect the film, (of course we'll probably film wherever we stay (if we want) and edit it on board etc. (Having just finished a movie we made around our albums 'Imagine' & 'Fly' – it's a beautiful <u>surreal</u> film, <u>very surreal</u>, <u>all music</u>, only about <u>two words</u> spoken in the whole thing! We know we are ready to make a major movie). Anyway it's just a thought, we'd always stay as near to land as possible, and of course, we'd take doctors etc, in case of any kind of bother. We'd always be able to get to a place where someone could fly off if they've had enough. The whole trip could take 3-4-5-6 months, depending how we all felt – all families, children whatever are welcome etc. Please don't think you <u>have to</u> go along with the boat trip, to be in the band. I just wanted to let you know everything we've been talking about. (I thought we'd <u>really</u> be <u>ready</u> to hit the road after such a <u>healthy restful rehearsal</u>.)

Anyway there it is, if you want to talk more please call us, or even come over here to New York. We're at the St. Regis, here til Nov. 30 at least (753-4500- ext/room 1701) all expenses paid of course! Or write. At least <u>think about it</u>, please don't be frightened, I understand paranoia, only too well, I think it could only do good for you, to work with people who love and respect you, and that's from all of us.

Lots of love to you both from

John & Yoko.

ʃ

Dear Eric and

i've been meaning to write or call you for a few weeks now. i think maybe writing will give you and yours more time to think.

You must know by now that John and i rate your music and yourself _very highly_, always have. you also know the kind of music we've been making and hope to make. Anyway the point is, after missing the Bangla-Desh concert, we began to feel more and more like going on the road, but not the way I used to with the Beatles, — night after night of torture. We mean to enjoy ourselves, take it easy, and maybe even _see_ some of the places we go to! We have many 'revolutionary' ideas for presenting shows that completely involve the audience — not just us 'superstars' 'up there'— blessing the people — but that's another letter really.

②

i'll get nerer to the point. We've asked Klaus
Jim Keltner, Nicky Hopkins — phil spector
even! to form a 'nucleus' group (Plastic
Ono band) — and between us all would
decide what — if any — augmentation' to
the group we'd like — eg saxs, vocal group'
~~whatever we like~~, they all ~~want to~~ agreed
so far — and of course we had YOU !!!
in mind as soon as we decided.
in the past when Nicky was working around
(Steven etc) bringing your girl/woman/wife
was frowned on — with us its the opposite,
Nicky's missus — will also come with us — on
stage if she wants (Yoko has ideas for her!)
— or backstage. Our upermost concern is
to have a happy group in body & mind.
Nobody will ~~be~~ asked to do anything ~~that~~
they don't want to, no-one will be held
to any contract of anysort — (unless they
wanted to of course!)

back to music. il've /we've long admired
your music — and always kept an eye
open to see what your up to of late. lately
i really feel that I /we can bring out
the best in you — (save kind of security
financial or otherwise I will help) but the
main thing is the music. I consider Klaus,
Jim, Nickey, Phil, Yoko, you could make
the kind of sound that could bring back
the Balls in rock 'n' roll.

        Both of us have been thru
the same kind of shit/pain that I know
you've had — and i know we could
help each other in that area — but mainly
Eric — i know i can bring out something
great — in fact greater in you that
has been so far evident in your music,
I hope to bring out the same kind of
great ness in all of us — which i know
will happen if /when we get together.

④ i'm not trying to pressure you in anyway and would quite understand if you decide against joining us, we would still love and ~~rus~~ respect you. We're not asking you for your 'name', i'm sure you know this – its your <u>mind</u> we want!

Yoko and i are not interested in earning bread from public appearances, but neither do we expect the rest of the band (who mostly have familys) to work for free – they/you must all be happy money wise as well – otherwise whats the use for them to join us. We don't ask you/them to <u>ratify</u> everything we believe politically – but we're certainly interested in 'revolutionizing' the world thru music, we'd love to 'do' Russia, china, Hungary Poland, etc. A friend of ours just got back from Moscow, and the kids over there are really hip – they have all the latest

Sounds on tape from giant radios
they have. 'Don't come² without your
guitar' was the message they sent us,
there are millions of people in the
East — who need to be exposed to
our kind of (freedom / music). We can
change the world — and have a ball at
the same time."
                    We don't want to work under
such pressure that we feel dead on stage
or have to pep ourselves up to live,
maybe we could do 2 shows a week
even, it would be entirely up to _us_.
One idea that i had which we've
discussed tentively (nothing definite)
is goes like this,
                    'a know we have to
rehearse sometime or other, i'm sick of
going on and jamming every live session.

i've also always wanted to go across
the Pacific from the U.S. thru all those
beautiful islands — across to Australia
New Zealand, Japan — wherever, you
know — Tahiti — Tonga — etc, so i came
up with <u>this</u>

How about a kind of
'Easy Rider' at sea. i mean we get
Emi or a same film co, to finance
a <u>big ship</u> with 30 people aboard
(including crew) — we take 8 track
recording equipment with us (mine
probably) movie equipment — and we
rehearse on the way over — record if we
want, play anywhere we fancy — Say
we film from L.A. to Tahiti, we stop
there if we want — maybe have the film
developed there — stay a week or as
long as we want — collect the film, (of

⑤

and edit it on board. etc.

'course we'll ~~bring it~~ probably film wherever
we stop (if we want). (Having just finished
a movie we made around ~~to~~ our albums
'imagine' 'fly' - it a beautiful surreal
film, very surreal, all music, only
about two words spoken in the whole
thing! we knew we are ready to make
a major movie). Anway it just a
thought, we'd always stay as near to
land as possible, and of course we'd
take Doctors etc, in case of any kind
of bother. we'd always be able to
get to a place where someone could
fly off if they're had enough. The
whole trip could take 3 - 4 - 5 - 6 months,
depending how we all felt - all familys
children whatever are ~~not~~ welcome etc.
Please don't think you have to go along
with the boat trip, to be in the band.

208

8.

i just we wanted to let you know
everything we've been talking about.
(9 thought we'd really be ready to
hit the road after such a healthy
rest_ful_ _rehearsal_)

anyway there it is, if
you want to talk more please call
us, or even come over here to N. York.
we're at the St. Regis here til Nov 30
at least (753-4500 - ext 1701) all
room
expenses paid of course! or write. At
least _think about it_, please don't be
frightened, i understand paranoia, only
to well, i think it could only do good for
you, and would bring to work with
people who love and respect you, and
that's from all of us.
, lots of love to you both from
John + Yoko.

YOU ARE A TRUE MAN

BRAM STOKER to WALT
WHITMAN
1876

In 1876, Walt Whitman
received a letter from a
fan who, like so many
others, had fallen in love
with his controversial,
groundbreaking collection of
poetry, *Leaves of Grass*, and
was keen to connect with its
creator. In fact, that young
government clerk was Bram
Stoker, future author of
Dracula – an immeasurably
influential horror novel
published 25 years later that
needs little introduction.
Included with Stoker's letter
was another missive – a far
lengthier, honest piece that
begins with an invitation to
burn the letter itself – that
was written four years
previous in draft form, but
which he had failed to send.
Both are reprinted here,
along with Whitman's reply.

Much to Stoker's delight, the
pair met in 1884, and twice
more before Whitman's
death.

Dublin, Feb. 14, 1876.

My dear Mr. Whitman.

I hope you will not consider this letter from an utter stranger a liberty. Indeed, I hardly feel a stranger to you, nor is this the first letter that I have written to you. My friend Edward Dowden has told me often that you like new acquaintances or I should rather say friends. And as an old friend I send you an enclosure which may interest you. Four years ago I wrote the enclosed draft of a letter which I intended to copy out and send to you—it has lain in my desk since then—when I heard that you were addressed as Mr. Whitman. It speaks for itself and needs no comment. It is as truly what I wanted to say as that light is light.

The four years which have elapsed have made me love your work fourfold, and I can truly say that I have ever spoken as your friend. You know what hostile criticism your work sometimes evokes here, and I wage a perpetual war with many friends on your behalf. But I am glad to say that I have been the means of making your work known to many who were scoffers at first. The years which have passed have not been uneventful to me, and I have felt and thought and suffered much in them, and I can truly say that from you I have had much pleasure and much consolation—and I do believe that your open earnest speech has not been thrown away on me or that my life and thought fail to be marked with its impress. I write this openly because I feel that with you one must be open. We have just had tonight a hot debate on your genius at the Fortnightly Club in which I had the privilege of putting forward my views—I think with success.

Do not think me cheeky for writing this. I only hope we may sometime meet and I shall be able perhaps to say what I cannot write. Dowden promised to get me a copy of your new edition and I hope that for any other work which you may have you will let me always be an early subscriber. I am sorry that you're not strong. Many of us are hoping to see you in Ireland. We had arranged to have a meeting for you. I do not know if you like getting letters. If you do I shall only be too happy to send you news of how thought goes among the men I know. With truest wishes for your health and happiness believe me,

Your friend
Bram Stoker

DRAFT

If you are the man I take you to be you will like to get this letter. If you are not I don't care whether you like it or not and only ask you to put it into the fire without reading any farther. But I believe you will like it. I don't think there is a man living, even you who are above the prejudices of the class of small-minded men, who wouldn't like to get a letter from a younger man, a stranger, across the world—a man living in an atmosphere prejudiced to the truths you sing and your manner of singing them. The idea that arises in my mind is whether there is a man living who would have the pluck to burn a letter in which he felt the smallest atom of interest without reading it. I believe you would and that you believe you would yourself. You can burn this now and test yourself, and all I will ask for my trouble of writing this letter, which for all I can tell you may light your pipe with or apply to some more ignoble purpose—is that you will in some manner let me know that my words have tested your impatience. Put it in the fire if you like—but if you do you will miss the pleasure of this next sentence, which ought to be that you have conquered an unworthy impulse.

A man who is uncertain of his own strength might try to encourage himself by a piece of bravo, but a man who can write, as you have written, the most candid words that ever fell from the lips of mortal man—a man to whose candor Rousseau's Confessions is reticence—can have no fear for his own strength. If you have gone this far you may read the letter and I feel in writing now that I am talking to you. If I were before your face I would like to shake hands with you, for I feel that I would like you. I would like to call you Comrade and to talk to you as men who are not poets do not often talk. I think that at first a man would be ashamed, for a man cannot in a moment break the habit of comparative reticence that has become a second nature to him; but I know I would not long be ashamed to be natural before you. You are a true man, and I would like to be one myself, and so I would be towards you as a brother and as a pupil to his master. In this age no man becomes worthy of the name without an effort. You have shaken off the shackles and your wings are free. I have the shackles on my shoulders still—but I have no wings. If you are going to read this letter any further I should tell you that I am not prepared to "give up all else" so far as words go. The only thing I am prepared to give up is prejudice, and before I knew you I had begun to throw overboard my cargo, but it is not all gone yet.

I do not know how you will take this letter. I have not addressed you in any form as I hear that you dislike to a certain degree the conventional forms in letters. I am writing to you because you are different from other men. If you were the same as the mass I would not write at all. As it is I must either call you Walt Whitman or not call you at all—and I have chosen the latter course. I don't know whether it is usual for you to get letters from utter strangers who have not even the claim of literary brotherhood to write you. If it is you must be frightfully tormented with letters and

I am sorry to have written this. I have, however, the claim of liking you—for your words are your own soul and even if you do not read my letter it is no less a pleasure to me to write it. Shelley wrote to William Godwin and they became friends. I am not Shelley and you are not Godwin and so I will only hope that sometime I may meet you face to face and perhaps shake hands with you. If I ever do it will be one of the greatest pleasures of my life.

If you care to know who it is that writes this, my name is Abraham Stoker (Junior). My friends call me Bram. I live at 43 Harcourt St., Dublin. I am a clerk in the service of the Crown on a small salary. I am twenty-four years old. Have been champion at our athletic sports (Trinity College, Dublin) and have won about a dozen cups. I have also been President of the College Philosophical Society and an art and theatrical critic of a daily paper. I am six feet two inches high and twelve stone weight naked and used to be forty-one or forty-two inches round the chest. I am ugly but strong and determined and have a large bump over my eyebrows. I have a heavy jaw and a big mouth and thick lips—sensitive nostrils—a snubnose and straight hair. I am equal in temper and cool in disposition and have a large amount of self control and am naturally secretive to the world. I take a delight in letting people I don't like—people of mean or cruel or sneaking or cowardly disposition—see the worst side of me. I have a large number of acquaintances and some five or six friends—all of which latter body care much for me.

Now I have told you all I know about myself. I know you from your works and your photograph, and if I know anything about you I think you would like to know of the personal appearance of your correspondents. You are I know a keen physiognomist. I am a believer of the science myself and am in an humble way a practicer of it. I was not disappointed when I saw your photograph—your late one especially. The way I came to like you was this. A notice of your poems appeared some two years ago or more in the Temple Bar magazine. I glanced at it and took its dictum as final, and laughed at you among my friends. I say it to my own shame but not to my regret for it has taught me a lesson to last my life out—without ever having seen your poems. More than a year after I heard two men in College talking of you. One of them had your book (Rossetti's edition) and was reading aloud some passages at which both laughed. They chose only those passages which are most foreign to British ears and made fun of them. Something struck me that I had judged you hastily. I took home the volume and read it far into the night. Since then I have to thank you for many happy hours, for I have read your poems with my door locked late at night, and I have read them on the seashore where I could look all round me and see no more sign of human life than the ships out at sea: and here I often found myself waking up from a reverie with the book lying open before me.

I love all poetry, and high generous thoughts make the tears rush to my eyes, but sometimes a word or a phrase of yours takes me away from the world around me and places me in an ideal land surrounded by realities more than any poem I ever read. Last year I was sitting on the beach on a summer's day reading your preface to the Leaves of Grass as printed in Rossetti's edition (for Rossetti is all I have got till I get the complete set of your works which I have ordered from

America). One thought struck me and I pondered over it for several hours—"the weather-beaten vessels entering new ports," you who wrote the words know them better than I do: and to you who sing of your own land of progress the words have a meaning that I can only imagine. But be assured of this, Walt Whitman—that a man of less than half your own age, reared a conservative in a conservative country, and who has always heard your name cried down by the great mass of people who mention it, here felt his heart leap towards you across the Atlantic and his soul swelling at the words or rather the thoughts.

It is vain for me to try to quote any instances of what thoughts of yours I like best—for I like them all and you must feel that you are reading the true words of one who feels with you. You see, I have called you by your name. I have been more candid with you—have said more about myself to you than I have ever said to any one before. You will not be angry with me if you have read so far. You will not laugh at me for writing this to you. It was with no small effort that I began to write and I feel reluctant to stop, but I must not tire you any more. If you ever would care to have more you can imagine, for you have a great heart, how much pleasure it would be to me to write more to you. How sweet a thing it is for a strong healthy man with a woman's eyes and a child's wishes to feel that he can speak so to a man who can be if he wishes father, and brother and wife to his soul.

I don't think you will laugh, Walt Whitman, nor despise me, but at all events I thank you for all the love and sympathy you have given me in common with my kind.

Bram Stoker

March 6, '76.

My dear young man,

Your letters have been most welcome to me—welcome to me as Person and as Author—I don't know which most—You did well to write me so unconventionally, so fresh, so manly, and so affectionately, too. I too hope (though it is not probable) that we shall one day meet each other. Meantime I send you my friendship and thanks.

Edward Dowden's letter containing among others your subscription for a copy of my new edition has just been received. I shall send the books very soon by express in a package to his address. I have just written E. D.

My physique is entirely shattered—doubtless permanently, from paralysis and other ailments. But I am up and dressed, and get out every day a little. Live here quite lonesome, but hearty, and good spirits.

Write to me again.

Walt Whitman

WHAT DO YOU TAKE ME FOR?

NANNI to EA-NASIR
1750 BC

Sitting behind a sheet of glass at the British Museum in London, inscribed on a clay tablet in an ancient script known as cuneiform, is solid proof of two things: firstly, that poor customer service – an affliction that somehow feels like a modern phenomenon – has actually been a plague on societies for at least 3775 long years, and secondly, that humans will never really change. For this is in fact a letter of complaint, sent by a furious man named Nanni to a Babylonian copper merchant called Ea-nasir, in which said customer makes very clear his dissatisfaction with the service experienced by his messengers. The letter was discovered in Southern Iraq, in a place then known as Ur.

Tell Ea-nasir: Nanni sends the following message:

When you came, you said to me as follows : "I will give Gimil-Sin (when he comes) fine quality copper ingots." You left then but you did not do what you promised me. You put ingots which were not good before my messenger (Sit-Sin) and said: "If you want to take them, take them; if you do not want to take them, go away!"

What do you take me for, that you treat somebody like me with such contempt? I have sent as messengers gentlemen like ourselves to collect the bag with my money (deposited with you) but you have treated me with contempt by sending them back to me empty-handed several times, and that through enemy territory. Is there anyone among the merchants who trade with Telmun who has treated me in this way? You alone treat my messenger with contempt! On account of that one (trifling) mina of silver which I owe you, you feel free to speak in such a way, while I have given to the palace on your behalf 1,080 pounds of copper, and umi-abum has likewise given 1,080 pounds of copper, apart from what we both have had written on a sealed tablet to be kept in the temple of Samas.

How have you treated me for that copper? You have withheld my money bag from me in enemy territory; it is now up to you to restore (my money) to me in full.

Take cognizance that (from now on) I will not accept here any copper from you that is not of fine quality. I shall (from now on) select and take the ingots individually in my own yard, and I shall exercise against you my right of rejection because you have treated me with contempt.

Facing page:
Clay tablet; letter from Nanni to Ea-nasir complaining that the wrong grade of copper ore has been delivered, 1750 BC

REMEMBER?

BREECE D'J PANCAKE to
JOHN CASEY
March 25th, 1979

Breece D'J Pancake's
promising career had only
just begun to take off when
he took his own life aged
26, with just six of his short
stories published, all to
great acclaim. It was no
surprise to those around
him that the posthumously
published *The Stories of
Breece D'J Pancake* was
nominated for a Pulitzer
Prize; even the great Kurt
Vonnegut called him "the
best writer, the most sincere
writer I've ever read". The
last letter Breece ever
wrote, seen here, was to
a close friend and mentor
who had championed him
from the beginning: Breece's
writing teacher at the
University of Virginia,
John Casey.

One Blue Ridge Lane
Charlottesville, Va.

John D. Casey
c/o Jane Casey
Department of English
Wilson Hall
University of Virginia

Dear John,

When you read this it really won't matter anymore, but I offer these thoughts the way a fossil comes back to haunt a geologist—but haunt isn't the right word, and I'm too stupid to think of another. But anyway . . .

Remember May, 1975? "God, why didn't you tell me . . . if I'd known you were this good, I'd have offered you a fellowship." I hadn't told you because I knew I wasn't. Then the summer of bad times when I pounded on doors, got fed-up, went fishing, and bingo they offered me a job sight unseen from Staunton, and bingo my father and my best friend croaked within a week of each other, and bingo I held on for dear life. I held on because of me, but I held on with the help of you. The night we went to see Ali murder Frazier in Manila, that night I nearly knocked your brains out with my driving into the parking-lot abutement. I was trying to think of some way to thank you for going with me to the gifts, and I forgot to hit the breaks.

Remember L_____? "I know you want me to tell you I've had a great time, but well, I've had a good time." And there were breakfasts with wheat cakes and lemon curd and spring mornings when I'd drive the VW from Staunton. I hit a "tree-rat," as Jane called it, but nobody was up to that for breakfast with lemon curd. And I drove home thinking what a wonderful day it had been, and how my father would want me to stop for coffee at least twice on the way home. I stopped three times for coffee, but when I got home my mother called to tell me Cousin _____ had dispatched his brains by a NY lake that morning. I wasn't all that sorry for Cousin _____.

Remember May, 1976? Jane said: "We got the house of my father—it has many bathrooms." I came over loaded in the VW for home, left you things one needs for long stays away—salt, coffee, whiskey, and a blanket. I spent the summer writing what would become "Trilobites," you wrote hopes of "Liberty." Later I came to Charlottesville, worked up the story, read a good novel in galley, met one Rod Kilpatrick. L___ died and went to heaven on somebody else's cross. I died over a girl who was dry as bean in bed but full of lush on the phone. She moved. I stayed.

Remember May, 1977? I wrote to say a story was sold. I got no answer. I worked frying hamburgers, selling golf balls. Richard had dinner with me before late Mass. I remembered you coming all the way here to welcome me to the Catholic faith. I missed you. I went home and started a story, then I found I would teach next year, so I started my lesson-plans. I finished the story and the lessons when you returned. The story wasn't good enough, and you helped me—soon it was good enough.

Remember Emily Miller? "Then Kerrigan said there weren't any virgins left in this day and time—but—I'm afraid—well he was wrong." So I decide she was right. I wanted to marry her, but later, when it became clear I would have no work, I wanted to become a padre. Me a padre? I loved this girl. Still, I had work, and you told me I'd get none. Still, I love this girl, and time flew its course. I sold another story: I called you on a winter's night and you were happy. Still, I love the girl.

Alright—maybe not.

Remember July, 1978? I went to the Southwest, and you went to Jane's Father's house. I loved the girl. I wrote several cards to you but the Post Office was on strike. I loved the girl. I went to a woman I knew in South Phoenix (blacks and Mexicans), but she told me I loved the girl. I went to a woman I knew in North Phoenix (lilly white), but she told me I loved the girl. I wrote you from a Big Boy counter on Central Ave., and I had no money, had no place to sleep, had no nothing. And "John, this is the last I'll ask." And it was. You were good enough to give me a clean bill of health with my dentist and then some.

So remember May, 1979? I can't. But as I see it, you'll go on as you have before I came. You're an honest man John Casey—honest at your heart—but what will you do for those who come after? Will you take a clean and simple writer like _____, and by giving him funds turn him into the slop _____ is made of? I could stay, I know, John, were I to beg—I might even have a job were I to stay one more year. Johnny, and you'll have to take a drink now, would you love me if I did? I love you. I love you because when my father and friend were dead you helped me hang on for dear life, told me I could write (and me damned if I hadn't done a passing job). Alright then, the bargain is settled, I can write, now, and nothing else matters. You've fought hard for me John—fought hard for five years, and please don't think that by my gruff manner and early temper I am any less the man for you. And by your fight, I hope something comes of me worthy of calling your own name to. I'm not good enough to work or marry, but I'm good enough to write.

Can you find a tear or two in these lines they are mine, and I will hope you shed them in Ireland this summer. Maybe we'll neither of us see Heaven, but if you can bring yourself to it, say a prayer for me (not in any church) under an Irish sky.

May God Bless and Go with You and Yours Always, John Casey.

(Signed, 'Breece')

I HOPE YOU DON'T FEEL
TOO DISAPPOINTED

ERIC IDLE to JOHN MAJOR
January 12th, 1993

One would imagine that Eric Idle, one-sixth of beloved comedy troupe Monty Python, and John Major, Prime Minister of the UK from 1990 to 1997, have nothing in common – but you would be wrong, for both Idle and Major were born on the same day: March 29th, 1943. In 1993, as their 50th birthdays approached, Idle took the opportunity to send the Prime Minister a brief letter.

The Rt.Hon. John Major M.P.
10 Downing Street
London SW1A.1AA

12th January 1993

Dear John Major,

On the 29th March you and I will both be fifty.

Has it ever occurred to you that, but for a twist of fate, I should be Prime Minister and you could have been the Man in the Nudge Nudge sketch from Monty Python?

I hope you don't feel too disappointed,

Happy birthday anyway,

Eric Idle

AN INSTRUMENT OF JOY

MARGARET MEAD to
ELIZABETH MEAD
January 11th, 1926

Margaret Mead was for
many years the leading
anthropologist on the
planet, thanks largely to
Coming of Age in Samoa,
a groundbreaking and
controversial book she wrote
after a research trip in 1925
in which a light was shone
on the previously alien lives
and relaxed sexual attitudes
of adolescent Samoan girls.
Although since contested,
Mead's findings were a
revelation, and in fact
have been credited with
influencing the sexual
revolution of the 1960s. In
1926, a year after setting
foot on the Samoan island of
T'au, Mead learnt of a sexual
awakening much closer to
home: that of her younger
sister, Elizabeth. This letter
of advice was her response.

Facing page:
American anthropologist
Dr Margaret Mead, 1928

Elizabeth dear, I've a good mind to punish you by writing back in pencil. You're a wretch to write in pencil on pink paper just when you're writing something very important that you particularly want me to read. Don't do it again.

I am glad you told me about the moonlight party, dear. It's the sort of thing that had to happen sometime and it might have been a great deal worse. As it was, it was a nice boy whom you like, and nothing that need worry you. There are two things I'd like to have you remember--or in fact several. The thrills you get from touching the body of another person are just as good and legitimate thrills as those you get at the opera. Only the ones which you get at the opera are all mixed up with your ideas of beauty and music and Life—and so they seem to you good and holy things. In the same way the best can only be had from the joys which life offers to our sense of touch (for sex is mostly a matter of the sense of touch) when we associate those joys with love and respect and understanding.

All the real tragedies of sex come from disassociation—either of the old maid who sternly refuses to think about sex at all until finally she can think about nothing else—and goes crazy—or of the man who goes from one wanton's arms to another seeking only the immediate sensation of the moment and never linking it up with other parts of his life. It is by the way in which sex—and under this I include warm demonstrative friendships with both sexes as well as love affairs proper with men—is linked with all the other parts of our lives, with our appreciation of music and our tenderness for little children, and most of all with our love for someone and the additional nearness to them which expression of love gives us, that sex itself is given meaning.

You must realize that your body has been given you as an instrument of joy—and tho you should choose most rigorously whose touch may make that instrument thrill and sing a thousand beautiful songs—you must never think it wrong of it to sing. For your body was made to sing to another's touch and the flesh itself is not wise to choose. It is the spirit within the body which must be stern and say—"No, you can not play on this my precious instrument. True it would sing for you. Your fingers are very clever at playing on such instruments—but I do not love you, nor respect you—and I will not have my body singing a tune which my soul cannot sing also." If you remember this, you will never be filled with disgust of any sort. *Any* touch may set the delicate chords humming—but it is your right to choose who shall really play a tune—and be very very sure of your choices first. To have given a kiss where only a handshake was justified by the love behind it—*that* is likely to leave a bad taste in your mouth.

And for the other part—about being boy crazy. Try to think of boys as people, some nice, some indifferent—not as a class. You aren't *girl* crazy are you? Then why should you be *boy* crazy? If a boy is an interesting *person* why, like him. If he isn't, don't. Think of him as an individual first and as a boy second. What kind of a person he is is a great deal more important than that he belongs to the other sex—after all so do some hundred million other individuals.

I am very proud of the way you are able to think thru the problems which life brings you—and of the way you meet them. And I consider it a great privilege to have you tell me about them. I'm so glad you are happy dear.

Very lovingly,

Margaret

WE PRESS YOU CLOSE AND KISS YOU WITH ALL OUR STRENGTH

ETHEL and JULIUS
ROSENBERG to THEIR SONS
June 19th, 1953

At New York's Sing Sing Prison on the evening of June 19th, 1953, married couple Ethel and Julius Rosenberg became the first Americans ever to be executed for espionage, sentenced to death thanks to a testimony from Ethel's brother, David Greenglass, which placed them at the centre of a Soviet spy ring. On the morning of their execution, Ethel and Julius wrote a letter to their two young sons, Robert and Michael. Three years earlier, whilst working on the Manhattan Project as a machinist, David had been arrested on suspicion of selling atomic secrets to a Soviet spy; keen to minimise his own punishment, he soon supplied names to the FBI and specifically recalled his sister typing out the stolen notes he had passed on. Years later, with his sister dead, David admitted that he had lied in court about her involvement in an effort to save the real typist, his pregnant wife, from imprisonment.

Facing page:
Michael Rosenberg reads
about his parents with his
brother Robert

June 19, 1953

Dearest Sweethearts, my most precious children,

Only this morning it looked like we might be together again after all. Now that his cannot be, I want so much for you to know all that I have come to know. Unfortunately, I may write only a few simple words; the rest your own lives must teach you, even as mine taught me.

At first, of course, you will grieve bitterly for us, but you will not grieve alone. That is our consolation and it must eventually be yours.

Eventually, too you must come to believe that life is worth the living. Be comforted that even now, with the end of ours slowly approaching, that we know this with a conviction that defeats the executioner!

Your lives must teach you, too, that good cannot really flourish in the midst of evil; that freedom and all the things that go to make up a truly satisfying and worthwhile life, must sometimes be purchased very dearly. Be comforted then that we were serene and understood with the deepest kind of understanding, that civilization had not as yet progressed to the point where life did not have to be lost for the sake of life; and that we were comforted in the sure knowledge that others would carry on after us.

We wish we might have had the tremendous joy and gratification of living our lives out with you. Your Daddy who is with me in these last momentous hours, sends his heart and all the love that is in it for his dearest boys. Always remember that we were innocent and could not wrong our conscience.

We press you close and kiss you with all our strength.

Lovingly,
DADDY AND MOMMY
JULIE   ETHEL

HOW DID YOU GET INVENTED?

ARCHBISHOP OF
CANTERBURY to LULU
March 24th, 2011

In 2011, journalist Alex
Renton's six-year-old
daughter, Lulu, wrote a brief
letter to God and tasked
her father with ensuring
that it reached the intended
recipient. Unsure of how to
deal with such a request,
Alex, a non-believer, sent
copies of the letter to family
members, Christian friends,
the local Scottish Episcopal
Church, the Church of
Scotland, and the Scottish
Catholic Church, all with
varying and unsatisfactory
degrees of success. It was
only when he wrote to the
Anglican Communion that
he finally received a letter
that so perfectly and gently
answered his daughter's
question. It was written
by Rowan Williams, then-
Archbishop of Canterbury.
Said Alex soon after:

"She listened quietly as I
read the Archbishop's letter
and it went down well. What
worked particularly was the
idea of 'God's story'.

'Well?' I asked when we
reached the end. 'What do
you think?' She thought
a little. 'Well, I have very
different ideas. But he has a
good one.'"

To God how did you get invented?

From Lulu

ARCHBISHOP
OF CANTERBURY

24 March 2011

Dear Lulu,

Your dad has sent on your letter and asked if I have any answers.

It's a difficult one! But I think God might reply a bit like this –

'Dear Lulu – Nobody invented me – but lots of people discovered me and were quite surprised. They discovered me when they looked round at the world and thought it was really beautiful or really mysterious and wondered where it came from. They discovered me when they were very very quiet on their own and felt a sort of peace and love they hadn't expected.

Then they invented ideas about me – some of them sensible and some of them not very sensible. From time to time I sent them some hints – specially in the life of Jesus – to help them get closer to what I'm really like.

But there was nothing and nobody around before me to invent me. Rather like somebody who writes a story in a book, I started making up the story of the world and eventually invented human beings like you who could ask me awkward questions!'

And then he'd send you lots of love and sign off.

I know he doesn't usually write letters, so I have to do the best I can on his behalf.

Lots of love from me too.

✝ Archbishop Rowan

WHY I AM AN ATHEIST

MINNIE PARRISH to BLUE-
GRASS BLADE
1903

In 1903, Kentucky-based
newspaper *Blue-grass
Blade* asked its readers to
write in and contribute to a
forthcoming feature named
"Why I am An Atheist".
Hundreds of letters soon
arrived and many were
subsequently reprinted in
the paper. Here is just one of
those replies. It was written
by Minerva Ola "Minnie"
Parrish, a 23-year-old
recently divorced mother
of four who later went on
to become one of the first
female doctors to practise
in North Texas. She passed
away in 1965.

Why I am an atheist

Because it has dawned upon me that it is right to be so, and upon
investigation I find no real evidence of the divine origin of the scriptures.
And because I cannot, as a refined and respectable woman, take to my
bosom as a daily guide a book of such low morals and degrading influences.
Written by a lot of priests, I cannot accept a salvation that is based wholly
upon the dreams of an ancient and superstitious people, with no proof save
blind faith.

Everything that so many people think transpires from the supernatural, and
many things that would really perplex the average mind, have a natural and
material foundation in the workings of the human mind; that is, things that
are not connected with our solar system.

It is ignorance of the scientific working of their own natures and mind that
keep so much "mystery" in the air; and as long as there is a mystery afloat
the people will ascribe it to the supernatural.

I am an Atheist because I know the Bible will not do to depend upon. I have
tried it, and found it wanting.

In fact, I found in the scriptures the origin of women's slayer, and that it was
one of God's main points to oppress women and keep them in the realms of
ignorance.

I am in the ranks of Liberalism because of its elevating principles, its broad
road to freedom of thought, speech, and investigation.

MINNIE O. PARRISH
23 years old
Leonard, Texas

Facing page:
Dr. Minerva Ola "Minnie"
Parrish

YOURS IN DISTRESS

ALAN TURING to NORMAN
ROUTLEDGE
February, 1952

Alan Turing was a human
being of exceptional
intelligence – a mathematical
genius – and worked as
one of the leading code-
breakers during World War
II. He is also considered to
be the "father of modern
computing" thanks to his
pioneering work in the
field of computer science.
In 1950, before the term
"artificial intelligence"
had been coined, he
posed the question, "Can
computers think?" and
proposed the Turing Test.
His achievements are
staggering. In 1952, he
was charged with gross
indecency after admitting to
a sexual relationship with
another man, and as a result
was told to choose either
imprisonment or chemical
castration as punishment. He
chose the latter. Alan Turing
was found dead on June 8th,
1954, a day after taking his
own life. He was aged just 41.

In 1952, shortly before
pleading guilty, Turing wrote
to his friend and fellow
mathematician, Norman
Routledge.

Hollymeade
Adlington Road
Wilmslow

My dear Norman,

I don't think I really do know much about jobs, except the one I had during the war, and that certainly did not involve any travelling. I think they do take on conscripts. It certainly involved a good deal of hard thinking, but whether you'd be interested I don't know. Philip Hall was in the same racket and on the whole, I should say, he didn't care for it. However I am not at present in a state in which I am able to concentrate well, for reasons explained in the next paragraph.

I've now got myself into the kind of trouble that I have always considered to be quite a possibility for me, though I have usually rated it at about 10:1 against. I shall shortly be pleading guilty to a charge of sexual offences with a young man. The story of how it all came to be found out is a long and fascinating one, which I shall have to make into a short story one day, but haven't the time to tell you now. No doubt I shall emerge from it all a different man, but quite who I've not found out.

Glad you enjoyed broadcast. Jefferson certainly was rather disappointing though. I'm afraid that the following syllogism may be used by some in the future.

Turing believes machines think
Turing lies with men
Therefore machines do not think

Yours in distress

Alan

Hollymeade
Adlington Rd
Wilmslow

[mid Feb. 1952 ?] AT

My dear Norman,

I don't think I really do know
much about jobs, except the one I had during the war,
and that certainly did not involve any travelling.
I think they do take on conscripts. It certainly involved
a good deal of hard thinking, but whether you'd be
interested I don't know. Philip was in the same
racket, and on the whole, I should say, didn't care
for it. However I am not at present in a state in
which I am able to concentrate well, for reasons
explained in next paragraph

I've now got myself into the kind of trouble
that I have always considered to be quite a
possibility for me, though I have usually rated it at

about 10:1 against. I shall shortly be pleading guilty to a charge of sexual offences with a young man. The story of how it all came to be found out is a long and fascinating one, which I shall leave to make into a short story one day, but have not time to tell you now. No doubt I shall emerge from it all a different man, but quite who I've not found out.

Glad you enjoyed broadcast. I certainly was rather disappointing now though. I'm rather afraid that the following syllogism may be used by some in the future

Turing believes machines think
Turing lies with men
Therefore machines do not think

Yours in distress

Alan

OH MY ASS BURNS LIKE FIRE!

MOZART to MARIANNE
November 5th, 1777

When he wasn't busy composing some of the most beautiful music ever to seduce the human ear, the legend that is Wolfgang Amadeus Mozart could often be found writing shockingly crude and often baffling letters to his family. The fine example seen here, admirably translated by Robert Spaethling, was penned to Mozart's 19-year-old cousin and possible love interest, Marianne – also known as "Betsie" ("little cousin") – in November of 1777, at which point the poop-loving musical genius was 21 years of age.

Note: The term "spuni cuni fait" was used in many of Mozart's letters. Its meaning is unknown.

Dearest cozz buzz!

I have received reprieved your highly esteemed writing biting, and I have noted doted that my uncle garfuncle, my aunt slant, and you too, are all well mell. We, too, thank god, are in good fettle kettle. Today I got a letter setter from my Papa Haha safely into my paws claws. I hope you too have gotten rotten my note quote that I wrote to you from Mannheim. So much the better, better the much so! But now for some thing more sensuble.

So sorry to hear that Herr Abbate Salate has had another stroke choke. But I hope with the help of God fraud the consequences will not be dire mire. You are writing fighting that you keep your criminal promise which you gave me before my departure from Augspurg, and will do it soon moon. Well, I will most likely find that regretable. You write further, indeed you let it all out, you expose yourself, you indicate to me, you bring me the news, you announce onto me, you state in broad daylight, you demand, you desire, you wish you want, you like, you command that I, too, should send you my Portrait. Eh bien, I shall mail fail it for sure. Oui, by the love of my skin, I shit on your nose, so it runs down your chin.

apropós. do you also have the spuni cuni fait?—what?—whether you still love me?—I believe it! so much the better, better the much so! Yes, that's the way of the world, I'm told, one has the purse, the other has the gold; whom do you side with?—with me, n'est-ce pas?—I believe it! Now things are even worse, apropós.

Wouldn't you like to visit Herr Gold-smith again?—but what for?—what?—nothing!—just to inquire, I guess, about the Spuni Cuni fait, nothing else, nothing else?—well, well, all right. Long live all those who, who—who—who—how does it go on?—I now wish you a good night, shit in your bed with all your might, sleep with peace on your mind, and try to kiss your own behind; I now go off to never-never land and sleep as much as I can stand. Tomorrow we'll speak freak sensubly with each other. Things I must you tell a lot of, believe it you hardly can, but hear tomorrow it already will you, be well in the meantime. Oh my ass burns like fire! what on earth is the meaning of this!—maybe muck wants to come out? yes, yes, muck, I know you, see you, taste you—and—what's this—is it possible? Ye Gods!—Oh ear of mine, are you deceiving me?—No, it's true—what a long and melancholic sound!—today is the write I fifth this letter. Yesterday I talked with the stern Frau Churfustin, and tomorrow, on the 6th, I will give a performance in her chambers, as the Furstin-Chur said to me herself. Now for something real sensuble!

A letter or letters addressed to me will come into your hands, and I must beg of you—where?—well a fox is no hare—yes there!—Now, where was I?—oh yes, now, I remember: letters, letters will come—but what kind of letters?—well now, letters for me, of course, I want to make sure that you send these to me; I will let you know where I'll be going from Mannheim. Now, Numero 2: I'm asking you, why not?—

I'm asking you, dearest numbskull, why not?—if you are writing anyway to Madame Tavernier in Munich, please include regards from me to the Mademoiselles Freysinger, why not?—Curious! why not?—and to the Younger, I mean Frauline Josepha, tell her I'll send my sincere apologies, why not?—why should I not apologize?—Curious!—I don't know why not?—I want to apologize that I haven't yet sent her the sonata that I promised, but I will send it as soon as possible, why not?—what—why not?—why shouldn't I send it?—why should I not transmit it?—why not?—Curious! I wouldn't know why not?—well, then you'll do me this favor;—why not?—why shouldn't you do this for me?—why not?, it's so strange! After all, I'll do it to you too, if you want me to, why not?—why shouldn't I do it to you?—curious! why not?—I wouldn't know why not?—and don't forget to send my Regards to the Papa and Mama of the 2 young ladies, for it is terrible to be letting and forgetting one's father and mother. Later, when the sonata is finished,—I will send you the same, and a letter to boot; and you will be so kind as to forward the same to Munich.

And now I must close and that makes me morose. Dear Herr Uncle, shall we go quickly to the Holy Cross Covent and see whether anybody is still up?—we won't stay long, just ring the bell, that's all. Now I must relate to you a sad story that happened just this minute. As I am in the middle of my best writing, I hear a noise in the street. I stop writing—get up, go to the window—and—the noise is gone—I sit down again, start writing once more—I have barely written ten words when I hear the noise again—I rise—but as I rise, I can still hear something but very faint—it smells like something burning—wherever I go it stinks, when I look out the window, the smell goes away, when I turn my head back to the room, the smell comes back—finally My Mama says to me: I bet you let one go?—I don't think so, Mama. yes, yes, I'm quite certain, I put it to the test, stick my finger in my ass, then put it to my nose, and—there is the proof! Mama was right!

Now farwell, I kiss you 10000 times and I remain as always your

Old young Sauschwanz
Wolfgang Amadé Rosenkranz
From us two Travelers a thousand
Regards to my uncle and aunt.
To every good friend I send
My greet feet; addio nitwit.
Love true true true until the grave,
If I live that long and do behave.

Mannheim, 5 November, 1777

1

Allerliebstes bestes Schwesterl!

Ich habe über mir so was, schreiben richtig erhalten sollen, und...

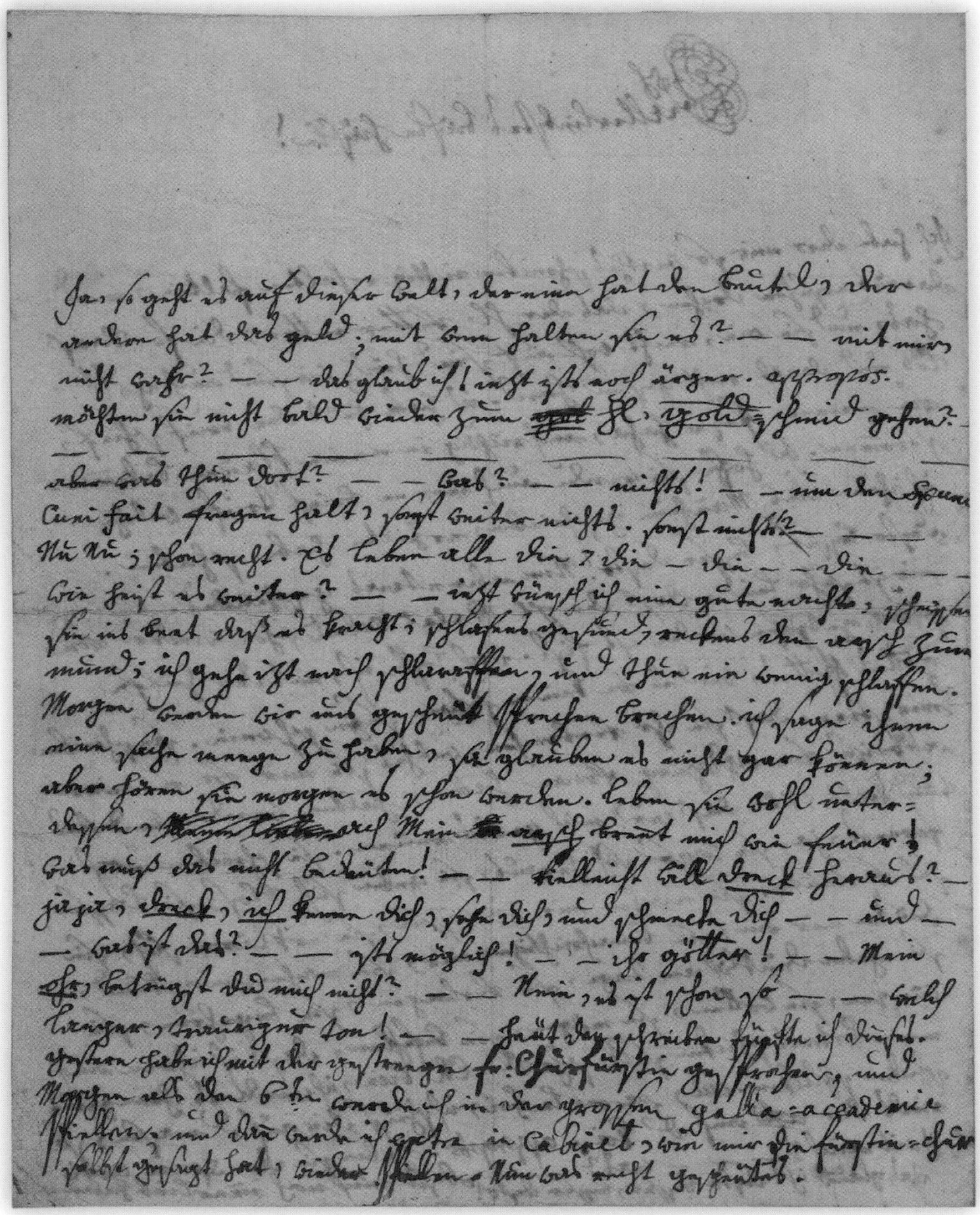

Ja, so geht es auf dieser welt, der eine hat den beutel, der
andern hat das geld; mit wem halten sie es? — — mit mir
nicht wahr? — — das glaub ich! nicht itzt noch ärger. apropos.
möchten sie nicht bald wieder zum ~~gol~~ H: gold=schmid gehen? —
— — — — — — — — — — — — — — —
aber was thun dort? — — was? — — nichts! — — um den spuni
cuni fait fragen halt, sonst weiter nichts. sonst nichts? — —
Nu nu; schon recht. Es leben alle die, die — die — — die — —
wie heist es weiter? — — itzt wünsch ich eine gute nacht, scheissen
sie ins bett dass es kracht; schlafens gesund, reckens den arsch zum
mund; ich gehe itzt noch schwanzen, und thue ein wenig schlafen.
Morgen werden wir uns gescheut sprechen brechen. ich sage ihnen
eine sache menge zu haben, sie glauben es nicht gar können;
aber hören sie morgen es schon werden. leben sie wohl unter=
dessen, ~~[illegible]~~ ach mein ~~a~~ arsch brennt mich wie feuer!
was muss das nicht bedeuten! — — vielleicht will dreck heraus? —
ja ja, dreck, ich kenne dich, sehe dich, und schmecke dich — — und —
— was ist das? — — ists möglich! — — ihr götter! — — Mein
ohr, betrügst du mich nicht? — — Nein, es ist schon so — — welch
langer, trauriger ton! — — heut den schreibe ich dieses.
gestern habe ich mit der gestrengen fr: Churfürstin gesprochen, und
Morgen als den 6ten werde ich in der grossen galla=academie
spiellen; und dann werde ich extra in cabinet, wie mir die fürstin=chur
selbst gesagt hat, wieder spiellen. Nun was recht gescheutes.

z: es wird ein brief, oder es werden briefe an mich ich ihnen händ kommen, wo ich sie bitte doch — — wer? — ja, kein fuchs ist kein Hase, ja das — Nun, wo bin ich den geblieben? — — ja, recht, logen komen z. — ja ja, sie werden komen — ja, wer? wer wird komen — ja izt fällt mir ein. briefe, briefe werden komen — aber was für briefe? — ja nu, briefe an mich halt, die bitte ich mir gewis zu schicken; ich werde ihnen schon nachricht geben wo ich von Mannheim weiter hin gehe, izt numero 2. ich bitte sie, warum nicht? — ich bitte sie — — — — — — — warum nicht? — deß wen sie schreiben an die Mad: da venier nach München schreiben, ein Compliment von mir an die 2 Mad:elles fränzsinger schreiben, warum nicht? — Curios! warum nicht? — — und die Jüngere, nämlich die sel: Josepha bitte ich halt recht um verzeihung, warum nicht? — warum sollte ich sie nicht um verzeihung bitten? — Curios! — ich bitte sie nicht warum nicht? — ich bitte sie halt recht sehr um verzeihung, deß ich ihr bisher die versprochene sonata noch nicht geschickt habe, aber ich werde sie, so bald es möglich ist überschicken. warum nicht? — — das? — — warum nicht? — — warum soll ich sie nicht überschicken? — warum soll ich sie nicht schicken? — Curios! ich bitte sie nicht warum nicht? — — warum nicht? — werden sie mir thun, — — nie, also, darum gefallen sie mir nicht thun? — — warum nicht? — — warum sollen sie mir nicht thun? — — warum nicht, Curios! ich thun? darnach zu thun, wen sie wollen, warum nicht? — — warum sollen ich sie ihnen nicht thun? — Curios! warum nicht? — ich bitte sie nicht warum nicht? — —

TERRY TOMA

DAWN POWELL to MABEL
POWELL POCOCK and
PHYLLIS POWELL COOK
April 15th, 1949

American author Dawn
Powell was born in Ohio in
1896. Her early childhood
was fraught with difficulty,
the pain caused by the death
of her mother when she was
seven sadly compounded
by the introduction of an
abusive replacement in
the form of her father's
aggressive new wife. But
Dawn persevered, going
on to become a prolific
writer of countless novels,
short stories and plays,
many of which remained
underappreciated until
long after her death, and
of hundreds of entertaining
letters that often bring
to mind the very best of
Dorothy Parker. In 1949,
after years of health
problems, doctors finally
removed from her chest a
teratoma – a type of tumour
often containing hair, bone,
and even eyes – and as she
recovered in hospital, with
nothing else to do, she wrote
to her sisters with a typically
amusing account of the
ordeal.

Dear Phyllis and Mabel:

Here I am--dismissed private nurses, washed my own hair and had my ass out for iron shots like a little beaver by 7 a.m. I could go home but Dr. Solley thinks I should have my blood count up with some iron and sleep.

Here is the family scandal I must now reveal. This here cyst (dermoid) or terra toma is a twin. That is, it is my own frustrated twin, a type of cyst that occurs (not very often) in the chest or other sections--even the head of a man or woman. It is made up of parts of various things--hair, teeth, sometimes an eye or a jawbone. It lives off your heart and lung and is "benign"--unless it gets overgrown and shoves out the organs you need which mine started to do. It was as large as a grapefruit and had cut off all but ⅓ of my lung space so it was about ready to shove me out. These twin cysts run in the family. (I shouldn't be surprised but what Grandma's choking spells, etc., indicated one.) They are simply parasites. Well, I was so pleased to hear about my twin Terry Toma that it kept me fascinated right along. It had the staff here fascinated too, so the operation--a five-hour job with three transfusions (3 pts. R.H. negative blood @ $105!)--had quite a gallery of chest experts. The surgeon is one of the best thoracic surgeons--Alexander Ada, a fine-looking, keen, very distinguished man about 45. The nurses who were witnesses said he lost six pounds, also that he was in my chest up to his shoulders. Collapsed a lung, removed a rib, then found cyst glued to heart so it took 45 minutes to slice it off there, then it was glued to lung. I was put on oxygen tank and had a tube draining my chest off and a needle infusing glucose in my arm and a behind full of penicillin jabs. In fact, it was something but I was not at all nervous because (a) I was in the best possible hands and (b) I didn't think I'd come out of it anyway so what could I do...?

Dr. Solley, the gay, sweet doctor in charge, is a best friend of my best friends the Murphys and Dr. Passos, so they are busy cabling him about me and it's nice to know the doctor is more than medically involved. I no longer need special nurses and today my entire bandage is removed. (The incision was made sort of below the right armpit toward the back--26 stitches.) Anyway, if it hadn't been for all they learned about chest surgery in the war, I would not be in this fine shape. If I had had it done before they wouldn't have known a lot of fancy precautionary touches. Anyway it just started growing and shoving this year, although Dr. Witt told me all about it 20 years ago with my first attack. I don't even need to be careful, Dr. Ada says. My twin thrives on whiskey, but all I'm giving him is steak and ice cream. Anyway I get all bandages off today. I had nine broken ribs before and probably Terry would keep cracking them if I let him. I was very glad on hearing of my twin that he hadn't popped out of my chest during a formal dinner party, me in my strapless and him grabbing my martini. I rather thought he'd come out saying, "Okay Louis, drop the gun."

Anyway, I breathe wonderfully as if I'd never breathed before. I didn't write Auntie May as I thought you'd tell her what was suitable for a growing girl. By the way Dr. Passos has been in several times after a trip he made for Life Magazine to Atlanta, Ga., also Johnson City, Tenn. He said the hills around J.C. were the most beautiful he'd ever seen. Is that your stomping ground?

I wish Dr. Ada could yank out Mabel's pyloris. I really am tired of pain and think Mabel should be promoted past it. I had my share of gas and rhubarb and soda. Anyway, you two ladies start looking in your chests for further twins. I was hoping Terry Toma had saved up a fortune for me. He's still being analyzed in the pathology dept., so I'm not sure what all he had in him but you'll both get your share, fair and square.

Much love,
Dawn

P.S. Joe is spending Easter with Jojo. I will go home Tuesday, I guess.

Facing page:
Author Dawn Powell at the
Cafe Lafayette, 1946

Letter No. 081

DO NOT REMAIN NAMELESS TO YOURSELF

RICHARD FEYNMAN to
KOICHI MANO
February 3rd, 1966

In 1966, nine years after
gaining his PhD with a
dissertation titled "The
Self-Energy of the Scalar
Nucleon", physicist Koichi
Mano wrote a congratulatory
letter to Richard Feynman,
the man who had originally
taught him at the California
Institute of Technology
and, more recently, joint
recipient of the Nobel
Prize in Physics for his
pioneering work in quantum
electrodynamics. Feynman
replied with an enquiry
about Mano's current job,
to which Mano responded
that he was "studying
the Coherence theory
with some applications
to the propagation of
electromagnetic waves
through turbulent
atmosphere [...] a humble
and down-to-earth type
of problem". Feynman
responded with this letter.

Facing page:
American theoretical physicist
Richard Feynman, 1965

Dear Koichi,

I was very happy to hear from you, and that you have such a position in the Research Laboratories.

Unfortunately your letter made me unhappy for you seem to be truly sad. It seems that the influence of your teacher has been to give you a false idea of what are worthwhile problems. The worthwhile problems are the ones you can really solve or help solve, the ones you can really contribute something to. A problem is grand in science if it lies before us unsolved and we see some way for us to make some headway into it. I would advise you to take even simpler, or as you say, humbler, problems until you find some you can really solve easily, no matter how trivial. You will get the pleasure of success, and of helping your fellow man, even if it is only to answer a question in the mind of a colleague less able than you. You must not take away from yourself these pleasures because you have some erroneous idea of what is worthwhile.

You met me at the peak of my career when I seemed to you to be concerned with problems close to the gods. But at the same time I had another Ph.D. Student (Albert Hibbs) was on how it is that the winds build up waves blowing over water in the sea. I accepted him as a student because he came to me with the problem he wanted to solve. With you I made a mistake, I gave you the problem instead of letting you find your own; and left you with a wrong idea of what is interesting or pleasant or important to work on (namely those problems you see you may do something about). I am sorry, excuse me. I hope by this letter to correct it a little.

I have worked on innumerable problems that you would call humble, but which I enjoyed and felt very good about because I sometimes could partially succeed. For example, experiments on the coefficient of friction on highly polished surfaces, to try to learn something about how friction worked (failure). Or, how elastic properties of crystals depends on the forces between the atoms in them, or how to make electroplated metal stick to plastic objects (like radio knobs). Or, how neutrons diffuse out of Uranium. Or, the reflection of electromagnetic waves from films coating glass. The development of shock waves in explosions. The design of a neutron counter. Why some elements capture electrons from the L-orbits, but not the K-orbits. General theory of how to fold paper to make a certain type of child's toy (called flexagons). The energy levels in the light nuclei. The theory of turbulence (I have spent several years on it without success). Plus all the "grander" problems of quantum theory.

No problem is too small or too trivial if we can really do something about it.

You say you are a nameless man. You are not to your wife and to your child. You will not long remain so to your immediate colleagues if you can answer their simple questions when they come into your office. You are not nameless to me. Do not remain nameless to yourself – it is too sad a way to be. Know your place in the world and evaluate yourself fairly, not in terms of your naïve ideals of your own youth, nor in terms of what you erroneously imagine your teacher's ideals are.

Best of luck and happiness.

Sincerely,
Richard P. Feynman

I SEE HIM IN THE STAR

EMILY DICKINSON to
SUSAN DICKINSON
October, 1883

Born in August of 1875 in Amherst, Massachusetts, Thomas Gilbert Dickinson was the third child of Susan and Austin Dickinson and by all accounts an adored member of their large family. Indeed, judging by the affection she showered upon him during his all-too-short existence, it was his smitten auntie and next door neighbour, celebrated poet Emily Dickinson, who was particularly taken with Thomas. Tragically, many hearts were forever broken on October 5th of 1883, when Thomas, still only eight, died following a battle with typhoid fever. Soon after, in the midst of attempting to deal with her own grief, Emily wrote what is arguably her greatest letter: one of condolence to her sister-in-law.

Dear Sue –

The Vision of Immortal Life has been fulfilled –
How simply at the last the Fathom comes! The Passenger and not the Sea, we find surprises us –
Gilbert rejoiced in Secrets –
His Life was panting with them – With what menace of Light he cried "Dont tell, Aunt Emily"! Now my ascended Playmate must instruct me. Show us, prattling Preceptor, but the way to thee!
He knew no niggard moment – His Life was full of Boon –
The Playthings of the Dervish were not so wild as his –
No Crescent was this Creature – He traveled from the Full –
Such soar, but never set –
I see him in the Star, and meet his sweet velocity in everything that flies – His Life was like the Bugle, which winds itself away, his Elegy an Echo – his Requiem Ecstacy –
Dawn and Meridian in one.
Wherefore would he wait, wronged only of Night, which he left for us –
Without a speculation, our little Ajax spans the whole –

Pass to thy Rendezvous of Light,
Pangless except for us –
Who slowly ford the Mystery
Which thou hast leaped across!

Emily –

Dear Sue.
The Vision
of. Immortal
Life has been
fulfilled.
How simply at
the last the
fathom comes!
The Passenger
and not the
Sea, we find
surprises us.
Gilbert rejoiced
in Secrets.
His Life was
panting with them.
With what menace

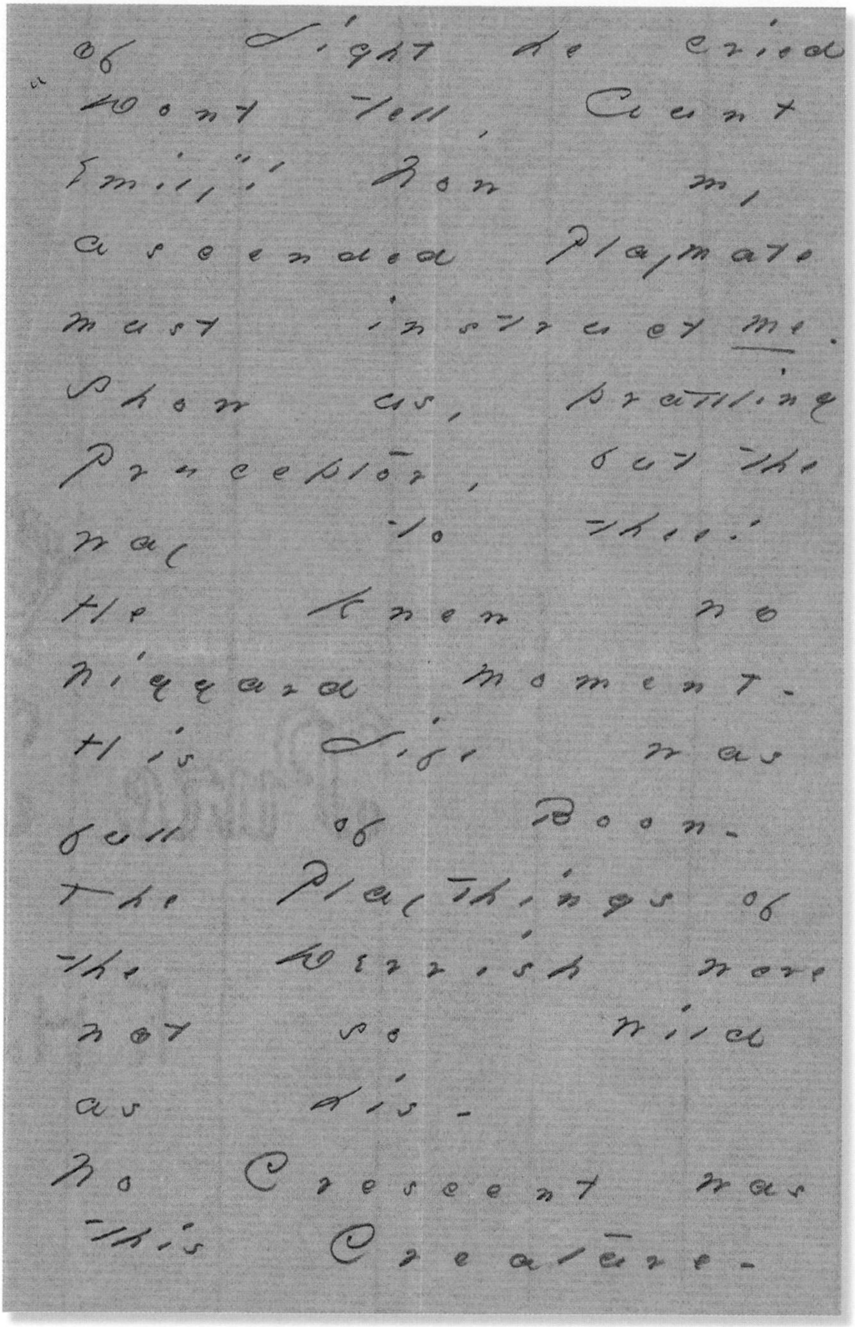

of Light he cried
"Wont tell, Count
Emili" her m,
ascended Playmate
must instruct me.
Show us, prattling
Preceptor, but the
way to thee!
He knew no
niggard moment.
His Life was
full of Boon.
The Playthings of
the Dervish were
not so rich
as his -
No Crescent was
this Creature -

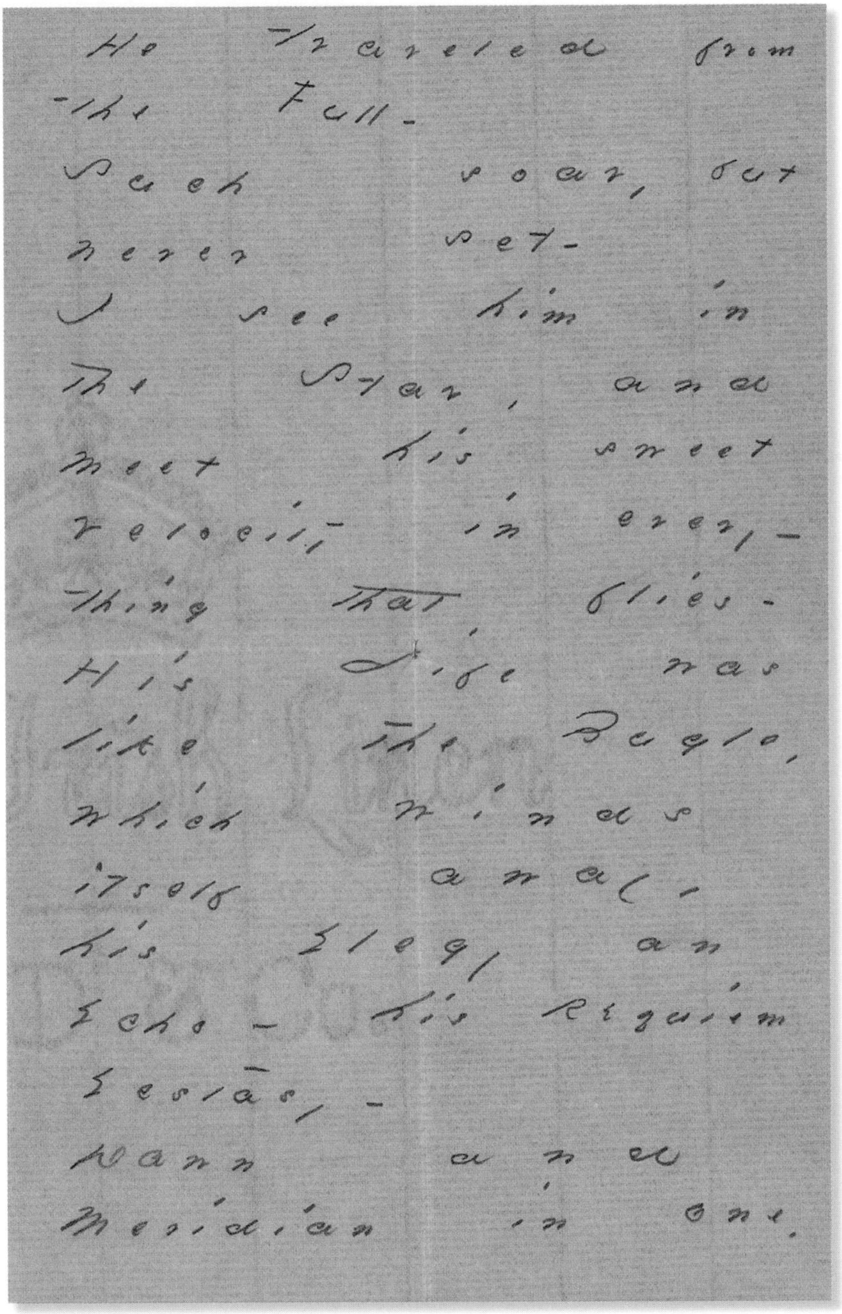

He traveled from
the Full -
Such soar, but
never set -
I see him in
the Star, and
meet his sweet
velocity in every -
thing that flies -
His life was
like the Bugle,
which winds
itself away,
his Elegy an
Echo - his Requiem
ecstasy, -
Dawn and
Meridian in one.

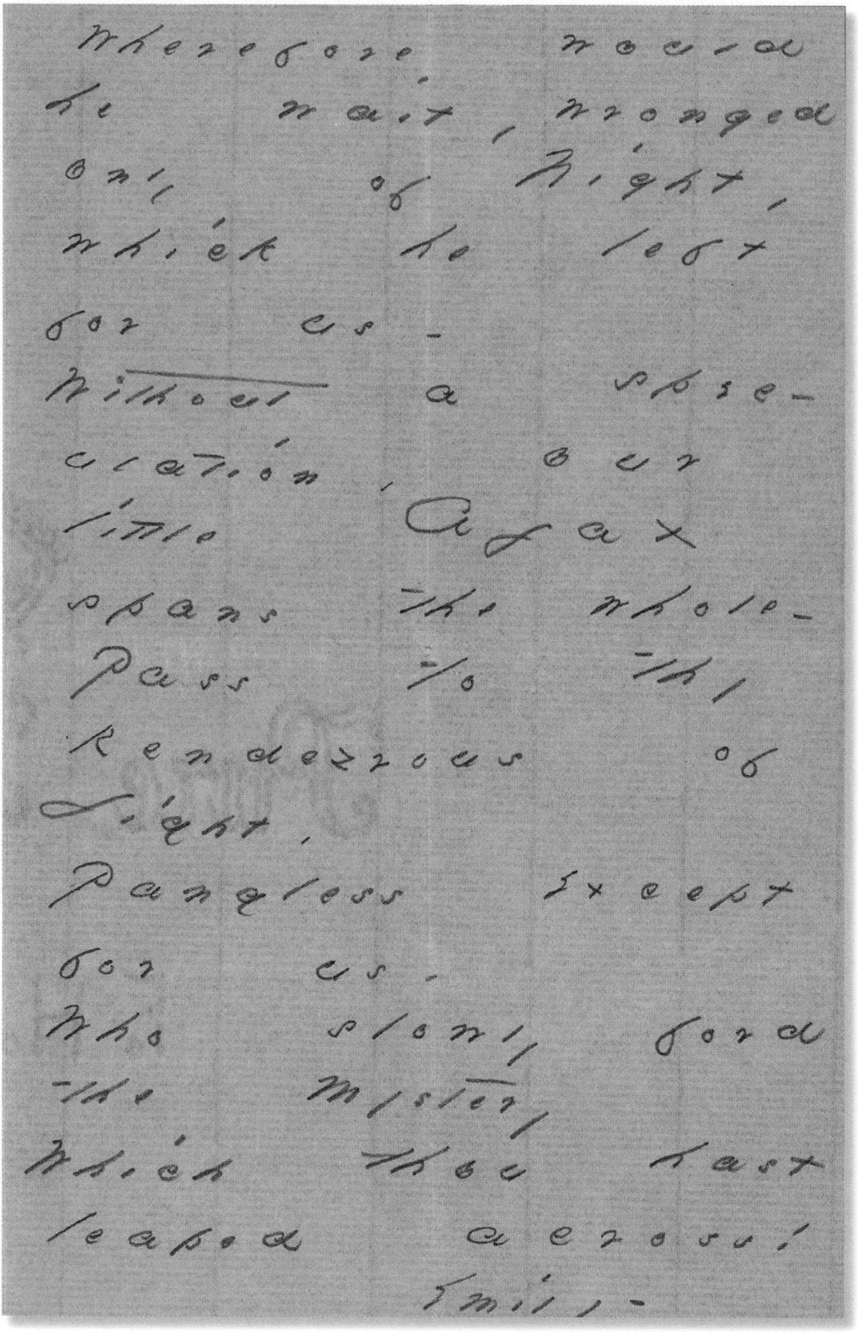

Wherefore need
he wait, wronged
only of Right,
which he left
for us –
Without a appre-
ciation, our
little Ajax
spans the whole-
Pass to thy
Rendezvous of
Light,
Pangless except
for us,
Who slow, ford
the Mystery
Which thou hast
leaped across -
Emi-

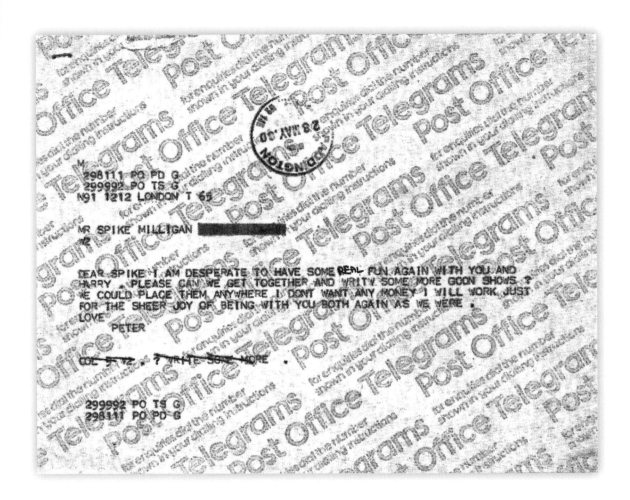

I AM DESPERATE TO HAVE SOME REAL FUN

PETER SELLERS to SPIKE MILLIGAN
May 28th, 1980

In January 1960, nine years and 250 episodes after first being introduced to a baffled but delighted audience, *The Goon Show*'s final instalment was broadcast on BBC radio, much to the dismay of its many fans. Written chiefly by Spike Milligan, the show's ten series had been a surreal mixture of sketches, music and general nonsense that went on to make stars of its three main actors – Milligan, Peter Sellers and Harry Secombe – and become one of British comedy's most influential and adored creations. Judging by this touching telegram, sent by an ill Sellers to his ex-co-stars in 1980, it wasn't just the listeners who mourned *The Goon Show*. Tragically, two months after sending it, hours before a planned reunion dinner with Milligan and Secombe, Sellers suffered a heart attack. He passed away two days later.

THE WHITE HOUSE

ABIGAIL ADAMS to HER
DAUGHTER
November 21st, 1800

In November of 1800, shortly
after her husband moved in,
55-year-old Abigail Adams
became the first First Lady
to live at the White House in
the newly designated capital
city, Washington D.C. Both
the house and city were still
unfinished but "habitable",
and Adams was clearly
frustrated. A few days
after arriving, she wrote
a letter to her daughter
and described the now
unimaginable scene.

Facing page:
Earliest known daguerrotype
of the White House, 1846

Washington, 21 November 1800

My Dear Child:

I arrived here on Sunday last, and without meeting with any accident worth
noticing, except losing ourselves when we left Baltimore and going eight or nine
miles on the Frederick road, by which means we were obliged to go the other eight
through woods, where we wandered two hours without finding a guide or the path.
Fortunately, a straggling black came up with us, and we engaged him as a guide to
extricate us out of our difficulty; but woods are all you can see from Baltimore until
you reach the city, which is only so in name. Here and there is a small cot, without
a glass window, interspersed amongst the forests, through which you travel miles
without seeing any human being. In the city there are buildings enough, if they
were compact and finished, to accommodate Congress and those attached to it; but
as they are, and scattered as they are, I see no great comfort for them. The river,
which runs up to Alexandria, is in full view of my window, and I see the vessels as
they pass and repass. The house is upon a grand and superb scale, requiring about
thirty servants to attend and keep the apartments in proper order, and perform the
ordinary business of the house and stables; an establishment very well proportioned
to the President's salary. The lighting of the apartments, from the kitchen to parlors
and chambers, is a tax indeed; and the fires we are obliged to keep to secure us
from daily agues is another very cheering comfort. To assist us in this great castle,
and render less attendance necessary, bells are wholly wanting, not one single one
being hung through the whole house, and promises are all you can obtain. This is
so great an inconvenience that I know not what to do, or how to do. The ladies from
Georgetown and in the city have many of them visited me. Yesterday
I returned fifteen visits--but such a place as Georgetown appears--why, our Milton
is beautiful. But no comparisons--if they will put me up some bells and let me have
wood enough to keep fires, I design to be pleased. I could content myself almost
anywhere three months; but surrounded with forests, can you believe that wood is
not to be had because people cannot be found to cut and cart it? Briesler entered
into a contract with a man to supply him with wood. A small part, a few cords only,
has he been able to get. Most of that was expended to dry the walls of the house
before we came in, and yesterday the man told him it was impossible for him to
procure it to be cut and carted. He has had recourse to coals; but we cannot get
grates made and set. We have, indeed, come into a new country.

You must keep all this to yourself, and, when asked how I like it, say that I write you
the situation is beautiful, which is true. The house is made habitable, but there is
not a single apartment finished, and all withinside, except the plastering, has been
done since Briesler came. We have not the least fence, yard, or other convenience,
without, and the great unfinished audience room I made a drying room of, to hang
up the clothes in. The principal stairs are not up, and will not be this winter. Six
chambers are made comfortable; two are occupied by the President and Mr. Shaw;

two lower rooms, one for a common parlor, and one for a levee room. Upstairs there is the oval room, which is designed for the drawing room, and has the crimson furniture in it. It is a very handsome room now; but, when completed, it will be beautiful. If the twelve years, in which this place has been considered as the future seat of government, had been improved, as they would have been if in New England, very many of the present inconveniences would have been removed. It is a beautiful spot, capable of every improvement, and the more I view it, the more I am delighted with it.

Since I sat down to write, I have been called down to a servant from Mount Vernon, with a billet from Major Custis, and a haunch of venison, and a kind, congratulatory letter from Mrs. Lewis, upon my arrival in the city, with Mrs. Washington's love, inviting me to Mount Vernon, where, health permitting, I will go before I leave this place.

Affectionately, your mother

YOUR ORGANIZATION HAS FAILED

ELEANOR ROOSEVELT to DAR
February 26th, 1939

Formed in 1890, the DAR (Daughters of the American Revolution) is an organisation whose members are all women descended from those who fought for American Independence, and in 1939, in accordance with a policy that prohibited African Americans from performing on their premises, they refused to allow celebrated musician Marian Anderson to sing at the DAR Constitution Hall. The decision caused uproar, but the DAR stood firm. As a result, and to everyone's surprise, First Lady Eleanor Roosevelt immediately resigned from the organisation by way of this letter and then invited Anderson to sing in front of the Lincoln Memorial. 75,000 people attended.

February 26, 1939.

My dear Mrs. Henry M. Robert, Jr.:

I am afraid that I have never been a very useful member of the Daughters of the American Revolution, so I know it will make very little difference to you whether I resign, or whether I continue to be a member of your organization.

However, I am in complete disagreement with the attitude taken in refusing Constitution Hall to a great artist. You have set an example which seems to me unfortunate, and I feel obliged to send in to you my resignation. You had an opportunity to lead in an enlightened way and it seems to me that your organization has failed.

I realize that many people will not agree with me, but feeling as I do this seems to me the only proper procedure to follow.

Very sincerely yours,
Eleanor Roosevelt

Facing page:
Celebrated American opera singer
Marian Anderson, c. 1950

THE CHAIRMAN
OF THE
CIVIL AERONAUTICS BOARD
WASHINGTON, D. C. 20428

June 16, 1977

MEMORANDUM

TO: Bureau and Office Heads
        Division and Section Chiefs

CC: Board Members

FROM: Chairman Alfred E. Kahn

SUBJECT: The Style of Board Orders and Chairman's Letters

One of my peculiarities, which I must beg you to indulge if I am to retain my sanity (possibly at the expense of yours!) is an abhorrence of the artificial and hyper-legal language that is sometimes known as bureaucratese or gobbledygook.

The disease is almost universal, and the fight against it endless. But it is a fight worth making, and I ask your help in this struggle.

May I ask you, please, to try very hard to write Board orders and, even more so, drafts of letters for my signature, in straightforward, quasi-conversational, humane prose -- as though you are talking to or communicating with real people. I once asked a young lawyer who wanted us to say "we deem it inappropriate" to try that kind of language out on his children -- and if they did not drive him out of the room with their derisive laughter, to disown them.

I suggest the test is a good one: try reading some of the language you use aloud, and ask yourself how your friends would be likely to react. (And then decide, on the basis of their reactions, whether you still want them as friends.)

I cannot possibly in a single communication give you more than a small fraction of the kinds of usages I have in mind. Here are just a few:

ON BUREAUCRATESE AND GOBBLEDYGOOK

ALFRED KAHN to HIS COLLEAGUES
June 16th, 1977

As a result of his influential stint as chairman of the now-defunct Civil Aeronautics Board in the 1970s, economist Alfred Kahn rightly became known as the "Father of Deregulation". However, he also made a lasting impression on many due to the wider publication – initially in the *Washington Star*, and then the *Post* – of this internal memo, sent by Kahn to his colleagues at the CAB shortly after taking the helm and circulated as a call for clearer written communications within the organisation. Little did Kahn know, but this document would soon attract praise from far and wide. According to Kahn's obituary in the *New York Times*, January 2011:

It generated a marriage proposal from a Boston Globe columnist, who gushed: "Alfred Kahn, I love you. I know you're in your late 50s and are married, but let's run away together." A Singapore newspaper suggested that Mr. Kahn be awarded a Nobel Prize. A Kansas City newspaper urged him to run for president. And, shortly after the memo's appearance, he was appointed to the usage panel of the American Heritage Dictionary, a position he held until his death.

1. One of our recent show cause orders contained this language: "all interested persons be and they hereby are directed to show cause. . . ." The underlined words are obviously redundant, as well as archaic.

2. Every time you are tempted to use "herein," "hereinabove," "hereinunder," or similarly, "therein" and its corresponding variants, try "here" or "there" or "above" or "below" and see if it doesn't make just as much sense.

3. The passive voice is wildly overused in government writing. Typically, its purpose is to conceal information: one is less likely to be jailed if one says "he was hit by a stone," than "I hit him with a stone." The active voice is far more forthright, direct, and humane. (There are, of course, some circumstances in which the use of the passive is unavoidable; please try to confine it to those situations.)

4. This one is, I recognize, a matter of taste: some people believe in maintaining standards of the language and others (like the late but unlamented editor of Webster's Third International) do not. But unless you feel strongly, would you please try to remember that "data" was for more than two thousand years and is still regarded by most literate people as plural (the singular is "datum"), and that (this one goes back even longer) the singular is "criterion," and "criteria" is plural. Also, that for at least from the 17th through most of the 20th century, "presently" meant "soon" or "immediately" and not "now." The use of "presently" in the latter context is another pomposity: why not "now?" Or, if necessary, "currently?"

5. Could you possibly try to make the introduction of letters somewhat less pompous than "this is in reference to your letter dated May 42, 1993, regarding (or concerning, or in regard to, or with reference to). . . ." That just doesn't sound as though it is coming from a human being. Why not, for example, "The practice of which you complain in your letter of May 42 is one that has troubled me for a long time." Or "I have looked into the question you raise in your letter of October 14, and am happy to be able to report . . . ." Or something like that?

6. Why use "regarding" or "concerning" or "with regard to," when the simple word "about" would do just as well? Unless you are trying to impress someone: but are you sure you want to impress anyone who would be impressed by such circumlocutions? There is a similar pompous tendency to use "prior to," when what you really mean is "before."

"Prior to" should be used only when in fact the thing that comes before is, in a sense, a condition of what follows, as in the expression "a prior condition."

I know "requesting," is considered more genteel than "asking," but "asking" is more forthright. Which do you want to be?

7. One of my pet peeves is the rampant misuse of "hopefully." That word is an adverb, and makes sense only as it modifies a verb, and means "with hope." It is possible to walk hopefully into a room, if one is going into the room with the hope of finding something (or not finding something) there. It is not intelligent to say "hopefully the criminal will make his identity known," because the meaning is not that he will do so with hope in his heart, and he is the subject of the verb "make."

8. My last imposition on you for today is the excessive use of "appropriate" or "inappropriate," when what the writer really means is either "legal" or "illegal," "proper" or "improper," "desirable" or "undesirable," "fitting" or "not fitting," or simply "this is what I want (or do not want) to do."

9. A final example of pomposity, probably, is this memorandum itself.

I have heard it said that style is not substance, but without style what is substance?

I THINK I NO HOW TO MAKE PEOPLE OR ANIMALS ALIVE

ANTHONY HOLLANDER to
BLUE PETER
June 29th, 1973

In June of 1973, spurred on by the recent discovery of a dying bird in his garden, nine-year-old Anthony Hollander wrote to the presenters of the BBC's much-loved children's television show *Blue Peter* and asked for assistance in his quest to "make people or animals alive". Soon after, an encouraging response arrived, written by the programme's editor, Biddy Baxter.

Thirty-five years later, in 2008, the very same Anthony Hollander, now Professor of Rheumatology and Tissue Engineering at the University of Bristol, played a key role in a record-breaking feat of surgery: the successful implantation of an artificially-grown windpipe into a 30-year-old Colombian woman named Claudia Castillo. He has since said of the letter and response:

"If [Biddy Baxter's] letter had shown any hint of ridicule or disbelief I might perhaps never have trained to become a medical scientist or been driven to achieve the impossible dream, and really make a difference to a human being's life. I remember being thrilled at the time to have been taken seriously. Actually, even nowadays I am thrilled when people take my ideas seriously."

29th June

Dear Val, Jhon, Peter and Lesslie,

This may seem very strange, but I think I no how to make people or animals alive. Why Im teling you is because I cant get the things I need.

A list of what I need.

1. Diagram of how evreything works. [inside youre body.]
2. Model of a heart split in half. [both halvs.]
3. The sort of sering they yous for cleaning ears. [Tsering must be very very clean.]
4. Tools for cutting people open.
5. Tools for stiches.
6. Fiberglass box, 8 foot tall, 3 foot width.

[DIAGRAM]

7. Picture of a man showing all the arteries.

Sorry but in number 6 in the list the box needs lid. If you do get them on 1st March I can pay £10, £11, £12, £13 or £14.

Send your answer to me,
[address redacted]

Love from
Anthony Peter Hollander

P.S. Could I please have all your Autographs.

2ª ᴱᴴ June,

Dear val, Jhon, Peter and Lesslie,

This, May seem very strange but I think I no how to make people or animals alive. Why Im teling you is because I cant get the things I need.

A List of what I need.

1; Diagram of how everything works, [inside youre body.]

2; Model of a heart split in half. [both halvs.]

3; The sort of sering they yous for cleaning ears, [sering must be very very clean.]

4; Tools for cutting people open.

5; Tools for stiches,

6; Fiberglass box, 8 foot tall, 3 foot width.

[8 foot]

3.?
foot

3 foot.

[8 foot]

7; Picture of a man showing all the Arteries.

P, t, Or

Sorry but in number 6
in the List the box needs a
lid. If you do get them on ~~Feb~~
~~March~~ ~~the~~ 1st March I can pay
~~they~~ £10, £11, £12, £13 or £14.
send your ~~at~~ answer to me
~~as your gra~~

Love ~~fro~~ from
Anthony peter
Hollander,

P.S. could I please have all
your Autographs,

cehre fue

August, 1973

Dear Anthony,

Thank you very much for your letter. It
was nice to hear from you again after such a
long time, and we are sorry we have been
delayed replying. We are receiving over
4,000 letters every week and are having
difficulty answering them as quickly as
we would like.

We were interested to hear that you think
you know how to make living people - and your
list of necessary items intrigued us! We are
sorry we can't help you at all, but we wondered
if you had thought of talking to your family
doctor - he might be glad to help you with
some diagrams and other information.

We are sending you a photograph of the "Blue
Peter" team - it has been signed specially for
you.

With best wishes from Valerie, John, Peter,
Lesley and all of us on the programme.

Yours sincerely,

(Biddy Baxter)
Editor, "Blue Peter"

Anthony Hollander,
7 Bigwood Road,
London, N.W.11.

P.S. "Blue Peter" will be back
on Monday, 10th September!

jo

Sir,

The publishers, Michael Joseph, have asked me to write my autobiography and I'd be grateful if you could give me any information about my whereabouts and behaviour between 1960 and 1974.

Jeffrey Bernard

Daily Mirror

Mirror Group Newspapers Limited

Holborn Circus London EC1P 1DQ
Switchboard: 01-353 0246
Direct Line: 01-822 3.**544**

Telegrams: Mirror London EC1
Telex: 27286

11 July 1975

Mr Jeffrey Bernard
39 Nottingham Place
W.1.

Dear Mr Bernard,

I read with interest your letter asking for information as to your behaviour and whereabouts between the years 1960-1974.

On a certain evening in September 1969, you rang my mother to inform her that you were going to murder her only son.

If you would like further information, I can put you in touch with many people who have enjoyed similar bizarre experiences in your company.

Yours sincerely,

MICHAEL J MOLLOY

Registered Office: Holborn Circus London EC1
A Company registered in England (No 168,660)
and a subsidiary of Reed International Limited

YOU RANG MY MOTHER

MICHAEL J. MOLLOY to JEFFREY BERNARD
July 11th, 1975

Famed journalist Jeffrey Bernard was married four times in his 65 years, but his one true love was Soho, London, and the many drinking holes that line its streets. More often than not one could find him propping up the bar at the Coach and Horses pub, cigarette in hand, delighting friends such as Dylan Thomas, Peter Cook and Ian Fleming with an endless stream of anecdotes, some of which also graced the weekly, booze-addled column he wrote for the *New Statesman*; he was also, thanks to his unwavering commitment to drunkenness and rowdiness, a regular character in the anecdotes of others. In 1975, after many approaches by different publishers, he finally agreed to write an autobiography – but there was a problem: he could remember very little of the past 15 years. With that in mind, he had a letter published in the *Spectator*, to which the editor of the *Daily Mirror* soon replied.

PEOPLE SIMPLY EMPTY OUT

CHARLES BUKOWSKI to
JOHN MARTIN
August 12th, 1986

In 1969, publisher John Martin offered to pay Charles Bukowski $100 each and every month for the rest of his life, on one condition: that he quit his job at the post office and become a full-time writer. Forty-nine-year-old Bukowski did exactly that, and just weeks after leaving work finished writing his first book, *Post Office,* a semi-autobiographical story in which Bukowski's fictional alter ego, Henry Chinaski, muddles through life as an employee of the US Postal Service. It was published by Martin's Black Sparrow Press in 1971. Fifteen years later, Bukowski wrote a letter to Martin and spoke of his joy at having escaped full-time employment.

Hello John:

Thanks for the good letter. I don't think it hurts, sometimes, to remember where you came from. You know the places where I came from. Even the people who try to write about that or make films about it, they don't get it right. They call it "9 to 5." It's never 9 to 5, there's no free lunch break at those places, in fact, at many of them in order to keep your job you don't take lunch. Then there's OVERTIME and the books never seem to get the overtime right and if you complain about that, there's another sucker to take your place.

You know my old saying, "Slavery was never abolished, it was only extended to include all the colors."

And what hurts is the steadily diminishing humanity of those fighting to hold jobs they don't want but fear the alternative worse. People simply empty out. They are bodies with fearful and obedient minds. The color leaves the eye. The voice becomes ugly. And the body. The hair. The fingernails. The shoes. Everything does.

As a young man I could not believe that people could give their lives over to those conditions. As an old man, I still can't believe it. What do they do it for? Sex? TV? An automobile on monthly payments? Or children? Children who are just going to do the same things that they did?

Early on, when I was quite young and going from job to job I was foolish enough to sometimes speak to my fellow workers: "Hey, the boss can come in here at any moment and lay all of us off, just like that, don't you realize that?"

They would just look at me. I was posing something that they didn't want to enter their minds.

Now in industry, there are vast layoffs (steel mills dead, technical changes in other factors of the work place). They are layed off by the hundreds of thousands and their faces are stunned:

"I put in 35 years..."

"It ain't right..."

"I don't know what to do..."

They never pay the slaves enough so they can get free, just enough so they can stay alive and come back to work. I could see all this. Why couldn't they? I figured the park bench was just as good or being a barfly was just as good. Why not get there first before they put me there? Why wait?

I just wrote in disgust against it all, it was a relief to get the shit out of my system. And now that I'm here, a so-called professional writer, after giving the first 50 years away, I've found out that there are other disgusts beyond the system.

I remember once, working as a packer in this lighting fixture company, one of the packers suddenly said: "I'll never be free!"

One of the bosses was walking by (his name was Morrie) and he let out this delicious cackle of a laugh, enjoying the fact that this fellow was trapped for life.

So, the luck I finally had in getting out of those places, no matter how long it took, has given me a kind of joy, the jolly joy of the miracle. I now write from an old mind and an old body, long beyond the time when most men would ever think of continuing such a thing, but since I started so late I owe it to myself to continue, and when the words begin to falter and I must be helped up stairways and I can no longer tell a bluebird from a paperclip, I still feel that something in me is going to remember (no matter how far I'm gone) how I've come through the murder and the mess and the moil, to at least a generous way to die.

To not to have entirely wasted one's life seems to be a worthy accomplishment, if only for myself.

yr boy,

Hank

A STRING OF VERITABLE PSYCHOLOGICAL PEACHES

CARL JUNG to JAMES JOYCE
September 27th, 1932

In 1932, renowned Swiss psychoanalyst Carl Jung wrote a largely critical piece for *Europäische Revue* on the subject of *Ulysses*, James Joyce's ground-breaking, controversial, and famously challenging novel. From Jung's essay:

I read to page 135 with despair in my heart, falling asleep twice on the way. The incredible versatility of Joyce's style has a monotonous and hypnotic effect. Nothing comes to meet the reader, everything turns away from him, leaving him gaping after it. The book is always up and away, dissatisfied with itself, ironic, sardonic, virulent, contemptuous, sad, despairing, and bitter [...] Yes, I admit I feel have been made a fool of. The book would not meet me half way, nothing in it made the least attempt to be agreeable, and that always gives the reader an irritating sense of inferiority.

In September of that year, Jung sent a copy of his article to Joyce along with a fascinating letter of which Joyce was both proud and infuriated. Interestingly, two years later Jung treated Joyce's daughter, Lucia, for schizophrenia; it was around this time that Joyce wrote in Jung's copy of *Ulysses*:

To Dr. C. G. Jung, with grateful appreciation of his aid and counsel. James Joyce. Xmas 1934, Zurich.

Küsnacht-Zürich

Seestrasse 228
September 27th 1932

James Joyce Esq.
Hotel Elite
Zurich

Dear Sir,

Your Ulysses has presented the world such an upsetting psychological problem that repeatedly I have been called in as a supposed authority on psychological matters.

Ulysses proved to be an exceedingly hard nut and it has forced my mind not only to most unusual efforts, but also to rather extravagant peregrinations (speaking from the standpoint of a scientist). Your book as a whole has given me no end of trouble and I was brooding over it for about three years until I succeeded to put myself into it. But I must tell you that I'm profoundly grateful to yourself as well as to your gigantic opus, because I learned a great deal from it. I shall probably never be quite sure whether I did enjoy it, because it meant too much grinding of nerves and of grey matter. I also don't know whether you will enjoy what I have written about Ulysses because I couldn't help telling the world how much I was bored, how I grumbled, how I cursed and how I admired. The 40 pages of non stop run at the end is a string of veritable psychological peaches. I suppose the devil's grandmother knows so much about the real psychology of a woman, I didn't.

Well, I just try to recommend my little essay to you, as an amusing attempt of a perfect stranger that went astray in the labyrinth of your Ulysses and happened to get out of it again by sheer good luck. At all events you may gather from my article what Ulysses has done to a supposedly balanced psychologist.

With the expression of my deepest appreciation, I remain, dear Sir,

Yours faithfully,
C. G. Jung

THE APPALLING HORROR

FLORENCE NIGHTINGALE to WILLIAM BOWMAN
November 14th, 1854

Florence Nightingale's influence in the world of nursing is impossible to quantify. Born in 1820 to a wealthy family, she knew from a young age that caring for the sick and vulnerable was her calling in life, much to the disapproval of her parents. Little did they know that their daughter would one day become the founder of modern nursing; she would also, most famously, train and take a team of nurses to Turkey in 1854 in order to care for the thousands of soldiers injured during the Crimean War, most of whom were languishing in unspeakably horrific conditions. It was there that she wrote this letter to Dr. William Bowman of King's College Hospital and described in great detail "the appalling horror". Such was her impact, Nightingale returned home a hero.

"I came out, Ma'am, prepared to submit to everything—to be put upon in every way—but there are some things, Ma'am, one can't submit to. There is caps, Ma'am, that suits one face and some that suits another's, and if I'd known, Ma'am, about the caps, great as was my desire to come out to nurse at Scutari, I wouldn't have come, Ma'am."

Speech of Mrs Lawfield, 5 November.

Barrack Hospital Scutari,
Asiatic Side
14 November 1854

Dear Sir

Time must be at a discount with the man who can adjust the balance of such an important question as the above—and I, for one, have none, as you will easily suppose when I tell you that, on Thursday last, we had 1715 sick and wounded in this hospital (among whom 120 cholera patients) and 650 severely wounded in the building called the General Hospital, of which we also have charge, when a message came to me to prepare for 570 wounded on our side of the hospital, who were arriving from the dreadful affair of 5 November at Balaclava, where were 1763 wounded and 442 killed, besides 96 officers wounded and 38 killed.

I always expected to end my days as hospital matron, but I never expected to be barrack mistress. We had but half an hour's notice before they began landing the wounded. Between 1 and 9 o'clock we had the mattresses stuffed, sewn up, laid down, alas! only upon matting on the floors, the men washed and put to bed, and all their wounds dressed. I wish I had time and I would write you a letter dear to a surgeon's heart, I am as good as a Medical Times.

But oh! you gentlemen of England who sit at home in all the well-earned satisfaction of your successful cases can have little idea from reading the newspapers of the horror and misery (in a military hospital) of operating upon these dying and exhausted men—a London hospital is a garden of flowers to it.

We have had such a sea in the Bosphorus and the Turks, the very men for whom we are fighting, carry our wounded so cruelly that they arrive in a state of agony. One amputated stump died two hours after we received him, one compound fracture just as we were getting him into bed, in all twenty-four cases on the day of landing. The dysentery cases have died at the rate of one in two. Then the day of operations which follows. I have no doubt that Providence is quite right and that the kingdom of hell is the best beginning for the kingdom of heaven, but that this is the kingdom of hell no one can doubt.

We are very lucky in our medical heads. Two of them are brutes and four of them are angels—for this is a work which makes either angels or devils of men, and of women too. As for the assistants, they are all cubs, and will, while a man is breathing his last breath under the knife, lament the "arrogance of being called up from the dinners by such a fresh influx of wounded." But wicked cubs grow up into good old bears, though I don't know how—for certain it is the old bears are good.

We have now four miles of beds—and not eighteen inches apart. We have our quarters in one tower of the barrack, and all this fresh influx has been laid down between us and the main guard in two corridors with a line of beds down each side, just room for one man to step between, and four wards.

Yet in the midst of this appalling horror (we are steeped up to our necks in blood) there is good. And I can truly say, like St Peter, "it is good for us to be here," though I doubt whether, if St Peter had been here, he would have said so.

As I went my night rounds among the newly wounded that first night there was not one murmur, not one groan—the strictest discipline, the most absolute silence and quiet prevailed—only the step of the sentry and I heard one man say, I was dreaming of my friends at home, and another said, And I was thinking of them. These poor fellows bear pain and mutilation with unshrinking heroism, and die or are cut up without a complaint.

Not so the officers, but we have nothing to do with the officers. The wounded are now lying up to our very door, and we are landing forty more from the Andes.

I take rank in the army as brigadier general, because forty British females, whom I have with me, are more difficult to manage than 4000 men. Let no lady come out here who is not used to fatigue and privation. For the Devonport sisters, who ought to know what self-denial is, do nothing but complain. Occasionally the roof is torn off our quarters, or the windows blown in, and we are flooded and under water for the night. We have all sick cookery now to do, and have got in four men for the purpose, for the prophet Muhammad does not allow us a female. And we are now able to supply these poor fellows with something besides the government rations. The climate is very good for the healing of wounds.

I wish you would recall me to Dr Bence Jones's remembrance when you see him, and tell him that I have had but too much occasion to remember him in the constant use of his dreadful presents. Now comes the time of hemorrhage and hospital gangrene, and every ten minutes an orderly runs and we have to go and cram lint into the wound till a surgeon can be sent for and stop the bleeding as well as we can.

In all our corridors I think we have not an average of three limbs per man—and there are two ships more "loading" at the Crimea with wounded—this is our phraseology. Then come the operations and a melancholy, not an encouraging list is this. They are all performed in the wards—no time to move them. One poor fellow, exhausted with hemorrhage, has his leg amputated as a last hope and dies ten minutes after the surgeons have left him. Almost before the breath has left his body it is sewn up in its blanket and carried away—buried the same day. We have no room for corpses in the wards. The surgeons pass on to the next, an excision of the shoulder joint—beautifully performed and going on well—ball lodged just in the head of the joint, and the fracture starred all round. The next poor fellow has two stumps for arms, and the next has lost an arm and leg.

As for the balls, they go in where they like and do as much harm as they can in passing—that is the only rule they have. The next case has one eye put out and paralysis of the iris of the other. He can neither see nor understand.

But all who can walk come in to us for tobacco, but I tell them that we have not a bit to put into our own mouths—not a sponge, nor a rag of linen, not an anything have I left. Everything is gone to make slings and stump pillows and shirts. These poor fellows have not had a clean shirt nor been washed for two months before they came here, and the state in which they arrive from the transport is literally crawling.

I hope in a few days we shall establish a little cleanliness—but we have not a basin nor a towel nor a bit of soap nor a broom. I have ordered 300 scrubbing brushes. But one half the barrack is so sadly out of repair that it is impossible to use a drop of water on the stone floors, which are all laid upon rotten wood, and would give our men fever in no time.

The next case is a poor fellow where the ball went in at the side of the head, put out one eye, made a hole in his tongue and came out in the neck. The wound was doing very nicely when he was seized with agonizing pain and died suddenly, without convulsion or paralysis. At the P.M . an abscess in the anterior part of the head was found as big as my fist—yet the man kept his reasoning faculties till the last. And nature had thrown out a false coat all round it.

I am getting a screen now for the amputations, for when one poor fellow— who is to be amputated tomorrow—sees his comrade today die under the knife, it makes impression, and diminishes his chance. But, anyway, among these exhausted frames the mortality of the operations is frightful.

We have erysipelas, fever and gangrene. And the Russian wounded are the worst. We are getting on nicely though in many ways. They were so glad to see us.

The senior chaplain is a sensible man, which is a remarkable providence. I have not been out of the hospital wards yet. But the most beautiful view in the world lies outside. If you ever see Mr Whitfield, the house apothecary of St Thomas', will you tell him that the nurse he sent me, Mrs Roberts, is worth her weight in gold.

There was another engagement on the 8th and more wounded, who are coming down to us. The text which heads my letter was expounded thus. Mrs Lawfield was recommended to return home and set her cap, vulgarly speaking, at somewhere else than here, but on begging for mercy, was allowed to make another trial. Mrs Drake is a treasure—the four others are not fit to take care of themselves nor of others in a military hospital. This is my first impression. But it may modify, if I can convince them of the absolute necessity of discipline and propriety in a drunken garrison…

This is only the beginning of things. We are still expecting the assault.

MISS FLORENCE NIGHTINGALE.   L.S.Cº.Nº123.

YOU ARE A
HOMOSEXUAL AND MAY
NEVER CHANGE

FELICIA BERNSTEIN to
LEONARD BERNSTEIN
Circa 1952

On September 10th of 1951,
29-year-old Chilean-born
actress and singer Felicia
Montealegre wed Leonard
Bernstein, 33, a musical
prodigy now considered one
of the most accomplished
conductors and composers
in history. By 1962 they had
three children and although
they separated towards the
end of their relationship,
Felicia and Leonard
remained married until her
death in 1978. The letter
seen here, written by Felicia
approximately a year after
the wedding, shines a light
on their marriage from a
different angle and concerns
an aspect of the relationship
of which she was seemingly
very understanding and
determined to accommodate:
Bernstein's sexuality.

Facing page:
Composer Leonard Bernstein
aged 36, 1955

Darling,

If I seemed sad as you drove away today it was not because I felt in any way deserted but because I was left alone to face myself and this whole bloody mess which is our "connubial" life. I've done a lot of thinking and have decided that it's not such a mess after all.

First: we are not committed to a life sentence—nothing is really irrevocable, not even marriage (though I used to think so).

Second: you are a homosexual and may never change—you don't admit to the possibility of a double life, but if your peace of mind, your health, your whole nervous system depend on a certain sexual pattern what can you do?

Third: I am willing to accept you as you are, without being a martyr or sacrificing myself on the L.B. altar. (I happen to love you very much—this may be a disease and if it is what better cure?) It may be difficult but no more so than the "status quo" which exists now—at the moment you are not yourself and this produces painful barriers and tensions for both of us—let's try and see what happens if you are free to do as you like, but without guilt and confession, please!

As for me—once you are rid of tensions I'm sure my own will disappear. A companionship will grow which probably no one else may be able to offer you. The feelings you have for me will be clearer and easier to express—our marriage is not based on passion but on tenderness and mutual respect. Why not have them?

I know now too that I need to work. It is a very important part of me and I feel incomplete without it. I may want to do something about it soon. I am used to an active life, and then there is that old ego problem.

We may have gotten married too soon and yet we needed to get married and we've not made a mistake. It is good for us even if we suffer now and make each other miserable—we will both grow up some day and be strong and unafraid either together or apart—after all we are both more important as individuals than a "marriage" is.

In any case my dearest darling ape, let's give it a whirl. There'll be crisis (?) from time to time but that doesn't scare me any more. And let's relax in the knowledge that neither of us is perfect and forget about being HUSBAND AND WIFE in such strained capital letters, it's not that awful!

There's a lot else I've got to say but the pill has overpowered me. I'll write again soon. My wish for the week is that you come back guiltless and happy.

F

I NEVER STUDIED GRACE

CHARLES LAMB to JACOB
VALE ASBURY
1830

One evening in 1830,
British essayist and poet
Charles Lamb attended a
party held by his friend and
doctor, Jacob Vale Asbury,
and Jacob's wife, Dorothy.
Never one to turn down an
alcoholic beverage, Lamb
proceeded to drink as much
as his body could hold and
soon lost all control of his
faculties; unable to move
more than a few inches, he
was eventually carried home
by a fellow guest. The next
day, having been forced by
his sister to ask forgiveness
for his behaviour, Lamb
wrote to his hosts with this
impressively unapologetic
letter of apology.

Dear Sir:

It is an observation of a wise man that "moderation is best in all things."
I cannot agree with him "in liquor." There is a smoothness and oiliness in wine
that makes it go down by a natural channel, which I am positive was made for
that descending. Else, why does not wine choke us? Could Nature have made that
sloping lane not to facilitate the downgoing? She does nothing in vain. You know
that better than I. You know how often she has helped you at a dead lift, and how
much better entitled she is to a fee than yourself sometimes, when you carry off the
credit. Still there is something due to manners and customs, and I should apologize
to you and Mrs. Asbury for being absolutely carried home upon a man's shoulders
through Silver Street, up Parson's Lane, by the Chapels (which might have taught
me better), and then to be deposited like a dead log at Gaffar Westwood's, who it
seems does not "insure" against intoxication. Not that the mode of conveyance is
objectionable. On the contrary, it is more easy than a one-horse chaise. Ariel in *The
Tempest* says

"On a Bat's back do I fly, after sunset merrily."

Now, I take it that Ariel must sometimes have stayed out late of nights.
Indeed, he pretends that "where the bee sucks, there lurks he," as much as to say
that his suction is as innocent as that little innocent (but damnably stinging when
he is provoked) winged creature. But I take it that Ariel was fond of metheglin,
of which the bees are notorious brewers. But then you will say, What a shocking
sight to see a middle-aged gentleman-and-a-half riding upon a gentleman's back
up Parson's Lane at midnight. Exactly the time for that sort of conveyance, when
nobody can see him, nobody but heaven and his own conscience; now, heaven makes
fools, and don't expect much from her own creation; and as for conscience, she and
I have long since come to a compromise. I have given up false modesty, and she
allows me to abate a little of the true. I like to be liked, but I don't care about being
respected. I don't respect myself. But, as I was saying, I thought he would have let
me down just as we got to Lieutenant Barker's coal shed (or emporium) but by a
cunning jerk I eased myself and righted my posture. I protest, I thought myself in a
palanquin, and never felt myself so grandly carried. It was a slave under me. There
was I, all but my reason. And what is reason? And what is the loss of it? And how
often in a day do we do without it, just as well? Reason is only counting, two and
two makes four. And if on my passage home, I thought it made five, what matter?
Two and two will just make four, as it always did, before I took the finishing glass
that did my business. My sister has begged me to write an apology to Mrs. A and
you for disgracing your party; now it does seem to me that I rather honored your
party, for everyone that was not drunk (and one or two of the ladies, I am sure,
were not) must have been set off greatly in the contrast to me. I was the scapegoat.
The soberer they seemed. By the way, is magnesia good on these occasions? I am
no licentiate, but know enough of simples to beg you to send me a draft after this

model. But still you will say (or the men and maids at your house will say) that it is not a seemly sight for an old gentleman to go home pickaback. Well, maybe it is not. But I never studied grace. I take it to be a mere superficial accomplishment. I regard more the internal acquisitions. The great object after supper is to get home, and whether that is obtained in a horizontal posture or perpendicular (as foolish men and apes affect for dignity) I think is little to the purpose. The end is always greater than the means. Here I am, able to compose a sensible rational apology, and what signifies how I got here? I have just sense enough to remember I was very happy last night, and to thank our kind host and hostess, and that's sense enough, I hope.

Charles Lamb

N.B.--What is good for a desperate headache? Why, patience, and a determination not to mind being miserable all day long. And that I have made my mind up to. So, here goes. It is better than not being alive at all, which I might have been, had your man toppled me down at Lieut. Barker's Coal-shed. My sister sends her sober compliments to Mrs. A. She is not much the worse.

Yours Truly,
C. Lamb

I DO NOT LIKE SCOLDING PEOPLE

KATHERINE MANSFIELD to
ELIZABETH BIBESCO
March 24th, 1921

Author Katherine Mansfield
and editor John Middleton
Murry met in 1911 and had
a turbulent relationship by
anyone's standards: by the
time they wed in 1918, they
had split several times and
seen other people; indeed,
the pattern continued
throughout their marriage.
Three years after marrying,
Mansfield wrote a stern
letter to fellow author
Princess Elizabeth Bibesco,
a woman who for some time
had been having an affair
with Murry. Mansfield could
deal with the infidelity; what
she couldn't stand, however,
were the love letters.

24 March, 1921

Dear Princess Bibesco,

I am afraid you must stop writing these little love letters to my husband while he
and I live together. It is one of the things which is not done in our world.

You are very young. Won't you ask your husband to explain to you the
impossibility of such a situation.

Please do not make me have to write to you again. I do not like scolding people
and I simply hate having to teach them manners.

Yours sincerely,

Katherine Mansfield

Facing page:
Writer Katherine Mansfield

MAKE YOUR SOUL GROW

KURT VONNEGUT to XAVIER
HIGH SCHOOL
November 5th, 2006

In 2006, a group of students at Xavier High School in New York City were given an assignment by their English teacher, Ms. Lockwood, that was to test their persuasive writing skills: they were asked to write to their favourite author and ask him or her to visit the school. It's a measure of his ongoing influence that five of those pupils chose Kurt Vonnegut, the novelist responsible for, amongst other highly respected books, *Slaughterhouse-Five*; sadly, however, he never made that trip. Instead, he wrote a wonderful letter. He was the only author to reply.

228 E 48 NYC 10017 212-688-2682 November 5, 2006

Dear Xavier High School, and Ms. Lockwood, and Messrs Perin, McFeely, Batten, Maurer and Congiusta:

I thank you for your friendly letters. You sure know how to cheer up a really old geezer (84) in his sunset years. I don't make public appearances any more because I now resemble nothing so much as an iguana.

What I had to say to you, moreover, would not take long, to wit: Practice any art, music, singing, dancing, acting, drawing, painting, sculpting, poetry, fiction, essays, reportage, no matter how well or badly, not to get money and fame, but to experience <u>becoming,</u> to find out what's inside you, <u>to make your soul grow.</u>

Seriously! I mean starting right now, do art and do it for the rest of your lives. Draw a funny or nice picture of Ms. Lockwood, and give it to her. Dance home after school, and sing in the shower and on and on. Make a face in your mashed potatoes. Pretend you're Count Dracula.

Here's an assignment for tonight, and I hope Ms. Lockwood will flunk you if you don't do it: Write a six line poem, about anything, but <u>rhymed.</u> No fair tennis without a net. Make it as good as you possibly can. But don't tell anybody what you're doing. Don't show it or recite it to anybody, not even your girlfriend or parents or whatever, or Ms. Lockwood. OK?

Tear it up into teeny-weeny pieces, and discard them into widely separated trash recepticals. You will find that you have already been gloriously rewarded for your poem. You have experienced becoming, learned a lot more about what's inside you, and you have made your soul grow.

God bless you all!

Kurt Vonnegut

THERE ARE NO REAL REWARDS FOR TIME PASSING

MARTHA GELLHORN to
ERNEST HEMINGWAY
June 28th, 1943

Martha Gellhorn is one of the most respected war correspondents ever known, having covered everything from the Spanish Civil War in the 1930s through to the U.S. invasion of Panama in 1989. It was at the beginning of her remarkable 60-year career, in 1936, that she met novelist Ernest Hemingway, and by 1940 they were married; however, they spent much of their four-year marriage apart with Hemingway keen to stay at home working on his novel and Gellhorn desperate to travel to and report from whichever war zone was within reach. Naturally, during such times they kept in touch by letter. In June 1943, miles apart, Gellhorn, restless, wrote to Hemingway and spoke of her fear of growing old.

June 28 1943

Bug my dearest:

How I long for you now. My cats are very good to me but fortunately or unfortunately they can neither read nor speak. I say to them: is it a good book; and they chase-chase over the table and roll with the electric wire and Friendless, with her dynamo purr, sits briefly on my lap.

I am enjoying Alicia who does the typing. She is surely the most unicellular female I have ever had dealings with. Today she said, 'Martha I hate men.' I believe it too: the way labor hates capital. She finds my books 'absorbing'; she loves Marc's 'reactions.' How odd it all is; how odd is life. Who ever would have thought that I, who started out with the dream of writing (and that dream at least never changed) and lived in a *maison de passe* alongside the Madeleine and romantically, self-consciously, bought a bunch of violets to wear, instead of buying breakfast, when I went looking for jobs (I was twenty), would end up here in this perfect safe beauty, finishing my fifth book. Alas. I do not want to grow old; not even if I write so much better, know more, and have an enviable instead of a rather shoddy uncertain life that only my posturing could dignify. I do not want to grow old at all. I want it so little that I would trade that wretched first book, right now, for this perhaps excellent fifth one: to have, included in the exchange, the fear and the surprise and the hope of twenty.

There are no real rewards for time passing. And I was not beautiful when I was young and no one said so and I never found myself so; and God knows it was a mean row to hoe. I have so much now that it startles me: blessings overflowing, and I had nothing then. But I don't really like what I know; I don't really care for wisdom and experience. I would rather believe, and beat out my brains, and believe some more. I do not like this safe, well-armed woman I have become. The loud bleating disheveled starry reckless failed girl was a better person.

I wish we could stop it all now, the prestige, the possessions, the position, the knowledge, the victory: and that we could by a miracle return together under the arch at Milan, with you so brash in your motorcycle sidecar and I, badly dressed, fierce, loving, standing in the street waiting for your picture to be taken. My God, how I wish it. I would give every single thing there now is to be young and poor with you, as poor as there was to be, and the days hard but always with that shine on them that came of not being sure, of hoping, of believing in fact in just the things we now so richly have. Well, shit I am a fool.

Where was I? I've had dinner now. I write the best letters and the worst books at night. Or maybe you don't think so? Perhaps, and very naturally, you would prefer the morning letters, the cheerful known thing. I am not cheerful and I never was, I have none of that truly inside me. But much practise and much fear have taught me how to hide, so I seem just about as comfortably unconscious as the next one. Only it's not true and I despise unconsciousness: I want life intense whether it's good or bad, but I never want it more than intense. I want to know it's happening, every minute of it.

Marriage is a rare thing, since it happens everywhere in nature and always has, since it is more an instinct than otherwise, it must be good. But it is a brutalization too. You've been married so much and so long that I do not really believe it can touch you where you live. That's your strength. It would be terrible if it did, since what you are is very much more important than the women you happen to be married to, and certainly more important than this institutionalized instinct. But it is an odd performance. One is safe: two people live together and know they will find each other at certain hours within some kind of walls. And slowly, for each other, they become the common denominator: they agree without words to lay off the fantasy and passion, the difficult personal private stuff: they find some common ground, which is green and smooth, and there they stay. And they may be quite odd and burning sort of people: like all the fancy ones of legend; Icarus and Prometheus and Leda and who else: but they are two people who have agreed to polish all the edges and keep their voice low and live. At what moment, together, can they be as wild and as free as they really are; as they are inside themselves where they never heard of an organized society and the serene considerate practical institution of marriage.

I would like to be young and poor in Milan, and with you and not married to you. I think maybe I have always wanted to feel some way like a woman, and if I ever did it was the first winter in Madrid. There is a sort of blindness and fervor and recklessness about that sort of feeling, which one must always want. I hate being so wise and careful, so reliable, so denatured, so able to get on. Possibly why I have always been happiest at wars (and also because I have never been hit) is that war is the greatest folly of all and it permits the participants to throw away all the working paraphernalia of life, and be fools too. If that is being fools? Depends on the values I guess.

I will almost bet twenty dollars that this letter makes you angry, my Bug. Doesn't it? What does she mean, you will say, complaining and crying for some other time, and place, and life? What the hell is the matter with that bitch: haven't I enough problems without her? But I am no problem, Bug, never think that. I am no problem. I have a brain locked inside the skull bones, as have all, and this is my affair. I only write to you as I now tonight feel or think because why not: we cannot be so married that we cannot speak.

Marty

```
                                    9 Orme Court,
                                    LONDON. W. 2.

                                    6th December, 1983

George Harrison Esq.,
26 Cadogan Square,
LONDON. SW1X. OJP.

Dear George,

You once said to me - the world is full of
arseholes, and I'm not one of them.   I have a
love for certain people and I have one for you,
but by sheer lack of contact it's running out.
I phone you frequently and never get a reply.
This is what you do, it's very simple;  you
stand in front of a telephone and you insert
your fingers in the holes and carry out a series
of numbers which have been given to you.   Of
course, if you are rich you have buttons, which
Irishmen usually sew on their coats.
Of course, if you are extremely rich you don't
have to get in touch with anybody, and that's what
I am worried about.   The funeral takes place
at Golders Green Crematorium, no flowers please,
just money.   You will recognise me, I am the
dead one.

                                    Love, light and peace,

                                    Spike Milligan.

P.S.   Thank you for sending the letter about the

                                    /Contd..
```

I AM THE DEAD ONE

SPIKE MILLIGAN to GEORGE
HARRISON
December 6th, 1983

The Beatles were huge fans of *The Goon Show*, the legendary comedy programme created by and starring Spike Milligan, Harry Secombe and Peter Sellers, and Lennon and co. cited it as an early influence on more than one occasion. The admiration was mutual, and the friendship between guitarist George Harrison and Spike Milligan was just one of the bonds that resulted; however, much to Milligan's annoyance, Harrison was almost impossible to get hold of by telephone – so much so that, in December of 1983, he instead wrote a letter.

Fender Guitar, believe it or not, I'm now playing
the Guitar, and the silly bastards who insure it
want living proof that it was a George Harrison
Guitar, and I said to them, it was a George Harrison
Guitar, but it is now mine.

LIKE A TREE IN FULL BEARING

CHARLOTTE BRONTË to W. S. WILLIAMS
December 25th, 1848

Charlotte Brontë was the eldest of the Brontë sisters, three creative English siblings born in the 19th century whose most successful novels, all three of which were published in the space of nine months, are now considered classics: Charlotte's *Jane Eyre*, Emily's *Wuthering Heights*, and Anne's *The Tenant of Wildfell Hall*. They are arguably the most famous of all literary families. In 1848, a year after the publication of her aforementioned magnum opus, Emily, the middle sister, died from tuberculosis; she was just 30 years old. A week later, Charlotte wrote to her publisher.

December 25th, 1848.

My dear Sir,—I will write to you more at length when my heart can find a little rest—now I can only thank you very briefly for your letter, which seemed to me eloquent in its sincerity.

Emily is nowhere here now, her wasted mortal remains are taken out of the house. We have laid her cherished head under the church aisle beside my mother's, my two sisters'—dead long ago—and my poor, hapless brother's. But a small remnant of the race is left—so my poor father thinks.

Well, the loss is ours, not hers, and some sad comfort I take, as I hear the wind blow and feel the cutting keenness of the frost, in knowing that the elements bring her no more suffering; their severity cannot reach her grave; her fever is quieted, her restlessness soothed, her deep, hollow cough is hushed for ever; we do not hear it in the night nor listen for it in the morning; we have not the conflict of the strangely strong spirit and the fragile frame before us—relentless conflict—once seen, never to be forgotten. A dreary calm reigns round us, in the midst of which we seek resignation.

My father and my sister Anne are far from well. As for me, God has hitherto most graciously sustained me; so far I have felt adequate to bear my own burden and even to offer a little help to others. I am not ill; I can get through daily duties, and do something towards keeping hope and energy alive in our mourning household. My father says to me almost hourly, "Charlotte, you must bear up, I shall sink if you fail me"; these words, you can conceive, are a stimulus to nature. The sight, too, of my sister Anne's very still but deep sorrow wakens in me such fear for her that I dare not falter. Somebody must cheer the rest.

So I will not now ask why Emily was torn from us in the fulness of our attachment, rooted up in the prime of her own days, in the promise of her powers; why her existence now lies like a field of green corn trodden down, like a tree in full bearing struck at the root. I will only say, sweet is rest after labour and calm after tempest, and repeat again and again that Emily knows that now.—Yours sincerely,

C. Brontë

Dr. Seuss
THE TOWER
La Jolla, California

May 12, 1957

Dear Howard:

       I am sorry to have been so long in answering your very friendly letter of April 13th. But I've been East. And the letter's been waiting me here in the West.

       Your theatre productions sound wonderful. And I am very proud that you dedicated it to me.. and performed so many of my stories in it.

       ....

       About giving you advice...pointers on how to properly write and illustrate a picture book...all I can say is this:
       This is a field in which no one can give you pointers <u>but yourself</u>.

       The big successes in this field all succeeded because they wrote and they wrote and they drew and they drew. They studied what they'd drawn and they studied what they'd written , each time asking themselves one question: <u>How can I do it better, next time?</u>

       To develop an individual style of writing and drawing, always go to <u>yourself</u> for criticsm. If you ask advice from too many other people, then you no longer are youself.

       The thing to do, and I am sure you will do it, is to keep up your enthusiasm! Every job is a lot of fun, no matter how much work it takes. If you'll plug away and do exactly what you are doing, making it better and better every month and every year...that you CAN be successful.

       The very best of luck to you!

       Your friend,

       Dr. Seuss

YOU GAVE ME A VALUABLE GIFT: YOU TOOK ME SERIOUSLY

HOWARD CRUSE to DR. SEUSS (and vice versa)
1957 onwards

During an illustrious career that saw him win multiple awards and worldwide recognition, Theodore Geisel published over 60 books, the majority of which he wrote and illustrated under the pen name Dr. Seuss. Despite his busy schedule, and just months after the release of *The Cat in the Hat*, Geisel set aside time to reply with a charming letter to a 13-year-old aspiring illustrator by the name of Howard Cruse. Naturally, Cruse was delighted, and wrote again two years later; yet again, Geisel replied. Such was the positive impact on Cruse that in 1985, 26 years later, he decided to write to the author one last time and thank him for his advice all those years ago. Again, Geisel replied.

As for Howard Cruse, his award-winning graphic novel, *Stuck Rubber Baby*, was published by DC Comics in 1995; a 15th anniversary edition was released in 2010.

Dr. Seuss

THE TOWER

La Jolla, California

June 12, 1959

Mr. Howard Cruse
P. O. Box 59
Springville, Alabama

Dear Mr. Cruse:

It was very pleasant to hear from you
again and to learn that your excitement is just as
high as ever, after two years.

I certainly think that the Famous Artists
Cartoon Course will help you a lot. This is one of the
few really top-drawer courses available in cartooning
in the United States.

AND, if you think you cringe when you
look at your scrapbook, you should see what I do. I
have been just cleaning house, and almost committed
suicide when I discovered my 1929 files.

Keep cringing away! The more you cringe
over your old stuff, the more that means you're going
ahead!

With every best wish,

T. S. Geisel

(DR. SEUSS)

TSG:em

January 3, 1985

Theodore Geisel/Dr. Seuss
The Tower
La Jolla, CA

Dear Mr. Geisel/Dr. Seuss,

If you peer at the two Xerox copies which are attached to this letter, you'll recognize them as your gracious responses to a thirteen/fifteen-year-old Alabama boy who wrote to you in 1957 and 1959. I told you about the puppet-show adaptations of Bartholomew and the Oobleck, and McElligot's Pool which I wrote and performed for neighborhood kids in my basement, and I confided that I hoped to grow up and write and illustrate children's books myself. As you can see, you gave me a valuable gift: you took me seriously.

It's been twenty-five years since the second of your two letters to me was written. During that time, I've often thought that I should write and thank you for the encouraging words which you offered me. On my fortieth birthday last May, I was given (at my request) The Butter Battle Book. I enjoyed seeing the world through your eyes again as much as I did when I was very young, and I appreciate your willingness to engage a truly serious and important subject within the children's book format.

I have not illustrated any children's books yet, but I have grown-up to be a cartoonist and humorous illustrator. My principal interest is in comic strips for adults, and I fill out my extra time doing spot drawings for magazines. My first book--a trade paperback collection of my comic strip Wendel--will be published at the end of 1985.

Although I couldn't claim to enjoy a hundredth of your own stature as an artist, I occasionally receive letters from youngsters not unlike the letters I wrote to you. And remembering the strength of the childhood dreams which are represented by such letters, I try very hard to do as you did and treat the young artist as a person with dignity. Thanks for showing me, in your work all through the years as well as in the particular letters you wrote to me, both how to be a wonderful artist and how to be a kind and supportive human being.

Yours sincerely,

Howard Cruse

THE MISERABLE'S NAME IS MAN

VICTOR HUGO to M. DAELLI
October 18th, 1862

Victor Hugo's *Les Misérables* is arguably one of the best-known novels of all time. Initially published in French in 1862, it tells the story of Jean Valjean, a prisoner of 19 years who, upon release, breaks parole in an attempt to rebuild his life and finds himself caring for a young girl who has turned to prostitution to support herself and her daughter – a situation further complicated by the fact that he is being doggedly pursued by a detective keen to return him to prison. The book has since been translated into every language imaginable, has graced countless "Best of" lists, and has been adapted for film, theatre and radio many times over – thanks, in no small part, to the universal themes at its core: redemption, love, forgiveness, and sacrifice. Very soon after its publication, Victor Hugo expanded on this very point by way of a letter written to M. Daelli, the publisher responsible for the novel's Italian translation.

HAUTEVILLE-HOUSE, October 18, 1862.

You are right, sir, when you tell me that Les Miserables is written for all nations. I do not know whether it will be read by all, but I wrote it for all. It is addressed to England as well as to Spain, to Italy as well as to France, to Germany as well as to Ireland, to Republics which have slaves as well as to Empires which have serfs. Social problems overstep frontiers. The sores of the human race, those great sores which cover the globe, do not halt at the red or blue lines traced upon the map. In every place where man is ignorant and despairing, in every place where woman is sold for bread, wherever the child suffers for lack of the book which should instruct him and of the hearth which should warm him, the book of Les Miserables knocks at the door and says: "Open to me, I come for you."

At the hour of civilization through which we are now passing, and which is still so sombre, the miserable's name is Man; he is agonizing in all climes, and he is groaning in all languages.

Your Italy is no more exempt from the evil than is our France. Your admirable Italy has all miseries on the face of it. Does not banditism, that raging form of pauperism, inhabit your mountains? Few nations are more deeply eaten by that ulcer of convents which I have endeavored to fathom. In spite of your possessing Rome, Milan, Naples, Palermo, Turin, Florence, Sienna, Pisa, Mantua, Bologna, Ferrara, Genoa, Venice, a heroic history, sublime ruins, magnificent ruins, and superb cities, you are, like ourselves, poor. You are covered with marvels and vermin. Assuredly, the sun of Italy is splendid, but, alas, azure in the sky does not prevent rags on man.

Like us, you have prejudices, superstitions, tyrannies, fanaticisms, blind laws lending assistance to ignorant customs. You taste nothing of the present nor of the future without a flavor of the past being mingled with it. You have a barbarian, the monk, and a savage, the lazzarone. The social question is the same for you as for us. There are a few less deaths from hunger with you, and a few more from fever; your social hygiene is not much better than ours; shadows, which are Protestant in England, are Catholic in Italy; but, under different names, the vescovo is identical with the bishop, and it always means night, and of pretty nearly the same quality. To explain the Bible badly amounts to the same thing as to understand the Gospel badly.

Is it necessary to emphasize this? Must this melancholy parallelism be yet more completely verified? Have you not indigent persons? Glance below. Have you not parasites? Glance up. Does not that hideous balance, whose two scales, pauperism and parasitism, so mournfully preserve their mutual equilibrium, oscillate before you as it does before us? Where is your army of schoolmasters, the only army which civilization acknowledges?

Where are your free and compulsory schools? Does every one know how to read in the land of Dante and of Michael Angelo? Have you made public schools of your barracks? Have you not, like ourselves, an opulent war-budget and a paltry budget of education? Have not you also that passive obedience which is so easily converted into soldierly obedience? military establishment which pushes the regulations to the extreme of firing upon Garibaldi; that is to say, upon the living honor of Italy? Let us subject your social order to examination, let us take it where it stands and as it stands, let us view its flagrant offences, show me the woman and the child. It is by the amount of protection with which these two feeble creatures are surrounded that the degree of civilization is to be measured. Is prostitution less heartrending in Naples than in Paris? What is the amount of truth that springs from your laws, and what amount of justice springs from your tribunals? Do you chance to be so fortunate as to be ignorant of the meaning of those gloomy words: public prosecution, legal infamy, prison, the scaffold, the executioner, the death penalty? Italians, with you as with us, Beccaria is dead and Farinace is alive. And then, let us scrutinize your state reasons. Have you a government which comprehends the identity of morality and politics? You have reached the point where you grant amnesty to heroes! Something very similar has been done in France. Stay, let us pass miseries in review, let each one contribute his pile, you are as rich as we. Have you not, like ourselves, two condemnations, religious condemnation pronounced by the priest, and social condemnation decreed by the judge? Oh, great nation of Italy, thou resemblest the great nation of France! Alas! our brothers, you are, like ourselves, Miserables.

From the depths of the gloom wherein you dwell, you do not see much more distinctly than we the radiant and distant portals of Eden. Only, the priests are mistaken. These holy portals are before and not behind us.

I resume. This book, Les Miserables, is no less your mirror than ours. Certain men, certain castes, rise in revolt against this book, – I understand that. Mirrors, those revealers of the truth, are hated; that does not prevent them from being of use.

As for myself, I have written for all, with a profound love for my own country, but without being engrossed by France more than by any other nation. In proportion as I advance in life, I grow more simple, and I become more and more patriotic for humanity.

This is, moreover, the tendency of our age, and the law of radiance of the French Revolution; books must cease to be exclusively French, Italian, German, Spanish, or English, and become European, I say more, human, if they are to correspond to the enlargement of civilization.

Hence a new logic of art, and of certain requirements of composition which modify everything, even the conditions, formerly narrow, of taste and language, which must grow broader like all the rest.

In France, certain critics have reproached me, to my great delight, with having transgressed the bounds of what they call "French taste"; I should be glad if this eulogium were merited.

In short, I am doing what I can, I suffer with the same universal suffering, and I try to assuage it, I possess only the puny forces of a man, and I cry to all: "Help me!"

This, sir, is what your letter prompts me to say; I say it for you and for your country. If I have insisted so strongly, it is because of one phrase in your letter. You write: –

"There are Italians, and they are numerous, who say: 'This book, Les Miserables, is a French book. It does not concern us. Let the French read it as a history, we read it as a romance.'" – Alas! I repeat, whether we be Italians or Frenchmen, misery concerns us all. Ever since history has been written, ever since philosophy has meditated, misery has been the garment of the human race; the moment has at length arrived for tearing off that rag, and for replacing, upon the naked limbs of the Man-People, the sinister fragment of the past with the grand purple robe of the dawn.

If this letter seems to you of service in enlightening some minds and in dissipating some prejudices, you are at liberty to publish it, sir. Accept, I pray you, a renewed assurance of my very distinguished sentiments.

VICTOR HUGO

Facing page:
French writer Victor Marie
Hugo, c. 1870

DALLAS COUNTY HOSPITAL DISTRICT

Office Memorandum
November 27, 1963

To: All Employees

At 12:38 p.m., Friday, November 22, 1963, President John F. Kennedy and Texas' Governor John Connally were brought to the Emergency Room of Parkland Memorial Hospital after being struck down by the bullets of an assassin.

At 1:07 p.m., Sunday, November 24, 1963, Lee H. Oswald, accused assassin of the late president, died in an operating room of Parkland Memorial Hospital after being shot by a bystander in the basement of Dallas' City Hall. In the intervening 48 hours and 31 minutes Parkland Memorial Hospital had:

1. Become the temporary seat of the government of the United States.

2. Become the temporary seat of the government of the State of Texas.

3. Become the site of the death of the 35th President.

4. Become the site of the ascendency of the 36th President.

5. Become site of the death of President Kennedy's accused assassin.

6. Twice become the center of the attention of the world.

7. Continued to function at close to normal pace as a large charity hospital.

What is it that enables an institution to take in stride such a series of history jolting events? Spirit? Dedication? Preparedness? Certainly, all of these are important, but the underlying factor is people. People whose education and training is sound. People whose judgment is calm and perceptive. People whose actions are deliberate and definitive. Our pride is not that we were swept up by the whirlwind of tragic history, but that when we were, we were not found wanting.

C. J. Price
Administrator

WE WERE NOT FOUND WANTING

CHARLES JACK PRICE to HIS STAFF
November 27th, 1963

On November 22nd of 1963, as he travelled by motorcade through Dealey Plaza in downtown Dallas, the 35th President of the United States, John F. Kennedy, was killed by the two bullets of a sniper hiding on the sixth floor of a nearby building; one of Kennedy's travelling companions, Governor of Texas Jack Connally, was also injured. Five days later, Charles Jack Price, then-Administrator of Parkland Memorial Hospital in Dallas, proudly sent a memo to all staff and made clear his appreciation for their professional conduct over the past week – a period during which, as the world's population looked on in abject horror, the hospital had dealt with the deaths of two people in particular on its premises: John F. Kennedy, and his assassin, Lee Harvey Oswald.

SHEER ENCHANTMENT

SOPHIE SCHOLL to LISA
REMPPIS
February 17th, 1943

Sophie Scholl was 22 years
old when she wrote this
optimistic letter to her
friend, Lisa Remppis, and
spoke of soon enjoying the
spring. Sadly, the next day
Sophie and her brother,
Hans – both members of the
White Rose, a non-violent
group of students who
actively opposed Hitler's
regime by circulating anti-
Nazi leaflets – were arrested
at Munich University for
handing out another batch
to passers-by. Within just
a week they had been
convicted of treason; a
few hours later they were
beheaded by guillotine.

Dear Lisa,

I've just been playing the Trout Quintet on the phonograph. Listening to the andantino makes me want to be a trout myself. You can't help rejoicing and laughing, however moved or sad at heart you feel, when you see the springtime clouds in the sky and the budding branches sway, stirred by the wind, in the bright young sunlight. I'm so much looking forward to the spring again. In that piece of Schubert's you can positively feel and smell the breezes and scents and hear the birds and the whole of creation cry out for joy. And when the piano repeats the theme like cool, clear, sparkling water – oh, it's sheer enchantment.

Let me hear from you soon.

Lots of love,
Sophie

I HAVE NEVER SEEN ANYTHING LIKE IT

BARNUM BROWN to
PROFESSOR OSBORN
August 12th, 1902

Born in Kansas in 1873, Barnum Brown was the "Indiana Jones of Paleontology" – a charismatic character who travelled the world hunting for the fossils of dinosaurs, and with great success. In August of 1902, whilst leading an expedition at the Hell Creek Formation in Montana, sponsored by the American Museum of Natural History, Brown wrote this letter to the museum's president, Professor Osborn. and spoke of, amongst other things, a collection of bones found in a small quarry, saying "I have never seen any thing like it from the Cretaceous." This was in fact the most famous discovery he would ever make, for he had actually found the first ever partial skeleton of the mighty Tyrannosaurus rex. Or so he thought. It later transpired that Brown had already discovered a Tyrannosaurus rex in 1900; he uncovered five in total during his incredible career.

My Dear Prof. Osborn:-

Your letter of July 20th received. I was greatly disappointed to hear that the Claosaurus turned out so poorly especially after all the labor and expense of getting it. I bared bones all over the blocks so that it would have been necessary to take out all the bones from the matrix in the field to determine what condition they were in while the femur ilium and pubis which lay in soft sand were in good state of preservation.

I greatly appreciate your criticism and every pound of matrix that we can possibly remove from these specimens will come off though it takes a great deal of valuable time from prospecting.

Quarry No 2 which contained Triceratops sacrum, scapula, humerus, ulna pubis vertebrae and ribs has been worked out and one load taken to Miles.

Quarry No 1 contains the femur, pubes, part of humerus, three vertebrae and two undetermined bones of a large Carnivorous Dinosaur not described by Marsh. The pubes are about five feet long. I have never seen any thing like it from the Cretaceous. These bones are embedded in flint-like blue sandstone concretions and require a great deal of labor to extricate.

I am now working out Sterrholophus skull which is a prize. Associated with skull are humerus, lower jaw, four phalanges fibula, tibia and frags. Part of these bones are in bad condition and in previous letter I described condition of skull. Prof Lull or I will go in with skull to insure its safety next week when Brooks leaves us. Brooks has been with us a little over a month, a fine fellow in camp and has proven useful in our work. I have received from the Museum five hundred dollars and have spent five hundred and seventy five dollars plus some small accounts not in yet not counting Prof Lull's salary. I purchased three good horses, a new wagon and camp equipage which will sell for nearly full value, about two hundred and seventy five dollars.

All provisions, lumber and plaster are very expensive so that I go as economical as possible. Plaster costs five dollars per barrel in Miles City so I use flour paste wherever practicable.

Please advise me what disposition to make of the outfit at end of season. I should not advise another seasons work in this immediate locality and it would seem to me a good plan to explore the Musselshell river at end of season. I propose to work out all material in immediate vicinity and then ride out Crooked Creek thirty miles east of here if nothing more shows up in Hell Creek.

Will make sections through to Missouri River as soon as these three specimens are out of the way which will give you data from Powder River to the Missouri River a distance of two hundred and seventy miles north and south and from Miles City to Porcupine Creek a hundred and two miles east and west.

The invertebrates I have collected will be a valuable acquisition. There is a small bed of leaves nearby which I calculate to collect also.

With regards to the Museum staff I am

Sincerely yours,

Barnum Brown

P.S. Advise me regarding freight of fossils.

American Museum of Natural History,

77th Street and Eighth Avenue.

Camp on Hell Creek
New York City, Aug 12 the 1902

My Dear Prof. Osborn :-

Your letter of July 25 th received. I was greatly disappointed to hear that the Clausaurus turned out so poorly especially after all the labor and expense of getting it. I bared bones all over the blocks so that it would have been necessary to take out all the bones from the matrix in the field to determine what condition they were in while the femur illium and pubis which lay in soft sand were in good state of preservation.

I greatly appreciate your criticism and every pound of matrix that we can possibly remove from these specimens will come off though it takes a great deal of valuable time from prospecting.

Quarry No 2 which contained Triceratops

Sacrum, scapula, humerus, ulna pubis vertebrae and ribs has bein worked out and one load taken to Miles.

Quarry No 1 containes the femur, pubes part of humerus, three vertebrae and two undetermined bones of a large Carnivorous Dinosaur not described by Marsh. The pubes are about five feet long. I have never seen any thing like it from the Cretaceous. These bones are embedded in flint-like blue sandstone concretions and require a great deal of labor to extricate.

I am now working out Stepholophus skull which is a prize. Associated with skull are humerus, lower jaw, four phalanges fibula, tibia and pays. Part of these bones are in bad condition and in previous letter I described andity of skull. Prof Lull or I will go in with skull to insure its safety next week when Brooks leaves us.

Brooks has been with us a little over a month, a fine fellow in camp, and has proven useful in our work.

I have received from the Museum five hundred dollars and have spent five hundred and seventy five dollars plus some small accounts not in yet not counting Prof. Lull's salary.

I purchased three good horses, a new wagon and camp equipage which will sell for nearly full value, about two hundred and seventy five dollars.

All provisions, lumber and plaster are very expensive so that I go as economical as possible. Plaster costs five dollars per barrel in Miles City, so I use flour paste wherever practicable

Please advise me what disposition to make of the outfit at end of season.

I should not advise another seasons work in this immediate locality and it would seem to me a good plan to explore the Musselshell river at end of season. I propose to work out all material in immediate vicinity and then ride out Crooked Creek thirty miles east of here if nothing more shows up on Hell Creek.

Will make sections through to Missouri River as soon as these three specimens are out of the way which will give you data from Powder River to the Missouri River a distance of two hundred and seventy miles north and south and from Miles City to Porcupine Creek a hundred and ten miles east and west.

The invertebrates I have collected will be a valuable acquisition. There is a small bed of leaves near by which I calculate to collect also.

With regards to the Museum staff I am

Sincerely yours

Barnum Brown

P.S. Advise me regarding freight of fossils.

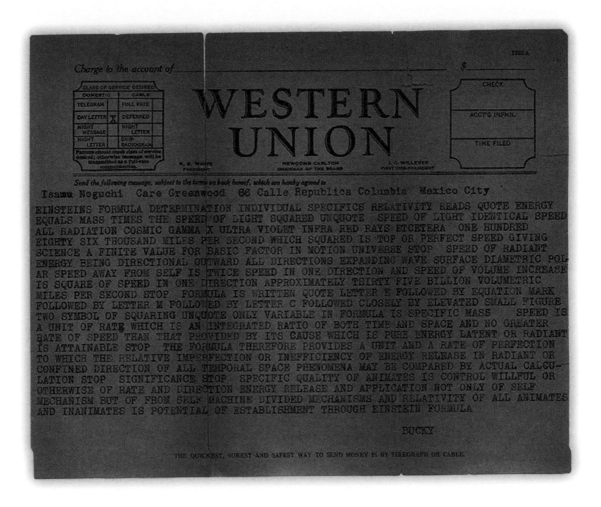

ENERGY EQUALS MASS TIMES THE SPEED OF LIGHT SQUARED STOP

BUCKMINSTER FULLER to ISAMU NOGUCHI

1936

In 1936, renowned sculptor Isamu Noguchi was in Mexico working on a 72-foot-long public mural when he hit a snag: for some reason, he couldn't precisely recall the famous formula, $E=mc^2$. Rather than risk a mistake, he decided to seek advice and wired his good friend, Buckminster Fuller — a world-famous architect and great admirer of Albert Einstein — for clarification. Rather than just respond with the equation, Fuller went the extra mile and soon sent a magnificent telegram to his friend in which he also explained it in 264 words.

7475 Hillside Avenue, Los Angeles, California
November 17, 1949

I THINK YOU'RE A DAMN FOOL

NORMAN MAILER to HIS
FATHER
November 17th, 1949

When 23-year-old Norman
Mailer left the US Army
in 1946 with three years'
service behind him, he
immediately began writing
his first book. In 1948, *The
Naked and the Dead* was
published to widespread
acclaim from critics and
readers alike, a war novel
that would sell hundreds
of thousands of copies in a
matter of months and make
a home for itself on the *New
York Times* Best Sellers list
for more than a year. His
success was instant. A year
after the book's publication,
with film rights recently sold
and praise still ringing in his
ears, Mailer received a letter
from his father, with news of
yet another gambling debt.
This was his reply.

Facing page:
*Novelist Norman Mailer in
Massachusetts, 2000*

Dear Pop,

If I ever had any doubt as to where I got my writing ability from, I know now finally that it comes from you. Your last letter was a masterpiece in which every line and every word is perfect — I doubt whether I have ever written two pages as good as that myself.

However, being a practitioner of the written word myself, I have come to understand a little about the emotional processes that go into writing, and so I find that I cannot accept your letter completely. For while it is a masterful document of the English colonel writing to his son about one of those bagatelles — a gambling debt — I finish it by reminding myself that you are not an English colonel but a Jewish accountant in Brooklyn, and that it is time you grew up.

I must confess that I have little hope in this direction. If I had I'd probably spend a great deal of time upbraiding you — I would scream about the three thousand dollars, would appeal to you as a grandfather (the money represents two years of college for Susan), would complain as a son (I figured out today that when I work in Hollywood for a thousand dollars a week, it represents after paying agent's and lawyer's fees, income tax, and subtracting living expenses, no more than three hundred dollars each seven days are saved. Thus this sum represents ten weeks of very unpleasant work to me.) But actually, I've always understood you better than Mother. There's no use upbraiding you because your eyes look away, your mind wanders, and your mouth gets sullen. One's a fool to nag a little boy.

So I'm not going to nag you, and I'm not going to frighten you, and I'm not going to scold you — I'm going to lay down several principles, and I'm going to hold to them until hell freezes over.

1) I am not going to pay the three thousand dollars to you. First of all the debt may well be a few hundred dollars less, and you put it in round figures to give yourself a little stake. I will pay it to the gambler or gamblers you owe it to, and I will also inform them at the same time that your credit will never be honored by me again, and they will be suckers to have you owe them ten bucks. So your next step, old boy, is to inform your creditors that they must write to me, and I will honor your debts — this time.

2) You are going on your own power to include Mother in your banking account with Mailer and Troll. If you don't do this, I am going to get another accountant. I'm fucked if I'm going to pay a fee like $1750 for the year, and have Mother get none of it. Apropos of this I would suggest that you're not really too clever. You have great talents at facing people at the penultimate moment and staring them down — as viz the time out here when you succeeded in making me feel ashamed of myself for considering the fee too high. Your performance was masterful that night, and I tip my hat to you, but I would also remind you that the memory of that evening is now dictating some of the tone of this letter. So that in the long run you were quite foolish.

3) You are not to consider this $3,000 as a debt to me. God Forbid. You would then go out, and try to win it back, and would find yourself owing me six thousand dollars.

4) If you start fooling around with the accounts of people like Flieg, I shall probably let you go to prison, but in any case I shall never speak to you again. And I shall tell Barbara everything.

5) I suggest that you sit down and attempt to understand a few fundamentals. You are never going to be a rich man, and if you could only realize that that is not important, and that you are loved by several people, you might be much closer to finding some internal peace. However, I offer this with no hope. You are a very neurotic man and I rather suspect that you almost enjoy the secret anxiety of carrying such secret debts and burdens as long as possible, relishing them the way a masturbator retires into the privacy of his own cock. But in any case whether you can work it out or not, I am giving you fair notice that I will never pay another gambling debt of yours. I am not soft like Mother, I have no illusions about you, and if every penny that is given to you has to be watched, I will not be afraid of your resentment, and bullied into giving you freedom again. You ought to understand by now, Pop, that I am not soft like Mother, that I am not at all sentimental, and that I can be ruthless if I have to. I lay down these conditions merely because I may not have the money in a few years, and I don't care to go into debt for anybody. There is no morality in this. I think you're a damn fool (the persistent question in my mind is Why doesn't he ever win?) and I am merely annoyed that I should have so stupid a father. (If there's any hope left for you it is that you will go off into a corner and indulge in masturbatory daydream about how you will show me some day. Because you never will. Face it.)

If I were a very healthy man I would give you a thousand dollars a year purely for gambling, much as one gives an alcoholic his quart for the day.

The purpose of this letter is to impress upon you indelibly that this is the last time. If you think Dave was hard in the past, don't try me again. I say this not because I consider myself a superior moral being to you — my own vices are quite the equal of yours — but because the situation is intolerable, and I do not intend to be burdened with it for the rest of my life.

When you answer me, I'll respect you more if you cut out all of the charm and all the English-colonel-writing-to-his-son kind of bullshit, and act as if you are writing to the man who understands you best in the world, and regards you with the distant sympathy we always feel for people who are exactly like ourselves.

Your son,
Norman

THE GREATEST MUSICAL PLEASURE I HAVE EVER EXPERIENCED

CHARLES BAUDELAIRE to
RICHARD WAGNER
February 17th, 1860

Early 1860, thousands visited
a grand Paris venue known
as the Salle Ventadour in
order to enjoy the music
of Richard Wagner, an
immeasurably influential
German composer who was
was in town to conduct three
concerts featuring extracts
from his various operas
– they included *The Flying
Dutchman*, *Lohengrin*, and
Tannhäuser. One member
of the audience who was
particularly taken with
the shows, despite having
been previously unfamiliar
with Wagner's work, was
noted French poet Charles
Baudelaire. In fact, he
was so impressed by what
he deemed "the greatest
musical pleasure [he had]
ever experienced", that
a few days after the last
performance, he wrote
Wagner a letter.

Dear Sir:

I have always imagined that however used to fame a great artist may be, he cannot be insensible to a sincere compliment, especially when that compliment is like a cry of gratitude; and finally that this cry could acquire a singular kind of value when it came from a Frenchman, which is to say from a man little disposed to be enthusiastic, and born, moreover, in a country where people hardly understand painting and poetry any better than they do music. First of all, I want to tell you that I owe you the greatest musical pleasure I have ever experienced. I have reached an age when one no longer makes it a pastime to write letters to celebrities, and I should have hesitated a long time before writing to express my admiration for you, if I did not daily come across shameless and ridiculous articles in which every effort is made to libel your genius. You are not the first man, sir, about whom I have suffered and blushed for my country. At length indignation impelled me to give you an earnest of my gratitude; I said to myself, "I want to stand out from all those imbeciles."

The first time I went to the Italian Theatre in order to hear your works, I was rather unfavorably disposed and indeed, I must admit, full of nasty prejudices, but I have an excuse: I have been so often duped; I have heard so much music by pretentious charlatans. But you conquered me at once. What I felt is beyond description, and if you will be kind enough not to laugh, I shall try to interpret it for you. At the outset it seemed to me that I knew this new music, and later, on thinking it over, I understood whence came this mirage; it seemed to me that this music was mine, and I recognized it in the way that any man recognizes the things he is destined to love. To anybody but an intelligent man, this statement would be immensely ridiculous, especially when it comes from one who, like me, does not know music, and whose whole education consists in having heard (most pleasurably, to be sure) some few fine pieces by Weber and Beethoven.

Next, the thing that struck me the most was the character of grandeur. It depicts what is grand and incites to grandeur. Throughout your works I found again the solemnity of the grand sounds of Nature in her grandest aspects, as well as the solemnity of the grand passions of man. One feels immediately carried away and dominated. One of the strangest pieces, which indeed gave me a new musical sensation, is the one intended to depict a religious ecstasy. The effect produced by the *Entrance of the Guests* and the *Wedding Fête* is tremendous. I felt in it all the majesty of a larger life than ours. Another thing: quite often I experienced a sensation of a rather bizarre nature, which was the pride and the joy of understanding, of letting myself be penetrated and invaded—a really sensual delight that resembles that of rising in the air or tossing upon the sea. And the music at the same time would now and then resound with the pride of life. Generally these profound harmonies seemed to me like those stimulants that quicken the pulse of the imagination. Finally, and I entreat you not to laugh, I also felt sensations which probably derive from my own turn of mind and my most frequent concerns. There is everywhere something rapt and enthralling, something aspiring to mount higher, something excessive and superlative. For example, if I may make analogies with painting, let me suppose I have before me a vast expanse of dark red. If this red stands for passion, I see it gradually passing through all the transitions of red and pink to the incandescent glow of a furnace. It would seem difficult, impossible even, to reach anything more glowing; and yet a last fuse comes and traces a whiter streak on the white of the background. This will signify, if you will, the supreme utterance of a soul at its highest paroxysm.

I had begun to write a few meditations on the pieces from Tannhäuser and Lohengrin that we listened to; but soon saw the impossibility of saying everything. Similarly, this letter could go on interminably. If you have been able to read it through, I thank you. It only remains for me to add a few words. From the day when I heard your music, I have said to myself endlessly, and especially at bad times, "If I only could hear a little Wagner tonight!" There are doubtless other men constituted like myself. After all, you must have been pleased with the public, whose instinct proved far superior to the false science of the journalists. Why not give us a few more concerts, adding some new pieces? You have given us a foretaste of new delights—have you the right to withhold the rest? Once again, sir, I thank you; you brought me back to myself and to what is great, in some unhappy moments.

Ch. Baudelaire

I do not set down my address because you might think I wanted something from you.

Vendredi 17 février 1860 -

Monsieur,

Je me suis toujours figuré que si accoutumé
à la gloire que fut un grand artiste, il n'était
pas insensible à un compliment sincère, quand ce
compliment était comme un cri de reconnaissance,
et enfin que le cri pouvait avoir une valeur
d'un genre singulier quand il venait d'un français
c'est à dire d'un homme peu fait pour l'action
d'aimer et né dans un pays où l'on ne s'entend
guère plus à la poésie et à la peinture qu'à
la musique. Avant tout, je veux vous dire que
si vous dois la plus grande jouissance musicale
que j'aie jamais éprouvée. Je suis d'un âge
où on ne s'amuse plus guère à écrire aux
hommes célèbres, et j'aurais hésité longtemps encore à vous
témoigner par lettre mon admiration si tous les
jours mes yeux ne tombaient sur des articles
indignes, ridicules, où on fait tous les efforts
possibles pour diffamer votre génie. Vous
n'êtes pas le seul être honnête, monsieur, à l'occasion duquel j'ai eu à souffrir et à rougir de mon
pays. Enfin l'indignation m'a poussé à vous ...
témoigner ma reconnaissance; je me suis dit :
je veux être distingué de tous ces imbéciles.

La première fois que je suis allé aux Italiens

pour entendre vos ouvrages, j'étais assez mal
disposé, et même j'avouerai, plein de mauvais
préjugés; mais si j'suis excusable; j'ai été si
souvent dupe; j'ai entendu tant de musique
de Charlatans à grandes prétentions. Par vous
j'ai été vaincu tout de suite, ce que j'ai éprouvé
est indescriptible, et si vous daignez ne pas
rire, j'essaierai de vous le rendre. D'abord il
m'a semblé que si connaissais cette musique, et
plus tard en y réfléchissant, j'ai compris d'où
venait le mirage; il me semblait que cette
musique était la mienne, et je la reconnaissais
comme tout homme reconnaît les choses qu'il est
destiné à aimer. Pour tout autre que pour un
homme d'esprit, cette phrase serait immensément
ridicule, surtout écrite par quelqu'un qui, comme
moi ne sait pas la musique, et dont toute l'éduca-
tion se borne à avoir entendu (avec grand plaisir,
il est vrai) quelques beaux morceaux de Weber
et de Beethoven.

Ensuite le caractère qui m'a principalement
frappé, ç'a été la grandeur. Cela représente le
grand, et cela pousse au grand. J'ai retrouvé
partout dans vos ouvrages la solennité des grands
bruits, des grands aspects de la nature, et la
solennité des grandes passions de l'homme. On
se sent tout de suite enlevé et subjugué. L'un
des morceaux les plus étranges et qui m'ont apporté
une sensation musicale nouvelle est celui qui

est destiné à peindre une extase religieuse.

L'effet produit par l'introduction des invités et par la fête nuptiale est immense. J'ai senti toute la majesté d'une vie plus large que la nôtre; autre chose encore : j'ai éprouvé souvent des sentiments d'une nature assez bizarre, c'est l'orgueil et la jouissance de comprendre, de me laisser pénétrer, envahir, volupté vraiment sensuelle et qui ressemble à celle de monter dans l'air ou de rouler sur la mer. Et la musique en même temps respirait quelquefois l'orgueil de la vie. Généralement les profondes harmonies me paraissaient ressembler à ces excitants qui accélèrent le pouls de l'imagination. Enfin, j'ai éprouvé aussi, et je vous supplie de ne pas rire, des sensations qui dérivent probablement de la tournure de mon esprit et de mes préoccupations fréquentes. Il y a partout quelque chose d'enlevé et d'enlevant, quelque chose aspirant à monter plus haut, quelque chose d'excessif et de superlatif. Par exemple, pour me servir de comparaisons empruntées à la peinture, je suppose devant mes yeux une vaste étendue d'un rouge sombre. Si ce rouge représente la passion, je le vois arriver graduellement, par toutes les transitions de rouge et de rose, à l'incandescence de la

journée. Il semblerait difficile, impossible
même d'arriver à quelque chose de plus
ardent; et cependant une dernière fusée veut
tracer un sillon plus blanc sur le blanc qui
lui sert de fond. Ce sera, si vous voulez, le
cri suprême de l'âme montée à son paroxysme.

J'avais commencé à écrire quelques méditations
sur les morceaux de Tannhoeuser et de
Lohengrin que vous avons entendus; mais
j'ai reconnu l'impossibilité de tout dire.

Ainsi je pourrais continuer cette lettre interminablement.
Si vous avez pu me lire, j'vous en remercie. Il ne
me reste plus à ajouter que quelques mots. Depuis
le jour où j'ai entendu votre musique, je me dis
sans cesse, surtout dans les mauvaises heures:
Si, au moins, je pouvais entendre ce soir un peu de
Wagner! Il y a sans doute d'autres
hommes faits comme moi. En somme vous avez dû
être satisfait du public dont l'instinct a été
bien supérieur à la mauvaise science des journalistes.
Pourquoi ne donneriez-vous pas quelques concerts encore
en y ajoutant des morceaux nouveaux? Vous nous
avez fait connaître un avant-goût de jouissances
nouvelles; avez-vous le droit de nous priver du reste
—Une fois encore, Monsieur, je vous remercie; vous m'avez
rappelé à moi-même et au grand, dans de mauvaises heures.

Ch. Baudelaire.

Je n'ajoute pas mon adresse, parceque vous croiriez
peut-être que j'ai quelque chose à vous demander.

Tennessee Williams
135 E. 58th Street
New York, NY

*Streetcar
motion picture*

148 - 9

October 29, 1950

Joseph Breen
Motion Picture Producers and Distributors of America
Los Angeles, Calif.

Dear Mr. Breen:

Mr. Kazan has just informed me that objections have been raised about the "rape scene" in "Streetcar" and I think perhaps it might be helpful for me to clarify the meaning and importance of this scene. As everybody must have acknowledged by now since it has been pointed out in the press by members of the clergy of all denominations, and not merely in the press but in the pulpit - "Streetcar" is an extremely and peculiarly moral play, in the deepest and truest sense of the term. This fact is so well known that a misunderstanding of it now at this late date would arouse widespread attention and indignation.

The rape of Blanche by Stanley is a pivotal, integral truth in the play, without which the play loses its meaning, which is the ravishment of the tender, the sensitive, the delicate by the savage and brutal forces in modern society. It is a poetic plea for comprehension. I did not beg the issue by making Blanche a totally "good" person, nor Stanley a totally "bad" one. But to those who have made some rational effort to understand the play, it is apparent that Blanche is neither a "dipsomaniac" nor a "nymphomaniac" but a person of intense loneliness, fallibility and a longing which is mostly spiritual for warmth and protection. I did not, of course, disavow what I think is one of the primary things of beauty and depth in human existence, which is the warmth between two people, the so-called "sensuality" in the love-relationship. If nature and God chose this to be the mean of life's continuance on earth, I see no reason to disavow it in creative work. At the same time, I know what taste is and what vulgarity is. I have drawn a very sharp and clear line between the two in all of the plays that I have had presented. I have never made an appeal to anything "low" or "cheap" in my plays and I would rather die than do so. Elia Kazan has directed "Streetcar" both on the stage and the screen, with inspired understanding of its finest values and an absolute regard for taste and propriety. I was fortunately able to see, in "rushes", all but the last three scenes of the picture before I left California. Mr. Kazan has given me a detailed description of the scenes I didn't see as they now exist on the screen. I am really amazed that any question should arise about censorship. Please remember that even in notoriously strict Boston, where the play tried out before Broadway, there was no attack on it by any responsible organ of public opinion, and on the screen the spiritual values of the play have been accentuated much more than they could be on the stage.

I KNOW WHAT TASTE IS AND WHAT VULGARITY IS

TENNESSEE WILLIAMS to JOSEPH BREEN
October 29th, 1950

In 1947, *A Streetcar Named Desire* premiered on Broadway to rapturous applause, glowing reviews and, the following year, numerous awards. Written by Tennessee Williams and directed by Elia Kazan with a cast that included Marlon Brando, Jessica Tandy, Kim Hunter, and Karl Malden, it ran for two successful years with few alterations. In 1951, a film version hit the big screen, adapted by Williams, directed by Kazan, and boasting largely the same cast. It went on to win four Academy Awards. But it wasn't all plain sailing. In 1950, the year before its release, the film ran afoul of the Motion Picture Production Code, who deemed a "pivotal" rape scene to be in breach of their guidelines. In response, Tennessee Williams wrote to the code's administrator, Joseph Breen.

The poetically beautiful and touching performance of a great visiting artist, Vivien Leigh, has dominated the picture and given it a stature which surpasses that of the play. "A Streetcar Named Desire" is one of the truly great American films and one of the very few really moral films that have come out of Hollywood. To mutilate it, now, by forcing, or attempting to force, disastrous alterations in the essential truth of it would serve no good end that I can imagine.

Please remember, also, that we have already made great concessions which we felt were dangerous to attitudes which we thought were narrow. In the middle of preparations for a new play, on which I have been working for two years, I came out to Hollywood to re-write certain sequences to suit the demands of your office. No one involved in this screen production has failed in any respect to show you the cooperation, and even deference, that has been called for. But now we are fighting for what we think is the heart of the play, and when we have our backs against the wall — if we are forced into that position — none of us is going to throw in the towel! We will use every legitimate means that any of us has at his or her disposal to protect the things in this film which we think cannot be sacrificed, since we feel that it contains some very important truths about the world we live in.

Sincerely,

Tennessee Williams

I WOULD LIKE TO GIVE YOU YOUR OWN HISTORY

JUAN GELMAN to HIS
GRANDCHILD
1995

In 1976, shortly after a coup
that saw the President of
Argentina, Isabel Martínez
de Perón, replaced by a
military dictatorship, the
life of celebrated Argentine
poet Juan Gelman darkened
immeasurably when his
son and daughter-in-law
– Marcelo, 20, and María
Claudia, an 18-year-old
expectant mother – were
kidnapped, just two of
approximately 30,000
people to go missing in
similar circumstances
under the new regime.
Gelman's subsequent
investigations confirmed
the worst, that both had
been killed, but also that
their baby had survived
and had been taken in by
foster parents in Uruguay.
Gelman was desperate to
meet his grandchild: this
letter, written in 1995 and
published in a national
newspaper, was the height
of his search.

Juan Gelman's grand-
daughter, Macarena, was
found in 1999. They met for
the first time the next year.
The Inter-American Court of
Human Rights later forced
Uruguay to admit publicly
the crimes against Maria,
Marcelo and Macarena
Gelman. The accompanying
photo shows Macarena
and Juan Gelman in 2012
after Uruguayan Prime
Minister Jose Mujica read a
statement to this effect.

An Open Letter to My Grandson or Granddaughter

Within the next six months you will turn nineteen. You would have been born one day in October 1976 in an army concentration camp, El Pozo de Quilmes, almost certainly. A little before or a little after they assassinated your father with a shot in the head from less than a half meter's distance. He was helpless and a military detail assassinated him, perhaps the same one that kidnapped him along with your mother in Buenos Aires that 24th of August, removing them to the concentration camp known as Automotores Orletti. It functioned right there in the neighborhood of Floresta, and the military christened it "The Garden."

Your father's name was Marcelo; your mother's, Claudia. Each was twenty years old at the time, and you were six months in your mother's womb when this happened. They moved her – and you within her – to Quilmes when she was about to give birth. She must have given birth there under the eyes of some doctor/accomplice of the military dictatorship. They took you from her then, and you were placed – it usually happened like this – in the hands of some sterile couple, military or police force, or some judge or journalist friendly to police or military. There was a sinister waiting list in those days for each concentration camp; those entered on it would wait to be paired with a child born of those prisoners who gave birth and who, with few exceptions, were assassinated immediately afterward.

Thirteen years have passed since the military left the government, and nothing is known of your mother. On the other hand, in a sixty-gallon oil drum which the military filled with sand and concrete and threw into the San Fernando River your father's remains were found thirteen years after the fact. He is buried now in La Tablada. At least in his case there is that much certainty.

It is very strange for me to be speaking of my children as your parents-who-never-were. I do not know if you are a boy or a girl. I know you were born. Father Fiorello Cavalli of the Secretariat of the Vatican State assured me of that fact in February 1978. What has been your destiny since, I ask myself. Conflicting ideas keep coming to me. On the one hand I have always found repugnant the idea of your calling "Daddy" some military or police gangster who stole you, or some friend of those who assassinated your father. On the other hand I have always wished that in whatever home you may have grown up you were well brought up and educated and loved a lot. Still, I have always thought there must be some hole, or failure in the love shown you, not so much because these parents are not your biological parents – as they say – but because they would have to have some awareness of your story and how they were involved in falsifying it. I suppose that you have been lied to a lot.

Then, too, I have wondered all these years what I would do if you were found – whether to drag you out of the home you knew; whether to speak with your adoptive parents and establish visiting rights, always on the basis of your knowing who you were and where you came from. The dilemma came up and circled around time and time again, whenever the possibility arose that the Grandmothers of the Plaza de Mayo had found you. I would work it out differently each time, according to your age at the moment. It would worry me that you'd be too small or not small enough to understand what had happened, to understand why your parents, whom you believed to be your parents, were not, even though you might want them to be. I was worried you would suffer a double wound that way, one that would cause structural damage to your identity as it was forming.

But now you are big. You will be capable of understanding who you are and of deciding what do to with who you are. The Grandmothers are there with their flesh-and-blood data banks that enable them to determine with scientific precision the origins of the children of the Disappeared. Your origins.

You are almost as old now as your parents were when they killed them, and soon you will be older than they got to be, they who have stayed twenty forever. They had dreams for you and for a world more suitable and habitable. I would like to talk to you about them and to have you tell me about yourself; to be able to recognize in you my own son and to let you find in me what I have of your father – both of us are his orphans. I would like to repair somehow this brutal severance or silence that has perpetrated the military dictatorship within the very flesh of my family. I would like to give you your own history, but not separate you from what you don't want to separate from. You are big now, as I said.

Marcelo and Claudia's dreams have not yet come true. Least of all for you, who were born, and who knows where and with whom you are? Perhaps you have the gray-green eyes of my son, or the chestnut-colored eyes of his wife that had a particular shine, tender and lively both. Who knows what you are like if you are a boy? Who knows what you are like if you are a girl? Maybe you'll be able to get yourself out of this mystery and into another one: a meeting with a grandfather who is waiting for you.

Facing page: Argentinean poet Juan Gelman kisses his granddaughter Macarena Gelman, 2012

312

THIS IS QUITE TRUE

EVELYN WAUGH to LAURA
WAUGH
May 31st, 1942

As World War II raged in May
of 1942, three years before
the publication of what has
since become his best-
known novel, *Brideshead
Revisited,* English author
Evelyn Waugh was in fact
a newly-assigned member
of the British Army's Royal
Horse Guards, a cavalry
regiment then stationed
in south-west Scotland to
which he had recently been
transferred. Back home,
in dire need of some light
relief, his wife of five years,
Laura, was steadfastly
holding fort whilst just
weeks away from giving
birth to their fourth child,
Margaret. Entertainment
soon arrived in the form of
a letter from her husband in
which he expertly and with
pitch-perfect comic timing
told the story of a tree stump
on the Earl of Glasgow's
estate.

31st May 1942

Darling

It was a great joy to get a letter from you. I thought you had been swallowed up in some Pixton plague.

Do you know Ellwoods address? I wrote to him care Harper – no answer.

Miss Cowles leaves tonight. Everyone except me will be sorry. I have had to arrange all her movements and it has been a great deal of trouble. She is a cheerful, unprincipled young woman. She wants to be made Colonel in chief of the commando so I have suggested Princess Margaret Rose instead. Bob eats out of my hand at the moment.

So No. 3 Cmdo were very anxious to be chums with Lord Glasgow so they offered to blow up an old tree stump for him and he was very grateful and he said don't spoil the plantation of young trees near it because that is the apple of my eye and they said no of course not we can blow a tree down so that it falls on a sixpence and Lord Glasgow said goodness you are clever and he asked them all to luncheon for the great explosion. So Col. Durnford-Slater D.S.O. said to his subaltern, have you put enough explosive in the tree. Yes, sir, 75 lbs. Is that enough? Yes sir I worked it out by mathematics it is exactly right. Well better put a bit more. Very good sir.

And when Col. D. Slater D.S.O. had had his port he sent for the subaltern and said subaltern better put a bit more explosive in that tree. I don't want to disappoint Lord Glasgow. Very good sir.

Then they all went out to see the explosion and Col. D.S. D.S.O. said you will see that tree fall flat at just that angle where it will hurt no young trees and Lord Glasgow said goodness you are clever.

So soon they lit the fuse and waited for the explosion and presently the tree, instead of falling quietly sideways, rose 50 feet into the air taking with it 1/2 acre of soil and the whole of the young plantation.

And the subaltern said Sir I made a mistake, it should have been 71/2 lbs not 75.

Lord Glasgow was so upset he walked in dead silence back to his castle and when they came to the turn of the drive in sight of his castle what should they find but that every pane of glass in the building was broken.

So Lord Glasgow gave a little cry & ran to hide his emotion in the lavatory and there when he pulled the plug the entire ceiling, loosened by the explosion, fell on his head.

This is quite true.

E

I SHALL EXPECT YOU, SISTER

CLAUDIA SEVERA to SULPICIA LEPIDINA
Circa AD102

First discovered near Hadrian's Wall in the 1970s, the Vindolanda tablets remain the oldest handwritten documents to have survived the test of time – delicate, wafer-thin sheets of wood on which the 2000-year-old everyday correspondence of families still breathes, offering invaluable insights into life in Roman Britain. Arguably the most famous of these time capsules is seen here: a letter written by Claudia Severa, wife of a fort commander, in which she invites Sulpicia Lepidina to her birthday party on the 11th September. This remarkable missive is one of the earliest examples of a woman's handwriting in Latin. The first part was dictated; the final section is in Claudia's hand. It now resides at the British Museum.

Claudia Severa to her Lepidina greetings. On 11 September, sister, for the day of the celebration of my birthday, I give you a warm invitation to make sure that you come to us, to make the day more enjoyable for me by your arrival, if you are present. Give my greetings to your Cerialis. My Aelius and my little son send him their greetings.

I shall expect you sister. Farewell, sister my dearest soul, as I hope to prosper, and hail.

Letter inviting Sulpicia Lepidina to a birthday party, Vindolanda, Britain, c.102AD

Letter No. 111

LET ME ALONE

KATHERINE ANNE PORTER
to HART CRANE
June 22nd, 1931

In March of 1931, shortly
before travelling to Mexico
to begin work on a follow-up
to his epic poem, *The Bridge*,
Hart Crane wrote to some
friends and told them that
he would be spending the
first week with his "old and
wonderful friend", novelist
Katherine Anne Porter, who
had lived there for some
time. Thanks to Crane's
increasingly drunken
and often violent nature,
even around those that he
loved, that friendship soon
crumbled, and just a few
months after he arrived in
the country, Porter could
see no other option but to
rid her life of him. This calm
but furious letter was her
goodbye. Sadly, Crane's
descent continued apace: a
year later, as he sailed back
to the US with no money or
creative inspiration to speak
of, he took his own life by
jumping into the Gulf of
Mexico.

Facing page:
Writer Katherine Anne Porter

Dear Hart:

First about the lunch. I was disappointed too, and sorry for your trouble, for it is trouble to have food for people who don't arrive. I waited too long at the Consulate, for of course they did not have my passports ready as they promised. This was my third trip to town, and I was so anxious to have it over I just sat and waited. Then the day being spoiled anyhow, I finished up some other tiresome errands, and had barely reached home when I heard myself being called, among other items, a whore and a fancy-woman and Gene a fancy-man, so I just turned about and went in again ... At other times when you were in the same state, you have mentioned my ancestry, upbringing, and habits of life in the same tone, with a peculiar insistence that grew comic, but still forced me to believe it was my existence you resented, rather than any superficial criticism such as friends make of one another.

This is a mystery to me, but not really interesting.

You know you have had the advantage of me, because I share the superstition of our time about the somewhat romantic irresponsibility of drunkenness, holding it a social offense to take seriously things said and done by a drunken person. Therefore I have borne to the limit of my patience with brutal behavior, shameless lying, hysterical raving, and the general sordid messiness of people who had not the courage to be as shabby as they wished when sober, for fear of consequences, but must hide behind liquor and be treated with indulgence. I have behaved badly when drunk, I know it, but never to my friends, nor they, when drunk, to me. I believe a drunken mood is as good a mirror as a sober one: your behavior to me when drunk falls too consistently into the same pattern, repeats itself too monotonously, for me to believe anything except what I do believe: that for whatever reasons, and you are welcome to any reasons you have, you bear a fixed dislike to me, of a very nasty kind. At first naturally I did not want to believe this, then it troubled me very much and I tried to get at the causes and cure them; now I merely am finished, quite, with this whole affair, and refuse to have anything more to do with it. I have lived in Greenwich Village also, as you know, but I was never involved there in such a meaningless stupid situation as this ... I have no taste for melodrama, and when I fight, it must be for something better than this.

I am by temperament no victim, and I wonder at your lack of imagination in picking on me as audience for exhibitions of this kind. I'm sorry about Peggy, but I suppose she has known persons who did not agree very well before now, and I see nothing in this to take sides about. I think that you like making mischief simply through idleness and restlessness, and you don't feel quite alive unless you are tearing at other personalities like a monkey ... Let me tell you plainly that this bores me, I see through it, and I won't have it. I have heard the astonishing tale of your treatment of the Spanish teacher, and your gratuitous insult to poor Miss Kelly, and I am beginning to believe that a sanitarium for the mentally defective is the proper place for you. If this is true, I should be sorry at having being angry at you. But I think it is time you grew up and stopped behaving like a very degenerate adolescent. You must either learn to stand on your own feet as a responsible adult, or expect to be treated as a fool. Your emotional hysteria is not impressive, except possibly to those little hangers-on of literature who feel your tantrums are a mark of genius. To me they do not add the least value to your poetry, and take away my last shadow of a wish to ever see you again ... Let me alone. This disgusting episode has already gone too far.

Katherine Anne

U.S. Department of Justice

Federal Bureau of Investigation

Washington, D.C. 20535

August 1, 1989

Mr. Gui Manganiello
National Promotions Director
Priority Records
Suite 800
6430 Sunset Boulevard
Hollywood, California 90028

Dear Mr. Manganiello:

A song recorded by the rap group N.W.A. on their album entitled "Straight Outta Compton" encourages violence against and disrespect for the law enforcement officer and has been brought to my attention. I understand your company recorded and distributed this album, and I am writing to share my thoughts and concerns with you.

Advocating violence and assault is wrong, and we in the law enforcement community take exception to such action. Violent crime, a major problem in our country, reached an unprecedented high in 1988. Seventy-eight law enforcement officers were feloniously slain in the line of duty during 1988, four more than in 1987. Law enforcement officers dedicate their lives to the protection of our citizens, and recordings such as the one from N.W.A. are both discouraging and degrading to these brave, dedicated officers.

Music plays a significant role in society, and I wanted you to be aware of the FBI's position relative to this song and its message. I believe my views reflect the opinion of the entire law enforcement community.

Sincerely yours,

Milt Ahlerich
Assistant Director
Office of Public Affairs

F**K THA POLICE

THE FBI to PRIORITY RECORDS
August 1st, 1989

Straight Outta Compton, the pioneering debut album from rap group N.W.A. (Niggaz Wit Attitude), remains to this day one of the most controversial records ever to have been recorded thanks to its explicit lyrics, misogyny, glorification of violence, and one song in particular: "Fuck tha Police". The release of such a record just a few years before the L.A. riots, at a time when tensions were already running high between the police and the black community, resulted in its being banned by most radio stations and the cancellation of their live shows. Then came a soon-to-be regretted letter from the FBI that was deemed to have crossed a line and which only served to intensify the public's interest in their music. The letter now sits in the Rock and Roll Hall of Fame in Cleveland. *Straight Outta Compton* has since sold many millions of copies.

I HAVE ALWAYS BEEN
TALKED ABOUT

ANSEL ADAMS to NANCY
NEWHALL
July 15th, 1944

It was in Yosemite National
Park in 1916 that Ansel
Adams, then aged 14 with
ambitions to become a
concert pianist, took a
photograph for the first
time using a Brownie box
camera given to him by
his father. He was bitten
by the bug immediately
and vowed to return to
Yosemite often, camera in
hand; thanks to this new
obsession, his imagined
musical career eventually
faded. Adams went on
to become an award-
winning photographer of
considerable standing,
famous for masterfully
shooting the American
landscape like no other
and producing numerous
handsome books filled with
his work. In July 1944, he
wrote a revealing letter
about his choice of career
to photography critic Nancy
Newhall, a friend who at the
time was beginning work on
a biography of Adams that
was eventually published
in 1963, titled *The Eloquent
Light.*

Yosemite National Park
July 15, 1944

My Dear Nancy,

Nice letter from the Overland Limited. Nice you saw Dorothea and Imogen. Sorry
you missed Wright. Hope you get home not too exhausted. Hope things are right
for you there. Let me know everything that happens. Am terribly interested, as you
know.

Did not really do much for you - not nearly what I had hoped to do. I think that we
will get a perspective on lots of problems one of these days. You really worked hard
most of the time.

I have always been talked about; in grammar school, as a kid, I was considered
"unusual" - not in my right mind, so to speak. Then, I lived "north of Lake St."
which automatically made me an aristocrat in relation to those who lived "south of
Lake." This distinction seemed to be based on the fact of two hideous stone pillars,
or pylons, which the real-estate development company set up to mark a perfectly
ordinary area as "exclusive"; the only sad gap in their logic is that the pylons were
built about eight years after my father "moved out there in the country." Hence,
my snootiness was thrust upon me. But I went through Hell at that time; was sent
to a private school for "adjustment," and otherwise enjoyed a rather irregular
youth. Of course, I was always aware that people talked about me. The fact that I
could do many things deftly and never was a "bad little boy" was not sufficient to
overcome the stronger fact that I was "different."

My father had a series of business misfortunes and things were not so hot for quite
a few years. As my father was about played out an old friend insisted he take us
to Yosemite for a vacation. This was in 1916. From that time on, things became
crystallized in a far more healthy way. In making the choice between music and
college, I still think I did the right thing, but others seem not to think so. Anyway,
here I am in photography; most of my friends of earlier days keep stressing their
regret I did not stay in music! My family said, "What!! you don't want to be
anything else but a photographer!!" That helped, of course. I was talked about
because:

> I could play AND photograph (something immoral about that!!)
> I wore a beard
> I knew a lot of artists
> I did not dance
> I dared to question the status-quo
> I became engaged to Virginia

I became dis-engaged to Virginia
I had too many girlfriends
I did not have enough girlfriends (something funny there, YES sir!!)
I married Virginia
I did not live in a garret
I moved to Yosemite
I liked Modern Art
I charged too much
I charged too little
I always did like women
Virginia should not have been so lenient
Virginia should have "understood" (think she has done a very good job of that kind of "understanding")
I drink too much
I can't follow the Commie line
I think expression is something in addition to politics and vice-versa
I'm a radical
I like to be reasonably precise (this seems to create immense annoyance)
I read PM
I know Ickes
I should be free
I should have some real responsibilities
I live in an ivory tower
I am complex
I am simple
I am rich as all get-out
I live off my wife
I live off my father
My work should be in line with my Tempo
I don't like people
I don't understand the BIG social problems of today
I'm precious

Nobody seems to inquire if I am actually any more or less happy than the average Homo sapien, any more or less adjusted to conditions, or figure out some objective appraisal. I have an answer which I think may suffice – perhaps it's just a rationalization, but here goes:

I know what I have in photography – what I have done, and what I believe I can do. In relation to most of my friends I have made a rather obvious success. Very few of my friends have made that kind of success. They fundamentally, subconsciously resent it. They would like to uncover the weak spots; set me up as they think I should be – put me in my place, in other words. Well, perhaps I am not ideally situated, personally, financially, creatively. But I am definitely NOT unhappy.

Facing page:
Ansel Adams in the Yosemite Valley, holding a Hasselblad camera, circa 1955

In fact, just about now I am happier than almost anyone I know. I would feel very bad to think I were not man enough to assume the normal responsibilities without adversely affecting my work. I am always violently in love with something – an idea, a person, a job. I am actually quite *un-moral;* my restraint in certain cases is not based on any personal moral inhibition, but on an objective appraisal of potential harm to the other, or others, concerned. I can't think of much I wouldn't do if it would not hurt anyone else. I think I have been most fortunate; after quite a few years of adjustments I find myself stable emotionally – to all outward appearances – fairly well set in a routine of daily life – terribly fond of my environment, terribly fond of my family. I have a huge program laid out, material obligations fairly well under control, hundreds and hundreds of friends. I do have distractions, worries, disappointments. But am I unique in that? I do not envy Stieglitz his life; it seems tragic to me – much more so than anything I have had to contend with. The fact that he has accomplished what he has is a miracle – the evidence of strength and clarity of purpose. Think how much more he gets talked about than I.

If the above sounds hopeless to you, write me what YOU think!!

Love and cheer!!
Ansel

Still in bed with the goddamn flu – but getting a lot done.

Facing Page: El Capitan,
Yosemite National Park,
California, 1952 by Ansel Adams

GROW UP AS GOOD REVOLUTIONARIES

CHE GUEVARA to HIS
CHILDREN
Circa 1965

In 1955, Argentinean-born
Che Guevara met Fidel
Castro and quickly joined
his efforts to oust Fulgencio
Batista as leader of Cuba – a
revolution in which he would
go on to play a major role,
and which would lead to
Guevara becoming Finance
Minister under Castro's rule.
By 1965, Guevara was keen
to spread his revolutionary
ideas: he began by travelling
to the Congo where he
unsuccessfully attempted
to train rebel forces in the
area; he then moved on
to Bolivia, where he was
ultimately captured by the
Bolivian Army and later
executed on the orders of
President René Barrientos.
Before he left for Bolivia, he
secretly visited his wife back
in Cuba and gave her this
letter, to be read by his five
children in the event of his
death.

Facing page:
Ernesto 'Che' Guevara and
wife Aleida March leaving for
their honeymoon, 1959

To my children

Dear Hildita, Aleidita, Camilo, Celia, And Ernesto,

If you ever have to read this letter, it will be because I am no longer with you. You practically will not remember me, and the smaller ones will not remember me at all.

Your father has been a man who acted on his beliefs and has certainly been loyal to his convictions.

Grow up as good revolutionaries. Study hard so that you can master technology, which allows us to master nature. Remember that the revolution is what is important, and each one of us, alone is worth nothing.

Above all, always be capable of feeling deeply any injustice committed against anyone, anywhere in the world. This is the most beautiful quality in a revolutionary.

Until forever, my children. I still hope to see you.

A great big kiss and a big hug from,

Papa

Above: Jessica and Unity
Mitford, 1923

WE HOPE YOU SHALL TRY...

JESSICA MITFORD to HERSELF
February 3rd, 1937

It was in 1937 that 19-year-old Jessica Mitford – one rebellious sixth of the legendary Mitford sisters and future celebrated journalist and author – turned her back on the comforts of her privileged home life in England and headed for war-torn Spain. To further complicate matters, she chose to elope with her lover Esmond Romilly, a Communist nephew of Winston Churchill whose ideals contrasted sharply with those of her stubborn, aristocratic family. Indeed, were it not for this forged letter, written to Jessica supposedly from a French friend, but in fact from Jessica herself, her mother may have stopped her from fleeing the nest entirely. Luckily, the ruse was a success and within days Jessica and Esmond were en route to the Spanish Civil War. They married the same year and remained so until Esmond, then fighting in WWII, was killed in action. Shortly after leaving home, Jessica wrote to her mother and confessed all. A telegram soon found its way to Esmond from the Mitfords' lawyers:

MISS JESSICA MITFORD IS A WARD OF COURT STOP IF YOU MARRY HER WITHOUT LEAVE OF JUDGE YOU WILL BE LIABLE TO IMPRISONMENT

The Mitfords eventually and reluctantly consented to the marriage.

Garmisch, Germany
February 3, 1937

Please excuse awful paper
Darling Decca,

Twin and I are so anxious to see you before you go off round the world. Now I have a suggestion to make--sorry it's such short notice, but do try and fall in. We have taken a house in Dieppe--that is, Auntie has taken it! We mean to make it the centre of a sort of motor tour to all the amusing places round. We are going there from Austria on Wednesday, and we should so love you to join us next weekend sometime if you could possibly manage it. There won't be much of a party--just two boys from Oxford and us three and Auntie. But if you don't mind that do try and come. Our address is 22, Rue Gambetta, Dieppe. So perhaps you could send a telegram to me there, if you can come. The boys (Dick and Leslie Cholmley) are coming by Saturday night boats so perhaps you could cross then, or if not on Sunday--anyway, just telegraph. Do you know them, by the way? I think you'll like them. We shall be so disappointed if you can't come; we could have asked you before, only we weren't sure of getting a house. Our house in London is successfully let--I hope yours is.

Much Love, Mamaine

P.S. We hope you will try...

I DON'T ENJOY THIS
WAR ONE BIT

DAVID FOSTER WALLACE to
DON DeLILLO
October 10th, 1995

In February of 1996, 33-year-old David Foster Wallace's highly anticipated second novel, his sprawling magnum opus *Infinite Jest,* was published to widespread coverage and acclaim. It has since been hailed a masterpiece on more than one occasion. Behind the scenes, however, Wallace was faced with a problem: although the quality of his writing was improving, he was having less fun in the process. Some months before it was unleashed on the public, Wallace saw that a copy was sent to Don DeLillo, an award-winning author and playwright for whom he held a great deal of respect; this letter soon followed.

10-10-95

Dear Don,

Since it's clear from your letters that you're a person nice, and since it's well-known that an overkeen sense of obligation tends to afflict the congenitally nice, I again want to implore you not to feel any obligation to read the BM any faster[1] than your own schedule and inclinations permit. If Little/Brown's Pietsch put blurb-pressure on you or something, I implore you to ignore it. I did not have the BM sent to you because I hoped for a blurb. I sent it to you because your own fiction is important to me and because I think you're smart and because, if you do end up reading it and end up saying anything to me about it, I stand a decent chance of learning something.

Your note of 9/19 was heartening and inspiring and also made me curious about several things. I would love to know what changes in yourself account for "And discipline is never an issue (as it was in earlier years)." I would love to know how this education of the will took place -- would that you could assure that it was nothing but a matter of time natural attritive/osmotic action, but I have a grim suspicion there's rather more to it. I'd love to know how the sentence quoted above stands in relation to "The novel is a fucking killer. I try to show it every respect."

As I understand your terms "discipline," "respect," "dedication," your thoughts have confirmed my belief that what usually presents in me as a problem with Discipline is actually probably more a problem with Dedication. I struggle very hard with my desires both to have Fun when writing and to be Serious when writing. I know that my first book was the most Fun I've ever had writing, but I know also that the only remotely Serious thing about it was that I very Seriously wanted the world to think I was a really good fiction-writer. I cringe, now, to look at how so much of my first stuff seems so excruciatingly obviously exhibitionistic and so Seriously approval-hungry.

I have no idea whether this will make any sense to you, or whether this stuff is too personal to me to make sense about, or whether in fact it's actually so banal and mill-run that seeming tormented about it or thinking I'm uniquely afflicted will seem to you grotesque. Fuck it -- an advantage to proofreading page-proofs (PP's) is that I'm too tired to care.

I think a certain amount of time and experience and pain have helped me -- somewhat -- with respect to the immature and selfish stuff. I think IJ is less self-indulgent and show-offy than anything I'd done before it, and that the stuff I've done since finishing IJ is even less ego-hobbled. Part of the improvement inside me, too, I think, is starting truly to "Respect" fiction and realize how very much bigger than I the art and enterprise are, to be able not just to countenance but live with how very very small a part of any Big Picture I am. Because I tend both to think I'm uniquely afflicted and to idealize people I admire, I tend to imagine you never having had to struggle with any of this narcissism or indulgence stuff, to imagine that the great gouts of Americana hurled daily at the page in the stoveless apartment of wherever you wrote it were as natively Disciplined and Respectful and humility-nourished as Libra or The Day Room. But now I rather hope that isn't so. I hope that in the course of your decades writing you've done and been subject to stuff that's helped make you a more Respectful writer. I would like to be a Respectful writer, I believe...though I know I'd far prefer finding out some way to become that w/o time and pain and the war of LOOK AT ME v. RESPECT A FUCKING KILLER.

Maybe what I want to hear is that this prenominate war is natural and necessary and a sign of Towering Intellect: maybe I want a pep-talk, because I have to tell you I don't enjoy this war one bit. I think my fiction is better than it

---

[1] (or at all, actually)

was, but writing is also less Fun than it was. I have a lot of dread and terror and inadequacy-shit, now, when I'm trying to write. I didn't used to. Maybe the terror is part of the necessary reverence, and maybe it's an inescapable part of the growing-up-as-a-writer-or-whatever process; but it can't -- cannot -- be the goal and terminus of that process. In other words there must be some way to turn terror into Respect and dread into a kind of stolidly productive humility.[2]

I have a hard time understanding how Fun fits into the Dedication-Discipline-Respect schema. I know that I had less fun doing IJ than I did doing earlier stuff, even though I know in my tummy that it's better fiction. I think I understand that part of getting older and better as a writer means putting away many of my more childish or self-gratifying notions of Fun, etc. But Fun is still the whole point, somehow, no? Fun on both sides of the writer/reader exchange? A kind of pleasure -- more rarified, doubtless, than M&M's or a good wank, but nevertheless pleasure? How do I allow myself to have Fun when writing without sacrificing Respect and Seriousness, i.e. going back to exhibitionism and show-offery and pointless technical acrobatics? I think one reason why I ask you this (though I know you not at all as a person, of course) is that your own fiction seems to me to marry Fun and Seriousness in a profound way, somehow -- a sense of Play that's somehow even Funner because it's not sophomoric or self-aggrandizing[3] or childish or even childlike. This is not coming across like I want it to; I can't make this clear. Maybe your work is this form of profound marriage only to and for me; maybe it's some weird subjective misprision that has to do with me and not your fiction; maybe you have no thoughts on how you've come to make (apparent) Respect and Dedication seem so fuck-all much (apparent) Fun. If you do have any thoughts -- together with a couple minutes to rub together -- I'd be grateful for them. I'm about as professionally flummoxed as I've ever been.

All Best Wishes,

Dave Wallace

---

[2] (You are heartily welcome to let me know what this way is, if you know what it might be.)

[3] I have in mind Mark Leyner when I refer to "self-aggrandizing Fun" -- I don't know whether you know his stuff, but he is the Prince of Darkness to me.

I SHALL ALWAYS BE WITH YOU

MILADA HORÁKOVÁ to HER DAUGHTER
June 26th, 1950

On June 8th of 1950, nine months after being arrested by the Czech secret police on suspicion of leading a plot to overthrow the Communist regime, 48-year-old socialist politician Milada Horáková was found guilty of "high treason" following a show trial that was broadcast on national radio, and in which she remained defiant. On the 27th of that month, despite international outcry and a petition signed by, amongst others, Albert Einstein and Winston Churchill, Milada Horáková was executed at Prague's Pankrác Prison. The night before her death, she wrote a letter to her 16-year-old daughter.

In 1991, President Václav Havel posthumously awarded Horáková the Order of Tomáš Garrigue Masaryk.

My only little girl Jana,

God blessed my life as a woman with you. As your father wrote in the poem from a German prison, God gave you to us because he loved us. Apart from your father's magic, amazing love you were the greatest gift I received from fate. However, Providence planned my life in such a way that I could not give you nearly all that my mind and my heart had prepared for you. The reason was not that I loved you little; I love you just as purely and fervently as other mothers love their children. But I understood that my task here in the world was to do you good by seeing to it that life becomes better, and that all children can live well. And therefore, we often had to be apart for a long time. It is now already for the second time that Fate has torn us apart. Don't be frightened and sad because I am not coming back any more. Learn, my child, to look at life early as a serious matter. Life is hard, it does not pamper anybody, and for every time it strokes you it gives you ten blows. Become accustomed to that soon, but don't let it defeat you. Decide to fight. Have courage and clear goals and you will win over life. Much is still unclear to your young mind, and I don't have time left to explain to you things you would still like to ask me. One day, when you grow up, you will wonder and wonder, why your mother who loved you and whose greatest gift you were, managed her life so strangely. Perhaps then you will find the right solution to this problem, perhaps a better one than I could give you today myself. Of course, you will only be able to solve it correctly and truthfully by knowing very, very much. Not only from books, but from people; learn from everybody, no matter how unimportant! Go through the world with open eyes, and listen not only to your own pains and interests, but also to the pains, interests and longings of others. Don't ever think of anything as none of your business. No, everything must interest you, and you should reflect about everything, compare, compose individual phenomena. Man doesn't live in the world alone; in that there is great happiness, but also a tremendous responsibility. That obligation is first of all in not being and not acting exclusive, but rather merging with the needs and the goals of others. This does not mean to be lost in the multitude, but it is to know that I am part of all, and to bring one's best into that community. If you do that, you will succeed in contributing to the common goals of human society. Be more aware of one principle than I have been: approach everything in life constructively—beware of unnecessary negation—I am not saying all negation, because I believe that one should resist evil. But in order to be a truly positive person in all circumstances, one has to learn how to distinguish real gold from tinsel. It is hard, because tinsel sometimes glitters so dazzlingly. I confess, my child, that often in my life I was dazzled by glitter. And sometimes it even shone so falsely, that one dropped pure gold from one's hand and reached for, or ran after, false gold. You know that to organize one's scale of values well means to know not only oneself well, to be firm in the analysis of one's character, but mainly to know the others, to know as much of the world as possible, its past, present, and future development. Well, in short, to know, to understand. Not to close one's ears before anything and for no reason—not even to shut out the thoughts and opinions of anybody who stepped on my toes, or even wounded me deeply.

Examine, think, criticize, yes, mainly criticize yourself don't be ashamed to admit a truth you have come to realize, even if you proclaimed the opposite a little while ago; don't become obstinate about your opinions, but when you come to consider something right, then be so definite that you can fight and die for it. As Wolker said, death is not bad. Just avoid gradual dying which is what happens when one suddenly finds oneself apart from the real life of the others. You have to put down your roots where fate determined for you to live. You have to find your own way. Look for it independently, don't let anything turn you away from it, not even the memory of your mother and father. If you really love them, you won't hurt them by seeing them critically—just don't go on a road which is wrong, dishonest and does not harmonize with life. I have changed my mind many times, rearranged many values, but, what was left as an essential value, without which I cannot imagine my life, is the freedom of my conscience. I would like you, my little girl, to think about whether I was right.

Another value is work. I don't know which to assign the first place and which the second. Learn to love work! Any work, but one you have to know really and thoroughly. Then don't be afraid of any thing, and things will turn out well for you.

And don't forget about love in your life. I am not only thinking of the red blossom which one day will bloom in your heart, and you, if fate favors you, will find a similar one in the heart of another person with whose road yours will merge. I am thinking of love without which one cannot live happily. And don't ever crumble love—learn to give it whole and really. And learn to love precisely those who encourage love so little—then you won't usually make a mistake. My little girl Jana, when you will be choosing for whom your maiden heart shall burn and to whom to really give yourself remember your father.

I don't know if you will meet with such luck as I, I don't know if you will meet such a beautiful human being, but choose your ideal close to him. Perhaps you, my little one, have already begun to understand, and now perhaps you understand to the point of pain what we have lost in him. What I find hardest to bear is that I am also guilty of that loss.

Be conscious of the great love and sacrifice Pepik and Veruska are bringing you. You not only have to be grateful to them...you must help them build your common happiness positively, constructively. Always want to give them more for the good they do for you. Then perhaps you will be able to come to terms with their gentle goodness.

I heard from my legal representative that you are doing well in school, and that you want to continue...I was very pleased. But even if you would one day have to leave school and to work for your livelihood, don't stop learning and studying. If you really want to, you will reach your goal. I would have liked for you to become a medical doctor—you remember that we talked about it. Of course you will decide yourself and circumstances will, too. But if you stand one day in the traditional alma mater and carry home from graduation not only your doctor's diploma, but also the real ability to bring people relief as a doctor—then, my little girl...your mother will be immensely pleased...But your mother would only be...truly happy, no matter where you stand, whether at the operating table, at the...lathe, at your child's cradle or at the work table in your household, if you will do your work skillfully, honestly, happily and with your whole being. Then you will be successful in it. Don't be demanding in life, but have high goals. They are not exclusive of each other, for what I call demanding are those selfish notions and needs. Restrict them yourself. Realize that in view of the disaster and sorrow which happened to you, Vera, Pepicek, grandmother and grandfather...and many others will try to give you what they have and what they cannot afford. You should not only not ask them for it, but learn to be modest. If you become used to it, you will not be unhappy because of material things you don't have. You don't know how free one feels if one trains oneself in modesty...how he/she gets a head start over against the feeble and by how much one is safer and stronger. I really tried this out on myself And, if you can thus double your strength, you can set yourself courageous, high goals...Read much, and study languages. You will thereby broaden your life and multiply its content. There was a time in my life when I read voraciously, and then again times when work did not permit me to take a single book in my hand, apart from professional literature. That was a shame. Here in recent months I have been reading a lot, even books which probably would not interest me outside, but it is a big and important task to read everything valuable, or at least much that is. I shall write down for you at the end of this letter what I have read in recent months. I am sure you will think of me when you will be reading it.

And now also something for your body. I am glad that you are engaged in sports. Just do it systematically. I think that there should be rhythmic exercises, and if you have time, also some good, systematic gymnastics. And those quarter hours every morning! Believe me finally that it would save you a lot of annoyance about unfavorable proportions of your waist, if you could really do it. It is also good for the training of your will and perseverance. Also take care of your complexion regularly—I do not mean makeup, God forbid, but healthy daily care. And love your neck and feet as you do your face and lips. A brush has to be your good friend, every day, and not only for your hands and feet; use it on every little bit of your skin. Salicyl alcohol and Fennydin, that is enough for beauty, and then air and sun. But about that you will find better advisors than I am.

Your photograph showed me your new hairdo; it looks good, but isn't it a shame to hide your nice forehead? And that lady in the ball gown! Really, you looked lovely, but your mother's eye noticed one fault, which may be due to the way you were placed on the photograph—wasn't the neck opening a little deep for your sixteen years? I am sorry I did not see the photo of your new winter coat. Did you use the muff from your aunt as a fur collar? Don't primp, but whenever possible, dress carefully and neatly. And don't wear shoes until they arc run down at the heel!

Facing page:
Milada Horáková at the time
of her arrest, 1949

Vazební fotografie M. Horákové (zdroj: ABS)

Are you wearing innersoles? And how is your thyroid gland? These questions don't, of course, require an answer, they are only meant as your mother's reminders. In Leipzig in prison I read a book—the letters of Maria Theresa to her daughter Marie Antoinette. I was very much impressed with how this ruler showed herself to be practical and feminine in her advice to her daughter. It was a German original, and I don't remember the name of the author. If you ever see that book, remember that I made up my mind at that time that I would also write you such letters about my experiences and advice. Unfortunately I did not get beyond good intentions.

Janinko, please take good care of Grandfather Kral and Grandmother Horakova. Their old hearts now need the most consolation. Visit them often and let them tell you about your father's and mother's youth, so that you can preserve it in your mind for your children. In that way an individual becomes immortal, and we shall continue in you and in the others of your blood.

And one more thing—music. I believe that you will show your gratitude to Grandfather Horak for the piano which he gave you by practicing honestly, and that you will succeed in what Pepik wants so much, in accompanying him when he plays the violin or the viola. Please, do him that favor. I know that it would mean a lot to him, and it would be beautiful. And when you can play well together, play me the aria from Martha: "My rose, you bloom alone there on the hillside," and then: "Sleep my little prince" by Mozart, and then your father's favourite largo: "Under your window" by Chopin. You will play it for me, won't you? I shall always be listening to you.

Just one more thing: Choose your friends carefully. Among other things one is also very much determined by the people with whom one associates. Therefore choose very carefully. Be careful in everything and listen to the opinions of others about your girlfriends without being told. I shall never forget your charming letter (today I can tell you) which you once in the evening pinned to my pillow, to apologize when I caught you for the first time at the gate in the company of a girl and a boy. You explained to me at that time why it is necessary to have a gang. Have your gang, little girl, but of good and clean young people. And compete with each other in everything good. Only please don't confuse young people's springtime infatuation with real love. Do you understand me? If you don't, aunt Vera will help you explain what I meant. And so, my only young daughter, little girl Jana, new life, my hope, my future forgiveness, live! Grasp life with both hands! Until my last breath I shall pray for your happiness, my dear child!

I kiss your hair, eyes and mouth, I stroke you and hold you in my arms (I really held you so little.) I shall always be with you. I am concluding by copying from memory the poem which your father composed for you in jail in 1940...

[There followed a poem written by her husband about the birth of their daughter-- since lost--and a reading list.]

P.S. THIS IS MY FAVORITE MEMO EVER

MATT STONE to THE MPAA
Circa 1999

Ever since it first aired on television in 1997, Matt Stone and Trey Parker's hugely popular animated comedy *South Park* has courted controversy due to its crude jokes, deliberate lack of tact, and the creators' steadfast refusal to self-censor or bow to external pressures. However, two years after the show debuted, a feature-length film was released – *South Park: Bigger, Longer & Uncut* – and in order for it to gain an R rating, Stone and Parker had no choice but to chop and change certain scenes. This legendary memo, from Stone to the MPAA, was sent along with the movie's second cut.

Date: [Illegible]
To: [Redacted]
From: Matt Stone
CC: [Redacted]
Re: MPAA cut #2

Here is our new cut of the *South Park* movie to submit to the MPAA. I wanted to tell you exactly what notes we did and did not address.

1. We left in both the "fisting" and the "rimjob" references in the counselor's office scene. We did cut the word "hole" from "asshole" as per our conversation.
2. We took out the entire "God has fucked me in the ass so many times..." It is gone.
3. Although it is not animated yet, we put a new storyboard in for clarification in the scene with Saddam Hussein's penis. The intent now is that you never see Saddam's real penis, he in fact is using dildos both times.
4. We have the shot animated that reveals the fact that Winona is not shooting ping-pong balls from her vagina. She is, in fact, hitting the balls with a ping-pong paddle.
5. We took out the only reference to "cum-sucking ass" in the film. It was in the counselor's office and we took it out.
6. We left in the scenes with Cartman's mom and the horse as per our conversation. This is the one joke we really want to fight for.

Call with any questions.

Matt

P.S. This is my favorite memo ever.

DEAR FRIENDS ALL

HENRY JAMES to 270
FRIENDS
April 21, 1913

In April of 1913, to celebrate
his 70th birthday, 270
friends of author Henry
James collectively paid for
two gifts for him: first, the
commission of a portrait
of James by John Singer
Sargent, and second, a
commemorative bowl
crafted by a prestigious
London silversmith. In reply,
James, never one to be
frugal with his sentences,
wrote a thank-you letter to
all 270 friends that perfectly
illustrates the ornate and
often verbose writing style
that continues to divide
audiences to this day.

21 Carlyle Mansions,
Cheyne Walk, S.W.

April 21st, 1913.

Dear Friends All,

Let me acknowledge with boundless pleasure the singularly generous and beautiful
letter, signed by your great and dazzling array and reinforced by a correspondingly
bright material gage, which reached me on my recent birthday, April 15th. It has
moved me as brave gifts and benedictions can only do when they come as signal
surprises. I seem to wake up to an air of breathing good will the full sweetness of
which I had never yet tasted; though I ask myself now, as a second thought, how
the large kindness and hospitality in which I have so long and so consciously lived
among you could fail to act itself out according to its genial nature and by some
inspired application. The perfect grace with which it has embraced the just-past
occasion for its happy thought affects me, I ask you to believe, with an emotion too
deep for stammering words. I was drawn to London long years ago as by the sense,
felt from still earlier, of all the interest and association I should find here, and I
now see how my faith was to sink deeper foundations than I could presume ever to
measure—how my justification was both stoutly to grow and wisely to wait. It is so
wonderful indeed to me as I count up your numerous and various, your dear and
distinguished friendly names, taking in all they recall and represent, that I permit
myself to feel at once highly successful and extremely proud. I had never in the
least understood that I was the one or signified that I was the other, but you have
made a great difference. You tell me together, making one rich tone of your many
voices, almost the whole story of my social experience, which I have reached the
right point for living over again, with all manner of old times and places renewed,
old wonderments and pleasures reappeased and recaptured—so that there is scarce
one of your ranged company but makes good the particular connection, quickens
the excellent relation, lights some happy train and flushes with some individual
colour. I pay you my very best respects while I receive from your two hundred
and fifty pair of hands, and more, the admirable, the inestimable bowl, and while I
engage to sit, with every accommodation to the so markedly indicated "one of you,"
my illustrious friend Sargent. With every accommodation, I say, but with this one
condition that you yourselves, in your strength and goodness, remain guardians of
the result of his labour—even as I remain all faithfully and gratefully yours,

HENRY JAMES

P.S. And let me say over your names.

[Followed by a list of the 270 subscribers.]

*Facing page: The portrait of
Henry James by John Singer
Sargent commissioned by his
friends, 1916*

Received S S

1984 MAY -9 AM 10: 36

Andy Smith

400 London Pride Road

Irmo, South Carolina 29063

April 18, 1984

Dear Mr. President,

    My name is Andy Smith. I am a seventh grade student at Irmo

Middle School, in Irmo, South Carolina.

    Today my mother declared my bedroom a disaster area. I would like

to request federal funds to hire a crew to clean up my room. I am

prepared to provide the initial funds if you will privide matching funds

for this project.

    I know you will be fair when you consider my request. I will be

awaiting your reply.

Sincerely yours,

Andy Smith

Andy Smith

MY MOTHER DECLARED MY BEDROOM A DISASTER AREA

ANDY SMITH to RONALD REAGAN
April 18th, 1984

As one would expect, Ronald Reagan was the recipient of thousands of letters each month during his presidency; a mailbag so voluminous, in fact, that a gang of patient volunteers were tasked with opening them all on his behalf and passing him approximately 30 each week to read and respond to. Letters arrived from all over the world and were written by human beings of all flavours: men, women, fans, critics, average Joes, celebrities, world leaders, and, as evidenced by this fine example, sent by a 13-year-old South Carolina boy called Andy Smith, children.

400 London Pride Road
Irmo, South Carolina 29063

April 18, 1984

Dear Mr. President,

My name is Andy Smith. I am a seventh grade student at Irmo Middle School, in Irmo, South Carolina.

Today my mother declared my bedroom a disaster area. I would like to request federal funds to hire a crew to clean up my room. I am prepared to provide the initial funds if you will provide matching funds for this project.

I know you will be fair when you consider my request. I will be awaiting your reply.

Sincerely yours,

[Signed]
Andy Smith

Norton, Kans.
March 6, 1921.

Mr. Measures Please Return to me. W. H. Meadowcroft

Mr. Edison.

Dear Sir:

Thank her very much Etc —

It is not always the privilege of a woman to thank personally the inventor of articles which make life liveable for her sex. I feel that it is my duty as well as privilege to tell you how much we women of the small town are indebted to you for our pleasures as well as our utmost needs. I am a college graduate and probably my husband is one of the best known surgeons between Topeka and Denver. I am an officer in the District of Women's Club as well as President of our Town Organization.

We have four children. The oldest lad expects to have a telegraph station in the Summer on the U.P. We have a large house so you see when doing practically all my own work, my duties are many and my activities most varied, yet I enjoy my labors and do not feel that I entirely neglect to get pleasure out of life. Positively as I hear my wash machine chugging along, down in the Laundry, as I write this it does seem as though I am entirely dependent on the fertile brain of one thousand miles away for every pleasure and labor saving device I have. The house is lighted by electricity. I cook on a Westinghouse electric range, wash dishes in an electric dish washer. An electric fan even helps to distribute the heat over part of the house. (at our private hospital electricity helps to heat some of the rooms). I wash clothes in an electric machine and iron on an electric mangle and with an electric iron. I clean house with electric cleaners. I rest, take an electric massage and curl my hair on an electric iron. Dress in a gown sewed on a machine run by a motor. Then start the Victrola and either study Spanish for a while or listen to Kreisler and Gluck and Galli Curci in almost heavenly strains, forgetting I'm living in a tiny town of two thousand where nothing much ever happens but am recalled when the automatic in my stove releases and know my dinner is now cooking. The Doctor comes home, tired with a days work wherein electricity has played almost as much part as it has at home, to find a wife not tired and dissatisfied but a woman waiting who has worked faithfully believing that work is beneficial and who is now rested and ready to serve the tired man and discuss affairs of the day. To play him a beautiful piece on the Victrola and possibly see a masterpiece at the "Movies."

Possibly he brings in a guest without warning but electricity and a pressure cooker save the day for the hostess. Indeed, I've entertained the Governor of our State and a dozen of our rep. citizens at a little more than an hours notice - at luncheon, but that was one of my pleasures, unexpected but none the less a real one.

Please accept the thanks Mr. Edison of one most truly appreciative woman. I know I am only one of many under the same debt of gratitude to you and while I also know you must have received the thanks of other women before yet a word may not be unwelcome to you. I believe men are like women after all and like to know that their labor is appreciated and I do think the World is inclined to be too parsimonius in its praises of work and value. Sincerely MRS. W. C. LATHROP

THANKS, MR. EDISON

W. C. LATHROP to THOMAS EDISON
March 6th, 1921

Thomas Edison is one of the most successful businessmen in history and arguably our most impressive inventor, with over 1000 patents to his name. During his 84 years he either invented or made major improvements to the phonograph, the motion picture camera, the incandescent light bulb, the alkaline battery, and many more of the modern technologies that we now take for granted, but which at the time drastically changed lives and made a huge impact. It's no real surprise, then, that as a result of his genius, 'The Wizard of Menlo Park' was the recipient of countless notes of appreciation from a diverse range of admiring fans. In March of 1921, he received such a letter from Mrs. W. C. Lathrop, a Kansas housewife whose daily routine had been improved immeasurably by his work.

THE MOST
EXTRAORDINARY SCENE

24/12/14.

CAPTAIN REGINALD JOHN
ARMES to HIS WIFE
December 24th, 1914

On Christmas Eve of 1914,
five months into World
War I, something amazing
happened: thousands of
British and German troops
on the Western Front
decided to put down their
weapons, rise from the
trenches, and greet each
other peacefully. In fact, for
the next few days, close to
100,000 men, British and
German, chatted, exchanged
gifts, sang carols and played
football. Most importantly,
they were even able to bury
their dead without fearing
for their own safety. On
the evening of December
24th, the first day of the
truce, Captain 'Jack' Armes
of the 1st Battalion North
Staffordshire Regiment
wrote to his wife and
described this incredible
occurrence. Armes did
return home to his family
after the war; he died in
1948.

I have just been through one of the most extraordinary scenes imaginable.
To–night is Xmas Eve and I came up into the trenches this evening for my tour of
duty in them. Firing was going on all the time and the enemy's machine guns were
at it hard, firing at us. Then about seven the firing stopped.

I was in my dug–out reading a paper and the mail was being dished out. It
was reported that the Germans had lighted their trenches up all along our front. We
had been calling to one another for some time Xmas wishes and other things. I went
out and they shouted "no shooting" and then somehow the scene became a peaceful
one. All our men got out of their trenches and sat on the parapet, the Germans did
the same, and they talked to one another in English and broken English. I got on
top of the trench and talked German and asked them to sing a German Volkslied,
which they did, then our men sang quite well and each side clapped and cheered the
other.

I asked a German who sang a solo to sing one of Schumann's songs, so he
sang "The Two Grenadiers" splendidly. Our men were a good audience and really
enjoyed his singing.

Then Pope and I walked across and held a conversation with the German
Officer in command. One of his men introduced us properly, he asked my name
and then presented me to his Officer. I gave the latter permission to bury some
German dead who are lying in between us, and we agreed to have no shooting until
12 midnight to–morrow. We talked together, 10 or more Germans gathered round.
I was almost in their lines within a yard or so. We saluted each other, he thanked me
for permission to bury his dead, and we fixed up how many men were to do it, and
that otherwise both sides must remain in their trenches.

Then we wished one another good night and a good night's rest, and a
happy Xmas and parted with a salute. I got back to the trench. The Germans sang
"Die Wacht Am Rhein", it sounded well. Then our men sang quite well "Christians
Awake", it sounded so well, and with a good night we all got back into our trenches.
It was a curious scene, a lovely moonlight night, the German trenches with small
lights on them, and the men on both sides gathered in groups on the parapets.

At times we heard the guns in the distance and an occasional rifle shot.
I can hear them now, but about us is absolute quiet. I allowed one or two men to
go out and meet a German or two half way. They exchanged cigars, a smoke and
talked. The Officer I spoke to hopes we shall do the same on New Year's Day. I
said "yes, if I am here." I felt I must sit down and write the story of this Xmas Eve
before I went to lie down. Of course no precautions are relaxed, but I think they
mean to play the game. All the same, I think I shall be awake all night so as to be on
the safe side. It is weird to think that to–morrow night we shall be at it hard again.
If one gets through this show it will be a Xmas time to live in one's memory. The
German who sang had a really fine voice.

Am just off for a walk round the trenches to see all is well. Good–night.

<u>Xmas</u> <u>Day.</u> We had an absolutely quiet night in front of us, though just to our right and left there was sniping going on. In my trenches and in those of the Enemy opposite to us were only nice big fires blazing, and occasional songs and conversation. This morning at the Reveille the Germans sent out parties to bury their dead. Our men went out to help, and then we all on both sides met in the middle, and in groups began to talk and exchange gifts of tobacco, etc. All this morning we have been fraternising, singing songs. I have been within a yard in fact to their trenches, have spoken to and exchanged greetings with a Colonel, Staff Officers and several Company Officers. All were very nice and we fixed up that the men should not go near their opponents' trenches, but remain about midway between the lines. The whole thing is extraordinary. The men were all so natural and friendly. Several photos were taken, a group of German Officers, a German Officer and myself, and a group of British and German soldiers.

The Germans are Saxons, a good–looking lot, only wishing for peace in a manly way, and they seem in no way at their last gasp. I was astonished at the easy way in which our men and theirs got on with each other.

We have just knocked off for dinner, and have arranged to meet again afterwards until dusk when we go in again and have [illegible] until 9 p.m., when War begins again. I wonder who will start the shooting! They say "fire in the air and we will", and such things, but of course it will start and to–morrow we shall be at it hard killing one another. It is an extraordinary state of affairs which allows of a "Peace Day". I have never seen men so pleased to have a day off as both sides.

Their Opera Singer is going to give us a song or two to–night and perhaps I may give them one. Try and imagine two lines of trenches in peace, only 50 yards apart, the men of of either side have never seen each other except perhaps a head now and again, and have never been outside in front of their trenches. Then suddenly one day men stream out and nest in friendly talk in the middle. One fellow, a married man, wanted so much a photo of Betty and Nancy in bed, which I had, and I gave him it as I had two: it seems he showed it all round, as several Germans told me afterwards about it. He gave me a photo of himself and family taken the other day which he had just got.

Well must finish now so as to get this off to–day. Have just finished dinner. Pork chop. Plum pudding. Mince pies. Ginger, and bottle of Wine and a cigar, and have drunk to all at home and especially to you, my darling one. Must go outside now to supervise the meetings of the men and the Germans.

Will try and write more in a day or two. Keep this letter carefully and send copies to all. I think they will be interested. It did feel funny walking over alone towards the enemy's trenches to meet someone half-way, and then to arrange a Xmas peace. It will be a thing to remember all one's life.

Kiss the babies and give them my love. Write me a long letter and tell me all the news. I hope the photos come out all right. Probably you will see them in some paper.

Yours,

[Signed]   JAKE.

24/12/14.

I have just been through one of the most extraordinary scenes imaginable. To-night is Xmas Eve and I came up into the trenches this evening for my tour of duty in them. Firing was going on all the time and the enemy's machine guns were at it hard, firing at us. Then about seven the firing stopped.

I was in my dug-out reading a paper and the mail was being dished out. It was reported that the Germans had lighted their trenches up all along our front. We had been calling to one another for some time Xmas wishes and other things. I went out and they shouted "no shooting" and then somehow the scene became a peaceful one. All our men got out of their trenches and sat on the parapet, the Germans did the same, and they talked to one another in English and broken English. I got on top of the trench and talked German and asked them to sing a German Volkelied, which they did, then our men sang quite well and each side clapped and cheered the other.

I asked a German who sang a solo to sing one of Schumann's songs, so he sang "The Two Grenadiers" splendidly. Our men were a good audience and really enjoyed his singing.

Then Pope and I walked across and held a conversation
with the German Officer in command.   One of his men introduced us properly, he asked my name and then presented me to
his Officer.   I gave the latter permission to bury some
German dead who are lying in between us, and we agreed to
have no shooting until 12 midnight to-morrow.   We talked
together, 10 or more Germans gathered round.   I was almost
in their lines within a yard or so.   We saluted each other,
he thanked me for permission to bury his dead, and we fixed
up how many men were to do it, and that otherwise both sides
must remain in their trenches.

Then we wished one another good night and a good night's
rest, and a happy Xmas and parted with a salute.   I got
back to the trench.   The Germans sang "Die Wacht Am Rhein",
it sounded well.   Then our men sang quite well "Christians
Awake", it sounded so well, and with a good night we all got
back into our trenches.   It was a curious scene, a lovely
moonlight night, the German trenches with small lights on
them, and the men on both sides gathered in groups on the
parapets.

At times we heard the guns in the distance and an
occasional rifle shot.   I can hear them now, but about
us is absolute quiet.   I allowed one or two men to go
out and meet a German or two half way.   They exchanged
cigars, a smoke and talked.   The Officer I spoke to hopes

- 2 -

346

we shall do the same on New Year's Day, I said "yes,
if I am here."   I felt I must sit down and write the
story of this Xmas Eve before I went to lie down.   Of
course no precautions are relaxed, but I think they mean
to play the game.   All the same, I think I shall be
awake all night so as to be on the safe side.   It is
weird to think that to-morrow night we shall be at it hard
again.   If one gets through this show it will be a Xmas
time to live in one's memory.   The German who sang had a
really fine voice.

An just off for a walk round the trenches to see all
is well.   Good-night.

Xmas Day.   We had an absolutely quiet night in
front of us, though just to our right and left there was
sniping going on.   In my trenches and in those of the
Enemy opposite to us were only nice big fires blazing,
and occasional songs and conversation.   This morning at
the Reveille the Germans sent out parties to bury their
dead.   Our men went out to help, and then we all on both
sides met in the middle, and in groups began to talk and
exchange gifts of tobacco, etc.   All this morning we
have been fraternising, singing songs.   I have been
within a yard in fact to their trenches, have spoken to
and exchanged greetings with a Colonel, Staff Officers
and several Company Officers.   All were very nice and

we fixed up that the men should not go near their
opponents' trenches, but remain about midway between
the lines.   The whole thing is extraordinary.   The
men were all so natural and friendly.   Several photos
were taken, a group of German Officers, a German
Officer and myself, and a group of British and German
soldiers.

The Germans are Saxons, a good-looking lot, only
wishing for peace in a manly way, and they seem in no
way at their last gasp.   I was astonished at the easy
way in which our men and theirs got on with each other.

We have just knocked off for dinner, and have
arranged to meet again afterwards until dusk when we
go in again and have some until 9 p.m., when War
begins again.   I wonder who will start the shooting!
They say "fire in the air and we will", and such
things, but of course it will start and to-morrow we
shall be at it hard killing one another.   It is an
extraordinary state of affairs which allows of a
"Peace Day".   I have never seen men so pleased to have
a day off as both sides.

Their Opera Singer is going to give us a song or
two to-night and perhaps I may give them one.   Try
and imagine two lines of trenches in peace, only 50
yards apart, the men of of either side have never seen
each other except perhaps a head now and again, and

have never been outside in front of their trenches.
Then suddenly one day men stream out and nest in friendly
talk in the middle.   One fellow, a married man, wanted
so much a photo of Betty and Nancy in bed, which I had,
and I gave him it as I had two: it seems he showed it
all round, as several Germans told me afterwards about it.
He gave me a photo of himself and family taken the other
day which he had just got.

Well must finish now so as to get this off to-day.
Have just finished dinner.   Pork chop.   Plum pudding.
Mince pies.   Ginger, and bottle of Wine and a cigar,
and have drunk to all at home and especially to you, my
darling one.   Must go outside now to supervise the meetings of the men and the Germans.

Will try and write more in a day or two.   Keep this
letter carefully and send copies to all.   I think they
will be interested.   It did feel funny walking over
alone towards the enemy's trenches to meet someone half-
way, and then to arrange a Xmas peace.   It will be a
thing to remember all one's life.

Kiss the babies and give them my love.   Write me a
long letter and tell me all the news.   I hope the photos
come out all right.   Probably you will see them in some
paper.

                    Yours,
                         (Signed)   JAKE.

- 5 -

British and German troops posing together, Christmas 1914

INDEX

Adams, Abigail 248
Adams, Ansel 321
Albini, Steve 12
Anderson, Marian 251
Andropov, Yuri 99, 137
Archbishop of Canterbury,
  The 224
Arkell, James 116
Armes, Steven 152
Asbury, Jacob Vale 270
Austen, Cassandra 176, 194
Austen, Jane 176, 194

Barker, George 18
Baudelaire, Charles 303
Baxter, Biddy 255
Beatles, The 163, 200, 278
Bernard, Jeffrey 259
Bernard, Jessie 69
Bernbach, Bill 196
Bernstein, Felicia 268
Bernstein, Leonard 268
Bibesco, Elizabeth 273
Blue-grass Blade 226
Blue Peter 255
Bowie, David 163
Bowman, Dr. William 264
Brave New World 32
Breen, Joseph 309
Brewster, Bertha 150
Brontë, Charlotte 280
Brontë, Emily 280
Brynner, Yul "Curly" 124
Bukowski, Charles 260
Bulwer, Lorina 159
Burroughs, William 142
Burton, Richard 60
Bush, Barabara 46
Bush, George H.W. 46

Camus, Albert 50
Capote, Truman 142
Carnegie Hall 36
Carr, Jeanne 23
Carson, Rachel 11

Cat Fancy 135
Chandler, Cissy 49
Chandler, Raymond 49
Chelsea Hotel, The 192
Churchill, Winston 52, 186
Civil Aeronautics Board, The
  252
Clancy, Tom 96
Clapton, Eric 200
Clemens, Orion 136
Clemens, Samuel 136
Cobain, Kurt 12
Coppola, Francis Ford 118
Covici, Pascal 123
Coward, Noël 124
Crane, Hart 318
Crumb, Robert 2
Cruse, Howard 282

Daelli, M. 286
Daily Mirror 259
Daily Telegraph 150
Daughters of the American
  Revolution (DAR) 251
Dave (family name unknown)
  140
Davis, Edward 80
de Souza, Louis 52
Dietrich, Marlene 124
Delaney, Shelagh 43
DeLillo, Don 330
Dickinson, Emily 242
Dickinson, Susan 242
Dickinson, Thomas Gilbert 242
Disney 164
Dodd, Sandra 163
Dowding, Hugh 186
Doyle, Brian 40
Dr. Seuss 46, 282
Du Bois, W.E.B. 144
Du Bois, Yolande 144
Dumbledore, Professor 152
Durrell, Gerald 72

E. Remington and Sons 136

Ea-nasir 214
Edison, Thomas 342
Einstein, Albert 93, 299, 332
El Pozo de Quilmes 311
Elbes, Lili 147
Elvenes, Lili 147
Entrance of Guests, The 303

FBI, The 320
Feuchtwanger, Lion 54
Feynman, Richard 240
Frampton, Hollis 4
Freeman, Dorothy 11
Fuller, Buckminster 299
Fullerton, Morton 184

Geisel, Theodore 282
Gellhorn, Martha 275
Gelman, Juan 311
Gelman, Macarena 311
Gelman, Marcelo 311
Gelman, María Claudia García
  311
Germain, Louis 50
Goldwyn, Samuel 164
Goodman Derrick & Co. 116
Goon Show, The 247, 278
Gottlieb, Gerda 147
Greenglass, David 222
Gregory, Alyse 70
Grey Advertising 196
Grohl, Dave 12
Grover, Hannah 92
Grover, Cato 92
Guevara, Aleida 326
Guevara, Camilo 326
Guevara, Celia 326
Guevara, Ernesto 'Che' 326
Guevara, Ernesto 326
Guevara, Hilda 326
Guggenheim, Harry 39
Gustafsson, Mats 2

Harrison, George 278

Helms, Dennis 189
Helms, Richard 189
Hemingway, Ernest 275
Henu 58
Hetepu 58
Hinton, S.E. 118
Hitler, Adolf 54, 186, 189, 291
Hogwarts School 152
Hollander, Anthony 255
Horáková, Jana 332
Horáková, Milada 332
Huxley, Aldous 32

Idle, Eric 218
In Cold Blood 142
Infinite Jest 330
Inkhenmet 58
Iy 58

James, Henry 185, 338
Jones, Reverend Charles
  Colcock 29
Jones, David 163
Joplin, Janis 93
Jorn, Asger 39
Joyce, James 262
Jung, Carl 262

Kahn, Alfred 252
Kawaguchi, Hirotsugu 111
Keith, Brian 140
Keller, Helen 36
Kennedy, John F. 290
Keyes, Mary 76
King Sequoia 23
Knight, Fanny 176

Lamb, Charles 270
Lathrop, W.C. 342
Le Guin, Ursula 158
Lenin, Vladimir 137
Lennon, John 200, 278
Lepidina, Sulpicia 316
Les Misérables 286
Lincoln, Abraham 16

Littlewood, Joan 43
London, Jack 156
Long Goodbye, The 49

Mailer, Isaac Barnett 300
Mailer, Norman 300
Mano, Koichi 240
Mansfield, Katherine 273
Major, John 218
Martin, John 260
Mary Poppins 164
Matsumoto, Keiichi 111
McCullogh, Fanny 16
McCullough, Lieutenant Colonel
    William 16
McGeorge, Lee 72
Mead, Elizabeth 220
Mead, Margaret 220
Milligan, Spike 247, 278
Misakian, Jo Ellen 118
Mitford, Jessica 329
Molloy, Michael J. 259
MoMA 4
Monarch butterflies 11
Moore, Annie 62
Moore, Noel 62
Mosley, Sir Oswald 146
Motion Picture Association of
    America (MPAA) 337
Mozart, Maria Anna (Marianne)
    231
Mozart, Wolfgang Amadeus
    231, 336
Muir, John 23
Murakami, Ryohei 112
Murry, John 273

Nanni 214
New Statesman, The 259
New York Symphony Orchestra,
    The 36
New Yorker 70, 123, 142, 170
Newaef 58
Nightingale, Florence 264
Nineteen Eighty-Four 32
Nirvana 12

Nobel Prize for Literature,
    The 50
Noguchi, Isamu 299
Novoselic, Krist 12
N.W.A. (Niggaz Wit Attitude) 320

Olmsted, Frederick Law 168
Olmsted, Henry 168
ONE 140
Ono, Yoko 200
Orwell, George 32
Osborn, Professor Henry
    Fairfield 292
Osler, Emma 126
Osler, Grace 126
Osler, Paul Revere 126
Osler, Sir William 126
Oswald, Lee H. 290
Outsiders, The 118

Parker, Dorothy 123, 237
Parkland Memorial Hospital,
    Dallas 290
Parrish, Minerva Ola "Minnie"
    226
Perkins, Maxwell 155
Plastic Ono Band 200
Plath, Sylvia 30
Portland Magazine 40

Pancake, Breece D'J 216
Porter, Katherine Anne 318
Potter, Beatrix 62
Powell, Dawn 237
Powell, Phyllis 237
Pressdram Ltd. 116
Price, Charles Jack 290
Priority Records 320
Private Eye 116

Radziewicz, John 158
Rand, Ayn 135
Reed, Virginia 76
Remppis, Lisa 291
Renton, Lulu 224
Richie, Donald 4

Roosevelt, Eleanor 251
Rosenberg, Ethel 222
Rosenberg, Julius 222
Rosewarne, Vivian 20
Routledge, Norman 228
Rowling, J.K. 152
Russell, Bertrand 146
Russell, Leonard 49

Sandburg, Carl 48
Sandburg, Margaret 48
Sargent, John Singer 338
Scholl, Sophie 291
Scriven, Abream 29
Scriven, Dinah 29
Sebkhotep 58
Sellers, Peter 247, 278
Sen 58
Shepsi 58
Sher 58
Shirai, Mariko 112
Silent Spring (Book) 11
Simoni, Giovan Simone
    Buonarroti 190
Simoni, Michelangelo di
    Lodovico Buonarroti 190
Simpson, Bart 46
Simpson, Homer 46
Simpson, Lisa 46
Simpson, Maggie 46
Simpson, Marge 46
Sing Sing Prison 222
Smith, Andy 340
Smart, Elizabeth 18
Smith, Samantha 137
South Park 337
Southey, Robert 166
Sparre, Andreas 147
Stoker, Bram 210
Stone, Matt 337
Streetcar Named Desire, A 309
Strunsky, Anna 156
Suffragettes, The 150

Tale of Peter Rabbit, The 62
Taste of Honey, A 43

Taylor, Elizabeth 60
Thomas, Caitlin 192
Thomas, Dylan 192, 259
Tiger Oil Company 80
Torturing the Saxaphone 2
Trice, Jack 44
Turing, Alan 228
Twain, Mark 136, 137
Tynan, Kenneth 142

Ulysses 262
University of Portland, The 40

Wagner, Richard 303
Wallace, David Foster 330
Walt Disney 164
Warner, Sylvia Townsend 70
Waugh, Evelyn 314
Waugh, Laura 314
Wedding Fête 303
Wegener, Einar 147
Wharton, Edith 184
White, Daisy 170
White, E.B. 170
White House, The 46, 101, 248
White, Joel 170
Whitman, Walt 210
Wilkinson, Bud 114
Wilkinson, Jay 114
Williams, Rowan 224
Williams, Tennessee 309
Williams, W.S. 280
Wolfe, Thomas 155
Wordsworth, Thomas 166
Wordsworth, William 166

Xavier High School 274

Yosemite National Park 23, 321
Yoshimura, Kazuo 112

ACKNOWLEDGEMENTS

By design, I am terrible at making books. Every fibre of my being works against such a feat. I have very little willpower; I leave everything until the very last minute; I am spectacularly disorganised. I rewrite everything at least ten times. I am paralysed by writer's block every single day. For every productive hour spent writing and researching, I could point to at least 100 that I have wasted in ways entirely unrelated to the magnificent book you now grasp. Indeed, the fact that you do hold such an impressive book in your hands is down to this: I have somehow managed to surround myself with people of seemingly unlimited talent, patience, and commitment, whose efforts I am often credited for. The most important of these is the person I fell in love with by letter in 2002 whilst we lived hundreds of miles apart: Karina, my beautiful, impossibly supportive wife and the mother of our gorgeous children. This book is for her.

I would also like to thank: everyone at Unbound, including my editor, Isobel Frankish, whose efforts on this book genuinely deserve some kind of award, as do her immaculate, life-saving spreadsheets; the permissions team of Gilly Vincent, Alice Brett and Louise Tucker, without whom this book would be a legal minefield; the world's greatest dancer, John Mitchinson; the always-inspiring Dan Kieran, Justin Pollard, Christoph Sander, Caitlin Harvey, Charlie Gleason, Georgia Odd, Lauren Fulbright, Phil Connor, Xander Cansell, Emily Shipp, DeAndra Lupu, Leo Byng and Louise Edwards; the team at Canongate, including: the force of nature that is Jamie Byng, Jaz Lacey-Campbell, Andrea Joyce, Anna Frame, Jenny Lord and Jenny Todd; the geniuses at Here Design, including Caz Hildebrand, Samantha Kerr, Julie Martin and Clare Lowther; everyone associated with Letters Live who hasn't already been mentioned, including Adam Ackland, Benedict Cumberbatch, Simon Garfield, Adam Selves and the countless performers who have helped to bring these letters to life on stage.

Also, thunderous applause to the following people: Rob "G-Funk" Gibbons, Stephen Fry, Matt Berry, Leo Barker, Guy Walters, Austin Kleon, Elbow, Biddy Baxter, Anthony Hollander, Matt Stone, Dave Robinson, Alicia Brindak, every single archivist in the world, and my friends and family.

Finally, thank you so much to two very important groups of people: all those who funded the creation of this book via Unbound, in doing so literally bringing it to life, and to all those who wrote the letters of note that are celebrated in this very book.

Dear Reader,

The book you are holding came about in a rather different way to most others. It was funded directly by readers through a new website: **Unbound**.

Unbound is the creation of three writers. We started the company because we believed there had to be a better deal for both writers and readers. On the Unbound website, authors share the ideas for the books they want to write directly with readers. If enough of you support the book by pledging for it in advance, we produce a beautifully bound special subscribers' edition and distribute a regular edition and e-book wherever books are sold, in shops and online.

This new way of publishing is actually a very old idea (Samuel Johnson funded his dictionary this way). We're just using the internet to build each writer a network of patrons. Here, at the back of this book, you'll find the names of all the people who made it happen.

Publishing in this way means readers are no longer just passive consumers of the books they buy, and authors are free to write the books they really want. They get a much fairer return too – half the profits their books generate, rather than a tiny percentage of the cover price.

If you're not yet a subscriber, we hope that you'll want to join our publishing revolution and have your name listed in one of our books in the future. To get started, just visit unbound.com.

Thank you for your support,

Dan, Justin and John
Founders, Unbound

SUBSCRIBERS

Unbound is a new kind of publishing house. Our books are funded directly by readers. This was a very popular idea during the late eighteenth and early nineteenth centuries. Now we have revived it for the internet age. It allows authors to write the books they really want to write and readers to support the writing they would most like to see published.

The names listed below are of readers who have pledged their support and made this book happen. If you'd like to join them, visit: www.unbound.co.uk.

Mary Abbene
Carole Adams
Geoff Adams
James Adonis
Phil Agius
Al and Andy
Wyndham Albery
Bruce Alcorn
Justine Alderman
Nancy Alderman
Moose Allain
Malcolm Allard
Errol Allcock
Craig Allen
Jamie Allen
Jim Allison
Abigail Amey
Evelyn Andrews
Igor Andronov
Andy Annett
Anonymous
Dave Appleby
Cheryl Arany
K. A. Arends
Sandra Armor
Heidi Armstrong
Barbara Arnest
Mark and Lauren Arnest
Miranda Arnold
Christine Asbury
Stuart Ashen
Fionna and Patrick Ashmore
Nesher Asner
Debbie Aspery
Samantha Atherton
Michael Atkins
Michael Atkinson
Rachel Atkinson
Steve Aukett
Alexandra Aulisi
James Austin

Marie Austin
Roby Austin
Kenneth Averill
Alicia Avina
Amal Awad
Juliana Babing
Kevin Bachus
Captain Badbeard
Cecilia Bailey
Tony Baines
A C Baird
David Baird
Chris Baker
Signe Gyrite Balch
Martina Baletkova
Paul Ball
Rob Ball
Ann Ballinger
Jason Ballinger
Annabelle Banbery
Andrew Bardsley
Clare Barker
Victoria Barnard
Allison Barrett
Charles Barry
Melanie Barry
Patrick Barry
Chris Bartlett
Iain Bartlett
Rosalind & Mark Bartlett
Matt Barton
Helen Bates
Ruth Anne Baumgartner
James Bay
Adam Baylis-West
Becky Baynes
Laura Bayzle
Rachael Beale
Claire Beaumont
Lynne Bebee
Lare Becker

Samuel Becker
Adam Becket
Sharon Belcher
Allie Bell
Margaret Bell
Owen Bell
Rachel Bell
Martin Bellamy
Claire Elizabeth Benjamin
Catharine A Benson
Catherine Benson
Theodore Bentley
Clare and Michael Berardi
Thor Berger
Ignacio Bergmann
Scott & Miranda Berridge
Paula Best
Karine B. Betti
William Bettridge-Radford
Matt, Terri & Joseph Betts
Owain Betts
Christine Bhatt
Nikki Bi
Joy Birck
Leigh & Philip Bird
Dorothy Birtalan
Nick Birtwistle
Kristine and Michael Blaess
Ruth Blanco
Billy Blanco-Usher
Danny Blanco-Usher
Karina Blanco-Usher
Jenni Block
Richard Block
Robbert Bloem
Lark Blum
Anne-Claire Bogle
Marion Bolt
Nicholas Bond
Robin Bonn
Thomas Bonnick

Gregory Boone
Richard Booty
Olga Parera Bosch
Phillipe Bosher
Jacques Bossonney
Nicky Bothoms
Graham Bould
Nikolaus Bourboulis
Karl Bovenizer
Glenys Bowe
Jules Bowes
Gavin Boyd
Geoff Boyle
Richard Boynton
Carrie Boysun
Kathryn Bracewell
Charlotte Bracuti
Claire Bradley
Colin Bradley
Emma Bradley
Alan Bradshaw
Kirstin Bradshaw
David Brady
Margaret Brady
John Brassey
Bev Bratton
Richard W H Bray
Howard Brazier
Lindsay Brechler
Sandie & Tony Brent
Petra Breunig
Neil Brewitt
Sophie Bridge
Janice Bridger
Phil Bright
John Brinsmead-Stockham
Barnaby Britton
Debra Brock
Matt Brockwell
Jane Brookes
Anne and Joe Brophy

Carl, Amanda and Hester Brown
Emma Brown
Helen Brown
Sue Brown
Kala Brownlee
Elizabeth Brownlie
Phil Bruce-Moore
Megan Bryan
Gareth Buchaillard-Davies
Matt & Louise Buchanan
Colm Buckley
Chris Budd
Lia Buddle
Jan Burbridge
Robert Burk
Jeremy Burke
Andrew Burne
Shelley and Joe Burnham
Johnny Burns
Jon Busby
Marcus Butcher
Michael N. Butera
Sharen Butrum
Kathryn Cairns
Joseph Camann
Chris Cameron
Crysta Campbell
Steve Campbell
Nick Campion
Rob Campion
Debra Campise
Alistair Canlin
Xander Cansell
Antonio Cantafio
Donna Capin
Chris Cardwell
Helen Carey
Lisa Carey
Victoria Cargill-James
Margot Carlson
Emma Carlsson
Susan Carpenter
John P Carr
Martin Carr
Kate Carroll
Kevin Carroll
Henry Carruthers
Chloe & Greg Carter
Christian Clarke Casarez
Cath Casburn
Gregory Cathcart
Chelsea Chadwick
Ravinder Chahil
Warwick chai
Rick Challener
Govinder Chambore

Arti Chandarana
Aaron Chandra
Paul Charlton
Dan Cheesbrough
Joe Cherry
Jody H. Y. Cheung
Naomi Chiffi
Rathika Chinnadurai
Brenda Chng
Tina Chopee
Christine
Chika Chukwujekwu
Ade Churchett
Gregory Ciotti
Paul Clancy
Danny Clarke
Dr Nick 'Sparky' Clarke
Emma Clarke
Frances Clarke
Jeroen Claus
Jane Clayton
Alex Cleave
Nick & Carey Clifford
Nic Close
Thom Clutterbuck
Claire Coady
Garrett Coakley
Alex Coats
Steph Coats
Melanie Cochran
Maya Cohan
Emma Cole
Pamela Collett
David Collier
Mhari Colvin
Audrey Comparet
Elaine Comyn, Ireland
Philip Connor
Andrea Cook
Edward Cook
Sarah Cook
David Cooke
Grace Elizabeth Cooke
Susan Cooklin
Julie Cooper
Marc Cooper
Sophie Cooper
Sarah Corbett
Jamie Corley
Sarah Corrigan
Jai Corti
James Cotton
Conrad Cotton-Barratt
Charlie Coulthard
Ana Luiza Couto
Mike Coventry

Peter Coventry
Jacqui Crawford
John Crawford
Anthony Creagh
Sarah Creed
Andrew Croker
Jennifer Crossland
Emma Crowe
Shannon Cullen
Shane Cullinane
Heather Culpin
Carl George Warren Cummings
Cornelia Gyrite Cummings
David Cummings
Martin Cunliffe
Matthew Cunliffe
Anne Cunningham
DJ Cunningham
Jim Curtis
Linda Curtis
Ruth Curtis
João Dabbur
Cornelia Daheim
Rod Dale
Stephen Daley
John Dalton
Breda Daly
Catherine Daly
David Dalzell
Duncan Danger
Howard Daniel
Victoria Dantanus
Heena Dave
Harriet Fear Davies
Matt & Owen Davies
Julia Davison
Tom Dawkins
Fiona Day
Clothilde Morgan de Rivery
Alison Deane
Jane Dear
Lindsey Dear
Marjan Debevere
Jonathan Debrick
Ana Catalina Decanini
Mary Decious
Benny Declerck
Jamie Dempster
Marcus Denny
Magdalena Derwojedowa
Michiel Devlieger
John Dexter
Nikhil Dhumma
Miranda Dickinson
Rosie Dickinson
Ritchie Djamhur

Leanna Dobson
Andy Doddington
Michael Dodds
Renee Doegar
Kate Donachie
Iain Donaldson
Julie Donaldson
Kristine Donly
Wendalynn P. Donnan
Kirsty Doole
Natalie Dorey
Eva Doubravska
Cressida Downing, The Book Analyst
Michele Doyle
Karin Drenth
Tracey Drost-Plegt
Andy Dudley
Natalie Duffy
Cordelia Dunai
Charis Dunn
Vivienne Dunstan
Claire and Kevin Durrant-Jones
Hugh Van Dusen
Keir Frederick Duthie
Kate Dyer
Thom Dyke
Tony (Tones) Earley
Echo
Mark Ecob
Daniel EC-Sigala
Colin Edgar
David Edwards
Meg Edwards
Toby Egelnick
Jennie Eggleston (and Tim & Alba)
Matthew Egglestone
Emma Eichhorn
Heike Ellinghaus
Victoria Elliott
Xanthe Elliott
Jonathan Ellis
Sophie Ellison
Kate Elms
Susan Emmens
Christian Eriksen
Soulla Tantouri Eriksen
Marigely Espinosa
Cath Evans
Dor Evans
gareth evans
Jack Evans
Jo Evans
Sara Evans
Thomas A. Evans

Jonathan Everall
Simon Everett
Joanna Fabling
Karen Faiers
Kristen Faiferlick
Pete Faint
Rachael Fairchild
Matt Fairhall
Peter Falconer
Jane Farey
Sarah Farley
Kimberly Farr
Elizabeth Farrell
Ewan Farry
Declan Fay
Ella Ferdenzi
Chris Ferebee
Matt Fiddes
James Fielden
Paul Fischer
Johann Flapsandwich
olivier Fleurot
Katy Flint
Émilie Floch
John Flook
Mia D. Fong
Steven Foreman
Gareth Forster
Nigel Forsyth
Oli Forsyth
Marco Fossati-Bellani
Anna Foster
David Foster
Sam Foulkes-Arnold
Evelina Fox
Julia Fox
Travis Fox
Stephanie Frackowiak
Miranda Franco
Ann Frank
Elizabeth Louise Franke
Isobel Frankish
Sarah Fraser
Alexandra Freddi
Graham Freeman
Mark Fry
Simon Gadd
Mark Gallagher
Orlagh Gallagher
Rosaleen Gallagher
Maggie Gallant
Mark Gamble
Martin Gamble
Maria Gannon
Paul Garbett
Penny Gardiner

Richard Garnett
Geoffrey Garoghan
Francesca L. Garrett
Glenn R. Garrett
Frank Garver
Carl Gaywood
Amro Gebreel
Saunders Gemma
Emma Giacon and Chris Helsen
Eric Gibbons
Jack & Ellie Gibbons
Rob & Joanne Gibbons
Don Gibson
Natalie Gill
William Gill
Dom Gittins
Laura Gittins
Mikey Gittins
Andy Gittos
Mikkel Gladhaug
Anne Glennie
Susan Godfrey
Xanthe Godwin-Summerfield
Barnaby Golden
Jeremy Goldsmith and Rebecca
    Laughton
Sophie Goldsworthy
Pierre Golpira
Elma Goncalves
Paul Goodison
Philip Goodman
Angus Goodwin
Mark Goodyear
Bharadwaj Gopinath
Ellen G Gordon
Alex Gosse
Robert Gottlieb
Zoe Gough
Claire Govier
Michele Govier
David Graham
Vasilica Grama
Voula Grand
David Grant
Laura Grant
Lucie Grant
Mark Krishan Gray
Fiona Green
James Green
Angela Greenfield
Rebecca Gregg
Kate Gregory
Jane Grievson
Richard Grievson
Zoe Griffith
Craig Griffiths

Stephen Griffiths
Tony Grigoriou
Alex Grinton
Frank Guerra
Nick Guerra
João Guerreiro
Aurelie Guidez
Robin Guise
Marek Gumienny
Amanda Gunn
Rich Gunn
Gina Guthrie
Alex Hackbart
Chloë Hackett
William Hackett-Jones
Katharine Halcrow
Alfie Hall
Kevin Hall
Sophie Hall
Katharine Halliwell
J C Hamilton
David Hancock
Stephen Hands
Jana Hannon
Emily Hanson-Coles
Mariann Hardey
Robyn Harding
Annie Hargreaves
Sean Harkin
Ruth Ann Harnisch
Andrew Harper
Ben J Harris
Jennifer Harris
Steve Harris
Jo Harris-Cooksley
Brian M. Harrison
A.F. Harrold
Mary M Hart
Steve Hartley
Caitlin Harvey
Dave Harvey
Kimberley Harvey
Dan Harwood
Gill Hastie
Joanne Haswell
Susanna Hauru
Malcolm Hay
Michael Haydock
Josh Hayes
Kate Haywood
Elspeth Head
Carol Heald
Natalie Hearn
Charlotte Heathcote
Tory Heazell
Margot Heesakker

Deborah Hefter
Helen & Patrick
Anne Hempstead
Vicky Hempstead
Brian Henderson
Hannah Henderson
Kevlin Henney
Alexander O. Henri
Henry, Syma and Ariana
Tatum Hensley Ð
Kirstie Hepburn
Vix Hepworth
Mark Herbert
Michael Herbert
D.A. Hernandez
Anna Hervé
Catherine Hibbitt
Patricia Hickey
Adrian Hickford
David Hilary
Joanne Hilburn
Gilbert Hill
Gregory Hill
Bernadette Hillman
Alexia Hill-Scott
Thomas Hilton
Matthew Hinchliffe
Faye Hindle-Lewis
Sigi Hirschbeck
Janet Hitchen
Cheryl Hodgkinson
Ingo Hofmann
Joanna Holland
Victor Holland
Pamela Hollenbeck
Yvonne Holm
Helen Hood
Amanda Hooper
Caroline Hope-Hawkins
David Hornby
Christopher Mark Horrocks
David John Horrocks
Bill Horton
Todd Hovis
Catherine Howard-Dobson
Eric Hsu
Jan Hudecek
Matt Huggins
Richard Hughes
Sali Hughes
William Hughes
Tony & Sonia Hunt
Jackie Hunter
Ray Hunter
Vanessa Hunter
Lee Hurst

Jennifer Hurstfield
Syahril Hussin
Nevil Hutchinson
Oli Hutt
Sylvia Huynh
Mo Ingham
Hannes Ingwersen
Louise Inward
Tim Irving
Lee Isaacsohn
Johari Ismail
Julie Jack
Tammy Jackson
Paula Jacunski
Sarah Jakes
Maxim Jakubowski
Louise Jallow
Christopher Robert Franklin
   James
Faye James
Clare Jamieson
Piet Jaspers
Mark Jefferson
Laura Jellicoe
Titus Jennings
Meagan Jensen
Jan Jewkes
JK & JY
Anne Johnsen
Christina Johnson
Dean Johnson
Georgie Johnson
Sandra Johnson
Tom Johnson
Adele Jolliffe
Sophie Jolliffe
Heather Jones
Helen Jones
Josie Jones
Karen Jones
Katie Jones
Lisa Jane Jones
Louisa Fry Jones
Martin Chad Jones
Meghan Jones
Rachel Catherine Jones
Robert Jones
Trish Jones
Joanne K
Martin Kane
Jørgen Kann
Tonya Kara
Katerina Kassela
Mayumi Kasuga
Nozomi Kawabata
Yvette Kehela

Carol Kehela-Marzouk
Steven Kehoe
Erik Keithley
Andrew Kelly
David Kelly
Martin Kelly
Steven Kelly
Scott Kennedy
John Kent
Julia Kenyon
Timothy Peter Keohane
Peter Kessler
Peter Kettle
Maika Keuben
Mobeena Khan
Rajesh Khatri
Lucy Kidson
Dan Kieran
Kevin Kieran
Simon King
Stephen Kinsella
Laura Kiralfy
Katrina Kirkby
Sarah Kirkland
Patricia Kitto
Doron Klemer
Ben Klomp
Fiona Klomp
Lorraine Knight
Richard Knowles
Juha Kolari
Gabe Krabbe
Seán Kretz
Andrew Kuchling
Jonas Kuehl
Nyasha Douglas Kunorubwe
Thando Natalia Kunorubwe
Stephan Kurz
Karl Kvarnström
Melanie La Barrie
Qiana R. La Croix
Cynthia Louise Lacey
Yvonne Lagorio
Fay Laing
Catherine Lake
Hannah Dell and Mark Lally
Dominique & Jean-Luc Laloë
Georgie Laming
Margit Lammertz
Peter Langdon
Valerie Langfield
Melissa Leilani Larson
Diana Laufenberg
David Laurie
Anna Lawrence
Sharon Lawrence

W Tom Lawrie
Wendy Lawson
Kim Le Patourel
Jimmy Leach
Jack R. Lebowitz
Kay Lee
James Leeper
Chloe Leila
Lillian Letran
Klim Levene
Elen Lewis
Monika Lewis
Rhyd Lewis
Ross Lewis
LexHands
Lidbert
Claire Liddle
Christina Wisbech Liebum
Otavio Lilla
Daniel Lim
Jennifer Lin
Hanna Lingman
Joonas Linkola
Robert Lischke
Paul Lisker
David Livingston
Sarah livingston
George Lloyd
James Lloyd
Chau-Yee Lo
Kari Long
Nate Long
Sarah Longman
Loo_Bee Loo_Bee
Lourdes Lopez
Isabell Lorenz
Gill French Lorimer
Florian Lottmann
Phillip Loughlin
Brian Loughnane
Anita Loveland
Stuart, Tara, Alexander, Giles
   and Phoebe-Rose Lowbridge
Alison Lowe
Andrew Lowe
Dianne Lowry
Adam Lucas
Lummers
Brian Lunn
Regina Lupoli
DeAndra Lupu
Debora Lustgarten
James Lydon
Mike Lynd
Nancy Lyons
Calvin Carson Ma

Ping Margaret Ma
SD JS Ma
Soong Ken Ma
Kirsty MacAlpine
Sam MacAuslan
Anne Macdonald
Sarah MacDonald
Louise Macdonald OBE
Neil Macehiter
Duncan MacGregor
Jonathan Macklin
Nick Maclean
Heather Macleod
Sarah Maddox
Andrew Magruder
Vipan Maini
Sharoz Makarechi
Deborah Makepeace
Elke Makowski
Jane Malcolm
Philippa Manasseh
Hedy Manders
Magdalena Wagner Manslau
Craig Mares
Michel Marks
Lisa Markwell
Fabien Marry
Graham Marshall
Jane Marshall
Dominick Marshall-Smith
Andrew Martin
Cally Martin
Nicholas Marum
Leslie Maslow
Dawn Mason
Roger Mathew
Alison May
Angela Mayes
John Mayhugh
Nicolas Mazzoli
Annalena McAfee
Lucy McCann
Tara McCausland
Pat Murphy McClelland
Stephen McConnell
Yarrow McConnell
Patrick McCormack
Wendy McCormack
Ewan McCowen
Janice McCreary
Caroline McDermott
Archie McDiarmid
Rob McDonald
Wanwen McFarlane-Cen
David McGeown
Bridget McGing

Helen McGovern
Siobhan McGrath
Neil McHugh
Anna McInerney
Carole McIntosh
Vi McIntosh
Gavin McKeown
Maureen Mckerrall
Alasdair McKinlay
Shelagh McKinlay
Carrie McKittrick
Eileen 'Mugs' McMahon
Rachel McMaster
Rachel McMaster
Roy McMillan
Iain McMullan
Angela & Martin McNamee
Steve McNay
Marie Therese McWalter
Chris Mead
Mary Megarry
Lena Megyeri
Lynne Mendoza
Ann Menke
Russell Metz
Alice Meynell
Richard Middleton-Kaplan
Louis Mikolay
Roger Miles
Melanie Lynn Miller
Michael Miller
Naomi Miller
Shannon Miller
William Miller
Tracy Miller and Paul Arnest
Lynne Milligan
Adam Mills
Robert Mills
Virginia Mills
Esther Milne
John Milner
Simon D Milner
Lady Charlotte Emily Mitchell
Lori Martin Mitchell
Ruth Mitchell
Clive Mitchelmore
John Mitchinson
Ronald Mitchinson
Stephanie Mlot
James Moakes
Andy Moffat
Linda Moir
Simon Monk
Renata Monnier
Jim Mooney
Christopher Daniel Moore

Alastair Moppett
Ben Moran
Helen Morgan-Jones
Rose Morley
Helen Morris
Milo F. S. Morris
Nancy Morris
Yves J. T. Morris
Anthea Morton-Saner
Clarissa Moschin
Alessia Mosci
Lucy and Julian Moss
Maryam Mossavar
Esther Mourits
Nicola Moxey
Victoria Muir
Pip Mulgrue
Sarah Mullarney
Kristen Mulvihill
Gavin Murdock
Faye Murfet
David Murphy
Kevin Peter Murphy
Ewen Murray
Lee & Christine Murray
Gethin J. Nadin
Stu Nathan
Carlo Navato
Astrid Vinsand Naver
Jessica Nelson
Scott Nelson
Cat Neshine
Caishnah Nevans
John New
Lisa Newman
Richard Newman
Jean Newsom
Adam Newton
Andy Nichol
Vic Nicholas
Michelle Nicholson
Tess Nicholson
Emily Nicol
Gary Nicol
Christopher Noel
Steven Noels
Stewart Nolan
Barney Nugent
Ethna Nugent
Jeffrey M. Nye
Enda O' Gara
Eimear O' Grady
Gwen Oakden
Neil Oatley
Jenny O'Connor-Madsen
Georgia Odd

Mike O'Dell
Andy Offor
Jenny O'Gorman
Chatrina O'Mara
Gerry ONeill
Craig O'Neill
Susan O'Reilly
Monica Ormonde
Jim Orrell
Lara Osmotherly
David Overend
Alaw Rhys Owen
Josh Owen
Louise Paddock
Julie Paice
Fernand Pajot
Jane Palmer
Mairi Palmer
Richard Palmer
Laarni Grace Paras
Avalon de Paravicini
Kevin Parker
Richard Parker
Luke Parks
Samantha Parnell
Emily Parsons
Mark Pashayan
Guy Pastorek
Inés Pastur de Dios
Angela Patel
Rima Patel
Matthew Paton
Damian Pattinson
Helen Paul
Jo-Anne Pawley
Clare Payne
Danielle Payne
Noah Payne-Frank
Carrie Peacock
Eric Pearce
Ben Pearson
Gemma Louise Pearson
Elizabeth Van Pelt
Alex Penfold
Guillermo Pérez-Hernández
Kevin Perry
Kate Pert
Vicky Pert
John H. Petrey
John Petrie
Fleur Phillips
Jay Phillips
Kerry Philpott
Amy Phung
Anna Pick
Cynda Pierce

Erin Pierce
Phil Pierce
Jane Pink
Francesca Pipe
Carlota Pires
Natasha Pitchacaren
Colette Pithie
Marco Piva-Dittrich & Solveig
    Dittrich-Piva
Russ Platt
Leza Plumb
Philip Podmore
Justin Pollard
Gemma Poole
Claire Poore
Cherie Porter
Kirstey Porter
Jennifer Potocnik
Matthew Potocnik
Jenny Pourian
Alison Collison Powell
Amy + Ben Powell
Jean Power
Amy Preece
Janet Pretty
Neil Pretty
Chris Price
Martin Price
Rhian Heulwen Price
arthur prior
Kate Pritchard
Jenny Pryer
Rebecca Pugh
Douglas J Purcell
Stephen Purse
Laura & Steve Pursglove
Michael Puskar
Elske van der Putten
Megan Quinn
Marleen Raaijmakers
Brady Rafuse
Ramaa Ramesh
Mark Ramirez
Jeanette Ramsden
Lane Rasberry
Rauf Rawson
Mark Reading
Colette Reap
Simon Reap
Aline Reed
Amy Rees
Bethan Rees
Phillip Reeves
Rebecca Regan
Helen Reid
David Reidy

Bia Reinach
G Rendle
Bruce Renny
Chuck Reuter
Teraza Rew
Kevin Reynolds
James Rhodes is Wonderful
Rafael Ramos Ribeiro
Hugh Richards
Tim & Lizzie Rickman
Jeffery Ricotttone
Karen Riden
Helen Ridgway
Clare Riding
Toni-Ann Riley
Maritza Rios-Ortiz
Jim & Jackie Robbins
Malcolm & Christine Robbins
Colin Roberts
Natalie Roberts
Wyn Roberts
Charlie Robertson
Ellen Robertson
Lauren Robertson
Philip Robertson
Suzanne Robey
Cassandra Naomi Robinson
Clive A. Robinson
Dan Robinson
Kiera Emily Robinson
Matthew Robinson
Rachael Robinson
Simon Robinson
Ben Rogers
Steve Ronksley
Naomi Roper
João Rosa
Robyn Roscoe
Rosemary Roscoe
Angela Rose
Roberto rosele
Katharine Roseveare, Martin &
   Lucas Raymond
Elizabeth Lucille Ross
Leon Ross
Laurie Roth
Matt Rotheram
Jessica Rowbottom
Harry Rowley
Jan Rowley
Geraldine Ruffier d'Epenoux
Isabela & Paul Ruskin
Allan P Russell
Benjamin Russell
Ruth & Nigel
Aedín Ryan

Anna Ryder
Anne Ryder
Stef S
Monique Sá
Hesham Sabry
M.E. Saenz
Amy Sakurai
Sara Salahub
Adam Sales
Miia 'Myrtti' Sample
Christoph Sander
John-Paul Sarni
Sarah Sarni
Shrikant R Sawant
Katie Sawyer
Tim Saxton
Neil Sayer
John Schebeck
Danny Scheinmann
Judith Schenck
Martin Scherer
Blair Schertenleib
Sabina Schiftar
Dagmar Schmitt
Caroline Schmitz
Eva Schnellbach
John Schoenbaum
Robbin Schroeder
Mary Ellen Schutz
Matthias Schwaab
Sarah Scoffin
Leslie Scott
Matthew Searle
Fiona Sedgwick
Ina Seidel
Tim Sell
Ugur Sendenel
James Hywel Sercombe
Branimira Sever
Shradha Shah & Jessy Mathew
Shruti Shalini
Katy Shanahan
Sophie Shanahan-Kluth
John Shand
Neil Sharma
Michael Douglas Sharp
Jacqui Sheldon
Mark Shepherd
Georgina Sheward
Kelvin Shewry
Emily Shipp
Kate Shires
Linda Shoare
Ben Short
Claire Shotter
Jack Sidey

Adam Signy
Susan Silver
Annelie Simmons
John Simpson
James von Simson
Melanie Sinclair
Victoria Singlehurst
Alex Sitaras
Jan Skakle
Jeremy Skillington
Susan Skipper
Rosie Slater
Sarah Slauson
Andy Slee
Keith Sleight
Matthew Sly
Andrew Smith
Catherine Smith
Catriona R Smith
Celia Armand Smith
Christopher Smith
Claire Smith
Don Smith
Helen Smith
Jacqueline Smith
Joe Saumarez Smith
Judy Smith
Leonie Smith
Patrick Milling Smith
Paul Smith
Roma Petra Noel Smith
Sneady
Barbara Snow
Rebecca Soglin
Lili Soh
Rachel Sommerville
Valerie Sonnenthal
Simon Soothill
Andrew Sorcini
Brad Sorensen
Mate Soric
Shawn Sou
Richard Soundy
Dave Sox
James Spackman
Kerri J Spangaro
Sam Harmsworth Sparling
Chris Spath
Philip Spedding
Lesli Speers
James Spencer
Robert Spencer
Helen Spicer
Matthew Spicer
Leigh Spriggs
Rachel Springett

Carol Staff
Amanda Stafford
Janice Staines
Pam Stanier
Tarrant Steele
Claudia Stehle
David Stelling
Richard Stephens
Gillian Stern
justin stevanz
Kelly Stevens
LeAnne Stevens
Helen J Stewart
Laura Stirling
Rosie Stirling
Helen Storm
Katie Stowell
Michael Strawson
Claire Lynne Strümpher
Bob Stuart
Kyle Sturgeon
Edmund Sumbar
Rachel Sumner
Yonga Sun
Philippe Surber
Mark Suret
Sharon Suter
Evelyn Sutherland
Keith Sutherland
Laura Sweetman
Silvia T
Kana Takahashi
James Tallis
Jennifer Tamir
Alison Tarry
Ezra Tassone
Helen Taylor
Joanne Taylor
Karen Taylor
Maisie Taylor
Mark Taylor
Rodney Taylor
Elizabeth Taylor-Mead
Will Thames
Andrea Thoene
Jayne Thomas
Lynda Thomas
Vanessa Thomas
Wayne Dilwyn Thomas
Pamela Thompson
Rachael, William and Anna
   Thompson
Simon Thompson
Tabitha Thompson
Ian Thompson-Corr
Jon Thomson

Scott Thomson
Joe Thorley
Amanda Thurman
Denise Tierney
Alice Tjiu
Aidan Tobin
James Tobin
Harry Todd
Sam Todd
Hayley Tolley
Victoria Tomlinson
Agnes Tongue
Andy Tootell
Alexandra Topping
Hernan Toro
Bob Townley
Sabrina Tozzi
Isla Traqauir
Tjarda Tromp
Andrew Truman
Linda P. Tupac Yupanqui
Nikki Turberville
Jim Turner
Michael Alastair Fearnley Turner
Sian Turner
Claudia H. L. Tye Tye
Eva Ullrich
Jamie Paige Washam Unaka
Gus Unger-Hamilton
John and Lindsay Usher
Karen Usher and Michael Franke
Luis Vallespin
Anna Vallesteros
Nikki Vane
Leila Varzideh
Samantha Vavrik
Boris Vellin
Mark Vent
Frances Versluys
Linda Verstraten & Pyter
   Wagenaar
Sarrah Vesselov
Arnar Ingi Viðarsson
David Vigar
Prashanthy Vigneswaran
Ulla-Maija Viitavuori
Robert Vincent
Isabel Vogt
Matus Vojtek
Nienke Vonsée
Jo W
Ian Wacogne
Nick Wadlow
Richard Wales
Dustin & Sara Waling
Claire Walker

Kirsty Walker
Stephen Walker
Steve Walker
Alistair Wallace
Steve Wallman
Natasha Walter
Sarah Walters
Shao Wang
Josie Ward
Lee Ward
Peter Ward
Kirsty Warriss
Sarah Wasley
Gail Watts
Simon Watts
Gemma Waughman
Tanya Weaver
David Webb
Monika Weber
Jess Weeks
Nick Wells
Anne Welsh
Tom Wexler
Simon Wheatley
Hannah Whelan
Paul Whelan
Levin Wheller
Joan Whent
Luiza Whitaker
Pete Whitby
Chantal White
Crispin White
Rosemary White
Simon White
Stephen White
Jacob Whitlow
David Whittle
Hayley Wickens
David Widdick
Andrew Wiggins
Thomas Wigley
David Wilf
Cary Wilkins
David Wilkinson
Andrea Williams
Daniel Williams
Jonathan Williams
Julian Williams
Marc Williams
Nick Williams
Rebecca Williams
Reshma Williams
Sarah Williams
Zoë-Elise Williamson
Jim Willis
Alexa Wilson

Carol Wilson
Joan Wilson
Kirsten Wilson
Rory Wilson
Sarah Wilson
Joke De Winter
Emma Winterschladen
Mary Wise
Gretchen Woelfle
Melissa Wong
Lee, Lisa and Eleanor Wood
Mark Woodward
Ryan Woodward
Hilary Woodward & Robert J.
   Kohlmeyer
Ben Wooliscroft
Tim Worwood
Paul Wray
Amanda Wright
Louise Wright
Steve Wright
Cindy Wu
Gerald Wyatt
Debbie Wythe
Nicholas Yates
Riana Yeates
Julia Yong
Sarah Young
Simon Young
Bo Yuen
Cindy Yuen
Vanessa Zainzinger
Anna Zammit
Jane Zara
Gabriele Zocchi

PERMISSION CREDITS

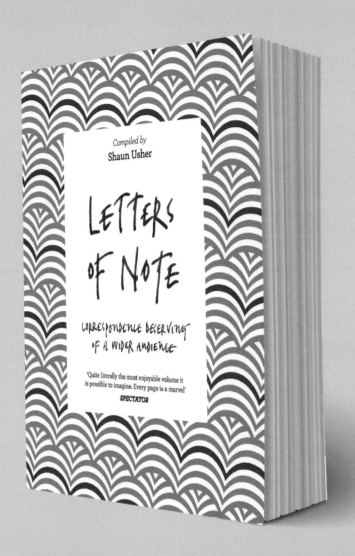

Compiled by
Shaun Usher

LETTERS
OF NOTE

CORRESPONDENCE DESERVING
OF A WIDER AUDIENCE

'Quite literally the most enjoyable volume it
is possible to imagine. Every page is a marvel'
SPECTATOR

'Addictive, like dipping into a bag of variously tempting assorted candies,
knowing that the next one will always bring surprise and pleasure'
New Yorker

'Beautiful and immensely satisfying'
Lauren Laverne, *Observer*